HYPERSPECTRAL DATA COMPRESSION

HYPERSPECTRAL DATA COMPRESSION

Edited by

Giovanni Motta
Brandeis University
Massachusetts, United States

Bitfone Corporation
United Staes

Francesco Rizzo
Brandeis University
Massachusetts, United States

University of Salerno
Italy

James A. Storer
Brandeis University
Massachusetts, United States

Library of Congress Cataloging-in-Publication Data

A C.I.P. Catalogue record for this book is available from the Library of Congress.

Hyperspectral Data Compression, Edited by Giovanni Motta, Francesco Rizzo and James A. Storer

   p.cm.

ISBN-10: (eBook) 0-387-25588-5
ISBN-13: 978-1-4419-3943-2   ISBN-13: (eBook) 978-0387-25588-0
Printed on acid-free paper.

CONTENTS

Preface

The interest in remote sensing applications and platforms (including airborne and spaceborne) has grown dramatically in recent years. Remote sensing technology has shifted from panchromatic data (a wide range of wavelengths merged into a single response), through multispectral (a few possibly overlapping bands in the visible and infrared range with spectral width of 100-200nm each), to hyperspectral imagers and ultraspectral sounders, with hundreds or thousands of bands. In addition, the availability of airborne and spaceborne sensors has increased considerably, followed by the widespread availability of remote sensed data in different research environments, including defense, academic, and commercial.

Remote sensed data present special challenges in the acquisition, transmission, analysis, and storage process. Perhaps most significant is the information extraction process. In most cases accurate analysis depends on high quality data, which comes with a price tag: increased data volume.

For example, the NASA JPL's *Airborne Visible/Infrared Imaging Spectrometer* (AVIRIS, http://aviris.jpl.nasa.gov) records the visible and the near-infrared spectrum of the reflected light of an area 2 to 12 kilometers wide and several kilometers long (depending on the duration of the flight) into hundreds of non overlapping bands. The resulting data volume typically exceeds 500 Megabytes per flight and it is mainly used for geological mapping, target recognition, and anomaly detection.

On the other hand, ultraspectral sounders such as the NASA JPL's *Atmospheric Infrared Sounder* (AIRS, http://www-airs.jpl.nasa.gov), which is recently becoming a reference in compression studies on this class of data, records thousands of bands covering the infrared spectrum and generates more than 12 Gigabytes of data daily. The major application of this sensor is the acquisition of atmospheric parameters such as temperature, moisture, clouds, gasses, dust concentrations, and other quantities to perform weather and climate forecast.

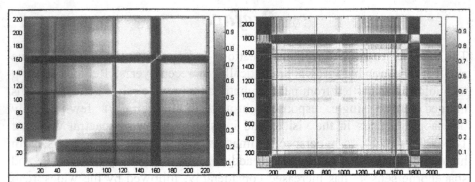

Absolute value of the correlation between spectral bands: AVIRIS, Moffett Field, scene 2 (left) and AIRS, Granule 9, Pacific Ocean, daytime (right).

Such volumes already exceed available transmission bandwidths. Efficient data compression allows real-time distribution of remote sensed data and reduces storage at the ground station. In many cases lossless compression is required at the archive level (e.g., for accurate climate monitoring in the case of ultraspectral sounders).

As in natural images, hyperspectral data present high correlation in the spatial dimension: adjacent locations have similar *spectral signatures*. Furthermore, there is a direct correspondence among bands or group of bands in the spectral dimension. For example, the figure above depicts the correlation coefficients (0 stands for no correlation, 1 for complete linear correlation) between spectral bands of two sample data volumes, one AVIRIS and one AIRS respectively.

This correlation seems to suggest that a simple extension of natural image compression algorithms to the hyperspectral data compression problem would suffice to achieve good performance. Unfortunately, the dynamic range of remote sensed data is much higher than natural images and statistics generally differ from one band to the other, and such extensions tend to lack effectiveness without further technical development.

This book provides a survey of recent results in the field of compression of remote sensed 3D data, with a particular interest in hyperspectral imagery. We expect this material to be of interest to researchers in a variety of areas, including multi dimensional data compression, remote sensing, military and aerospace image processing, homeland security, archival of large volumes of scientific and medical data, target detection, and image classification.

Chapter 1 addresses compression architecture and reviews and compares compression methods. Chapter 2 through 4 focus on lossless compression (where the decompressed image must be bit for bit identical to the original). Chapter 5 (contributed by the editors) describes a lossless algorithm based on vector quantization with extensions to near lossless and possibly lossy compression for efficient browsing and pure pixel classification. Chapters 6 deals with near lossless compression while Chapter 7 considers lossy techniques constrained by almost perfect classification. Chapters 8 through 12 address lossy compression of hyperspectral imagery, where there is a tradeoff between compression achieved and the quality of the decompressed image. Chapter 13 examines artifacts that can arise from lossy compression.

Acknowledgements

The editors would like to thank the authors for their contributions to this book, and have designated all income from the sale of this book to be donated to the IEEE Foundation;

   http://www.ieee.org/organizations/foundation/html/about.html

                                        G. Motta, F. Rizzo, and J. A. Storer, 6/1/2005

An Architecture for the Compression of Hyperspectral Imagery

Mark R. Pickering and Michael J. Ryan

School of Information Technology and Electrical Engineering
The University of New South Wales
Australian Defence Force Academy

1. INTRODUCTION

Modern hyperspectral sensors have both high spatial resolution and high spectral resolution covering up to several hundred bands. The economics of transmission and storage of the resultant large volume of data collected by such sensors means that image compression will become an essential feature of systems incorporating hyperspectral sensors. Efficient compression techniques are therefore required for the coding of remotely sensed images, particularly for those that are to be transmitted directly to the ground and distributed to users.

Image compression techniques fall broadly into two main categories: lossless and lossy compression, depending on whether the original image can be precisely re-generated from the compressed data. In lossless compression, no information is discarded; compression results from a more efficient storage of the information. In lossy coding, information is discarded, leading to much higher compression ratios. The type of information that can be discarded, however, will depend on which data is unnecessary for a given application. Since this is rarely known in the point of compression (particularly for data for general use) there is still a significant role for lossless compression in the transmission and storage of hyperspectral data.

Perhaps the most useful role of lossy techniques is in the initial analysis of hyperspectral data where large areas of data are evaluated to select smaller areas for more detailed evaluation. In that case, to reduce the cost of purchase of this data and the storage required to retain and process it, a suitable distortion measure could be used to produce lossy data at an acceptable distortion level and at much reduced image sizes. The low-resolution data could be available at dramatically reduced purchase price, transmission times and storage requirements. Having identified the areas of interest, a smaller amount of high-resolution data could be procured, transmitted, stored and evaluated. Central to lossy compression, therefore, is the development of a suitable distortion measure so that the performance of an algorithm on lossy data produces results, from which its performance on the original data can be inferred.

Many hyperspectral compression algorithms proposed in the literature have concentrated solely on the problem of producing the maximum compression ratio for the minimum value of a mean distortion measure. There is strong evidence that these mean distortion measure values have little or no correlation to the degradation in accuracy when the compressed data is used for classification.

For future improvements to be made in the area of hyperspectral image compression, two main deficiencies of current systems need to be addressed. First a suitable distortion measure that accurately estimates the degradation in classification accuracy for the compressed data is required. Second such a distortion measure must be incorporated into a compression algorithm that is designed as a complete system that incorporates the possible classification applications of the compressed data.

Some candidate distortion measures are discussed and evaluated in the following section. In Section 3, a suitable architecture for a complete compression system is described. Section 4 provides a brief overview of the theory behind many of the compression algorithms from the literature. Section 5 summarizes the majority of these contributions and finally in Section 6 conclusions are drawn and some possible future directions are outlined.

2. A SUITABLE DISTORTION MEASURE FOR COMPRESSION OF HYPERSPECTRAL IMAGERY

The principal difficulty in lossy image compression is to code an image with as few symbols as possible while ensuring that the quality of the reconstructed image can be maintained at some acceptable standard. The decision as to which information to discard must therefore be informed by some understanding of the effect on the quality of the reconstructed image, which in turn requires some measure of image quality or of the level of distortion introduced by the compression process. This problem is similar to that faced in the compression of video sequences, so it is useful to briefly discuss distortion measures for video compression.

2.1 Distortion Measures for Compression of Video Sequences

For video sequences, the acceptable standard for quality of reconstruction is set by the receiver of the image—the human observer. That is, the image must still look acceptable. Early researchers in video compression therefore recognised that an understanding of the human visual system [1-4] would aid in the identification of an image quality measure that corresponded to the way in which the human visual system assesses image fidelity [5]. With such a measure it would be possible to rate definitively the fidelity of an image-coding scheme in comparison with some standard. Furthermore, if the measure were an analytic function, it would be possible to employ it as a goal or objective function for optimisation of the parameters of the coding scheme [6].

Some rudimentary facts are known about the human visual system. Visual perception of distortion is sensitive to variations in luminance, rather than absolute luminance values. [7] It is most sensitive to mid-frequencies and least sensitive to high wavelengths. [8] In addition, visual perception of distortion is less sensitive to large luminance changes [9,10] and the relative sensitivity of the human visual system has a bandpass characteristic with respect to spatial frequencies. The spatial frequencies masking studies by Stromeyer and Julesz [11] suggest that the visual system is relatively tuned to different spatial frequencies; an idea supported by experimental results [3,12,13].

Since the pioneering work of Budrikis [5], Stockham [14] and Mannos and Sakrison [15], many attempts have been made to derive suitable distortion measures based on the various models of the human visual system, resulting in a large array of candidate measures. Examples are: general norms such as absolute error, the cube root of the sum of the cubic errors, and maximum error, as well as variations to include linear weightings. Linear weightings have been included in an attempt to incorporate properties of the human visual system such as sensitivity to edges, insensitivity to textures and other masking effects. [16]

Despite these investigations, however, an accurate visual model has not been found since visual perception is still not well understood. Consequently, an accurate distortion measure has not been produced, since it is only through the development of more sophisticated visual models that more objective distortion criteria can be developed with consequent improvement in coding efficiency [17]. The most appropriate test of video coding is whether the quality of the reconstructed image is adequate, a decision best made by the viewer.

Therefore, the ultimate test of video coding for many applications is subjective rating by human observers who can examine the reconstructed images from a number of compression techniques and make a comparison to choose the most acceptable standard. Measurement of image quality ultimately depends therefore upon subjective evaluations, either directly or indirectly through distortion measures based on the results of subjective tests [18]. This reliance is such that international standards for subjective tests have been introduced with recommendations from the CCIR [19]. The use of subjective tests does not greatly assist in the coding process where decision have to be made on a pixel-by-pixel or a block-by-block basis during the process of coding, rather than as some subjective assessment once compression and reconstruction are complete. As an aid during the coding process, it is commonplace in video coding to use distortion measures such as the mean square error (MSE) during the coding process as well as an objective means of comparing coding techniques.

Despite the lack of a theoretical foundation for its use, MSE has been used extensively in video coding because it is mathematically tractable, is easily computed, and has some intuitive appeal since large errors are given more importance than small ones. MSE is a poor criterion for coding video images, however, as it is not subjectively meaningful and does not correlate well with subjective ratings [6]. Additionally, similar levels of distortion can lead to a large spread in reported subjective quality [20]. A common fault with MSE as a distortion measure is that the minimisation of a mean error may still result in a strong visual artefact in the reconstructed image, if all of the error is concentrated in a small, but important, region. The unsuitability of an MSE-based distortion measure can also be observed when it is noted that a perfect reconstruction with a 1-pixel shift in any direction will lead to a high MSE, but the viewer will not see any degradation.

2.2 Distortion Measures for Coding for Quantitative Analysis

The human viewer of reconstructed video images has no specific task to perform when viewing the presented frames. An objective distortion measure must therefore be related to the general human visual system, rather than to any specific function. This does not apply to all types of image compression, however. In the compression of hyperspectral data for quantitative analysis, where the receiver of the encoded images will not only be a human viewer but will also be one of a range of automated algorithms. In that case it is particularly important for a suitable distortion measure to be determined in the context of the remote-sensing application that will make use of the data. On reconstruction, the accuracy of the results from those algorithms can only be as accurate as the reconstructed data. Most applications are still not perfected on the original data and will require the best available accuracy in compressed data. The key to this problem is the identification of a suitable distortion measure that can be applied during the compression process. Put simply, the distortion measure must be able to be used to determine which data can be discarded during lossy compression.

However, the information that can be discarded for one particular application may be necessary for use in another. Since the distortion measure is used to decide what information to discard during lossy compression, a general distortion measure is required that can be applied even though the application to be applied to the reconstructed image is not known in advance. Therefore, for the compression of hyperspectral imagery, it is more appropriate to minimise a distortion measure that reflects the loss in *scientific value* of the original data. Unfortunately such quantitative measures do not exist, either for specific applications or for general application to hyperspectral imagery.

Appropriate criteria have been developed, however, for a suitable distortion measure for the lossy compression of images required for quantitative analysis [21]. Table 1 lists these criteria and compares them to those relevant to a distortion measure for coding for viewing [22].

While the first and second criteria are the same for the coding of video as well as hyperspectral data, the third and fourth criteria are significantly different.

The requirement for a distortion measure to be *quantitatively meaningful* for quantitative remote-sensing analysis is significantly different from the video requirement to be *subjectively meaningful*. The principal reason for the difference is that the reconstructed data is not put to the same use. When coded video data is viewed, the distortion measure can take into account that the eye is a very forgiving receiver due to its substantial ability to integrate spatial information. Large errors are therefore less important, provided there are few such large errors that are surrounded by pixels with errors of small magnitude. Unlike video data, hyperspectral data is invariably processed by an algorithm which, unlike the human eye, is likely to be sensitive to all formes of large errors, whether they are isolated or not. For remote-sensing applications, a suitable distortion measure therefore must, in a quantitative way, reflect the loss in scientific value of the original data, rather than protect its subjective quality.

Viewing	Quantitative Analysis
mathematically tractable to permit analysis	mathematically tractable to permit analysis
computable in real time	computable in real time (although not as essential as for viewing)
subjectively meaningful so that large or small errors correspond to bad or good quality	quantitatively meaningful in that differences in the coded image correspond to the same relative magnitude of differences in the original image
-	independent of the application to be applied to the coded data

Table 1: Distortion measure criteria for video viewing [22] and quantitative analysis [21].

Further, a suitable distortion measure for quantitative analysis must be *application-independent*. Not only is the human eye very forgiving as a receiver, but most viewers' eyes have very similar characteristics. Consequently, what pleases a small cross-section of viewers will no doubt please the majority. In coding data to be used in remote-sensing applications, however, the reconstructed data could be subjected to quantitative analysis by one of a wide range of computer-based algorithms, each of which may require a different level of accuracy depending on the remote-sensing application. A general distortion measure for remotely sensed data must therefore be able to accommodate the diverse requirements of a range of algorithm-based end-user applications.

For example, it may be possible to develop a distortion measure for a remote-sensing application such as maximum likelihood classification. Yet, such a measure is not necessarily suitable to any other remote-sensing application. Consequently, although for different reasons, a general distortion measure is equally as difficult to achieve for remote-sensing applications as it has been for video coding.

2.3 A Suitable Distortion Measure

Since a general theoretical distortion measure is unlikely to be developed for remote-sensing applications in the short term, a suitable compromise distortion measure must be found. The answer will depend on the end-user application which, as identified earlier, could be in a variety of forms. The lossy compression of the image must not prejudice the use of, or conversely favour, any one of the possible applications.

The distortion measure must also produce predictable results in the performance of each remote-sensing application for reconstructed data with a given level of distortion. By determining a particular remote-sensing algorithm's performance on reconstructed data in the presence of the given level of distortion, an application scientist should be able to infer the performance of the algorithm on the original (undistorted) data.

This requirement is very important as the compressed data is of little value unless the performance of a remote-sensing algorithm on the original data can be inferred by observing the performance of the algorithm on data distorted to any particular degree. The requirement also implies that the performance of the algorithm gracefully degrades as the level of coding distortion increases.

2.3.1 The Suitability of Mean Distortion Measures

Mean distortion measures are not suitable since they cannot be obtained directly because a decision on a mean distortion level cannot be made on a pixel-by-pixel basis. In video coding, it is normal to accommodate this difficulty by encoding on a pixel-by-pixel basis using scalar quantization, which can be predicted to result in a desired mean distortion across the image. The other difficulty with a mean distortion measure is that the specification of a mean level of distortion gives a general indication of the distortion in the image but does not give any indication of the specific magnitude of the errors in any particular spatial or spectral portion of the image. Mean distortion measure therefore are of little assistance in the application of a quantitative algorithm.

Additionally, in almost all quantitative applications, algorithms make decisions based on local information such as pixel values. A mean distortion measure provides an indication of the distribution of errors, but does not assist the algorithm to make local decisions because it provides no information as to the specific location and magnitudes of errors. Such information can only really be provided by an absolute distortion measure that indicates something quantitative about both the local and global distortion in an image.

2.3.2 The Suitability of Absolute Distortion Measures

In addition to giving precise information about local distortion, *absolute distortion* measures are able to be applied on a pixel-by-pixel basis as the image is being encoded. Two possible absolute distortion measures are: *maximum absolute distortion* and *percentage maximum absolute distortion*.

The maximum absolute distortion (MAD) measure [21] guarantees that every pixel $\hat{\mathbf{B}}(x, y, t)$ in the reconstructed image is within a maximum distance d of its original value $\mathbf{B}(x,y,t)$, where d is in absolute brightness value terms. This MAD measure is inflexible, however, as it takes no account of the original magnitude of $\mathbf{B}(x,y,t)$. Pixels with small original values will therefore have a larger relative error in the reconstructed image than will pixels that had large original values. A suitable distortion measure must be relative to the original pixel intensity. The best way of achieving this is to use a percentage absolute distortion measure.

The percentage maximum absolute distortion (PMAD) measure [21] guarantees that every pixel $\hat{\mathbf{B}}(x, y, t)$ in the reconstructed image is within a maximum distance of $p*100$ percent to its original value $\mathbf{B}(x,y,t)$. This PMAD distortion measure appears to be the most suitable for application to lossy compression for quantitative analysis. It gives a direct indication of the loss of scientific value for a particular level of distortion and is able to be implemented on a pixel-by-pixel basis. It also offers the best potential to produce predictable results in a range of applications.

A similar measure to PMAD, the percentage maximum absolute error (PMAE), was used by Motta et al [23].

Once a suitable distortion measure has been determined it then needs to be incorporated into a compression algorithm that has been designed as a complete system. A suitable architecture for such a system is described in the following section.

3. A SUITABLE ARCHITECTURE FOR THE COMPRESSION OF HYPERSPECTRAL DATA

This basic architecture for a hyperspectral compression system is shown in Figure 1. This architecture consists of the following components; pre-processing, compression, post-processing and classification.

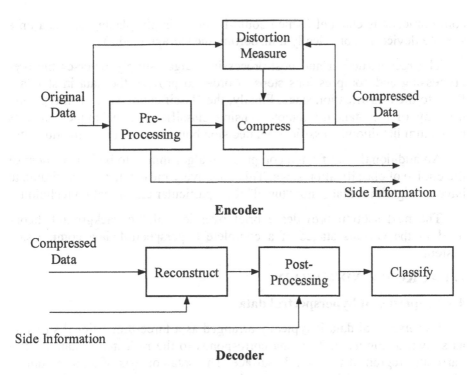

Figure 1: The encoder and decoder architecture for a complete hyperspectral compression system.

The pre-processing stage typically involves applying some simple reversible process, that can easily be communicated to the decoder via side information, in order to improve the performance of the compression algorithms that follow. Some examples of preprocessing that have been proposed in the literature are band re-ordering and normalization, principle component analysis and pre-clustering.

The compression stage comprises the use of one of the standard image compression techniques, such as vector quantization or transform coding, that have been modified to suit the three-dimensional nature of hyperspectral imagery. The compression stage should use a suitable distortion measure to determine the effect of the compression algorithm on the final application of the reconstructed data. This final application is typically some form of classification. The compression stage may also require the generation of side information that is required at the encoder to reconstruct the data. After compression the compressed data is then transmitted via some communications channel (which could involve simply placing the data on a storage device and physically transporting the storage media).

The reconstruction and post-processing stages simply reverses the pre-processing and compressions steps in order to provide the data in standard form to the classification stage. Finally, the classification stage will typically use any of the standard remote sensing classification techniques such as maximum likelihood classification, decision boundary feature extraction, etc.

An additional goal for the compression algorithm is to be independent of the choice of classification stage. This effectively means that it is desirable to have an algorithm that is not "tuned" for a particular classification technique.

The next section provides a brief overview of the background theory used in the various stages of a complete hyperspectral data compression system.

4. BACKGROUND THEORY

4.1 Properties of hyperspectral data

Hyperspectral data is typically arranged as a three-dimensional structure as shown in Figure 2. The data corresponds to the reflected radiation off a particular region of the Earth's surface. The data consists of a large number of two dimensional images with each different image corresponding to the radiation received by the sensor at a particular wavelength. These images are often referred to as *band images* or simply *bands* since they correspond to reflected energy in a particular frequency band.

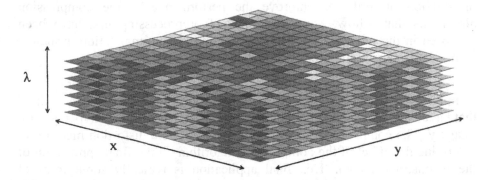

Figure 2: The three-dimensional structure of hyperspectral data.

An alternative way of viewing hyperspectral data is to use the data from the same pixel location in each band image and create a multidimensional *pixel vector* as shown in Figure 3. Each element of the pixel vector corresponds to the reflected energy with a particular wavelength from the same physical location on the Earth's surface.

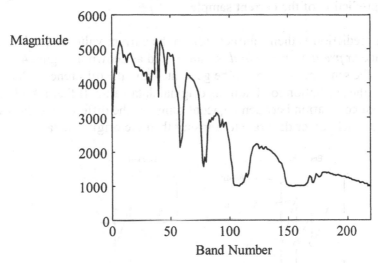

Figure 3: A typical hyperspectral pixel vector.

All pixel vectors formed from hyperspectral data in this way will exhibit some similarity due to the energy-absorbing properties of the Earth's atmosphere. For example, all vectors will show a characteristic reduction in energy at frequencies where electromagnetic energy is absorbed by water in the atmosphere.

4.2 Differential Pulse Code Modulation (DPCM)

Early investigations into the compression of hyperspectral imagery were based on the data compression technique known as Differential Pulse Code Modulation (DPCM).

The term *Pulse Code Modulation* (PCM) refers to the process of sampling an analogue waveform and converting the sampled data values into binary numbers. *Differential* PCM refers to sending the difference between successive samples rather than the original data values. A more general term for this type of compression algorithm is *predictive coding*.

In predictive coding a part of the original data which has already been sent to the decoder is used to predict the current value to be coded. The prediction is typically a data value that is spatially, temporally or spectrally adjacent to the current value. These values are used as a prediction on the basis that, in naturally occurring signals such as audio, photographic images etc., there is usually a high degree of correlation between successive sample values and hence the previous sample in time, space or frequency will make a good prediction of the current sample.

The prediction is then subtracted from the current value and only the difference or *prediction residual* is transmitted as shown in Figure 4. At the decoder the same prediction can be generated and the difference value is added to the prediction to obtain the original data value. If there is a large amount of correlation between adjacent samples, the difference values will require a much lower data rate to transmit than the original data.

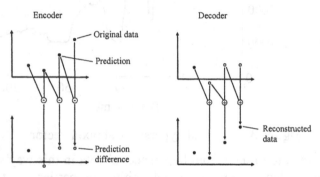

Figure 4: Predictive coding.

In hyperspectral predictive coding, a linear combination of values from pixels that are spatially and spectrally adjacent to the current pixel is typically used as the prediction. An example of the pixel elements that could be used to predict the current pixel value is shown in Figure 5. Note that only those pixel elements that have previously been coded and transmitted to the decoder can be used to predict the current pixel value.

For the case shown in Figure 5, the prediction value x_0' would be given by

$$x_0' = a_1 x_1 + a_2 x_2 \ldots a_9 x_9$$

where $a_0 \ldots a_9$ are usually referred to as the *prediction coefficients*. In some cases the prediction coefficients can be chosen adaptively using the pixel values surrounding the current pixel to be predicted.

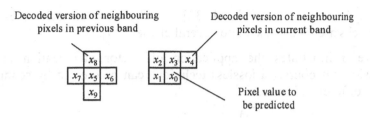

Figure 5: A possible set of prediction pixels used in hyperspectral DPCM coding.

For practical implementations of hyperspectral DPCM compression there are usually some constraints on the amount of data that can be held in the processor memory at any instant in time. Consequently, there is usually only a small portion of the data available to the DPCM compression algorithm at any instant in time. Consequently, the order in which the data is supplied to the compression algorithm will determine which pixels are available to be used in the prediction process. There are two main formats for arranging the order of the data supplied to the coder: *band-interleaved-by-line* (BIL) in which all bands of the current line plus a few preceding lines are available, and *band-sequential* (BSQ) in which all lines of the current band plus a few preceding bands are available.

4.3 Vector Quantization (VQ)

The first step in image vector quantization is the decomposition of the image into a set of vectors. Second, a subset of the input vectors is chosen as a training set. In the third step, a codebook is generated from the training set, normally with the use of an iterative clustering algorithm. Finally, the codeword for the closest code vector in the codebook is found for each input vector and the codeword is transmitted. Therefore, the four stages of vector quantization are: *vector formation, training set generation, codebook generation* and *quantization*.

Many different methods have been proposed to decompose an image into a set of vectors. Examples include the colour components of a pixel, the intensity of spatial blocks of pixels, spatial blocks of intensity values normalised by the mean and variance [24], spectral and spatial blocks [25], three dimensional (spatial/spectral) blocks formed from image sequences [26], blocks formed by subtracting the sample mean from the input spatial vectors [27–29], the transformed coefficients of a block of pixels [30], the adaptive linear predictive coding (LPC) coefficients for a block of pixels

[31], inter-frame difference signal [32] and classification techniques where spatial blocks are categorised into several classes [33].

Figure 6 illustrates the application of vector quantization to lossy compression. Of course, a lossless technique can be created by sending the complete difference image.

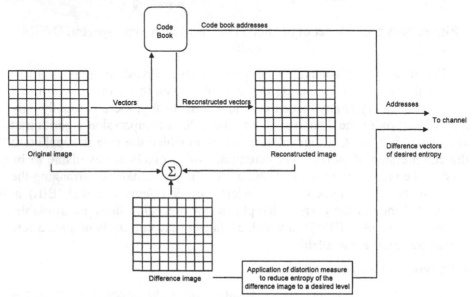

Figure 6: Lossy coding by vector quantization.

An example of the vector quantization process is shown in Figure 7 for a set of 2-dimensional data vectors. Figure 7 (a) shows the data points obtained by plotting the two elements of each data vector against each other. In Figure 7 (b) the full circles show the position of the codebook vectors for a four-vector codebook. The *clusters* of data vectors that would be quantized to each of the four codebook vectors are shown as empty circles, diamonds, crosses and squares respectively. For each original data vector, the index of the closest codebook vector will be transmitted along with the difference between the codebook vector and the original vector. The VQ compression process can be adapted by varying the number and length of the codebook vectors and the accuracy of the transmitted difference vectors.

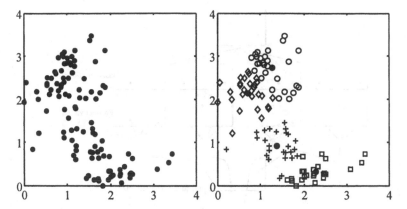

Figure 7: (a) Data points obtained by plotting the two elements of a two-dimensional data vector against each other. (b) full circles – codebook vectors for a four-vector VQ codebook; circles, diamonds, crosses and squares – data points belonging to the clusters for each codebook vector.

4.4 Transform coding

In transform coding, the original sample values are multiplied by a set of *basis vectors* to produce a set of product values as shown in Figure 8. For simpler transforms, the basis vectors are typically sampled sinusoids of increasing frequency. The product values are then added together, and the resulting *coefficients* indicate the frequency content of the original waveform. If the original sample values are similar in shape to the basis vectors then the product values will be mostly positive and the sum of the product values will be a large positive number. If the basis vector and the original signal do not have similar shape then the sum of the product values will be close to zero. If adjacent samples in the original data are highly correlated then many of the higher frequency coefficients will be close to zero and the coefficients can be transmitted or stored with fewer bits than the original samples.

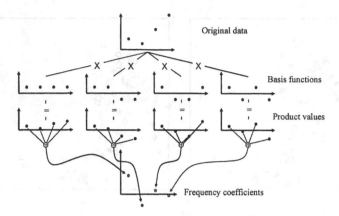

Figure 8: The transform coding process.

At the decoder, each basis vector is multiplied by its corresponding coefficient and the resulting scaled basis vectors are added together to produce the original samples as shown in Figure 9. Often only a small number of low frequency coefficients are needed to produce a good quality reproduction of the original data.

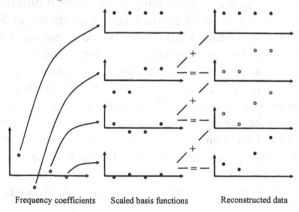

Frequency coefficients   Scaled basis functions   Reconstructed data

Figure 9: The transform decoding process.

For the transform process to be completely reversible the basis vectors are required to be *orthonormal*. A set of orthonormal basis vectors must satisfy the following condition:

$$\mathbf{t}'_p \mathbf{t}_q = \begin{cases} 0 & \text{when } p \neq q \\ 1 & \text{when } p = q \end{cases}$$

where **t** denotes a column basis vector.

To illustrate this property of orthonormality, consider a set of 2 basis vectors in 2-dimensional space. For these basis vectors to be orthonormal they must have a magnitude of 1 and the angle between them must be 90°.

4.4.1 The Karhunen-Loeve Transform (KLT)

The KLT is theoretically the most efficient transform at maximizing the amount of energy contained in the smallest number of coefficients. The basis vectors for the KLT are generated for each particular data set using the statistical properties of the data. More specifically the basis vectors are derived from the covariance matrix of the data.

The elements of this covariance matrix $r_{i,j}$ are given by:

$$r_{i,j} = \sum_{k=1}^{N} (x_{i,k} - \bar{x})(x_{j,k} - \bar{x}) \quad \text{for } i, j = 1 \ldots B$$

where $x_{i,k}$ denotes the k th data value in band i, N is the number of pixels in each band image and B is the number of spectral bands. The basis vectors for the KLT are then the eigenvectors of the covariance matrix and hence are the columns of the matrix $\mathbf{T}$ that satisfies the equation:

$$\mathbf{RT} = \mathbf{TD}$$

where $\mathbf{R}$ is the covariance matrix and $\mathbf{D}$ is a diagonal matrix of eigenvalues of $\mathbf{R}$.

One way of visualizing the transform process is to view it as an axes rotation in B dimensional space where B is the length of the basis vectors. For example, consider a set of two-dimensional data vectors. Figure 10 (a) shows the data points obtained by plotting the two elements of each data vector against each other. The KLT basis vectors for the data shown in Figure 10 (a) are $\mathbf{t}_1 = [-0.46 \quad 0.89]$ and $\mathbf{t}_2 = [0.89 \quad 0.46]$. If these basis vectors are used as a new coordinate system, as shown in Figure 10 (b), the transformed data now has maximum variance along the $\mathbf{t}_1$ axis and minimum variance along the $\mathbf{t}_2$ axis.

This property of the KLT is useful for compression since it means that coefficients which correspond to the directions of minimum variance can be discarded and the resulting error at the decoder will be minimized.

For example, if only c_1 were transmitted, the data rate would be halved and the resulting error between the compressed and original data would be the minimum possible error for that number of coefficients.

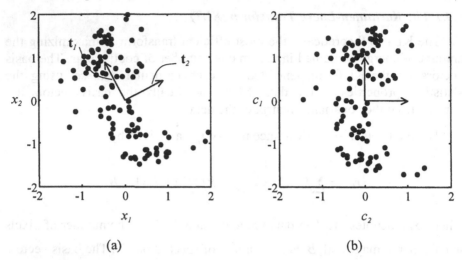

Figure 10: (a) Data points obtained by plotting the two elements of a two-dimensional data vector against each other. (b) Data points obtained by plotting the two coefficients of the basis vectors against each other.

The KLT process is essentially identical to Principal-component Analysis (PCA) where the transform is used to reduce the dimensionality of the data. If data from many dimensions in the original data space is highly correlated PCA allows the data for these dimensions to be represented using a single dimension in the transformed coordinate system.

The disadvantage of the KLT is that it is data-dependent and the optimal basis vectors must be recalculated and transmitted as side information. This problem can be overcome by using a fixed set of basis vectors that are known to both the encoder and decoder. A common transform that uses such a set of fixed basis vectors is the Discrete Cosine Transform (DCT).

4.4.2 The Discrete Cosine Transform (DCT)

The DCT is a sub-optimal transform that is commonly used in image and video compression. It has been shown that if some assumptions are made about the statistics of typical image data then the DCT basis vectors are almost identical to the basis vectors that would be produced by the KLT.

The equation for the basis vectors of the DCT is:

$$t_{m,u} = k_u \sqrt{\frac{2}{N}} \cos\left(\frac{(2m+1)u\pi}{2N}\right) \quad \text{for} \quad m,u = 0,1,\ldots B-1$$

where $t_{m,u}$ is the mth element of the uth basis vector and

$$k_u = \begin{cases} \dfrac{1}{\sqrt{2}} & u = 0 \\ 1 & \text{otherwise} \end{cases}.$$

4.4.3 The Discrete Wavelet Transform

The discrete wavelet transform is essentially a subband filtering process as shown in Figure 11. The input data signal is filtered to produce low-pass and high-pass filtered versions of the input signal. The outputs of the decomposition filters are then subsampled by a factor of two to produce a critically sampled set of subband samples. These subband samples then form the representation of the signal in the wavelet transform domain and are usually referred to as wavelet coefficients. The basis vectors of a wavelet transform are subsampled and shifted versions of the impulse response of the filter used in the subband filtering process.

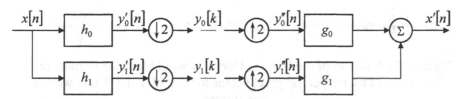

Figure 11: One-dimensional, single-level wavelet decomposition and reconstruction process.

To produce the reconstructed data signal, the subband samples are first upsampled by a factor of two and then filtered to produce reconstructed low-pass and high-pass versions of the original signal. The outputs of the reconstruction filters are then summed to produce the final reconstructed signal.

The two-channel decomposition process can be repeated on the low-pass subband samples of a previous filtering stage to provide a multi-resolution decomposition of the original signal. For two-dimensional data such as images, one-dimensional wavelet transforms in the horizontal and vertical directions are typically applied.

4.4.4 A Comparison of The Basis Vectors Produced by Different Transforms

Figure 12 shows a subset of the basis vectors that would be used to transform a 220 element hyperspectral pixel vector, for each of the transforms described above. It should be noted that the KLT basis vectors will vary for different data sets and the wavelet basis vectors will vary with the particular filter and the number of decomposition levels used.

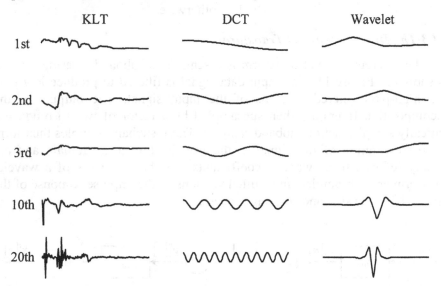

Figure 12: A subset of the basis vectors that would be used to transform a 220 element hyperspectral pixel vector for the KLT, DCT and wavelet transforms.

4.5 Linear mixture analysis

In the technique known as linear mixture analysis it is assumed that the hyperspectral data contains a number of *target* pixel vectors or *pure* pixel vectors (usually referred to as *end-members*). All other pixel vectors in the data are then expressed as a linear combination of these end-members plus some error or noise. Hence any pixel vector in the data can be represented using the equation:

$$x = \mathbf{M}\alpha + n$$

where x is the pixel vector and n is a column vector of noise values. The matrix $\mathbf{M}$ is given by

$$M = \begin{bmatrix} t_1 & t_2 & \cdots & t_p \end{bmatrix}$$

where t_i are the end-members. The column vector α is given by:

$$\alpha = \begin{bmatrix} \alpha_1 & \alpha_2 & \cdots & \alpha_p \end{bmatrix}'$$

where α_i are the abundance fractions for the corresponding end-members.

Extra constraints are typically placed on the abundance fractions so that they are always non-zero and the abundance fractions for a given pixel vector always sum to one. Compression is achieved by observing that each original pixel vector can be approximated by the linear combination of a small number of end-members.

If the end-members are chosen in a supervised way, linear mixture analysis allows classes containing only a few pixels to be represented in the compressed domain.

4.6 Entropy Coding

Entropy coding is usually the final process in any compression algorithm. It involves converting the data produced by the previous coding stages into a stream of binary codewords. The two main techniques used in entropy coding are Huffman coding and arithmetic coding.

In Huffman coding the data values to be transmitted are represented as a pre-defined alphabet of *symbols* or *messages*. The probability that each message will be transmitted is measured and a unique pattern of bits called a *codeword* is allocated to each message. These codewords have different lengths and the shortest codewords are allocated to the messages with highest probability while longer codewords are allocated to messages which occur relatively infrequently. In this way, the *average* number of bits to be transmitted will be less than if all messages were allocated a codeword of the same length.

There are two main disadvantages of Huffman coding. First, the codewords to be used are fixed and must be known to the coder and decoder. This means that Huffman coding cannot easily adapt to a change in the probability distribution of the messages to coded. Second, the smallest codeword that can be used is one bit long. In cases when a particular message occurs very frequently this can lead to an inefficient use of the available data rate.

These two problems can be overcome by using arithmetic coding. Arithmetic coding is a relatively new entropy coding technique that allows highly frequent messages to be coded with an average of less than one bit per message. It achieves this by considering messages to be transmitted in fixed-length groups and producing a single codeword that describes the particular combination of messages which appear in the group. In this way a group of ten messages with high probability, for example, could be transmitted with a codeword of less than ten bits in length. Arithmetic coding typically recalculates the statistics of the data during the coding process and hence can adapt to the changing probabilities of each message. The disadvantage of arithmetic coding is that it is computationally more complex than Huffman coding.

5. CONTRIBUTIONS FROM THE LITERATURE

5.1 Pre-Processing Techniques

5.1.1 Band Re-Ordering For Spectral DPCM

Tate [34] showed that by rearranging the order in which bands were coded a higher inter-band correlation could be achieved. Consequently, when using DPCM coding on the re-ordered data, smaller prediction residuals resulted when adjacent bands were included in the prediction process. The only extra cost of the technique was the requirement to transmit the re-ordering map to the decoder as side information. This overhead was far outweighed by the reduction in data rate of the prediction residuals.

5.1.2 Coefficient Pre-Emphasis Based On Discriminating Power

Lee and Choi [35] used statistical measures to determine the discriminating power (the ability to distinguish one class from all others) of each vector in a set of KLT basis vectors. The coefficients of these basis vectors were then weighted according to their discriminating power. The data was then reconstructed using these weighted basis vectors and the resulting "pre-enhanced" data was compressed using a wavelet transform. The weighted coefficients were then entropy coded using a 3-D SPIHT algorithm [36] (see section 5.2.4).

5.2 Compression Techniques

5.2.1 DPCM

Roger and Cavenor [37] performed the initial investigations on the lossless compression of AVIRIS images in 1996 using spatial-spectral DPCM. Their algorithm used a fixed set of prediction coefficients and Rice coding of the prediction residuals (Rice coding is an early form of arithmetic coding). Compression ratios of 1.6–2.0:1 were reported for a wide range of AVIRIS images.

Lossless JPEG or JPEG-LS [38] is a DPCM compression algorithm included as part of the original JPEG standard. It was designed to losslessly code continuous-tone photographic images. Lossless JPEG has been used as a benchmark for comparison purposes when coding hyperspectral images. Since it was designed for two-dimensional images however, JPEG-LS can only use prediction pixels from the same line when using the BIL format or the same band when using the BSQ format.

Aiazzi et. al. [39] developed a spatial-spectral DPCM algorithm which used fuzzy logic to choose the prediction coefficients. A context-based arithmetic coder was used as the entropy coder for the prediction residuals. Results provided for bands 12–41 of the Cuprite AVIRIS image showed up to 20% better compression ratio for the fuzzy DPCM algorithm when compared with lossless JPEG.

Another DPCM coder that was originally developed for continuous-tone images is the Context-based Adaptive Lossless Image Coding (CALIC) algorithm developed by Wu and Memon [40]. The CALIC algorithm uses the gradient of spatially adjacent pixels to select prediction coefficients from a number of pre-determined configurations. The surrounding gradient is also used to determine the statistics required for entropy coding of the prediction residuals. Wu and Memon later developed a 3-D version of CALIC for coding hyperspectral imagery that incorporated previous bands into the prediction process [41].

Mielikainen and Tovainen [42] developed a spectral DPCM coder which allowed the prediction coefficients to be chosen based on the membership of the current pixel in a pre-determined cluster. The membership of a particular cluster also determined the statistics used in the entropy coder. Their algorithm showed similar performance to Aiazzi's Fuzzy DPCM alogrithm for BSQ data but without the requirement for causality in the bands presented to the prediction algorithm.

Magli et. al. modified the CALIC algorithm to use multiple previous bands in the prediction process. They compared the new M-CALIC algorithm with JPEG-LS [38], 2-D CALIC [40] , 3-D CALIC [41] and fuzzy DPCM [39] for the Jasper, Cuprite, Moffet and Lunar AVIRIS images. Their results show that, on data in BIL format, the new M-CALIC algorithm outperforms other state-of-the art algorithms including 3-D CALIC for lossless and near-lossless applications.

5.2.2 VQ

Vector quantization for the compression of speech and images has been extensively investigated [43]. Investigations on multispectral imagery were carried out as early as 1975 by Hilbert [44] with the compression of Landsat imagery (albeit in the context of clustering for classification). Since hyperspectral images can be considered as a group of brightness vectors in the spectral domain, they would immediately seem ideal for compression by vector quantization.

Due to the wide dynamic range of hyperspectral images, however, normalization of the input vectors is required to aid the performance of the vector quantizer.

Ryan and Arnold [45] investigated a number of normalisation techniques for lossless coding: *mean/residual VQ (M/RVQ)* [27], where the mean was subtracted from the input vector; *normalised VQ* [24], where data was converted to vectors with zero mean and unit standard deviation; *gain/shape VQ* [46], where a shape vector is formed by dividing the original brightness vector by its Euclidean norm; and *mean-normalised vector quantization (M-NVQ)* [45], in which input vectors are pre-processed by normalising them in accordance with the average internal reflectance (or mean) of each vector. M-NVQ was selected as the preferred technique for lossless compression due principally to its low contribution to the overhead compared with the other techniques. M-NVQ produced compression performances approaching the theoretical minimum compressed image entropy of 5 bits/pixel. Images were compressed from original image entropies of between 8.28 and 10.89 bits/pixel to between 4.83 and 5.90 bits/pixel. Lossless M-NVQ performed slightly better than the DPCM results of Roger and Cavenor [37].

Ryan and Arnold [21] also applied M-NVQ to lossy coding using the PMAD distortion measure. The effect of lossy compression was then investigated on the maximum likelihood classification of hyperspectral images, both directly on the original reconstructed data and on features extracted by the decision boundary feature extraction technique [47]. The effect of the PMAD measure was determined on the classification of an image reconstructed with varying degrees of distortion. Despite some anomalies caused by challenging discrimination tasks, the classification accuracy of both the total image and its constituent classes remains predictable as the level of distortion increases. Although total classification accuracy is reduced from 96.8% for the original image to 82.8% for the image compressed with 4% PMAD, the loss in accuracy is not significant (less that 8%) for most classes other than those that present a challenging classification problem. Yet the compressed image was one seventeenth the size of the original.

Motta et al [23] employed a locally optimum partitioned VQ based on a locally adaptive partitioning algorithm that is shown to perform comparably with a more expensive globally optimum one that employs dynamic programming. This technique was extended [48] through the employment of context based DPCM concatenated with LPVQ to provide extremely fast decoding (albeit at the cost of more complex encoding).

Pickering and Ryan [49] improved M-NVQ with the development of an optimised spatial M-NVQ followed by spectral DCT where the parameters for the overall algorithm were optimised jointly. Optimised spatial M-NVQ/spectral DCT was shown to produce compression ratios of between 1.5 and 2.5 times better than those obtained by the optimised spatial M-NVQ technique alone. The improved M-NVQ algorithm was also shown to provide compression ratios of up to 43:1 without a significant loss in classification accuracy.

Jia et al [50] developed a fast classification technique for hyperspectral data that has been compressed using VQ. The cluster space representation of the codebook indices is used for training data representation allowing the class separability to be assessed quantitatively. Experiments using AVIRIS data showed that classification accuracy obtained from the compressed data was comparable to the accuracy achieved when using the original data. In a similar approach, Ramasubramanian and Kanal [51] simply classified by mapping codebook indices onto classes.

Jia and Richards [52] extended the fast classification algorithm of [50] to develop a complete compression system based on a cluster-space representation of the hyperspectral data. The system encoder uses unsupervised VQ of spectral KLT coefficients to determine clusters based on the codebook indices. The codebook indices were then transmitted and used in the fast classification process at the decoder. The classification accuracy of this technique was shown to be comparable with using a Maximum Likelihood classifier on KLT coefficients of the original data.

Canta and Poggi [53] developed a form of gain-shape vector quantization for low bit rate encoding of multi-spectral images in which three-dimensional blocks of data were quantized as the Kronecker product of a spatial-shape codevector and a spectral gain codevector. While the Kronecker-representation gain-shape VQ (KR-GSVQ) is suboptimal with respect to VQ, the encoding strategy was shown to be over 100 times more computationally efficient than unconstrained VQ, and over ten times more computationally efficient than direct gain-shape VQ.

Qian et al [54] developed a fast VQ technique, multiple subcodebook algorithm (MSCA), for lossy compression by spatially segmenting the hyperspectral image first and using codebooks local to each spatial region. The overall processing speed of compression could be improved by a factor of around 1000 at an average fidelity penalty of 1 dB.

Qian [55] also developed a fast VQ technique for hyperspectral imagery by making use of the fact that in the full search of the generalised Lloyd algorithm (GLA) for vector quantization a training vector does not require a search to find the minimum distance partition if its distance to the partition is improved in the current iteration compared to that of the previous iteration. The resulting method is simple producing a large computational saving for compression fidelity as good as the GLA.

5.2.3 DCT

Baizert et. al. [56] showed that, for lossless and near lossless compression, using a 3-D DCT approach provided improved compression ratios when compared with the spatial M-NVQ/ spectral DCT algorithm in [49].

5.2.4 Wavelet

Compression algorithms that use the wavelet transform can be divided into two main groups. These two groups differ in the type of entropy coding applied to the coefficients produced by the wavelet transform process. The two types of entropy coding are: *zero-tree* coding and *context-based* coding.

In both algorithms, the wavelet coefficients are represented as bit planes i.e. the most-significant bit for every coefficient is coded first, followed by the next most significant bit for each coefficient, and so on. Both algorithms also use arithmetic coding to produce codewords that represent the bits comprising each bit-plane. Hence the messages to be coded by the arithmetic coder have only two possible values; zero or one. An arithmetic coder requires that the probability of each message to be transmitted be known and it is in this aspect of the coding process where the two algorithms differ.

In zero-tree coding the bit values for each bit-plane are coded in order from lowest frequency band to highest frequency band. The bits occurring in the same spatial position for each band are combined to form an inverted tree of bit values. This representation provides good compression since it is quite common for many of the high frequency branches of the tree to be zero and this is indicated at the last non-zero node of the tree. The most well-known implementation of the zero-tree approach is the set partitioning in hierarchical trees (SPIHT) algorithm [57].

In context-based coding, the probability that the value of current bit to be coded is zero is estimated using immediately adjacent bit values in the current bit-plane and in more significant bit-planes. This approach also provides good compression since regions of the image containing low frequency information will produce mostly zero bit in all bit-planes. The context-based approach has been adopted in the JPEG-2000 image compression standard [58].

Pal et. al. [59] investigated the effects on classification accuracy after hyperspectral imagery had been compressed using a spectral KLT followed by spatial compression using the JPEG-2000 algorithm. Their results showed that over 99% of pixels were classified in an identical manner to the original data for compressed data rates of 0.125 bits per pixel. Lim et. al. showed similar results using a spectral KLT followed by SPIHT coding of the spatial wavelet coefficients [60] and also with a 3-D version of the SPIHT algorithm [61].

Lee et. al. [62] compared several techniques with different spectral compression methods followed by spatial compression of the spectral coefficients using the JPEG-2000 coder. The spectral compression techniques employed were the DCT, KLT and Wavelet transform coing as well as a spectral DPCM approach. Their results showed that for decoded images requiring the same bit-rate to transmit, the KLT produced decoded images with the highest PSNR, followed by DCT, Wavelet and DPCM in that order.

Tang et. al. [63] developed a modified SPIHT algorithm that used an asymmetric tree structure with a different type of decomposition in the spectral dimension. Their results showed that using the new tree structure provides a 0.5 to 1.0 dB improvement in PSNR over the 3-D SPIHT and 3-D JPEG-2000 algorithms.

Wang et. al. [64] developed a simple non-adaptive filtering approach to estimate the probability of zero bits in bit-planes of quantized wavelet coefficients. This technique, known as *tarp* filtering, is similar to the context-based estimation used in JPEG-2000 but in tarp filtering the probability estimates do not rely on patterns in the surrounding bits. Instead the variance of adjacent bits is used to predict areas of all zeros or all ones. Their results show that 3-D tarp filtering provides similar performance to 3-D JPEG-2000 and 3-D SPIHT but with a much simpler implementation.

5.3 Linear Mixture Analysis

Rupert et. al. [65] used the mean of clusters found by unsupervised clustering as end-members. An iterative process was then used to determine the optimal set of abundance fractions and end-members that reduced the noise to a predetermined level. The abundance fractions were then coded losslessly.

Bowles et. al. [66] modified this idea by extrapolating the mean of clusters found by unsupervised clustering to determine end-members that may not have been contained in the original data set. The abundance maps were spatially compressed using a 2-D spatial wavelet transform.

Plaza et. al. [67] used a new extended morphological filtering approach to find end-members based on spatially coherent regions of the image. Their results showed significantly improved classification accuracy when compared with other techniques for determining end-members.

Du and Chang [68] developed a complete compression system based on linear mixture analysis. The system consists of an unsupervised method for determining end-members and abundance fractions. The abundance fractions for each pixel are transmitted and used to reconstructed version of the original data. The system provides comparable compression and classification accuracy when compared with using a spectral-only KLT.

6. CONCLUSIONS AND FUTURE DIRECTIONS

The descriptions of the hyperspectral compression algorithms given in the previous section indicate that most of the approaches provide results for mean distortion measures such as PSNR. However there is strong evidence that such distortion measures have little or no correlation to the degradation in accuracy when the compressed data is used for classification. Hence there is a strong argument for the requirement of new and more meaningful measures of compression induced distortion.

The PMAD measure proposed by Ryan and Arnold [21] and the similar PMAE measure proposed by Motta et. al. [23] provide a starting point toward a more meaningful distortion measure. However these measures still only provide weak estimates of how the compressed data will behave during the classification process. A more promising approach was demonstrated by Faulconbridge et. al. in [69] where hyperspectral data was compressed in a controlled manner based on the estimated reduction in classification accuracy. In this technique parts of the data that were estimated to provide little benefit to separating classes were compressed more heavily than other parts of the data which were estimated to be important to the final classification process. Their results showed that, when compared with the use of a mean distortion measure, classification accuracy for each class and the overall accuracy could be degraded in a much more controlled manner. The algorithm proposed in [69] was implemented using a heuristic approach, however, and could be improved with the development of an analytical measure of the importance of individual data components to any final classification application.

Once a more meaningful distortion measure has been developed, it should be an integral part of the compression process and provide a reliable estimate of the degradation in classification accuracy for a particular amount of compression. This serves two purposes; first, users who do not require a high level of classification accuracy can choose to work with much smaller file sizes and data rates. Second, the compression process can be actually targeted at reducing file size without degrading classification performance rather than satisfying some measure of the average error in the image. Some examples from the previous section that have been developed in this way are the compression systems proposed by Du and Chang [68] and Jia and Richards [52].

Finally, to summarize these concluding remarks, for future improvements in hyperspectral image compression, a complete system design approach should be adopted that includes an appropriate distortion measure providing meaningful feedback at the encoder. Further work is needed in the areas of suitable distortion measures and in compression algorithms that can provide an accurate mapping between compression ratio and degradation in classification accuracy.

7. REFERENCES

[1]   Jelinek F., *Probabilistic Information Theory*, Chapter 4, McGraw Hill, New York, 1968.
[2]   Seyler A. and Budrikis Z., "Detail Perception after Scale Change in

Television Image Processing", *IEEE Transactions on Information Theory*, IT-11, pp. 31–43, 1965.

[3] Hall C. and Hall E., "A Non-linear Model for the Spatial Characteristics of the Human Visual System", *IEEE Transactions on Systems, Man and Cybernetics*, SMC-7, pp. 161–170, Mar. 1977.

[4] Pratt W., *Digital Image Processing*, Wiley, New York, 1978.

[5] Budrikis Z., "Visual Fidelity Criterion and Modeling", *Proceedings of the IEEE*, vol. 60, no 7, pp. 771–779, Jul. 1972.

[6] Pratt W.K, *Image Transmission Techniques*, Academic Press, New York, 1979.

[7] Hecht S., "The Visual Discrimination of Intensity and the Weber-Fechner Law", *Journal of General Physiology*, pp. 235–267, 1924.

[8] Sakrison D., "On the Role of the Observer and a Distortion Measure in Image Transmission", *IEEE Transactions on Communications*, COM-25, pp. 1251–1266, 1977.

[9] Limb J. and Rubinstein C., "On the Design of a Quantizer for DPCM Coders: A Functional Relationship Between Visibility, Probability and Masking", *IEEE Transactions on Communications*, COM-26, pp. 573–578, 1978.

[10] Netravali A. and Prasada B., "Adaptive Quantization of Picture Signals Using Spatial Masking", *Proceedings of the IEEE*, vol. 65, pp. 536–548, 1977.

[11] Stromeyer C. and Julesz B., "Spatial-Frequency Masking in Vision: Critical Bands and Spread of Marking", *Journal of the Optical Society of America*, vol. 62, no. 10, pp. 1221–1232, Oct. 1972.

[12] Campbell F., "Visual Acuity Via Linear Analysis", *Proceedings of the Symposium on Information Processing in Sight Sensory Systems*, Pasadena, CA, Nov. 1965.

[13] Davidson M., "Perturbation Approach to Spatial Brightness Interaction in Human Vision", *Journal of the Optical Society of America*, vol. 58, pp. 1300–1309, 1968.

[14] Stockham T., "Image Processing in the Context of a Visual Model", *Proceedings of the IEEE*, vol. 60, no. 7, pp. 828–842, Jul. 1972.

[15] Mannos J. and Sakrison D., "The Effects of a Visual Fidelity Criterion on the Encoding of Images", *IEEE Transactions of Information Theory*, IT-20, no. 4, pp. 525–536, Jul. 1974.

[16] Murakami T., et al, "Vector Quantizer of Video Signals", *Electronic Letters*, vol. 7, pp. 1005–1006, Nov. 1982.

[17] Netravali A. and Limb J., "Picture Coding: A Review", *Proceedings of the IEEE*, vol. 68, no. 3, pp. 366–406, Mar. 1980.

[18] Chen S. and Wang Y., "Vector Quantization of Pitch Information in Mandarin Speech", *IEEE Transactions on Communications*, vol. 38, no. 9, pp. 1317–1320, Sep. 1990.

[19]   CCIR, *Method for Subjective Assessment of the Quality of Television Pictures*, 13th Plenary Assembly, Recommendation 500, vol. 11, pp. 65–68, 1974.

[20]   Limb J., "Distortion Criteria of the Human Viewer", *IEEE Transactions on Systems, Man and Cybernetics*, SMC-9, no. 12, pp. 778–793, 1979.

[21]   Ryan M. and Arnold J, "Lossy Compression Of Hyperspectral Data Using Vector Quantization", *Remote Sensing of Environment*, vol. 61, no. 3, pp. 419–436, Sep. 1997.

[22]   Gray R., et al, "Distortion Measures for Speech Processing", *IEEE Transactions on Acoustics, Speech and Signal Processing*, ASSP-28, no. 4, pp. 367–376, Aug. 1980.

[23]   Motta G., Rizzo F., and Storer J., "Compression Of Hyperspectral Imagery", *Data Compression Conference*, pp. 333–342, 25-27 Mar. 2003.

[24]   Murakami T., Asai K. and Yamazaki E., "Vector Quantizer of Video Signals", *Electronic Letters*, vol. 7, pp. 1005–1006, Nov. 1982.

[25]   Boucher P. and Goldberg M., "Colour Image Compression by Adaptive Vector Quantization", *Proceedings IEEE International Conference on Acoustics Speech and Signal Processing*, San Diego, pp. 29.6.1–29.6.4, Mar. 1984.

[26]   Goldberg M. and Sun H., "Image Sequence Coding by Three-dimensional Block Vector Quantization", *IEE Proceedings*, vol. 135, pt. F, no. 5, pp. 482–487, Aug. 1986.

[27]   Baker R. and Gray R., "Image Compression Using Non-adaptive Spatial Vector Quantization", *Conference Record of the 16th Asilomar Conference on Circuits, Systems, Computers*, pp. 55–61, Oct. 1982.

[28]   Baker R. and Gray R., "Differential Vector Quantization of Achromatic Imagery", *Proceedings of the International Picture Coding Symposium*, pp. 105–106, Mar 1983.

[29]   Budge S. and Baker R., "Compression of Colour Digital Images Using Vector Quantization in Product Codes", *Proceedings IEEE International Conference on Acoustics, Speech*, Signal Processing, pp. 129–132, Mar. 1985.

[30]   Blain M. and Fischer T., "A Comparison of Vector Quantization Techniques in Transform and Subband Coding of Imagery", *Image Communication*, vol. 3, pp. 91–105, 1991.

[31]   Sun H. and Goldberg M., "Image Coding using LPC with Vector Quantization", *Proceedings of the IEEE International Conference on Digital Signal Processing*, Florence, pp. 508–512, Sep. 1984.

[32]   Murakami T. et al, "Interframe Vector Coding of Colour Video Signals", *Proceedings of the International Picture Coding Symposium*, Jul. 1984.

[33]   Ramamurthi B. and Gersho A., "Classified Vector Quantization of Images", *IEEE Transactions on Communications*, vol. 34, no. 11, pp. 1105–1115, Nov. 1986.

[34]   Tate S., "Band Ordering In Lossless Compression Of Multispectral Images," *IEEE Transactions on Computing*, vol. 46, pp. 477–483, Apr. 1997.

[35]   Chulhee Lee and Euisun Choi, "Compression Of Hyperspectral Images With Enhanced Discriminant Features", *IEEE Workshop on Advances in Techniques for Analysis of Remotely Sensed Data*, pp. 76–79, 27–28 Oct. 2003.

[36]   Kim, B., Xiong, Z., and Pearlman, W. A.., "Low Bit-rate Scalable Video Coding With 3-D Set Partition in Hierarchical Trees (3-D SPIHT)," *IEEE Tranactions on Circuits and Systems for Video Technology*, vol. 10, pp. 1374–1387, Dec. 2000.

[37]   Roger R. and Cavenor M., "Lossless Compression of AVIRIS Images", *IEEE Transactions on Image Processing*, vol. 5, no. 5, pp. 713–719, May 1996.

[38]   Weinberger M., Seroussi G., and Sapiro G., "The LOCO-I Lossless Image Compression Algorithm: Principles and Standardization into JPEG-LS," *IEEE Transactions on Image Processing*, vol. 9, pp. 1309–1324, Aug. 2000.

[39]   Aiazzi B., Alba P., Alparone L., and Baronti S., "Lossless Compression Of Multi/Hyper-Spectral Imagery Based On A 3-D Fuzzy Prediction", *IEEE Transactions on Geoscience and Remote Sensing*, vol. 37, no. 5, pp. 2287–2294, Sept. 1999.

[40]   Wu X. and Memon N., "Context-based, Adaptive, Lossless Image Coding," *IEEE Transactions on Communications*, vol. 45, pp. 437–444, Apr. 1997.

[41]   Wu X. and Memon N., "Context-based Lossless Interband Compression— Extending CALIC," *IEEE Transactions on Image Processing*, vol. 9, pp. 994–1001, Jun. 2000.

[42]   Mielikainen J. and Toivanen P., "Clustered DPCM for The Lossless Compression of Hyperspectral Images", *IEEE Transactions on Geoscience and Remote Sensing*, vol. 41, no. 12, pp. 2943–2946, Dec. 2003.

[43]   Gersho A. and Gray R., *Vector Quantization and Signal Compression*, Kluwer Academic Publishers, Norwell MA, 1990.

[44]   Hilbert E., "Joint Pattern Recognition / Data Compression Concept for ERTS Hyperspectral Data", *Efficient Transmission of Pictorial Information*, SPIE, vol. 66, pp. 122–137, Aug. 1975.

[45]   Ryan M. and Arnold J., "The Lossless Compression of AVIRIS Images by Vector Quantization", *IEEE Transactions on Geoscience and Remote Sensing*, vol. 35, no. 3, pp. 546–550, May 1997.

[46]   Ramamurthi B. and Gersho A., "Image Vector Quantization With a Perceptually Based Classifier", in *Proceedings of the IEEE International Conference on Acoustics, Speech, Signal Processing*, San Diego, CA, vol. 2, pp. 32.10.1–32.10.4, Mar. 1984.

[47]   Lee C. and Landgrebe D., "Feature Extraction on Decision Boundaries", *IEEE Transactions on Pattern Analysis and Machine Intelligence*, vol. 15, no. 4, pp. 388–400, 1993.

[48]   Rizzo F., Carpentieri B., Motta G., and Storer J., "High Performance Compression of Hyperspectral Imagery With Reduced Search Complexity In The Compressed Domain", *Data Compression Conference*, pp. 479–488, 23–25 March 2004.

[49]   Pickering M. and Ryan M., "Efficient Spatial-Spectral Compression Of Hyperspectral Data", *IEEE Transactions on Geoscience and Remote Sensing*, vol. 39, no. 7, pp. 1536–1539, Jul. 2001.

[50]   Jia X., Ryan M., and Pickering M., "Fast Classification of V-Q Compressed Hyperspectral Data", *IEEE Geoscience and Remote Sensing Symposium IGARSS '01*, vol. 4, pp. 1862–1864, 9–13 Jul. 2001.

[51]   Ramasubramanian D. and Kanal, L., "Classification of Remotely Sensed Images in Compressed Domain", *IEEE Workshop on Advances in Techniques for Analysis of Remotely Sensed Data*, pp. 249–253, 27–28 Oct. 2003.

[52]   Jia X. and Richards J., "Efficient Transmission and Classification of Hyperspectral Image Data", *IEEE Transactions on Geoscience and Remote Sensing*, vol. 41, no. 5, pp. 1129–1131, May 2003.

[53]   Canta G. and Poggi G., "Kronecker-Product Gain-Shape Vector Quantization For Multispectral And Hyperspectral Image Coding", *IEEE Transactions on Image Processing*, vol. 7, no. 5, pp. 668–678, May 1998.

[54]   Shen-En Qian, Hollinger A.B, Williams D., and Manak D., "Vector Quantization Using Spectral Index-Based Multiple Subcodebooks For Hyperspectral Data Compression", *IEEE Transactions on Geoscience and Remote Sensing*, vol. 38, no. 3, pp. 1183–1190, May 2000.

[55]   Qian S.-E., "Hyperspectral Data Compression Using a Fast Vector Quantization Algorithm", *IEEE Transactions on Geoscience and Remote Sensing*, accepted for future publication, 2004.

[56]   Baizert P., Pickering M. and Ryan M., "Compression of Hyperspectral Data By Spatial/Spectral Discrete Cosine Transform", *IEEE Geoscience and Remote Sensing Symposium IGARSS '01*, vol. 4, pp. 1859–1861, 9-13 Jul. 2001.

[57]   Said A. and Pearlman, W., "A New, Fast, And Efficient Image Codec Based On Set Partitioning In Hierarchical Trees," *IEEE Transactions on Circuits and Systems for Video Technology*, vol. 6, pp. 243–250, Jun. 1996.

[58]   Taubman, D. and Marcellin, M., "*JPEG2000: Image Compression Fundamentals, Standards and Practice*," Boston, MA, Kluwer, 2002.

[59]   Pal M., Brislawn C. and Brumby S., "Feature Extraction From Hyperspectral Images Compressed Using The JPEG-2000 Standard", *Fifth IEEE Southwest Symposium on Image Analysis and Interpretation*, pp. 168–172, 7–9 Apr. 2002.

[60]   Sunghyun Lim, Kwang Hoon Sohn and Chulhee Lee, "Principal Component Analysis for Compression of Hyperspectral Images", *IEEE Geoscience and Remote Sensing Symposium IGARSS '01*, vol. 1, pp.97–99, vol.1, 9-13 Jul.

2001.

[61]   Sunghyun Lim, Kwanghoon Sohn and Chulhee Lee, "Compression For
       Hyperspectral Images Using Three Dimensional Wavelet Transform", *IEEE
       Geoscience and Remote Sensing Symposium IGARSS '01*, vol. 1, pp. 109–111,
       9–13 Jul. 2001

[62]   Lee, H., Younan N. and King R., "Hyperspectral Image Cube Compression
       Combining JPEG-2000 and Spectral Decorrelation", *IEEE Geoscience and
       Remote Sensing Symposium IGARSS '02*, vol. 6, pp. 3317–3319, 24–28 Jun.
       2002.

[63]   Tang X., Cho S. and Pearlman W., "3D Set Partitioning Coding Methods In
       Hyperspectral Image Compression", *International Conference on Image
       Processing*, vol. 2, pp. 239–242, 14–17 Sept. 2003

[64]   Yonghui Wang, Rucker J. and Fowler J., "Three-dimensional Tarp Coding
       For The Compression Of Hyperspectral Images", *IEEE Geoscience and
       Remote Sensing Letters*, vol. 1, no. 2, pp. 136–140, Apr. 2004.

[65]   Rupert S., Sharp M., Sweet J. and Cincotta E., "Noise Constrained
       Hyperspectral Data Compression", *IEEE Geoscience and Remote Sensing
       Symposium IGARSS '01*, vol. 1, pp. 94–96 vol. 19-13, Jul. 2001.

[66]   Bowles J., Wei Chen and Gillis D., "ORASIS Framework—Benefits To
       Working Within The Linear Mixing Model", *IEEE Geoscience and Remote
       Sensing Symposium IGARSS '03*, vol. 1, pp.96–98, 21–25 July 2003.

[67]   Plaza A., Martinez P., Perez R. and Plaza J., "A New Approach To Mixed
       Pixel Classification Of Hyperspectral Imagery Based On Extended
       Morphological Profiles", *Pattern Recognition*, vol. 37, no. 6, pp. 1097–1116,
       Jun. 2004.

[68]   Du Q. and Chang C-I, "Linear Mixture Analysis-based Compression for
       Hyperspectral Image Analysis", *IEEE Transactions on Geoscience and
       Remote Sensing*, vol. 42, no. 4, pp. 875–891, Apr. 2004.

[69]   Faulconbridge R., Pickering M., Ryan M., and Jia X., "A New Approach to
       Controlling Compression-Induced Distortion of Hyperspectral Images", *IEEE
       Geoscience and Remote Sensing Symposium IGARSS '03*, vol. 3, pp. 1830–
       1832, 21–25 Jul. 2003.

Lossless Predictive Compression of Hyperspectral Images

Hongqiang Wang and Khalid Sayood
Department of Electrical Engineering
University of Nebraska, Lincoln

1 Introduction

After almost three decades of successful data acquisition using multispectral sensors the first space based hyperspectral sensors were launched in 2000 on the NASA EO-1 satellite. However, airborne hyperspectral sensors such as AVIRIS, among others, have been generating useful data for many years. The advent of the space-borne ALI and Hyperion sensors as well as the successes of AVIRIS presage the development of many more hyperspectral instruments. Furthermore the success of multispectral imagers such as the Enhanced Thematic Mapper Plus (EMT+) on the LANDSAT-7 mission and the modestly named 36 band MODIS (Moderate Resolution Imaging Spectroradiometer) instrument aboard the *Terra* satellite and the *Aqua* spacecraft promises the deployment of significant numbers of other such instruments. The use of multispectral and hyperspectral sensors, while opening the door to multiple applications in climate observation, environmental monitoring, and resource mapping, among others, also means the generation of huge amounts of data that needs to be accommodated by transmission and distribution facilities that cannot economically handle this level of data. This means that compression, always a pressing concern [1], is now imperative. While in many cases the use of lossy compression may be unavoidable, it is important that the design always include the possibility of lossless recovery. Much effort usually has gone into the reduction of noise in the instruments. The voluntary addition of noise due to compression can be a bitter pill to swallow.

Compression is needed, and can be applied, in several different places from where the images are acquired to the end-user. At the point of acquisition compression may be required under several different scenarios. The satellite carrying the sensor may not be in continuous contact with ground stations. In the interval between contacts the data has to stored on board. If these intervals are of any significant length the amount of data generated is likely to be very high and compression becomes imperative. Any compression at this point has to be lossless. Even if there is relatively frequent contact between the satellite and the ground station if the portion of the bandwidth available to the instrument is less than the raw data rate again compression is required, and again this compression has to be lossless. Once the data is on the ground it needs to be archived. This is another point at which lossless compression may be needed. Finally, the data has to be distributed to end-users. Depending on the amount of data desired by a particular end-user compression may or may not be required. Furthermore, depending on the application of interest to the end-user this compression can be lossy or lossless. Thus, while it can be argued for certain applications that given a stringent enough distortion constraint lossy compression may be possible there are many scenarios in which only lossless compression will be acceptable. Various lossless compression schemes based on transform coding, vector quantization [2, 3], and predictive coding have been proposed. In this chapter we examine a number of lossless compression schemes based on predictive coding.

Most lossless compression schemes include prediction as part of the algorithm. Strong local correlations in the image allow prediction of the pixel being encoded. The difference between the pixel and the prediction, known as the prediction error or prediction residual, usually has a much lower first order entropy than the pixel itself and therefore, can be encoded with fewer bits. Well known predictive lossless image compression techniques developed for use with natural images include CALIC (*Context-based Adaptive Lossless Image Compression*) [4, 5] and LOCO-I (*Low Complexity Lossless Compression for Images*) [6] which is part of JPEG-LS, the ISO/ITU standard for lossless and near-lossless compression of images. These, as well as others, have their three dimensional counterparts. In recent years, various lossless hyperspectral image compression schemes using reversible integer wavelet transforms have been proposed. These include EZW (*Embedded Zerotree Wavelet*) [7] and SPIHT (*Set Partitioning in Hierarchical Trees*) compression [8]. These schemes takes advantage of the fact that when an image is decomposed based on its frequency the coefficients at higher frequency are closely related to the coefficients at lower frequency. Wavelet decomposition and predictive coding can be combined in two ways. The prediction error residuals can be encoded using a wavelet coder [9], or the decomposition of the images can be used as a preprocessing step prior to prediction.

In the following we describe some of the more popular predictive coding schemes as they have been applied to hyperspectral compression.

2   Predictive Coding - Overview

Compression algorithms depends on the underlying model of data we are dealing with. For speech data, which can be modeled by a mechanism that is fundamentally similar across individuals, it is relatively easy to obtain a model that generates the data in a standard way. This leads to the development of speech compression algorithms. However, for image data, the absence of a single generative mechanism means that it is very difficult to seek a single mode to be used for image compression. The problem can be circumvented to some extent by focusing on the sink or user, of the information, rather than the source. If images aims for human perception, they are likely to contain quasi-consent regions encoded by edges or regions of short transitions. We can model this as high frequency which consists of the edges combined with low frequency signal or the background. This view leads to approaches which decompose the image prior to further modeling, such as wavelet transform coding. A somewhat different approach is to focus on local relationships between pixels. This approach naturally leads to predictive coding algorithms which encode the difference between a prediction of the value of the pixel being encoded and the pixels itself.

Image compression algorithms based on predictive coding generally use local modes to generate a prediction of the pixel being encoded. The input to the predictor are pixels available to both encoder and the decoder. The prediction error is then encoded with respect to a probability model. For instance, differential pulse code modulation (DPCM) schemes are usually employed for lossless compression of two-dimensional (2-D) image. This generally consists of a spatial prediction followed by an entropy coder for the residual images. Given the neighborhood pixels are causal, i.e. those pixels are already known for both encoder and decoder, a predictor can be designed such that the prediction is optimized in the sense of minimum mean squared error (MMSE) over the entire image. This can be done by using standard linear combination, or regression method. If the data is stationary, such prediction would be optimum. For speech signals, we can make an assumption that they are stationary within a short segment, and it demonstrated that this assumption can result in very good results. Unfortunately, the assumption is generally not true for image data. As a consequence, it is not possible to figure out a single model which can capture all local structures in images, and most modern lossless image compression algorithms employ multiple predictors to capture the local relationships in different parts of the images, or explore the underlying data structure in a progressive manner. For instance, rather than use a uniform linear prediction model, ADPCM, updates the coefficients of predictors as long as new data is available. Another method is to switch between various predictors based on the local context or by combing the various predictions in some manner. This point has been demonstrated by the CALIC algorithm and the LOCO-I algorithm used in JPEG-LS standard.

For hyperspectral images, an additional source of richness is the existence of two types of correlation: spatial correlation between adjacent pixels in a band, and spectral correlation between adjacent bands. We can view this increase in the size of the neighborhood as an extension from 2-D prediction to 3-D prediction. However, this extension is not always straightforward and the direct extension of a 2D method to three dimensions may not always provide much benefit, and can at times be detrimental. As such, it is necessary to develop predictors specialized for the application 3-D hyperspectral images.

A significant improvement in coding performance of predictive coding algorithms used with hyperspectral images can be obtained if the bands are reordered to enhance the band-to-band predictability [10]. The motivation behind this idea is that the reflection intensity of the frequency components by materials in the earth generally are not monotonically increasing or decreasing. As the reordering has to be done offline this enhancement is not always possible.

3 3-Dimensional Adaptive Differential Pulse Coded Modulation (ADPCM)

Adaptive Differential Pulse Code Modulation for lossless compression of AVIRIS images was first proposed by Roger and Cavenor in 1996 [11]. The various predictors in the 3-D ADPCM algorithm exploited spectral (interband) correlation, spatial (intraband) correlations, and the combination of spectral and spatial correlation for the lossless compression of AVIRIS images. The residual images obtained were then coded by using various variable length codes.

Similar to most lossless predictive coding schemes, the method has two stages, predictive decorrelation (which produces the residuals) and residual encoding. The residual image is obtained by taking the difference between the pixel values and their prediction values. The residual encoding primarily exploited Rice codes [12]. Two other forms of variable length coding were also evaluated.

3.1 Predictors for Image Decorrelation

Five predictors shown in Table 1 were used in this work. (The authors indicate that these five were selected from a set of 25 candidates). These predictors are causal, that is, the pixels values used for predictions are all available to both the encoder and the decoder. The predictors prefixed with "SA" are spatial predictors, or intraband predictors, and the predictors prefixed with "SE" are spectral predictors, or interband predictors. The predictors with a prefix of "SS" are spatial and spectral predictors which explore both spatial and spectral correlations.

Two of the five predictors have constant coefficients, while three predictors whose names contain an "o" have variable coefficients which are obtained by minimizing the variance of the prediction errors within each row. These coefficient are obtained by the least-squares minimization of $\sum_{j=1}^{n} (\hat{x}_{i,j,\lambda} - x_{i,j,\lambda})^2$, where n is the number of pixels in a row, i denotes the row, j denotes the column, and λ denotes the spectral band. The coefficients a, b, c, and d must be transmitted as header information to the decoder for decompression purpose. In the algorithm, a is quantized using 16 bits, and b, c, and d are quantized using 12bits for transmission.

3.2 Encoding of Residuals

The residual images are further entropy encoded. A simple variable length code, the Rice code, and two other variable length codes based on Huffman codes are evaluated. Rice codes have been shown to be the optimum codes for the information sources with a geometric distribution [12]. They are also very simple to implement in hardware. The residuals within each row are assumed

Predictor	Formula for Predictor $\hat{x}_{i,j,\lambda}$
SA-2RC	$(x_{i-1} + x_{i,j-1,\lambda})/2$
SS-1	$x_{i,j-1,\lambda} + x_{i,j,\lambda-1} - x_{i,j-1,\lambda-1}$
SE-o1B	$a + bx_{i,j,\lambda-1}$
SE-o2B	$a + bx_{i,j,\lambda-1} + cx_{i,j,\lambda-2}$
SS-o1	$a + bx_{i,j-1,\lambda} + cx_{i,j,\lambda-1} + dx_{i,j-1,\lambda-1}$

Table 1: Definition of Five Predictors

to have a geometric distribution and the Rice codes are then applied to each individual rows.

Two other variable length codes based on Huffman codes are evaluated. The first one is semi-static Huffman coding with truncation. The advantages of these codes is that the coding allows for an uncertain range of residuals. However it needs codebooks to be constructed to match the data's statistics. This necessarily means that the coding is a two-pass scheme. The second one is dynamic Huffman coding in which the Huffman code tables are updated as the compression proceeds. To improve the compression performance, eight codebooks are used in the algorithm and the residuals for each row are assigned to a codebook according to their statistics.

The authors provide compression ratios obtained by using 5 predictors, 10 AVIRIS hyperspectral images, and three variable length codes. It demonstrated that the predictor SA-2RC that only uses spatial correlations is the poorest, even though among the (old) JPEG predictors [13] it performs the best for 2D natural images. The SS-1 predictor which exploits both spectral and spatial correlation works much better than the SA-2RC. The best performance is obtained by using the three optimized predictors.

The overall compression ratio for the typical hyperspectral images are in the range of 1.6 -2.0:1. The methods can provide 1.0-1.8 bits/pixels more compression than the best of the JPEG predictors. They also perform better than the prediction tree approach of Memon et al. [14].

4 Interband Context-based, Adaptive, Lossless Image Codec (CALIC)

CALIC operates by exploiting local structure in images in an exhaustive fashion both for prediction and for context coding of the residuals. Since its introduction in 1995, CALIC has remained at the forefront in terms of compression performance. Two dimensional CALIC, was extended to 3-dimensional hyperspectral images by Wu and Memon [15]. The three dimensional CALIC was then improved upon by Magli et al. [16]. We present how the prediction in CALIC is extended from 2-D to 3-D and how spectral correlation is used to improve the prediction.

4.1 Intraband CALIC

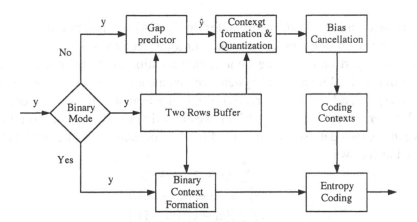

Figure 1: Schematic description of the CALIC image coding system

CALIC operates in two modes: a binary mode and a continuous-tone mode as shown in Fig.1. In the continuous-tone mode, predictive coding is used, therefore, it is the continuous tone mode that is of interest to us. In this mode the encoder obtains a prediction which is adjusted based on the local gradients. The prediction is then further adjusted based on the context in which the pixel occurs. The performance of the predictor in similar contexts is monitored and any bias in the prediction computed. This bias is then removed from the prediction. The prediction error is then encoded using a context based variable length coder, either a Huffman coder or an arithmetic coder.

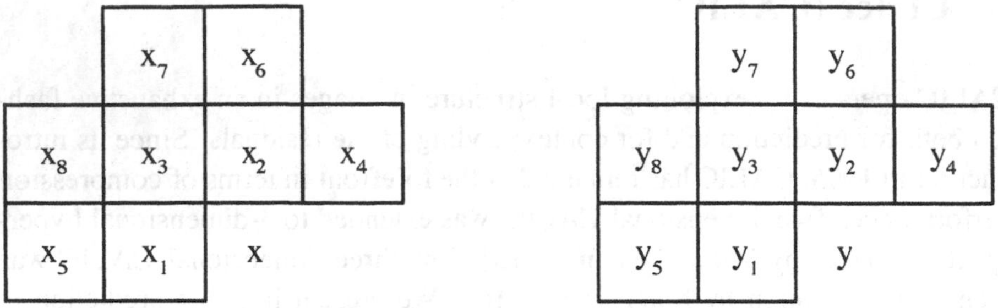

	x_7	x_6		
x_8	x_3	x_2	x_4	
x_5	x_1	x		

	y_7	y_6		
y_8	y_3	y_2	y_4	
y_5	y_1	y		

Figure 2: Labelling of neighboring pixels used in prediction and modeling.

4.2   Interband CALIC

The predictor in 3D CALIC incorporates the 2D CALIC predictor in a correlation-driven adaptive prediction framework. For a particular pixel y, we trace back to its counterpart pixel x at the same spatial location in the reference band, as shown in Fig. 2. With a causal system we assume all the pixels in the pixel set $Y = [y_1, y_2, \cdots, y_n]^T$ and $X = [x_1, x_2, \cdots, x_n]^T$ are available to both the encoder and decoder, except the pixel y, which we are trying to predict. The correlation between the two data sets is measured by the correlation coefficient which is defined as follows

$$\wp = \frac{\sum\limits_{i=0}^{n} [(x_i - \bar{x})(y_i - \bar{y})]}{\sqrt{\sum\limits_{i=0}^{n} [(x_i - \bar{x})^2 (y_i - \bar{y})^2]}} \tag{1}$$

where $\bar{x}$ is the mean of x_i, and $\bar{y}$ is the mean of y_i, i = 0, 1, ..., n.

If the correlation is very high this means that we can use the pixels in the previous band around the spatial location of the pixel being encoded to form the prediction. In particular, let

$$A = \begin{bmatrix} x_1 & y_1 \\ x_2 & y_2 \\ x_3 & y_3 \\ \vdots & \vdots \\ x_n & y_n \end{bmatrix} \tag{2}$$

and assume that x and y satisfy a linear relationship as

$$y = \alpha x + \beta \tag{3}$$

where α is the gain and β is the offset. Using standard linear regression techniques, the system that minimizes the error (in the sense of mean square error) can be obtained by

$$[\alpha, \beta] = (A^T A)^{-1} A^T Y \tag{4}$$

where A^{-1} is the inverse matrix of A, and A^T is the transpose of the matrix A.

Thus, $\hat{y} = \alpha x + \beta$ can be used as a predictor of y if the correlation coefficient $\wp$ is sufficiently high. A variation of the predictor as follows is used when there is a sharp edge at y:

$$\hat{y} = \frac{|x - x_2|\hat{y}_h + |x - x_1|\hat{y}_v}{|x - x_2| + |x - x_1|} \tag{5}$$

where

$$\hat{y}_h = y_1 + \alpha(x - x_1) \tag{6}$$

$$\hat{y}_v = y_2 + \alpha(x - x_2) \tag{7}$$

This predictor is based on horizontal and vertical gradients computed in the reference band. As the various bands are imaging the same physical location it is very likely that an edge in the reference band will occur at the same location as an edge in the current band.

Because the reflectance of different materials can be strikingly different in different spectral bands, the correlation between the bands can exhibit significant variation across the image. In the regions where the correlation between neighboring bands is low it is much better to use an intraband predictor. Switching between interband and intraband predictors can be performed by monitoring the local correlation. As this correlation is available to both encoder and decoder there is no need for any side information. The threshold for switching in this work was set at 0.5.

As in the case of the original CALIC algorithm, the three dimensional extension also includes a bias cancellation step. The bias in the predictions occurring in various quantized contexts is computed on an ongoing basis and subtracted from the prediction. The number and size of the contexts in the 3D version is different from the 2D version. However, the contexts are used in the same way. The prediction residual is encoded using context based arithmetic coders.

The interband CALIC is compared with the intraband CALIC and LOCO-I on various multispectral images and it outperforms both of them by an appreciable margin. More than a 20% compression gain can be obtained for typical multi-spectral images.

Magli et al. [16] extend this work by noting that the 3D CALIC proposed in [15] does not make full use of the spectral resolution available in hyperspectral images. They show that the performance of 3-D CALIC can be significantly improved by taking account of the fact that in hyperspectral images spectral prediction can be enhanced by taking into account multiple bands. They do so by creating a reference band in which the $(i, j)^{th}$ pixel of the reference band used to predict the pixels in the kth spectral band is given by

$$y_{i,j}^k = \gamma_1 + \gamma_2 x_{i,j}^{k-1} + \gamma_3 x_{i,j}^{k-2}$$

where $x_{i,j}^{k-1}$ and $x_{i,j}^{k-2}$ are the pixels in the same spatial location in the previous two bands. The coefficients γ_i are obtained by minimizing $||x_{i,j}^k - (\gamma_1 + \gamma_2 x_{i,j}^{k-1} + \gamma_3 x_{i,j}^{k-2}||_2^2$. The reference band pixel $y_{i,j}^k$ is then refined by adding to it the average difference between the previous band and the previous reference band. They further optimize the parameters of 3D CALIC for hyperspectral images and show significant gains over the original 3D CALIC proposal.

5   Optimum Linear Prediction

Given a sample x_k and a set of "past" samples $\{x_{k-1}, x_{k-2}, \ldots, x_{k-M}\}$, we can obtain the optimum linear prediction $\hat{x}_k$ for x_k as

$$\hat{x}_k = \sum_{i=1}^{M} \alpha_i x_{k-i}$$

where α_i are solutions of the Yule-Walker equations

$$\alpha = R^{-1} P$$

where $\alpha = [\alpha_1, \alpha_2, \ldots, \alpha_M]^T$, R is the autocorrelation matrix with

$$R[i, j] = E[x_{k-i} x_{k-j}] \qquad i, j = 1, 2, \ldots, M$$

and P, known in the filtering literature as the steering vector is given by

$$P[i] = E[x_k x_{k-i}] \qquad i = 1, 2, \ldots, M$$

The problem with applying this approach to hyperspectral image compression is that the images are statistically nonstationary. One way to get around this problem is to partition the hyperspectral images into sets which are quasi-stationary. Aiazzi et al [17] use a fuzzy clustering scheme to partition the hyperspectral data into clusters. They then compute optimal predictors for each cluster. The final prediction is obtained as a weighted sum where the weights correspond to membership in the clusters. Mielikainen and Toivanen [18] obtain the clustering by using the LBG algorithm [19] and then obtain the coefficients for a quasi-linear predictor. Rizzo et al. [20] use a membership function to separate the pixels into two groups, a group for which intraband prediction is used and a group for which interband prediction is used.

5.1   JPEG-7 Prediction

In this section we present a very simple lossless compression scheme which takes advantage of the similarity of local structure of spectral bands in a much more ad-hoc manner than in the schemes described previously. This method was originally proposed for the prediction of color band in lossless video compression [21]. Before we describe the hyperspectral compression scheme, we review the JPEG lossless compression schemes.

The previous JPEG lossless still compression standard [13] provided eight different predictive schemes from which users can select. The first scheme makes no prediction. The next seven are listed below. Three of the seven are one-dimensional predictors, and others are 2-D prediction schemes. Here $I(i,j)$ is the (i,j)th pixel of the original image and $\hat{I}(i,j)$ is predicted value for the (i,j)th pixel.

$$1 \qquad \hat{I}(i,j) = I(i-1,j) \tag{8}$$

$$2 \qquad \hat{I}(i,j) = I(i,j-1) \tag{9}$$

$$3 \qquad \hat{I}(i,j) = I(i-1,j-1) \tag{10}$$

$$4 \quad \hat{I}(i,j) = I(i,j-1) + I(i-1,j) - I(i-1,j-1) \tag{11}$$

$$5 \quad \hat{I}(i,j) = I(i,j-1) + (I(i-1,j) - I(i-1,j-1))/2 \tag{12}$$

$$6 \quad \hat{I}(i,j) = I(i-1,j) + (I(i,j-1) - I(i-1,j-1))/2 \tag{13}$$

$$7 \qquad \hat{I}(i,j) = (I(i,j-1) + I(i-1,j))/2 \tag{14}$$

Different images can have different structures that can be best exploited by one of the eight modes of prediction. If the compression is performed in offline mode, all eight predictors can be tried and the one that gives the best compression is used. The mode information is stored as header information in the compressed file for the decoding purpose.

The JPEG-7 predictors can be extended to 3-D hyperspectral image compression. As we have discussed before, strong correlations exist between adjacent bands. However, strong correlation between two bands does not mean that the pixel values between two bands are similar. In addition, the computation cost is very high if we calculate the correlation coefficient for each windowed local region. Due to these two factors, we might look at the problem from another perspective and pursue a relatively simple way to deal with the similarity. If strong correlation exists, the relationship between the pixel and its surrounding pixels are similar. Therefore, rather than use the pixels in the reference band to estimate the pixel in the current band, we take the pixels in the reference band to select an appropriate predictor among all these seven JPEG predictors, and the predictor is used for the prediction of the corresponding pixel in the current band. The selection criteria is the predictor that minimizes the prediction error in the reference band. This leads to a simple adaptive predictive coding schemes. Surprisingly, it this prediction schemes works very well when the dynamic range of the pixels is relatively small. For example, the average residual band entropy for the cuprite89 image using this very simple scheme is around 4.6 bits/pixel, which compares favorably with some of the more complex schemes.

5.2   Correlation-based Conditional Average Prediction (CCAP)

The optimal estimate (in the sense of MMSE) of a random variable X given a set of observation Y_i is known to be the conditional expectation of X given Y_i

$$E[x|Y_i] = \sum xP[X = x|Y_1 = y_1, y_2, \cdots, y_N] \tag{15}$$

Therefore, the optimal predictor of the value of a pixel is

$$E[X_{i,j}|\{X_{i-l,j-m}\}^{i,j}_{(l,m)=(1,1)}]$$

the conditional expected value. In practice we can assume that the pixel $X_{i,j}$ is conditionally independent of pixels that are some distance from it and hence the conditional variables can be limited to pixels in the causal neighborhood, or causal context, of $X_{i,j}$. For jointly Gaussian processes the conditional expectation can be expressed as a linear combination of the observation. However, for the non-Gaussian case the computation of the conditional expectation requires the availability of the conditional probability density function. In the case of image pixels it would be difficult to assume that the process under consideration is Gaussian. Slyz and Neuhoff [22] reduce the size of the problem by replacing the conditioning variables with their vector quantized representation. However, vector quantization of the neighborhoods leads to an apriori ad-hoc partitioning of the conditioning space which can result in significant loss of information.

In the area of text compression Cleary and Witten [23] developed a blending approach for estimating the conditional probabilities in their development of the prediction-with-partial-match (PPM) algorithm. This approach implicitly replies on the fact that the textual information contains many exact repeats. As this situation is not duplicated in natural images the algorithm used in PPM cannot be applied directly to the problem of generating predictions. Fortunately, while we do not have exact repeats as in textual data our objectives are also not the same. We are interested in an expected value which can be estimated using a sample mean.

Given a pixel $x_{i,j}$, let $C_{i,j}$ be the set of pixels in the causal context of $x_{i,j}$ For convenience, we put an ordering on these pixels so we refer to them as $x_1^{i,j}, x_2^{i,j}, \cdots, x_k^{i,j}$. Given a particular set of value $\alpha = (\alpha_1, \alpha_2, \cdots, \alpha_k)$, define

$$C_k(\bar{\alpha}) = \{x_{l,m} : x_1^{l,m} = \alpha_1, x_2^{l,m} = \alpha_2, \cdots, x_k^{l,m} = \alpha_k\} \qquad (16)$$

Then we can estimate $E[X_{i,j}|x_{l,m} : x_1^{l,m} = \alpha_1, x_2^{l,m} = \alpha_2, \cdots, x_k^{l,m} = \alpha_k]$ by the sample mean

$$\hat{\mu}_{X|\alpha} = \frac{1}{\|C_k(\bar{\alpha})\|} \sum_{x \in C_k(\bar{\alpha})} x \qquad (17)$$

where $\| \cdot \|$ denote the cardinality.

Before we use this method in practice, we need to address several issues. We need to decide on the size and composition of the causal context. We need to decide on how large $\|C_k(\bar{\alpha})\|$ should be to make $\hat{\mu}_{X|\alpha}$ a good estimate and we need to decide what to do when $\|C_k(\bar{\alpha})\|$ is not a large enough for $\hat{\mu}_{X|\alpha}$ to be a valid estimate.

To address these issues, first we define the MED predictor used in JPEG-LS to be the default predictor for the first band. Given the nomenclature of Fig.2 the prediction using the MED algorithm is as follows:

$$\hat{X} = \begin{cases} \min(x_2, x_1), & \text{if } x_3 \geq \max x_2, x_1; \\ \max(x_2, x_1), & \text{if } x_3 \leq \min x_2, x_1; \\ x_1 + x_2 - x_3. & \text{otherwise.} \end{cases} \qquad (18)$$

Second, we use the JPEG 7 prediction as the default prediction if the number of valid estimates is not sufficient, i.e., $\|C_k(\bar{\alpha})\|$ is small or even zero. As the set $\|C_k(\bar{\alpha})\|$ is built using the past history of the image, the information about the size of the set is available to both the encoder and decoder. The decoder can perform exactly the same procedures as the encoder was doing. The size of $\|C_k(\bar{\alpha})\|$ required for a valid estimate was determined empirically by conducting experiments with a test set of images.

The question about the size and composition of the context, and the definition of context match is somewhat more difficult. As might be expected using a large context generally leads to a better prediction. However, when a larger

context is used it is less likely to have been encountered in the history of the
image. It is somewhat reasonable to use a larger context first and if there are not
sufficient matched to this context in the history we shift to a smaller context,
similar to the way the PPM performs context match. However, it is found that
contexts of sizes greater than 4 or contexts less than 4 give only marginal gains
over the smaller contexts and it also shows that there is no much improvement
if we use dynamical context composition and size, rather than fixed contest
composition and size. Therefore, context size is fixed to 4.

5.3   Algorithm Parameters

The definition for a context match is a critical part of the algorithm. There are
two methods available. Given a sequence of pixels $Y = y_1^{i,j}, y_2^{i,j}, \cdots, y_k^{i,j}$, which
take on the set of value $\beta = \beta_1, \beta_2, \cdots, \beta_k$, we declared the pixel $y_{l,m}$ to be a
member of $C_k(\bar{\alpha})$ if:

- $|\alpha_i - \beta_i| \leq T_1$, $i = 1, 2, \cdots,, k$, or

- $\wp < T_2$, where $\wp$ is the correlation coefficient between Y and β_i.

Note that neither of these matches partition the space of conditioning contexts into disjoint sets as would be the case if we used a vector quantizer to
reduce the number of contest. Ideally, the context match based on the first definition should give a good match performance, given the data is stationary. And
experiments show that it did work greater than GAP predictor of CALIC and
most other prediction methods for stand-alone 2-D still image compression,
in terms of entropy. However, when applied to hyperspectral images, context
matches based on the first definition did not provide any improvements in compression. This can be explained by noticing that although the correlation can
be very strong between two bands, the difference between corresponding pixels values are not small. In other words, if we use the linear mode described in
Section 4.2, either the gain factor α or the offset β is typically very large for hyperspectral images. As a consequence, the context match according to the first
criteria does not work as well as we had expected from experiments conducted
using single band natural images. Therefore, we use the second definition to
perform the context match. Next a context search area needs to be specified. It
is usually beneficial if we search a particular context within a windowed search

area from its adjacent bands, as shown in Figure 3. Alternatively, we can use the pixel in the same spatial location in the reference bands to perform the context match, rather than use a search window which contains more pixels. It would be reasonable to assume that this should work as each individual pixel location represents the same material on the earth and they should have strong correlation. However, our experiments show that the most correlated pixels in reference bands are not always in the same location as the pixel to be predicted. As a result, it is reasonable to use a search window instead of a single pixel.

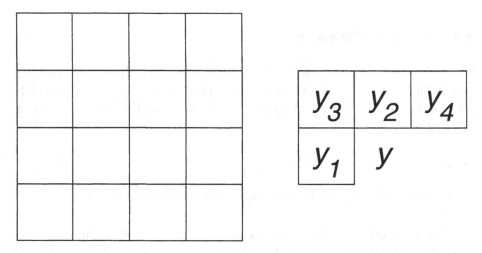

Figure 3: Context Search Window

If such a match is found, what we need to do now is to obtain the prediction. It looks very straightforward if we use the linear model to get the prediction. However, experiment shows that in terms of entropy of residual images, this method is inferior to the simple predictor by just taking a scaled neighboring pixel as follows:

$$\bar{y} = \frac{x}{x_1} * y_1 \tag{19}$$

Therefore, for each pixel to be predicted, the algorithm goes back to the previous bands and calculates the correlation coefficient for each pixel within the window. If the correlation coefficient is greater than a threshold, we then use Equation 19 to obtain a prediction value.

Considering the nonstationary property of hyperspectral images, only one prediction value is not sufficient. As such, we extend the search area and find more than one such context matches and their predictions, and take the average of those prediction values as the prediction value, as described by Equation 17.

To find the value of $C_k(\bar{\alpha})$ for which the estimate $\hat{\mu}_{X|\alpha}$ is valid we ran a series of experiments by varying the correlation coefficient threshold T_2 for a valid context match, the number of bands and the window size to be searched. Experiments show that the best performance in terms of average band entropy is obtained if we take 5 bands, constrain the search window as 3×3 pixels, and set the value of T_2 to 0.95.

Figure 4: pixel labelling for correlation-based context match

5.4 Results

The average band entropy of various residual AVIRIS images by using the JPEG7 predictors and conditional average images is shown in Table 2. As we can see, the entropy difference between both methods for the cuprite89 image is marginal. However, for other images, we can see that the performance of CCAP is much better than that of JPEG7. The reason for this is that the intensity variation between adjacent bands in the cuprite89 image is very small, and the dynamic range of pixels is within a much narrower range, as compared with other images. In all these images, most of the computed correlation coefficients between neighboring bands are close to 1, that is, the bands are strongly correlated. However, cuprite89 has a small gain factor and offset between adjacent bands and JPEG7 works much better in this situation. The reflectance property is solely determined by the materials in the earth that were sensed situations in which the dynamic ranges are very large are common for hyperspectral images. the CCAP is able to catch such spectral structures much better than JPEG7 predictors.

The residual images can be encoded by any entropy coder, such as arith-

Image	Cuprite89	JASPER92	LA92	MF92	SUN 92
JPEG7	4.64	6.8	7.7	7.5	7.4
CCAP	4.55	6.26	5.69	6.55	4.64

Table 2: Average band entropy obtained from JPEG7 and CCAP

metic codes. Similar to CALIC, the residual entropy can be further reduced by bias cancellation as well as band reordering. The final compression ratio can be improved by using a context-based arithmetic coder.

5.5 Summary

Here is the summary of how the algorithm performs prediction.

- JPEG-LS prediction is used for the first band.

- In the following bands, search for the context match in the previous bands and calculate the correlation coefficient for each pixel in the search window.

- Determine whether JPEG7 or CCAP is used according to the correlation coefficient and its threshold, and the number of valid predictions.

- If JPEG7 is used, 7 predictors based on previous band are used for the prediction of the current pixel.

- Otherwise, the CCAP is used for prediction.

- Entropy of the residual images can be further reduced by exploiting bias cancellation.

- The final residual images can then be encoded by a context-based entropy coder, such as the arithmetic coder.

6 Conclusion

We have presented a number of different predictive coding schemes for the compression of hyperspectral images. While the schemes differ in the details of their implementation their outline is essentially the same. Each algorithm tries to approximate the ideal case of stationary data for which optimal predictors can be computed. The approximations can be viewed as attempting to partition the data space into sets within which the stationarity assumption can be applied with some level of plausibility. The extent to which these algorithms function or fail depends upon the validity of their assumption. There is clearly much more work to be done before we can claim that the problem of predictive lossless compression has been solved.

References

[1] K. Sayood. Data Compression in Remote Sensing Applications. *IEEE Geoscience and Remote Sensing Newsletter*, (84):7–15, September 1992.

[2] M.J. Ryan and J.F. Arnold. The Lossless Compression of AVIRIS Images by Vector Quantization. *IEEE Transactions on Geoscience and Remote Sensing*, Vol 35:546–550, March 1997.

[3] G. Motta, F. Rizzo, and J.A. Storer. Compression of Hyperspectral Imagery. In *Proceedings of the Data Compression Conference, DCC '03*. IEEE, 2003.

[4] X. Wu, N.D. Memon, and K. Sayood. A Context Based Adaptive Lossless/Nearly-Lossless Coding Scheme for Continuous Tone Images. ISO Working Document ISO/IEC SC29/WG1/N256, 1995.

[5] X. Wu and N.D. Memon. CALIC - A Context Based Adaptive Lossless Image Coding Scheme. *IEEE Transactions on Communications*, May 1996.

[6] M. Weinberger, G. Seroussi, and G. Sapiro. The LOCO-I Lossless Compression Algorithm: Principles and Standardization into JPEG-LS. Technical Report HPL-98-193, Hewlett-Packard Laboratory, November 1998.

[7] J.M. Shapiro. Embedded Image Coding Using Zerotrees of Wavelet Co-
     efficients. *IEEE Transactions on Signal Processing*, SP-41:3445–3462,
     December 1993.

[8] A. Said and W.A. Pearlman. A New Fast and Efficient Coder Based on
     Set Partitioning in Hierarchical Trees. *IEEE Transactions on Circuits and
     Systems for Video Technologies*, pages 243–250, June 1996.

[9] A.C. Miguel, A.R. Askew, A. Chang, S. Hauck, R.E. Ladner, and E.A.
     Riskin. Reduced Complexity Wavelet-Based Predictive Coding of Hyper-
     spectral Images for FPGA Implementation. In *Proceedings of the Data
     Compression Conference, DCC '04*. IEEE, 2004.

[10] S.R. Tate. Band Ordering in Lossless Compression of Multispectral Im-
     ages. *IEEE Transactions on Computers*, pages 477–483, April 1997.

[11] R.E. Roger and M.C. Cavenor. Lossless Compression of AVIRIS Images.
     IEEE Transactions on Image Processing, pages 713–719, May 1996.

[12] R. F. Rice, P. S. Yeh, and W. Miller. Algorithms for a very high speed
     universal noiseless coding module. Technical Report 91-1, Jet Propul-
     sion Laboratory, California Institute of Technology, Pasadena, Califor-
     nia., February 1991.

[13] G. K. Wallace. The JPEG still picture compression standard. *Communi-
     cations of the ACM*, 34:31–44, April 1991.

[14] N.D. Memon, K. Sayood, and S.S.. Magliveras. Lossless Compression of
     Multispectral Image Data. *IEEE Transactions on Geoscience and Remote
     Sensing*, 32:282–289, March 1994.

[15] X. Wu and N.D. Memon. Context Based Lossless Intraband Adaptive
     Compression - Extending CALIC. *IEEE Transactions on Image Process-
     ing*, 9:994–1001, June 2000.

[16] E. Magli, G. Olmo, and E. Quacchio. Optimized Onboard Lossless and
     Near-Lossless Compression of Hyperspectral Data Using CALIC. *IEEE
     Geoscience and Remote Sensing Letters*, 1:21–25, January 2004.

[17] B. Aiazzi, P. Alba, L. alparone, and S. Baronti. Lossless Compres-
     sion of Multi/Hyper-spectral Imagery Based on 3-D Fuzzy Prediction.

IEEE Transactions on Geoscience and Remote Sensing, 37:2287–2294, September 1999.

[18] J. Mielikainen, P. Toivanen, and A. Kaarna. Linear Prediction in Lossless Compression of Hyperspectral Images. *Optical Engineering*, 42:1013–1017, April 2003.

[19] Y. Linde, A. Buzo, and R. M. Gray. An algorithm for vector quantization design. *IEEE Transactions on Communications*, COM-28:84–95, Jan. 1980.

[20] F. Rizzo, B. Carpentieri, G. Motta, and J.A. Storer. High Performance Compression of Hyperspectral Imagery with Reduced Search Complexity in the Compressed Domain. In *Proceedings of the Data Compression Conference, DCC '04*. IEEE, 2004.

[21] N.D. Memon and K. Sayood. Lossless Compression of Video Sequences. *IEEE Transactions on Communications*, Vol 44:1340–1345, October 1996.

[22] M.J. Slyz and D.L. Neuhoff. A Nonlinear VQ-based Predictive Lossless Image Coder. In *Proceedings of the Data Compression Conference, DCC '94*. IEEE, 1994.

[23] J. G. Cleary and I. H. Witten. Data compression using adaptive coding and partial string matching. *IEEE Transactions on Communications*, 32(4):396–402, 1984.

Lossless Hyperspectral Image Compression via Linear Prediction

Jarno Mielikainen, Pekka Toivanen
Lappeenranta University of Technology
Finland

1 Introduction

Remote sensing involves the acquisition of information about a scene or an object without physical contact with it. Materials comprising the various objects in the scene reflect, absorb and emit electromagnetic radiation depending on their molecular composition and shape. By using the radiation over a broad spectral band, the spectrum can be used to identify materials. Hyperspectral sensors are imaging spectrometry sensors, which divide the waveband into hundreds of contiguous narrow bands for analysis [24]. Hyperspectral images provide much richer and finer spectral information than traditional multispectral images do. An example of a hyperspectral image can be seen in Figure 1.

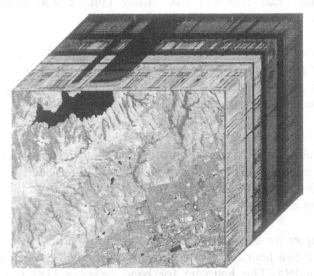

Figure 1: False-color image of a 224-channel AVIRIS hyperspectral image [22].

The hyperspectral imaging data is in the visible or near-infrared part of the spectrum. Huge volumes of daily-generated data can be handled only with the help of efficient compression algorithms. The main purpose for hyperspectral images are pattern/target recognition and classification. If the original quality of the data suffers from the use of lossy compression, then recognition/classification accuracy also suffers. That is not what scientists using the data want, and therefore, lossless compression is a better alternative

Hyperspectral satellite images require enormous amounts of space. NASA's project EOS (the Earth Observing System) will generate data at an unprecedented rate. It has been estimated are that EOS satellites will generate well over a terabyte of data every day, most of it being hyperspectral image data. Given the large volume of hyperspectral image data that will be generated each day, the use of robust data compression techniques will be beneficial to data transfer and archive [11].

On the other hand, hyperspectral infrared sounders provide very accurate information about the atmosphere, clouds and surface parameters. The physical retrieval of these geophysical parameters involves the inverse solution of the radiative transfer equation and it is a mathematically ill-posed problem, i.e. the solution is sensitive to the error or noise in the data. Therefore, data loss resulting from lossy compression schemes is not acceptable, in this case either [16].

Lossless compression techniques involve no loss of information [1]. They are used for applications that cannot tolerate any difference between the original and reconstructed data. Lossless compression of hyperspectral images can be seen as consisting of three steps:

1. Band ordering.
2. Modeling, which extracts information on the redundancy of the data and describes this redundancy in the form of a model.
3. Coding describes the model and how it differs from the data using a binary alphabet.

In this Chapter we concentrate mostly on band ordering and modeling. We will present a fast heuristic for the band ordering and three types of linear prediction models. The heuristic for band ordering [18] is explained in

Section 2. Section 3 presents an adaptive prediction [8] model. In adaptive prediction both the compressor and decompressor recompute prediction coefficients for all the pixels. Therefore, the prediction coefficient values do not need to be sent to the decompressor as it can recompute the same values as the compressor. The delta-coding approach [9] is presented in Section 4. Delta-coding refers to a method in which a simple difference is computed between values, so that both the compressor and decompressor can get the same values without any additional information. Section 5 presents clustered prediction [10]: a static prediction is performed separately inside each cluster. Static prediction refers to a method in which the prediction coefficients are precomputed and sent to the decompressor.

2 Band Ordering

In this Section we present a heuristic for the band reordering scheme. The proposed ordering heuristic uses a correlation factor to examine interband similarity. When a 3D image has been split into a set of 2D bands, the interband similarity can be measured. The correlation factor has been chosen to characterize the interband similarity due to its simplicity. The correlation function takes two vectors as an input and computes the real number in the range [-1.0; 1.0], where 1.0 indicates that the input vectors are totally identical. The correlation coefficient $r_{A,B}$ between image bands A and B is calculated as follows:

$$r_{A,B} = \frac{\sum_{j=0}^{\frac{M}{D}} \sum_{i=0}^{\frac{N}{D}} \left(A_{j \cdot D, i \cdot D} - \overline{A}\right)\left(B_{j \cdot D, i \cdot D} - \overline{B}\right)}{\sqrt{\sum_{j=0}^{\frac{M}{D}} \sum_{i=0}^{\frac{N}{D}} \left(A_{j \cdot D, i \cdot D} - \overline{A}\right)^2 \sum_{j=0}^{\frac{M}{D}} \sum_{i=0}^{\frac{N}{D}} \left(B_{j \cdot D, i \cdot D} - \overline{B}\right)^2}}, \tag{1}$$

where M is the number of rows and N is the number of columns in the image; $\overline{A}$ and $\overline{B}$ denote the mean values of the bands A and B computed for every D^{th} pixel, respectively. Each Dth pixel in the spatial directions is used for the computation of the correlation coefficients. If D equals 1, the exact value of the correlation between the two image bands is computed; otherwise Equation (1) results in a correlation estimate. The larger the D, the faster the reordering phase of the algorithm; however, at the same time, the estimation accuracy is reduced.

The algorithm's next step is band ordering. The problem of the optimal image band reordering is equivalent to the problem of finding a minimum spanning tree (MST) in weighted graphs [13]. The computed matrix of the interband similarity coefficients above is considered a matrix of weight coefficients for the graph, where the graph vertices denote the image band numbers and the edges indicate whether there is a direct connection between two vertices. Prim's algorithm is known to be efficient for constructing an MST in weighted undirected graphs [11]. The algorithm in our case has been reversed aiming to achieve the maximum weight tree instead of the minimum spanning tree. The output of the algorithm is a set of band numbers corresponding to the path that indicates how image bands should be rearranged in order to achieve the best compression results. Eventually bands with higher correlation coefficients are allocated together.

Alternatively, reordering can be performed as suggested in [11] by compressing each band by using all the other bands as predicting bands one at a time. A directed graph is formed from the sizes of the encoded residual bands. The optimal band reordering is achived by computing a minimum spanning tree for the above-mentioned directed graph using Edmond's algorithm [14].

3   Adaptive Prediction

The purpose of the linear prediction technique is to exploit redundancy in both the spectral and spatial dimensions of the image. The whole procedure is a two-pass technique. At first, each pixel is predicted using the values of the pixels from its causal neighborhood, known as the sample set. In the algorithm, two different sample sets are involved; an example of the sample sets is shown in Figure 2.

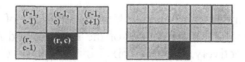

Figure 2: An example of the sample sets.

At first, the prediction for all the bands is performed using both sample sets. Then residuals between the original and the predicted bands are calculated. Then for each spatial position, a sum of the absolute values of the residuals over the bands is calculated and the sample set, which gives a smaller sum, is used for the spatial position during the second pass; i.e. for each spatial position one of the two possible sample sets is selected.

The predicted pixel value $\hat{p}_{r,c,b}$ at location (r, c, b), where r and c are spatial coordinates and b is a spectral coordinate, can be computed using the following equation:

$$\hat{p}_{r,c,b} = \left\lfloor a_{r,c,b} p_{r,c,b-1} + \frac{1}{2} \right\rfloor. \tag{2}$$

The prediction coefficient $a_{r,c,b}$ is computed as follows

$$a_{r,c,b} = \frac{1}{Q} \frac{\sum\limits_{(x,y)\in S} p_{r-y,c-x,b}}{\sum\limits_{(x,y)\in S} p_{r-y,c-x,b-1}}, \tag{3}$$

where S is the sample set; Q is the number of pixels in the sample set. For example, when the leftmost sample set in Figure 2 is used the coefficient $a_{r,c,b}$ can be computed according to

$$a_{r,c,b} = \frac{1}{4} \frac{p_{r,c-1,b} + p_{r-1,c-1,b} + p_{r-1,c,b} + p_{r-1,c+1,b}}{p_{r,c-1,b-1} + p_{r-1,c-1,b-1} + p_{r-1,c,b-1} + p_{r-1,c+1,b-1}} \tag{4}$$

Thus, the neighboring pixels are utilized in order to compute the current pixel value. As the number of pixel values used in the estimation of the prediction coefficients is small, the number of coefficients in the prediction model must be also small, one in this case. Once the predicted image is estimated, residual images can be found as a difference between the original and the predicted bands. Further residuals are coded using a range coder [2]. A non-adaptive range coder has been used and therefore the frequencies for all the residual bands have to be stored. For the pixels that do not have a large enough causal neighborhood and therefore cannot be predicted, we calculated the difference between consecutive bands, which along with other compression parameters is compressed as side information using a general-purpose text compression program, PPMD [28].

4 Delta-coding

Vector quantization (VQ) is a popular asymmetric technique also suitable for data compression [1,3,4]. While VQ compression is normally computationally demanding, decompression is a computationally inexpensive table lookup process. The performance of the VQ techniques depends largely on the quality of the codebook used in coding the data. However, there exist several methods for generating a codebook [3]. We used the most popular one known as the Generalized Lloyd Algorithm (GLA) [6] that produces a locally optimal codebook. Following vector quantization, the reconstructed image is subtracted from the original image in order to obtain a residual image. The difference between consecutive bands in the residual image is calculated and a difference image is formed. The residual image can be reconstructed using the first band of the residual and all the bands of the difference image.

Vector quantization consists of three stages. The first step is the decomposition of the image into a set of vectors. The second step is codebook generation. The last stage is index selection.

For the codebook generation phase we used the GLA.

The codebook generation phase can be formally defined as follows: given M k-dimensional input vectors, $v_i=(v_{i1},v_{i2},...,v_{ik})$, $(i=1,...,M)$, we are looking for a set of N k-dimensional codebook vectors, $u_j=(u_{j1},u_{j2},...,u_{jk})$, $(j=1,...,N)$, that minimize the sum of the squared distances of every input vector to its closest code vector:

$$D(v,u) = \sum_{i=1}^{M} d(v_i, u_{m(i)}), \tag{5}$$

where $m(i)$ is the index of the closest code vector of the input vector with index i under the distance metrics, $d(v,u)$.

For the distance metrics $d(v,u)$, we used the squared Euclidean distance:

$$d(v,u) = \|v - u\|^2 = \sum_{i=1}^{k} (v_i - u_i)^2, \tag{6}$$

The GLA algorithm iteratively generates the codebook, which is only a locally optimal solution to Equation (5). Initially, the size of the codebook is one and its only code vector is set to the arithmetic mean of all the input vectors, v_i, $i=1,...,M$. At every iteration step, r, the size of the codebook is doubled by duplicating all the codebook vectors and adding a small perturbance, $\varepsilon \in \mathfrak{R}^k$, to the duplicates. For every input vector v_i, the nearest code vector u_j under distance metrics $d(v_i, u_j)$ is determined. Then, each code vector, u_j, is assigned the arithmetic mean of all input vectors, v_i, the closest code vector of which is u_j. If there exists a codebook vector, u_j, that is not the nearest to any input vector, v_j, the codebook vector is reassigned in such a way that the unused codebook vector is moved to the neighborhood of often used codebook vectors. The codebook error, $D^p(v,u)$, during the iteration, p, is calculated. If the relative error of the codebook errors between two iterations,

$$\frac{D^p(v,u) - D^{p-1}(v,u)}{D^p(v,u)} \tag{7}$$

is smaller than a given tolerance, the local optimum for a codebook has been found.

In the index selection phase, for each input vector, v_i, the closest code vector in the codebook, u_j, is found and a table containing the indices formed.

In order to form a difference image, the difference between consecutive bands in the residual image is calculated:

$$d_i = b_{i-1} - b_i, \qquad\qquad (8)$$

where i is the band number, and b_i the value of band i.

The residual image can be reconstructed using the first band of the residual image and all the bands of the difference image:

$$b_i = b_{i-1} - d_i. \qquad\qquad (9)$$

The first band's residuals and other bands' differences are entropy coded, one band at a time. Also both the index and codebook values are separately entropy coded. The frequency tables that are used by entropy coders are grouped into one data set and are entropy coded by an 8-bit entropy coder.

Also, several approaches for speeding up the VQ process have been developed [25-27].

5 Clustered Prediction

The clustered prediction presented in this Section can be seen as an extension of the VQ from the previous section. That fact will become apparent after a brief explanation. First, we change one stage in the general prediction framework presented in Section 1; we divide the lossless compression of hyperspectral images into three components: clustering, prediction and coding. The optimal band order selection stage is unnecessary since we are using many previous bands in the prediction. The clustering stage refers to the recognition of clusters so that the entropy that results from the subsequent procedure is minimized. The prediction is performed using a linear predictor. All the pixels used to make the prediction have the same spatial location as the current pixel and the coefficients are optimized to minimize the mean squared error inside each cluster, i.e. the optimization is performed for each cluster separately. The error is the difference between the predicted and actual value. Therefore, the procedure can be seen as a clustered linear prediction.

The resulting residual band is entropy coded using a range coder [2] with a separate model for each cluster. Hence, the cluster is used as the context for the adaptive entropy coder, in addition to the band. We set out to use different linear predictors for different areas in the image. The size of the side information for the cluster indexes would have been too large if we had used separate clustering for each band; therefore, we clustered the spectra. There are

$$\frac{1}{m!}\sum_{i=0}^{m}(-1)^{m-i}\binom{m}{i}i^{N}, \tag{10}$$

possible ways of partitioning N spectra into m clusters [5]. The evaluation of all the possible partitions is computationally infeasible. Furthermore, the evaluation of each clustering would require the computation of optimal linear prediction coefficients for all the clusters, the computation of the difference between the predicted and real values and the entropy coding of the residual. Therefore, we used the following procedure that only approximates the optimal clustering. We first cluster our spectral data according to their spectra using the well known GLA [6] method. The cluster indices are stored using delta-coding, i.e. the differences between the indices are saved instead of the indices themselves.

For each band, the linear prediction is computed in such a way that the prediction coefficients minimize the expected value of the squared error inside each cluster, i.e. we solve a multiple linear regression model for each of the clusters for every band. The prediction function is a linear function

$$\hat{p}_{x,y,z} = \left\lfloor \sum_{i=1}^{M} a_{z,c,i}\, p_{x,y,z-i} + b_{z,c} + 1/2 \right\rfloor, \qquad (11)$$

where $p_{z,y,x}$ is the value in band z in the spatial location $(x,\ y)$, M is the number of bands that are used in prediction, $a_{z,c,i}$, $i=1..M$ and $b_{z,c}$ are the prediction coefficients and offsets for cluster c in band z, respectively. The coefficients are quantized to 16-bit values using uniform quantization. The resulting residual band is entropy coded with a range coder [2] using a separate model for each cluster. Hence, the cluster is used as the context for the adaptive entropy coder, in addition to the band. Each band is also entropy coded without prediction, and if the size of the entropy coded band without prediction is smaller than it is with prediction, the band is stored without prediction. The observation that the compression ratio can be improved if some bands are not predicted is based on the absorption of wavelengths of certain bands in the atmosphere.

The clustered prediction method can be seen as an extension of a method presented in Section 4. In Section 4, residuals after VQ were predicted using the following predictor

$$\hat{p}_{x,y,z} = p_{x,y,z-i}. \qquad (12)$$

In the clustered prediction method, the step in VQ, at which the cluster centers are subtracted from the spectra, is unnecessary as we use the clusters as the context for the entropy coder instead of using a context-free entropy coder as in Section 4. If the cluster centers were subtracted from the spectra we would only be subtracting a constant which does not change the entropy.

6 Experimental Results

Hyperspectral sounder data can be generated from either an interferometer or a grating sounder. The AIRS instrument aboard NASA's Aqua spacecraft employs 49.5 degree cross-track scanning with a 1.1 degree instantaneous field of view [16]. The daily-generated AIRS data is divided into 240 granules; each of them includes 2,378 infrared channels in the 3.74 to 15.4

μm region of the spectrum. The granules obtained consist of 135 scan lines containing 90 cross-track footprints per scan line; thus there are a total of 135 x 90 = 12,150 footprints per granule [16].

For the compression studies 10 granules, five daytime (DT) and five nighttime (NT), have been simulated from the data obtained from NASA AIRS observations on September 6, 2002, in the following way. First of all, the 270 channels that occurred only in the AIRS sounder have been excluded in order to make the AIRS data more genetic to other hyperspectral sounders. Then the 16-bit raw radiances were converted into brightness temperatures and scaled as unsigned 16-bit integers to ensure 0.01 Kelvin accuracy, which is appropriate for the sounder data compression [17]. Thus, each resulting granule is saved as a binary file, arranged as 2,108 channels, 135 scan lines and 90 pixels for each scan line with [16]. The data is available via anonymous ftp [15].

The performance of the band ordering heuristic from Section 2 has been measured in terms of a compression ratio and compression time using 10 selected AIRS granules. The tests were performed on an AMD Barton XP 2600+ PC. The actual prediction method is adaptive prediction, which is explained in Section 3.

Table I shows the average compression/decompression times for different prediction orders. The number 42 after the dash refers to the maximum number of bands used to determine the optimal band ordering. In other words, 21 bands before the current band and 21 bands after the current band along the image spectra were used to form the weight matrix for the Edmond's algorithm. This number of bands was used because it gives the same compression ratio as the proposed method. For the correlation-based band ordering the computation of the correlation coefficients, MST, and the prediction and encoding phases require 10.11s, 0.03s, 4.67s and 8.45s on average, respectively.

Natural Order	Correlation Order	Optim.- 42	Optim. order
14.0/8.7	23.3/8.2	379.1/8.3	20298.7/8.1

TABLE I: Average compression/decompression times [s] for different prediction orders.

In Table II the actual compression ratios are shown both for the band-ordering heuristic and optimal ordering suggested in [11] using the same dataset. This optimal order obtains 1% higher results in terms of compression ratio; however, the computational time is 871 times longer than in the case of the correlation-based band reordering presented in Section 2. On the other hand, when the number of bands used to predict the current band is limited, the optimal-ordering algorithm [11] shows exactly the same compression ratio as the correlation-based method. It has been empirically found that for the 10 test granules the required number of bands is 42. In this case, the optimal band reordering proposed in [11] demonstrated a 13 times slower computational speed than the correlation-based ordering.

The correlation-based ordering has been compared with the natural band ordering, as well. It is worth noticing that natural band ordering does not imply any reordering before prediction, which in turn results in 40% time savings compared to the correlation-based ordering algorithm. But the correlation-based ordering demonstrates 5% higher compression ratios, which outweighs this drawback.

Granule #	Natural Order	Corr. Order	Optim.-42	Optim. Order
9	2.088	2.179	2.182	2.210
16	2.013	2.115	2.111	2.133
60	1.950	2.070	2.062	2.083
82	2.023	2.111	2.110	2.129
120	1.945	2.027	2.027	2.042
126	2.041	2.157	2.158	2.184
129	1.991	2.067	2.066	2.087
151	2.088	2.169	2.176	2.202
182	1.934	2.035	2.034	2.036
193	2.045	2.149	2.147	2.170
Average	2.012	2.108	2.107	2.127

TABLE II: Compression ratios for different prediction orders for the 10 tested granules.

Next, we will show some additional results for the same sounder data using spectral prediction from Section 5. In this case, we are not clustering the spectra as the spatial size of the images is so small that clustering would bring no advantage at all. Figure 2 shows a stacked area plot of the overall contributions of the residual and side information as the function of the prediction length (*M*). Figure 3 shows compression ratios for different values of M. The best value for *M* was empirically determined to be 32. Figure 4 depicts the compression and decompression times for different values of *M*.

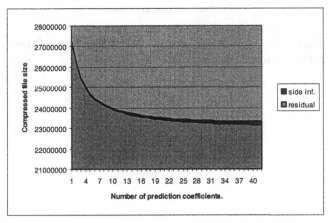

Figure 2: Compressed file size as a function of the coefficients of linear prediction. [21]

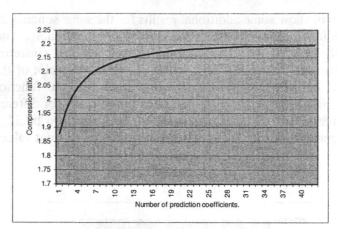

Figure 3: Compression ratio as a function of the coefficients of linear prediction. [21]

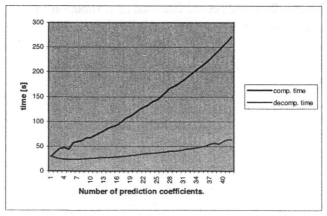

Figure 4: Compression and decompression times as functions of the coefficients of linear prediction. [21]

Finally, Table III compares the results for adaptive linear prediction (ALP)[8], spectral prediction (SP) [21], CALIC-3D[19] and M-CALIC-3D [20].

ALP	SP	CALIC-3D	M-CALIC-3D
2.00	2.19	2.06	2.09

TABLE III: Average compression Ratios For HES Images.

The performance of the methods presented in Sections 3-5 is measured in the form of compression ratios using 13 images from the Airborne Visible InfraRed Imaging Spectrometer (AVIRIS) 97 image set [22]. AVIRIS covers the solar-reflected portion of the electromagnetic spectrum: 0.41 μm to 2.45 μm in 10 nm bands. The AVIRIS instrument consists of four spectrometers that view a 20-square-meter spot on the ground from a flight altitude of 20 km. This spot is simultaneously viewed in all the spectral bands. A spatial image is formed by moving the spectrometers perpendicular to the direction of the aircraft. [23]

The images were taken from four areas: Jasper Ridge, California, Moffet Field, California, Lunar Lake, Nevada, and Cuprite, Nevada. The spatial size of the images was 614 by 512 and they contained 224 bands. The compression ratio is measured as the size of the original file divided by the size of the compressed file. Therefore, the overhead is included in the quoted compression ratios.

Table IV shows the average compression ratios for the above-mentioned image set.

Adaptive Prediction	Vector Quantization	Clustered Prediction
3.23	3.03	3.43

TABLE IV: Average compression Ratios For AVIRIS 97 Images.

References:

[1] K. Sayood, *Introduction to Data Compression*, University of Nebraska-Lincoln, Morgan Kaufmann Publishers, Academic Press, 2000.

[2] G. N. Martin, "Range encoding: an algorithm for removing redundancy from a digitalized image", *Proceedings. of Video and Data Compression Conference*, 1979.

[3] A. Gersho and R. M. Gray, *Vector Quantization and Signal Compression*, Boston, MA: Kluwer, 1992.

[4] R. Gray, and D. Neuhoff, "Quantization", *IEEE Transactions on Information Theory*, Vol. 44, Oct. 1998, pp. 2325-2383.

[5] S. Theodoridis, K. Koutroumbas, *Pattern recognition*, San Diego: Academic Press, 1999.

[6] Y. Linde, A. Buzo, R. Gray, "An Algorithm for vector quantization design", *IEEE Transactions on Communications*, 28, 1980, pp. 84-95.

[7] M. Lundqvist's implementation of the range coder. [Online]. Available: http://w1.515.telia.com/~u51507446, 20.9.2004.

[8] J. Mielikainen, P. Toivanen, and A. Kaarna, "Linear Prediction in Lossless Compression of Hyperspectral Images", *Optical Engineering*, Vol. 42, No. 4, pp. 1013-1017, April 2003.

[9] J. Mielikainen, P. Toivanen, "Improved Vector Quantization for Lossless Compression of AVIRIS Images", *Proceedings of the 11th European Signal Processing Conference (EUSIPCO-2002)*, Toulouse, France, September 3-6, 2002.

[10] J. Mielikainen, P. Toivanen, "Clustered DPCM for the Lossless Compression of Hyperspectral Images", *IEEE Transactions on Geoscience and Remote Sensing*, Vol. 41, No. 12, pp. 2943-2946, December 2003.

[11] S. R. Tate, "Band ordering in lossless compression of multispectral images", *IEEE Tranactions on.Comput*ers Vol. 46, No. 4, 1997, pp. 477–483.

[12] S. Baase, A. V. Gelder, *Computer Algorithms: Introduction to Design and Analysis*, Addison-Wesley, 1988.

[13] P. W. Purdom, Jr., C. A. Brown, *The analysis of algorithms*, Oxford University Press, 1995.

[14] J. Edmonds, "Optimum branchings", *J. Research of the National Bureau of Standards*, 71B, pp. 133-240, 1967.

[15] AIRS data, anonymous ftp. Available: ftp://ftp.ssec.wisc.edu /pub/bormin/HES, cited 28.9.2004.

[16] B. Huang, A. Ahuja, H. L. Huang, T. J. Schmit, R. W. Heymann, "Improvements to Predictor-based Methods in Lossless Compression of 3D Hyperspectral Sounding Data via Higher Moment Statistics", *WSEAS Transactions on Electronics*, Vol. 1, No. 2, pp. 299-305, April 2004.

[17] B. Huang, H. L. Huang., H. Chen., A. Ahuja, K. Baggett., T. J. Smith, R.W. Heymann, "Data Compression Studies for NOAA Hyperspectral Environmental Suite (HES) using 3D Integer Wavelet Transforms with 3D Set Partitioning in Hierarchical Trees", *Proceedings. of the SPIE International Symposium on Remote Sensing*, pp. 255-265, 2003.

[18] P. Toivanen, O. Kubasova, J. Mielikainen, "Correlation Based Band Ordering Heuristic for Lossless Compression of Hyperspectral Sounder Data", Accepted for Publication in *IEEE Geoscience and Remote Sensing Letters*, 2004.

[19] X. Wu and N. Memon, "Context-Based, Lossless Interband Compression – Extending CALIC", *IEEE Transactions on Image Processing*, Vol. 9, pp. 994-1001, June 2000.

[20] E. Magli, G. Olmo, E. Quacchio, "Optimized Onboard Lossless and Near Lossless Compression of Hyperspectral Data Using CALIC", *IEEE Geoscience and Remote Sensing Letters*, Vol. 1, No. 1, pp. 21-25, January 2004.

[21] J. Mielikainen, O. Kubasova, P. Toivanen, "Spectral DPCM for Lossless Compression of 3D Hyperspectral Data", *WSEAS Transactions on Systems*, Vol. 3, Issue 5, pp. 2188-2193, July 2004.

[22] AVIRIS 97 data. Available: http://aviris.jpl.nasa.gov/html/aviris.freedata.html, cited 28.9.2004.

[23] W. Porter, H. Enmark, "A system overview of the airborne visible/infrared imaging spectrometer (AVIRIS)", *Proceedings of SPIE*, Vol. 834, 1997, pp. 22-31.

[24] G. Shaw, D. Manolakis, "Signal Processing for Hyperspectral Image Exploitation", *IEEE Signal Processing Magazine*, Vol. 19, No. 1, January 2002, pp. 12-16.

[25] S. Ra, J. Kim, "A fast mean-distance-ordered partial codebook search algorithm for image vector quantization", *IEEE Transactions on Circuits and Systems II: Analog and Digital Signal Processing*, Vol. 40, No. 9, September 1993, pp. 576–579.

[26] T. Kaukoranta, P. Franti, O. Nevalainen., "A fast exact GLA based on code vector activity detection", IEEE *Transactions on Image Processing*, pp. 1337-1342, Vol. 9, No. 8, August 2000.

[27] P. Zhibin, K. Kotani, T. Ohmi, "A unified projection method for fast search of vector quantization", IEEE *Signal Processing Letters*, pp. 637- 640, Vol. 11, No. 7, July 2004.

[28] D. Shkarin, "PPM: One Step to Practicality", *Data Compression Conference*, Snowbird, Utah, pp. 202-211, 2002.

Lossless Compression of Ultraspectral Sounder Data

Bormin Huang, Alok Ahuja, and Hung-Lung Huang

Space Science and Engineering Center, University of Wisconsin-Madison

1. INTRODUCTION

In the era of contemporary and future ultraspectral sounders such as
Atmospheric Infrared Sounder (AIRS) [7], Cross-track Infrared Sounder
(CrIS) [9], Infrared Atmospheric Sounding Interferometer (IASI) [40],
Geosynchronous Imaging Fourier Transform Spectrometer (GIFTS) [52], and
Hyperspectral Environmental Suite (HES) [26], better inference of
atmospheric, cloud and surface parameters is feasible. An ultraspectral
sounder generates an unprecedented amount of three-dimensional (3D) data,
consisting of two spatial and one spectral dimension. For example, the HES
is the next-generation NOAA/NESDIS Geostationary Operational
Environmental Satellite (GOES) sounder, slated for launch in the 2013
timeframe. It would be either a Michelson interferometer or a grating
spectrometer, with high spectral resolution (over one thousand infrared
channels with spectral widths on the order of 0.5 wavenumber), high
temporal resolution (better than 1 hour), high spatial resolution (less than
10km) and hemispheric coverage. Given the large volume of 3D data that
will be generated by an ultraspectral sounder each day, the use of robust data
compression techniques will be beneficial to data transfer and archive.

There exist differences between ultraspectral sounder data and
hyperspectral imager data in terms of application areas and subsequent user
constraints on the data compression. The hyperspectral imager data (e.g. the
well-known AVIRIS data [6, 43]) has hundreds of bands in the visible or
near-infrared regions with major application categories of anomaly detection,
target recognition and background characterization [50]. Lossy compression
is usually acceptable for imager data as long as the tolerance limits in
application-specific metrics are met [46]. These metrics include those that
signify scientific loss for end users [42, 45], content-independent metrics

[51], and even visual comparisons [18]. On the other hand, the ultraspectral sounder data has over a thousand channels in the infrared region with the main purpose of retrieving atmospheric temperature, moisture and trace gases profiles, surface temperature and emissivity, and cloud and aerosol optical properties for better weather and climate prediction. The physical retrieval of these geophysical parameters from the sounder data via the inverse solution of the radiative transfer equation is a mathematically ill-posed problem [25], which is sensitive to the data quality. Therefore there is a need for lossless or near-lossless compression of ultraspectral sounder data to avoid potential retrieval degradation of geophysical parameters due to lossy compression. Here, near-lossless compression implies that the error spectrum between the reconstructed data set and original data set is significantly less than the sensor noise spectrum.

This chapter explores lossless compression of ultraspectral sounder data. These investigations are divided into transform-based, prediction-based, and clustering-based methods. The ultraspectral sounder data features strong correlations in disjoint spectral regions affected by the same type of absorbing gases at various altitudes. To take advantage of this fact, a bias-adjusted reordering (BAR) data preprocessing scheme [29] is devised that is applicable to any 2D compression method. We begin with a description of the ultraspectral sounder data used.

2. ULTRASPECTRAL SOUNDER DATA

The ultraspectral sounder data could be generated from either a Michelson interferometer (e.g. CrIS, IASI and GIFTS) or a grating spectrometer (e.g. AIRS). Compression is performed on the standard ultraspectral sounder data set that is publicly available via anonymous ftp [1]. It consists of ten granules, five daytime and five nighttime, selected from representative geographical regions of the Earth. Their locations, UTC times and local time adjustments are listed in Table 1. This standard ultraspectral sounder data set adopts the NASA AIRS digital counts on March 2, 2004. The AIRS data includes 2378 infrared channels in the 3.74 to 15.4 μm region of the spectrum. A day's worth of AIRS data is divided into 240 granules, each of 6 minute durations. Each granule consists of 135 scan lines containing 90 cross-track footprints per scan line; thus there are a total of 135 x 90 = 12,150 footprints per granule. More information regarding the AIRS instrument may be acquired from the NASA AIRS website [2].

Granule 9	00:53:31 UTC	-12 H	(Pacific Ocean, Daytime)
Granule 16	01:35:31 UTC	+2 H	(Europe, Nighttime)
Granule 60	05:59:31 UTC	+7 H	(Asia, Daytime)
Granule 82	08:11:31 UTC	-5 H	(North America, Nighttime)
Granule 120	11:59:31 UTC	-10 H	(Antarctica, Nighttime)
Granule 126	12:35:31 UTC	-0 H	(Africa, Daytime)
Granule 129	12:53:31 UTC	-2 H	(Arctic, Daytime)
Granule 151	15:05:31 UTC	+11 H	(Australia, Nighttime)
Granule 182	18:11:31 UTC	+8 H	(Asia, Nighttime)
Granule 193	19:17:31 UTC	-7 H	(North America, Daytime)

Table 1: Ten selected AIRS granules for ultraspectral sounder data compression studies.

The digital count data ranges from 12-bit to 14-bit for different channels. Each channel is saved using its own bit depth. To make the selected data more generic to other ultraspectral sounders, 271 bad channels identified in the supplied AIRS infrared channel properties file are excluded, assuming that they occur only in the AIRS sounder. Each resulting granule is saved as a binary file, arranged as 2107 channels, 135 scan lines, and 90 pixels for each scan line. Figure 1 shows the AIRS digital counts at wavenumber $800.01 cm^{-1}$ for the 10 selected granules on March 2, 2004. In these granules, coast lines are depicted by solid curves, and multiple clouds at various altitudes are shown as different shades of gray pixels.

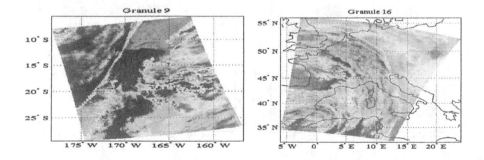

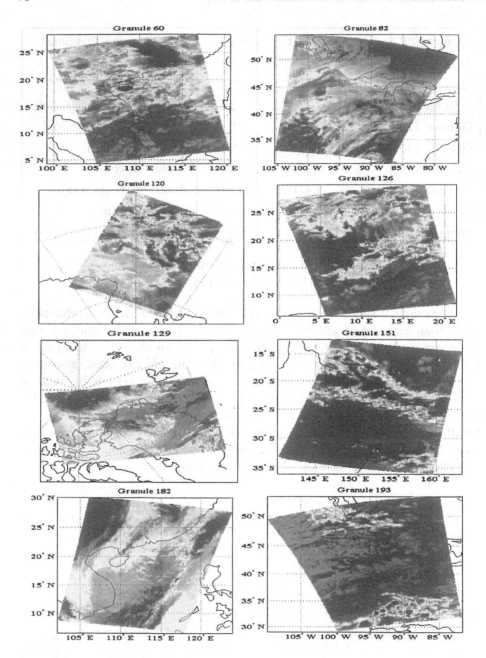

Figure 1: AIRS digital counts at wavenumber 800.01cm^{-1} for the ten selected granules on March 2, 2004.

3. DATA PREPROCESSING SCHEME

Ultraspectral sounder data features strong correlations in disjoint spectral regions affected by the same type of absorbing gases. Figure 2 shows an example of the dominant absorbing gases in different spectral regions.

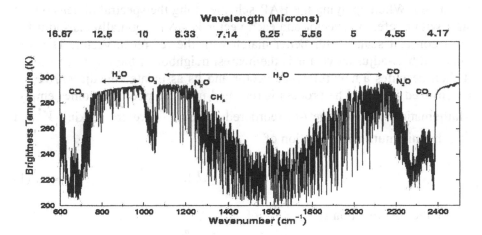

Figure 2: Dominant absorbing gases in the infrared spectrum of the 1976 US Standard Atmosphere.

The Bias-Adjusted Reordering (BAR) scheme [29] takes advantage of this unique spectroscopic characteristic of ultraspectral sounder data. When combined with a 3D compression scheme (e.g. 3D SPIHT [47, 54]), the BAR scheme reorders the spectral channels, each of which corresponds to a 2D spatial frame. It explores the spectral correlations among disjoint channels, resulting in compression gains. When the BAR scheme is combined with a 2D compression scheme (e.g. 2D JPEG2000 [4], 2D JPEG-LS [3], 2D CALIC [59]), the 3D sounder data is first made two-dimensional by converting the two spatial dimensions into one dimension via a continuous scan (e.g. horizontal, vertical and diagonal zigzag scans, spiral scan, Peano scan [61]) that smoothens the transition of data samples from one line to another. The BAR scheme is then applied along the spectral and/or spatial dimension. In doing so, it can explore the spectral correlations among disjoint channels, and/or the spatial correlations of disjoint geographical regions affected by the same type of absorbing gases or clouds.

Consider a 3D ultraspectral data cube of size n_c by n_x by n_y. For 2D compression, it is reshaped into a 2D data of size n_c by n_s via a continuous scan, where $n_s = n_x \times n_y$. When data are spectrally reordered, there are n_c vectors, each with n_s components. Let S be the pool of the vectors not yet reordered. When applying the BAR scheme along the spectral dimension we start with a reference vector and each vector $V \in S$ is optimally bias-adjusted by a constant scalar b for better match with the reference vector. The best matched bias-adjusted vector is the nearest neighbor of the reference vector. It then becomes a new reference vector and its associated unadjusted vector is removed from S. The process is repeated until the pool S becomes empty. Mathematically, given the i-th reordered vector $\tilde{V}^i$, we are seeking V^* and b^*, the minimum norm solution of

$$\min_{\substack{V \in S \\ b \in \mathbb{R}}} f^i(V,b), \tag{1}$$

where the cost function is

$$f^i(V,b) = \left\| \tilde{V}^i - V - b \right\|^2 = \sum_{k=1}^{n_s} (\tilde{v}_k^i - v_k - b)^2 . \tag{2}$$

Then the $(i+1)$-th reordered vector is simply

$$\tilde{V}^{i+1} = V^* + b^*.$$

The optimal value b^* is obtained by

$$\left. \frac{\partial f^i(V,b)}{\partial b} \right|_{b=b^*} = 0, \tag{3}$$

which yields

$$b^* = \frac{1}{n_s} \sum_{k=1}^{n_s} (\tilde{v}_k^i - v_k) = \langle \tilde{V}^i \rangle - \langle V \rangle, \tag{4}$$

where $\langle \, \rangle$ is the mean of a vector over its components. The b^* represents the bias between the two vectors $\tilde{V}^i$ and V.

Applying Eq. (4) to Eq. (2) yields the following cost function

$$f_{b^*}^i(V) = \sum_{k=1}^{n_s} (\tilde{v}_k^i - v_k)^2 - \frac{1}{n_s}\left[\sum_{k=1}^{n_s}(\tilde{v}_k^i - v_k)\right]^2, \tag{5}$$

or

$$f_{b^*}^i(V) = \left\| \tilde{V}^i - V \right\|^2 - n_s\left(\langle\tilde{V}^i\rangle - \langle V\rangle\right)^2, \tag{6}$$

and the bias-adjusted reordering problem is reduced to finding the minimum norm solution V^* of

$$\min_{V \in S} f_{b^*}^i(V). \tag{7}$$

For lossless compression, the b^* is rounded to the nearest integer $[\![b^*]\!]$, and the $(i+1)$-th reordered vector becomes

$$\tilde{V}^{i+1} = V^* + [\![b^*]\!]. \tag{8}$$

Similarly, the BAR scheme can be applied along the spatial dimension. In this case, there are n_s vectors, each with n_c components. A horizontal zigzag (Boustrophedon) scan has been used to convert the ten 3D granules into 2D before compressing the data with the 2D compression algorithms like JPEG2000, JPEG-LS, and CALIC.

The effects of the BAR scheme can be gauged by looking at the reordered 2D data patterns in the spectral-spatial domain. Figure 3 shows such an example for granule 82. Comparing Fig. 3(a) with Fig. 3(b), we can see that the data pattern is smoother along the spectral dimension after spectral reordering. This results in a higher compression ratio for Fig. 3(b). Similarly, the spatially reordered data in Fig. 3(c) is smoother than that in Fig. 3(a) along the spatial dimension. Fig 3(d) depicts the reordering along both dimensions that produces a smoother transition along both dimensions. Moreover, the bias adjustment has reduced the dynamic range of the reordered data as visualized by the reduction of grayscale intensities. Following the BAR preprocessing, significant compression gains have been reported on 3D SPIHT, 2D JPEG2000, 2D JPEG-LS and 2D CALIC in [28]. Investigations are underway for applying the BAR scheme to the 3D versions of these schemes.

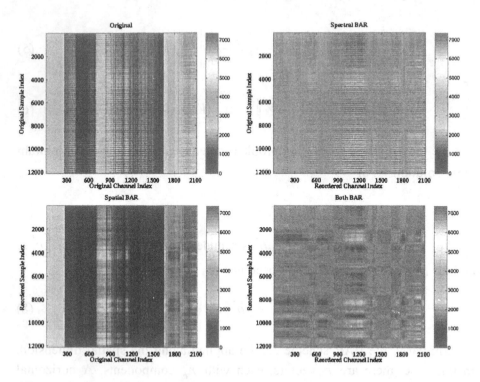

Figure 3: Examples of 2D data distributions (a) of the original granule; (b) after applying spectral BAR; (c) after applying spatial BAR; (d) after applying spectral BAR followed by spatial BAR.

Figure 4 shows the sorting indices plotted against the original indices in the cases of spectral BAR for four granules. The sorting indices are quite different from the original indices as judged by their great deviation from the straight line. This shows the natural channel order given by the spectral wavelengths do not possess optimal correlation in neighboring channels. In the BAR scheme, a given starting channel produces its own unique list of reordering indices. Subsequently, the compression ratios are different for the BAR scheme using different starting channels. An investigation of the effects of the starting channel has been conducted in [30]. It was shown that any starting channel may be used without compromising the compression ratio significantly for the ultraspectral sounder data.

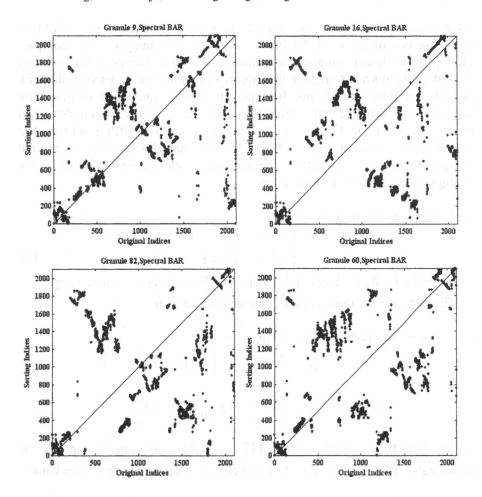

Figure 4: Spectral BAR sorting indices for various AIRS digital counts
granules.

4. COMPRESSION METHODS

4.1 Transform-based Methods

Transforms such as the wavelet transform [15] and the Principal Component
Analysis [11] are explored for compression of ultraspectral sounder data.
Various methods based on these transforms are highlighted in this section.

4.1.1 Wavelet Transform: The wavelet transform has been a successful tool in image compression. It features multiresolution analysis with compact support and linear computation times. Wavelet compression exploits redundancies in scale to reduce the information stored in the wavelet domain. Invertible wavelet transforms that map integers to integers have important applications in lossless data compression. The discrete wavelet transform can be implemented via the lifting scheme [53, 16]. The lifting scheme has several desirable advantages that include low complexity, linear execution time, and in-place computation. The integer wavelet transform based on the lifting scheme consists of three steps:

1) the lazy wavelet transform:

$$h_0[n] = x[2n+1],$$
$$l_0[n] = x[2n].$$
(9)

where $x[n]$, $h_0[n]$ and $l_0[n]$ are the discrete input data, the high-pass coefficients and the low-pass coefficients, respectively.

2) one or more dual and primal lifting steps:

$$h_i[n] = h_{i-1}[n] - \left\lfloor \left(\sum_k s_i[k] l_{i-1}[n-k] \right) + \frac{1}{2} \right\rfloor,$$

$$l_i[n] = l_{i-1}[n] - \left\lfloor \left(\sum_k t_i[k] h_i[n-k] \right) + \frac{1}{2} \right\rfloor.$$
(10)

where the filter coefficients $s_i[k]$ and $t_i[k]$ may be computed by factorization of a polyphase matrix of any perfect reconstruction filter bank.

3) rescaling:

$$l[n] = \frac{l_N[n]}{K},$$
$$h[n] = K \cdot h_N[n].$$
(11)

The inverse is obtained by reversing the above steps with the corresponding sign flips.

The filter coefficients need not be integers, but are generally rational with power-of-two denominators allowing all divisions to be implemented using binary shifts. Figures 5 and 6 show the forward and inverse wavelet transforms using the lifting scheme, respectively [8]. The wavelet transform can be extended to multiple dimensions by use of separable filters [32]. Each dimension is filtered and down-sampled alternatively.

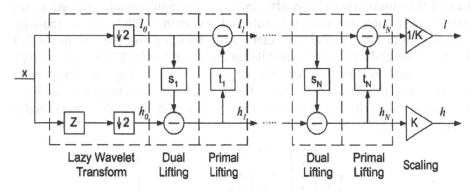

Figure 5: Forward wavelet transform using the lifting scheme.

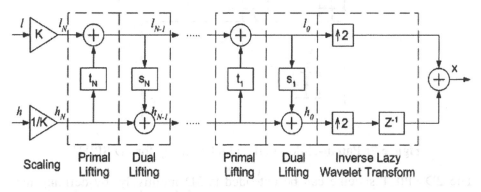

Figure 6: Inverse wavelet transform using the lifting scheme.

4.1.1.1 3D Set Partitioning in Hierarchical Trees (SPIHT) with the BAR preprocessing

SPIHT [47] is an embedded coding algorithm that performs bit-plane coding of the wavelet coefficients. It is a refinement of the embedded zerotree wavelet (EZW) scheme [48, 49, 8], providing better compression while also featuring faster encoding and decoding times. Extensions to 3D have been proposed in [54, 17]. Huang et al. [26] developed a version of 3D SPIHT to tackle irregular-sized 3D data, the dimensions of which need not be divisible by 2^N, where N is the levels of wavelet decomposition being performed.

After the wavelet transform, the coefficients can be represented by use of a tree structure using the SPIHT algorithm. The advantage of this structure lies in the observation that coefficients are better magnitude-ordered as we move downward through the subband pyramid. SPIHT uses spatially oriented trees to describe the relationship between the parents on higher levels to the children and grandchildren on lower levels. These relationships can be seen in the 2D wavelet decomposition of Fig. 7. Progressive transmission is achieved by use of two passes, the sorting pass and the refinement pass, that send wavelet coefficients with the highest magnitudes first.

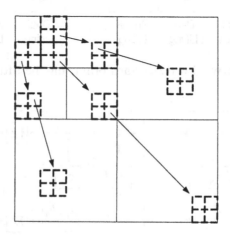

Figure 7: Parent-child interband relationship for 2D SPIHT.

The 2D SPIHT scheme can be extended to 3D intuitively, by defining the parent-child interband relationships as illustrated [8] in Fig. 8.

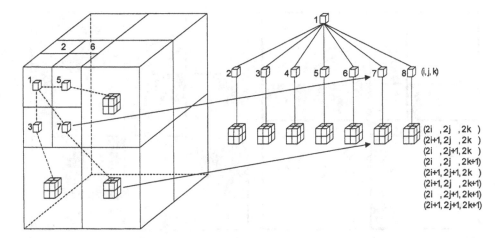

Figure 8: Parent-child interband relationship and locations for 3D SPIHT.

4.1.1.1.1 General Consideration for 3D Irregular Data: We extend the SPIHT scheme to deal with the ultraspectral sounder data that is not of regular size, i.e. each dimensions length of the 3D data set may not be divisible by 2^N, where N is the number of levels of wavelet decomposition. For an irregular data set the number of children varies for each parent node and not all combinations of child nodes are possible. It can be shown that {1, 2, 3, 4, 6, 9} are the allowable child combination set for 2D irregular data, whereas {1, 2, 3, 4, 6, 8, 9, 12, 18, 27} for 3D irregular data. In contrast, the allowable numbers of children for 2D and 3D regular data are 4 and 8, respectively. Figure 9(a) shows {1, 2, 3, 6, 9} as the possible numbers of children for 2D irregular data whereas Fig. 9(b) shows {1, 2, 4}. The SPIHT scheme for irregular data requires additional amount of memory storage and CPU time for tracking the more complicated parent-child relationship.

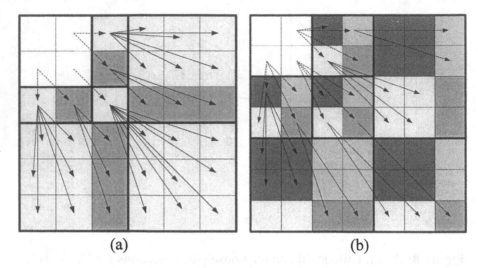

(a)   (b)

Figure 9: Examples of allowable parent-child relations for 2D irregular data.

4.1.1.1.2 Application of BAR + SPIHT to ultraspectral sounder data:
Various 3D integer wavelet transforms were used on the ten AIRS granules
followed by the 3D SPIHT method and arithmetic coding [33,58]. The
compression ratios thus obtained are shown in Fig. 10. As can be seen,
different choices of wavelet transforms produce different compression ratios.
For compression gains, the granules were reordered using spectral BAR
preprocessing. Figure 11 shows the compression ratios of the 3D SPIHT
method with BAR preprocessing. Comparing Fig. 11 with Fig. 10, it is seen
that the compression ratios obtained for all ten granules are significantly
higher with spectral BAR followed by 3D SPIHT than using 3D SPIHT
alone.

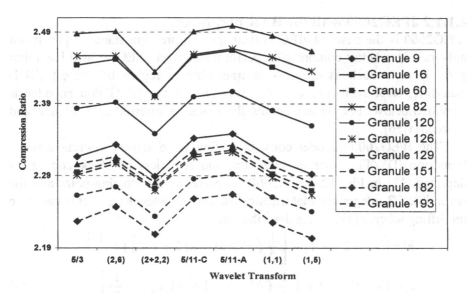

Figure 10: Compression ratios of ten granules using different wavelet transforms and 3D SPIHT.

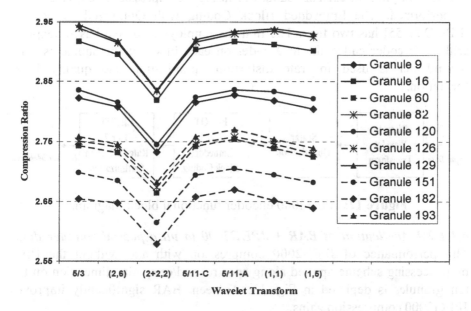

Figure 11: Compression ratios of ten granules after spectral BAR using different wavelet transforms and 3D SPIHT.

4.1.1.2 JPEG2000 with the BAR preprocessing

JPEG2000 is the new ISO/IEC still-image compression standard [4]. It not only provides better compression performance over JPEG, it also has other good features such as progressive transmission, region of interest (ROI) encoding, error resilience etc. An overview of the JPEG2000 encoder is provided below. For further details the reader is referred to Taubman and Marcellin [56].

The JPEG2000 encoder consists of four main stages: discrete wavelet transform (DWT), scalar quantization, and two tiers of block coding, as depicted [12] in Fig. 12. JPEG2000 supports the 9/7 floating-point and the reversible 5/3 integer wavelet transforms. The 5/3 integer wavelet is based on the lifting scheme [49] and is described by

$$h[n] = x[2n+1] - \left\lfloor \frac{1}{2}\left(x[2n] + x[2n+2]\right) + \frac{1}{2} \right\rfloor$$

$$l[n] = x[2n] + \left\lfloor \frac{1}{4}\left(h[n-1] + h[n]\right) + \frac{1}{2} \right\rfloor. \tag{12}$$

The scalar quantization is implemented with the quantization step size possibly varying for each subband. For lossless compression, no quantization is performed. The Embedded Block Coding with Optimized Truncation (EBCOT) [55] has two tiers. The first tier employs a context based adaptive arithmetic coder called the MQ coder on each block of the subbands. The second tier is used for rate distortion optimization and quality layer formation.

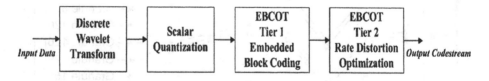

Figure 12: JPEG2000 encoder functional block diagram.

4.1.1.2.1 Application of BAR + JPEG2000 to ultraspectral sounder data: The performance of JPEG2000 compression with and without the BAR preprocessing scheme applied along spectral and/or spatial dimension on the ten granules is depicted in Fig. 13. As seen, BAR significantly improves JPEG2000 compression gains.

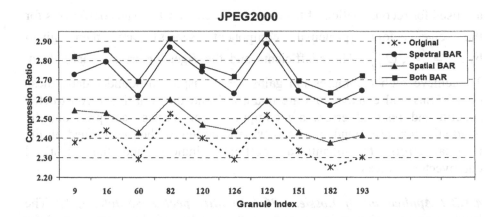

Figure 13: Compression ratios for JPEG2000 with and without BAR for ten tested granules.

4.1.2   Lossless Principal Component Analysis

The Principal Component Analysis (PCA) or the Karhunen-Loève transform (KLT) has long been used in applications pertaining to hyperspectral images such as feature extraction, dimensionality reduction, and pattern recognition [11]. The principal components are the eigenvectors of the data covariance matrix. PCA has been used for lossy compression of hyper spectral imager data [19, 24, 34]. Lossless compression of ultraspectral sounder data via PCA is investigated below.

For 3D ultraspectral sounder data with size n_c by n_x by n_y, we reshape it into a 2D with $n_s = n_x \times n_y$ vectors. Each vector V_i is a spectrum. The covariance matrix is given by

$$\Gamma = \frac{1}{n_c - 1} \sum_{i=1}^{n_s} (V_i - \mu_i)(V_i - \mu_i)^T \tag{13}$$

where μ_i is the mean spectrum. The principal components are obtained from the eigendecomposition of Γ:

$$\Gamma = Q \Lambda Q^T \tag{14}$$

where $Q = [Q_1, Q_2, \dots Q_{n_c}]$ is the matrix of eigenvectors and Λ is the diagonal matrix of the corresponding eigenvalues. To compress the ultraspectral sounder data, only n eigenvectors with the largest n eigenvalues are used for reconstruction of the data set, where $n < n_c$. The coefficients for the eigenvectors (principal component scores) are then given by $c_{ij} = \langle V_i, Q_j \rangle$. The coefficients and the eigenvectors are real-valued. To achieve higher compression gains for ultraspectral sounder data, these coefficients and eigenvectors are quantized and the resulting reconstructed spectra and residual errors are computed. For lossless compression, the residual errors are rounded. The arithmetic coding is then performed on the residual errors, the quantized coefficient indices, and the quantized eigenvectors indices.

4.1.2.2 Application of Lossless PCA to ultraspectral sounder data: The lossless compression ratio depends on the number of eigenvectors used for reconstruction. The choice of this number represents a tradeoff between the size of side information and magnitude of the residual errors. Figure 14 shows the average lossless compression ratios over all ten granules with different numbers of eigenvectors. The maximum compression ratio is found with 60 eigenvectors. The compression ratios of the ten granules using lossless PCA with 60 eigenvectors are shown in Table 2.

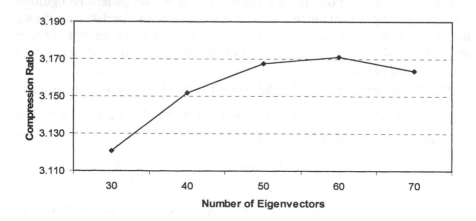

Figure 14: Average Lossless PCA compression ratios for different number of eigenvectors.

Granule	PCA
9	3.19
16	3.19
60	3.18
82	3.20
120	3.16
126	3.17
129	3.22
151	3.14
182	3.10
193	3.16
Average	**3.17**

Table 2: Compression ratios using Lossless PCA with 60 eigenvectors for ten granules.

4.2   Prediction-based Methods

4.2.1   JPEG-LS with the BAR preprocessing

The ISO/IEC working group released a new standard for the lossless/near-lossless compression of continuous-tone images in 1999, popularly known as JPEG-LS [3]. Near-lossless compression is controlled through an integer valued threshold representing the maximum permissible absolute difference between each original pixel value and its decompressed value. As shown in Fig. 15, the JPEG-LS encoder is composed of four main stages: prediction, context modeling, error encoding, and run mode [57].

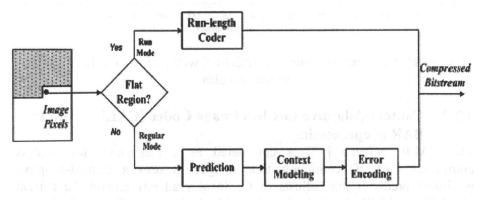

Figure 15: JPEG-LS encoder block diagram.

The predictor is based on local edge detection and is a function of the neighborhood values. The context modeling employs three local gradients to characterize the neighborhood of the pixel being predicted. To further reduce the context model, each of these local gradients is quantized to obtain 9 quantization indices. The error encoding is done via a Golomb code [21]. A length-constrained Golomb code is used to avoid excessively large code words from being produced. The run mode is used to capture local redundancy in homogeneous regions. In this mode, the pixels are run-length encoded using a reference value.

4.2.1.1 Application of BAR + JPEG-LS to ultraspectral sounder data: The 3D data set is converted to 2D using a horizontal zigzag scan. Figure 16 show the compression ratios of JPEG-LS with and without the BAR preprocessing scheme applied along spectral and/or spatial dimension on the ten granules. It is seen that the combination of BAR+JPEG-LS significantly outperforms JPEG-LS applied alone.

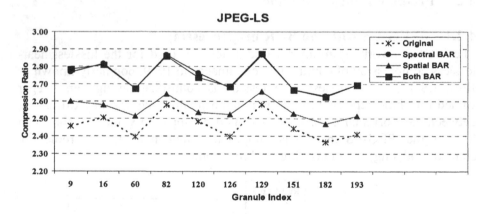

Figure 16: Compression ratios for JPEG-LS with and without BAR for ten tested granules.

4.2.2   Context-Adaptive Lossless Image Codec (CALIC) with the BAR preprocessing

The CALIC scheme [59] is considered as a benchmark for lossless compression of 2D continuous-tone images. It uses a context-adaptive nonlinear predictor that adjusts to the local gradients around the current pixel. Figure 17 illustrates the functional block diagram of CALIC [59].

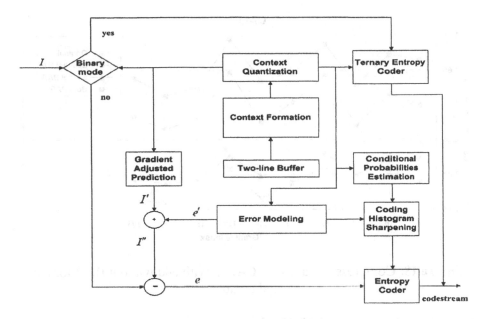

Figure 17: Schematic description of the CALIC encoder.

The binary mode of CALIC is performed on the image regions where the number of intensity values is no more than two. In the continuous mode, the system has four major components: gradient-adjusted prediction, context selection and quantization, error modeling, and entropy coding. Gradient-adjusted prediction is performed using a nonlinear predictor that adapts to the intensity gradients near the predicted pixel. An empirically chosen formula is used to calculate the prediction errors. Context selection and quantization facilitates further decorrelation. Error modeling is used to achieve further compression. Entropy coding is context-based with usage of conditional error probabilities.

4.2.2.5 Application of BAR + CALIC to ultraspectral sounder data: The compression ratios obtained by using CALIC with and without the BAR preprocessing scheme applied along spectral and/or spatial dimension are depicted in Fig. 18. As seen, BAR+CALIC significantly outperforms CALIC.

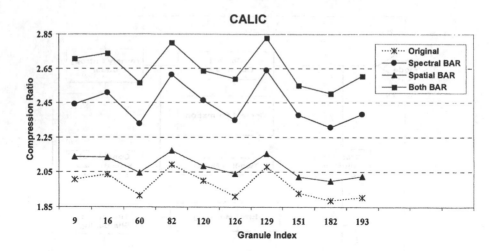

Figure 18: Compression ratios for CALIC with and without BAR for ten tested granules.

4.3   Clustering-based Methods

Vector Quantization (VQ) [23] has been used for hyperspectral imager data compression [5, 41, 10, 19, 39]. To reduce the computational burden for ultraspectral sounder data compression, we investigated the Predictive Partitioned VQ (PPVQ) [27]. This scheme falls under the category of predictive vector quantization [13, 20]. An open-loop design methodology [20] is used such that the predictor is designed independently of the VQ codebooks. Different vector quantizers are designed for each partition. The PPVQ scheme consists of four steps that are outlined below.

i) Linear Prediction: The simple idea of linear prediction is to represent a pixel as the linear combination of a set of neighboring pixels [60, 35, 38, 37] to reduce the data variance. For ultraspectral sounder data, the spectral correlation is generally much stronger than the spatial correlation. Therefore, we predict a channel as a linear combination of neighboring channels. The problem can be formulated in the matrix form:

$$\hat{X} = X_p A \qquad (15)$$

where $\hat{X}$ is the column vector representing the current channel, X_p is the matrix of neighboring channels, and A is the column vector of the prediction coefficients. The least-squares solution to Eq. (15) yields the prediction coefficients

$$A = (X_p^T X_p)^\dagger (X_p^T \hat{X}) \qquad (16)$$

where the superscript † represents the pseudo-inverse that deals with the case of the matrix being ill-conditioned [22]. The prediction error is the difference between the original channel vector and its predicted counterpart.

ii) Channel Partitioning: The bit depth of each channel varies after taking the prediction step. To reduce the computational burden, channels with the same bit depth of prediction error are assigned to the same partition and VQ is applied to each partition separately.

iii) Vector Quantization: In vector quantization, we group each partition of multidimensional data into a number of clusters and each cluster is represented by a single vector which is the codeword of the cluster. The set of all codewords in each partition forms its codebook. In this study, each codeword is a partial spectrum within a partition. The codebook is designed using the well-known Linde-Buzo-Gray (LBG) algorithm [36]. After the codebook is designed, data of the same partition is replaced by its corresponding codeword. The difference between the original data and its codeword is the quantization error. For lossless compression, the codebooks are rounded.

iv) Entropy Coding: A context-based adaptive arithmetic coder is used to encode the VQ codebooks, data quantization indices, and quantization errors.

Huang et al. [31] also developed a fast precomputed vector quantization (FPVQ) scheme with optimal bit allocation. Unlike previous bit allocation algorithms [44, 14] that may yield a sub-optimal solution, the proposed bit allocation algorithm guarantees to find the minimum of the cost function under the constraint of a given total bit rate. Numerical experiments upon the NASA AIRS data have shown that the FPVQ scheme gives high compression ratios for lossless compression of ultraspectral sounder data.

4.3.1 Application to ultraspectral sounder data: Figure 19 shows the original and linear prediction residual images for three channels of Granule 193 using $N=32$ predictors. The randomness of the prediction residuals indicates that they are decorrelated quite well.

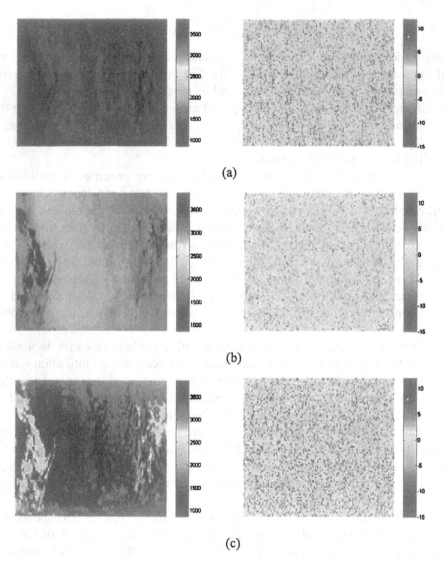

Figure 19: (a) Original and prediction residual scenes for wavenumber 800.01 cm^{-1} of Granule 193; (b) Same as (a) except for wavenumber 1330.4 cm^{-1}; (c) Same as (a) except for wavenumber 2197 cm^{-1}.

For comparison with PPVQ, we also investigate the Differential Partitioned VQ (DPVQ) and Partitioned VQ (PVQ) schemes. In the DPVQ scheme, the spectral difference between successive neighboring channels is calculated. The rest of the steps viz. channel partitioning, vector quantization and entropy coding are the same as those used in the PPVQ scheme. In the PVQ scheme, channels are partitioned according to their original bit-depths, followed by vector quantization and entropy coding. Table 3 shows the compression ratios achieved by these schemes. As seen, the PPVQ scheme significantly outperforms DPVQ and PVQ.

Granule	PVQ	DPVQ	PPVQ
9	2.23	2.85	3.35
16	2.25	2.88	3.36
60	2.01	2.75	3.30
82	2.37	2.94	3.39
120	2.13	2.80	3.31
126	2.07	2.76	3.29
129	2.38	2.91	3.38
151	2.03	2.73	3.26
182	1.96	2.64	3.22
193	2.04	2.73	3.27
Average	**2.15**	**2.80**	**3.31**

Table 3: Compression ratios for partitioned VQ, DPVQ, and PPVQ on ten granules.

5 CONCLUSIONS

The compression of ultraspectral sounder data is better to be lossless or near-lossless to avoid potential degradation of the geophysical retrieval in the associated ill-posed problem. Transform-based, prediction-based, and clustering-based methods for lossless compression of ultraspectral sounder data have been presented. It is shown that the compression ratios of ultraspectral sounder data via the standard state-of-the-art algorithms (e.g. 3D SPIHT, 2D JPEG2000, 2D CALIC, 2D JPEG-LS etc.) can be significantly improved when combining the BAR preprocessing scheme. We also report the promising compression results for the ultraspectral sounder data using various approaches such as lossless PCA and Predictive Partitioned Vector Quantization (PPVQ).

6 REFERENCES

[1]   ftp://ftp.ssec.wisc.edu/pub/bormin/Count.

[2]   http://www-airs.jpl.nasa.gov

[3]   ISO/IEC 14495-1 and ITU Recommendation T.87, 1999. Information Technology – lossless and near-lossless compression of continuous-tone still images.

[4]   ISO/IEC 15444-1, 2000. Information technology - JPEG2000 image coding system-part 1: Core coding system.

[5]   Abousleman G.P., M.W. Marcellin, and B.R. Hunt, 1997. Hyperspectral image compression using entropy-constrained predictive trellis coded quantization. *IEEE Transactions on Image Processing*, Vol. 6, No. 4, pp. 566-573.

[6]   Abousleman G.P., 1999. Adaptive coding of hyperspectral imagery. In *Proceedings of the 1999 IEEE International Conference on Acoustics, Speech, and Signal Processing (ICASSP)*, Vol. 4, pp. 2243 -2246.

[7]   Aumann H.H., and L. Strow, 2001. AIRS, the first hyper-spectral infrared sounder for operational weather forecasting. In *Proceedings of IEEE Aerospace Conference*, Vol. 4, pp. 1683-1692.

[8]   Bilgin A, G. Zweig, M.W. Marcellin, 2000. Three-dimensional image compression with integer wavelet transforms. *Applied Optics*, Vol. 39, No. 11, pp. 1799-1814.

[9]   Bloom H.J., 2001. The Cross-track Infrared Sounder (CrIS): a sensor for operational meteorological remote sensing. In *Proceedings of the 2001 International Geoscience and Remote Sensing Symposium (IGARSS)*, Vol. 3, pp. 1341-1343.

[10]   Canta G.R., and G. Poggi, 1998. Kronecker-product gain-shape vector quantization for multispectral and hyperspectral image coding. *IEEE Transactions on Image Processing*, Vol. 7, No. 5, pp. 668-678.

[11]   Chang C.-I., and Q. Du, 1999. Interference and noise-adjusted principal components analysis. *IEEE Transactions on Geoscience and Remote Sensing*, Vol. 37, No. 5, pp. 2387-2396.

[12]   Chung-Jr L, K.-F. Chen, H.-H. Chen, and L.-G. Chen, 2003. Analysis and architecture design of block-coding engine for EBCOT in JPEG 2000. *IEEE Transactions on Circuits and Systems for Video Technology*, Vol. 13, No. 3, pp. 219-230.

[13] Cuperman V., and A. Gersho, 1982. Adaptive differential vector coding of speech. In *Proceedings of IEEE GLOBECOM*, pp. 1092-1096, December.

[14] Cuperman V., 1993. Joint bit allocation and dimensions optimization for vector transform quantization. *IEEE Transactions on Information Theory*, Vol. 39, No. 1, pp. 302–305.

[15] Daubechies I., 1992. *Ten Lectures on Wavelets*. CBMS-NSF Regional Conference Series in Applied Mathematics, vol. 61, SIAM, Philadelphia, PA, 1992.

[16] Daubechies I. and W. Sweldens, 1998. Factoring wavelet and subband transforms into lifting steps. *Journal of Fourier Analysis and Applications*, Vol. 4, No. 3, 247-269.

[17] Dragotti P.L., G. Poggi, A.R.P. Ragozini, 2000. Compression of multispectral images by three-dimensional SPIHT algorithm. *IEEE Transactions on Geoscience and Remote Sensing*, Vol. 38, No. 1, pp. 416-428.

[18] Eckstein, B.A., R. Peters, J.M. Irvine, R. Ritzel, R. Hummel, 2000. Assessing the performance effects of data compression for SAR imagery. In *Proceedings of the 2000 IEEE Applied Imagery and Pattern Recognition Workshop*, pp. 102-108.

[19] Gelli G., and G. Poggi, 1999. Compression of multispectral images by spectral classification and transform coding. *IEEE Transactions on Image Processing*, Vol. 8, No. 4, pp. 476-489.

[20] Gersho A., and R.M. Gray, 1992. *Vector Quantization and Signal Compression*. Norwell, Mass: Kluwer Academic.

[21] Golomb S. W., 1966. Run-length encoding. *IEEE Transactions on Information Theory*, Vol. IT-12, pp. 399–401.

[22] Golub G. H. and C.F. Van Loan, 1996. *Matrix Computations*. John Hopkins University Press.

[23] Gray R.M., 1984. Vector Quantization. In *IEEE Acoustics, Speech, and Signal Processing Magazine*, Vol.1, pp. 4-29.

[24] Hoffman R.N., and D.W. Johnson, 1994. Application of EOF's to multispectral imagery: data compression and noise detection for AVIRIS. *IEEE Transactions on Geoscience and Remote Sensing*, Vol. 32, No. 1, pp. 25-34.

[25] Huang B., W. L. Smith, H.-L. Huang, and H. M. Woolf, 2002. Comparison of linear forms of the radiative transfer equation with analytic Jacobians, *Applied Optics*, Vol. 41, No. 21, pp. 4209-4219.

[26] Huang B., H.-L. Huang, H. Chen, A. Ahuja, K. Baggett, T. J. Schmit, and R. W. Heymann, 2003. Data compression studies for NOAA hyperspectral environmental suite using 3D integer wavelet transforms with 3D set partitioning in hierarchical trees. In *SPIE International Symposium on Remote Sensing Europe, 8-12 Sept. 2003, Barcelona, Spain, Proceedings of SPIE,* Vol. 5238, pp. 255-265.

[27] Huang B., A. Ahuja, H.-L. Huang, T. J. Schmit, and R. W. Heymann, 2004. Predictive partitioned vector quantization for hyperspectral sounder data compression. In *SPIE Annual Meeting, 2-6 August 2004, Denver, Proceedings of SPIE,* Vol. 5548, pp. 70-77.

[28] Huang B., H.-L. Huang, A. Ahuja, H. Chen, T.J. Schmit, R.W. Heymann, 2004. Lossless data compression for infrared hyperspectral sounders – an update. In *SPIE Annual Meeting, 2-6 August 2004, Denver, Proceedings of SPIE,* Vol. 5548, pp. 109-119.

[29] Huang B., A. Ahuja, H.-L. Huang, T. J. Schmit, and R. W. Heymann, 2004. Lossless compression of 3D hyperspectral sounding data using context-based adaptive lossless image codec with Bias-Adjusted Reordering. *Optical Engineering,* Vol. 43, No. 9, pp. 2071-2079.

[30] Huang B., A. Ahuja, H.-L. Huang, T. J. Schmit, and R. W. Heymann, 2004. Effects of the starting channel for spectral reordering on the lossless compression of 3D ultraspectral sounder data. In *SPIE International Asia-Pacific Symposium, 8-11 Nov. 2004, Honolulu, Hawaii, Proceedings of SPIE,* Vol. 5655, pp. 353-363.

[31] Huang B., A. Ahuja, H.-L. Huang, T. J. Schmit, and R. W. Heymann, 2005. Fast precomputed VQ with optimal bit allocation for lossless compression of ultraspectral sounder data. To appear In *Proceedings of the 2005 IEEE Data Compression Conference.*

[32] Kovačević J., and W.Sweldens, 2000. Wavelet families of increasing order in arbitrary dimensions. *IEEE Transactions on Image Processing,* Vol. 9, No. 3, pp. 480-496.

[33] Langdon G.G., 1984. An introduction to arithmetic coding. *IBM Journal of Research and Development,* Vol. 28, pp. 135-139.

[34] Lee H.S., N.-H. Younan, and R.L. King. 2000. Hyperspectral image cube compression combining JPEG 2000 and spectral decorrelation. In *Proceedings of the IEEE International Geoscience and Remote Sensing Symposium (IGARSS),* Vol. 6, pp. 3317-3319.

[35] Li X. and M. Orchard, 2001. Edge-directed prediction for lossless compression of natural images. *IEEE Transactions on Image Processing,* Vol. 10, No. 6, pp. 813-817.

[36] Linde Y., A. Buzo, and R.M. Gray, 1980. An Algorithm for Vector Quantizer Design. *IEEE Transactions on Communications*, Vol. COM-28, pp. 84-95.

[37] Mielikainen J., P. Toivanen, and A. Kaarna, 2003. Linear prediction in lossless compression of hyperspectral images, *Optical Engineering*, Vol. 42, No. 4, pp. 1013-1017.

[38] Motta G., J.A. Storer, and B. Carpentieri, 1999. Adaptive linear prediction lossless image coding. In *Proceedings of the 1999 IEEE Data Compression Conference*, pp. 491-500.

[39] Motta G., F. Rizzo, and J.A. Storer, 2003. Compression of hyperspectral imagery. In *Proceedings of the 2003 IEEE Data Compression Conference*, pp. 333-342.

[40] Phulpin T., F. Cayla, G. Chalon, D. Diebel, and D. Schlüssel, 2002. IASI onboard Metop: Project status and scientific preparation. In *12th International TOVS Study Conference, Lorne, Victoria, Australia*, pp. 234-243.

[41] Qian S.-E., A.B. Hollinger, D. Williams, and D. Manak, 1996. Fast 3-D data compression of hyperspectral imagery using vector quantization with spectral-feature-based binary coding. *Optical Engineering*, Vol. 35, No. 11, pp. 3242-3249.

[42] Qian S.-E., A.B. Hollinger, M. Dutkiewicz, H. Tsang, H. Zwick, J.R. Freemantle, 2001. Effect of lossy vector quantization hyperspectral data compression on retrieval of red-edge indices. *IEEE Transactions on Geoscience and Remote Sensing*, Vol. 39, No. 7, pp. 1459-1470.

[43] Qian S.-E., B. Hu, M. Bergeron, A. Hollinger, and P. Oswald, 2002. Quantitative evaluation of hyperspectral data compressed by near lossless onboard compression techniques. In *Proceedings of the 2002 International Geoscience and Remote Sensing Symposium (IGARSS)*, pp. 1425-1427.

[44] Riskin E.A., 1991. Optimal bit allocation via the generalized BFOS algorithm. *IEEE Transactions on Information Theory*, Vol. 37, No. 2, pp. 400-402.

[45] Ryan M.J., and J.F. Arnold, 1998. A suitable distortion measure for the lossy compression of hyperspectral data. In *Proceedings of the IEEE International Geoscience and Remote Sensing Symposium (IGARSS)*, Vol. 4., pp. 2056-2058.

[46] Saghri J.A., A.G. Tescher, and J.T. Reagan, 1995. Practical Transform Coding of Multispectral Imagery. In *IEEE Signal Processing Magazine*, Vol. 12, No. 1, pp. 32-43.

[47] Said A., and W.A. Pearlman, 1996. A new, fast, and efficient image codec based on set partitioning in hierarchical trees. *IEEE Transactions on Circuits and Systems for Video Technology*, Vol. 6, No. 3, pp. 243-250.

[48] Shapiro J.M., 1993. Embedded image coding using zerotrees of wavelet coefficients. *IEEE Transactions on Signal Processing*, Vol. 41, No. 12, pp. 3445-3462.

[49] Shapiro J.M., 1995. *Apparatus and method for compressing information.* United States Patent Number 5,412,741, Issued May 2, 1995.

[50] Shaw G.A., and H-h. K. Burke., 2003. Spectral Imaging for Remote Sensing. In *Lincoln Laboratory Journal,* Vol. 14, No. 1, pp. 3-28.

[51] Shen S. S., J.E. Lindgren, P.M. Payton, 1993. Effects of multispectral compression on machine exploitation. In *Twenty-Seventh Asilomar Conference on Signals, Systems, and Computers*, Vol. 2, pp. 1352-1356.

[52] Smith W.L., F.W. Harrison, D.E. Hinton, H.E. Revercomb, G.E. Bingham, R. Petersen, and J.C. Dodge, 2002. GIFTS - the precursor geostationary satellite component of the future Earth Observing System. In *Proceedings of the 2002 International Geoscience and Remote Sensing Symposium (IGARSS)*, Vol. 1, pp 357-361.

[53] Sweldens W., 1996. The lifting scheme: A custom-design construction of biorthogonal wavelets. *Journal of Applied and Computational Harmonic Analysis*, Vol. 3, No. 2, pp. 186-200.

[54] Tang X., S. Cho, and W.A. Pearlman, 2003. Comparison of 3D set partitioning methods in hyperspectral image compression featuring an improved 3D-SPIHT. In *Proceedings of the 2003 Data Compression Conference,* p. 449.

[55] Taubman D., 2000, High performance scalable image compression with EBCOT. *IEEE Transactions on Image Processing*, Vol. 9, No. 7, pp. 1158-1170.

[56] Taubman D. and M. Marcellin, 2002. *JPEG2000: Image Compression Fundamentals, Standards and Practice.* Kluwer Academic, Norwell.

[57] Weinberger M.J., G. Seroussi, and G. Sapiro, 2000. The LOCO-I lossless image compression algorithm: principles and standardization into JPEG-LS. *IEEE Transactions on Image Processing*, Vol. 9, No. 8, pp. 1309-1324.

[58] Witten I.H., R.M. Neal, and J. Cleary, 1987. Arithmetic coding for data compression. *Communications of the ACM*, Vol. 30, No. 6, pp. 520-540.

[59] Wu X., 1997. Context-based, adaptive, lossless image coding. *IEEE Transactions on Communications*, Vol. 45, No. 4, pp. 437–444.

[60] Wu X., and K. Barthel, 1998. Piecewise 2D autoregression for predictive image coding. In *Proceedings of the International Conference on Image Processing (ICIP)*, Vol. 3, pp. 901-904.

[61] Yang K.M., L. Wu, and M. Mills, 1988. Fractal based image coding scheme using peano scan. In *Proceedings of the 1988 International Symposium on Circuits and Systems*, Vol. 3, pp. 2301-2304.

Locally Optimal Partitioned Vector Quantization of Hyperspectral Data

G. Motta[1,2], F. Rizzo[1,3], J. A. Storer[1]

[1]Brandeis University, Waltham, MA 02453
[2]Bitfone Corporation, Laguna Niguel, CA 92677
[3]Università degli Studi di Salerno, Baronissi SA, Italy

I. INTRODUCTION

An increasing number of scientific instruments acquire data in the form of three dimensional *data cubes*, i.e., two-dimensional matrices of vectors. Typical examples are body imaging medical instruments, multi-, hyper- and ultraspectral imagers, and microwave sounders measuring volumetric parameters like atmospheric temperature and pressure.

Compressing these data presents a challenge for the currently standardized general purpose compressors. Beside the three-dimensional nature of the measurements, which exhibit correlation along each dimension, individual samples have 16 bit or higher precision. Current state-of-the-art lossless compressors do not perform well on data sources with large alphabets.

Lossless compression is often required for data collection and archiving due to the cost of the acquisition and transmission process and due to the fact that original data may be needed for unforeseen analyses or further elaboration. Conversely, the distribution of the data to the final users can benefit from lossy modes both to speed up transmission, since the final users may not need all measurements at their full precision, and to provide multiple levels of service where higher quality data can be made available on demand. Consequently, it would be desirable to have a single compressor that could scale to data cubes of arbitrary size while supporting lossless, near lossless and lossy compression modes.

Traditional approaches to the compression of hyperspectral imagery are based on differential prediction via DPCM [1-3], vector quantization [4-7], or dimensionality reduction through principal component analysis [8, 9]. Inter-band linear prediction based on least square optimization has been proposed by Mielikäinen et alii [10]; this compression method optimizes, for each sample, the parameters of a linear predictor with spatial and spectral support. A more complex least-square optimized scheme combined with a vector quantizer has been presented by Mielikäinen and Toivanen [11]. Rizzo et alii [12] have recently introduced a purely spectral linear prediction with efficient entropy coding and an intra-band prediction mode for noisy bands.

The authors have studied a compression algorithm based on partitioned vector quantization [13, 14], where one dimension of the cube is treated as a single vector, partitioned and quantized. Partitioning the vector into subvectors of (possibly) different lengths is necessary because of the possibly large number of components. Subvectors are individually quantized with appropriate codebooks. The adaptive partitioning uses a novel locally optimal algorithm and provides a tool to reduce the size of the source alphabet. The design converges to a local optimum that has been experimentally shown to achieve performance close to global optima found by costly and time-consuming dynamic programs.

In this chapter a detailed description of such a method, named *locally-optimal partitioned vector quantizer* or LPVQ, is given. After introducing the necessary notation and reviewing vector quantization, the design of the LPVQ codebook is described in detail followed by a description of the entropy coding stage and experimental results. Besides the competitive compression, LPVQ has the advantage that the quantization indices retain important information on the original scene; it is shown here how this information can be used to browse the image and select regions of interest. Furthermore, by bounding the quantization error on each sample, an algorithm to speed up the pure-pixel classification is introduced. The Euclidean distance between a target pixel and a pixel of the image can be computed 90 percent of the time from the pixel indices via a lookup table; only the remaining 10 percent of the time is it necessary to decompress the residual error. Even if vector quantizers are typically complex, a careful choice of the size of the dictionary can make the VQ section of the encoder fast enough that even an implementation on a general-purpose hardware can achieve real-time compression. A hardware implementation is also relatively simple. The bottleneck of LPVQ is constituted by the entropy encoder. In the final section, the effect of replacing the arithmetic encoder with a low complexity lossless data compressor is discussed.

II. VECTOR QUANTIZATION

Vector quantization (or in short VQ) is probably the oldest and most general source coding technique. Shannon proved in his *source coding theorem* [15] that VQ has the property of achieving asymptotically the best theoretical performance on every data source.

Since vector quantization generalizes scalar quantization to multi-dimensional inputs (vectors), scalar quantizers are introduced first.

A *scalar quantizer* is defined by:

- An encoding function $E(x)$ that maps an input point x from the real line $\mathfrak{R}$ to an integer index;
- A decoding function $D(i)$ that maps an index i to one of a set of representative real numbers called quantization levels.

By means of these two functions, any real number can be approximated by one of a small set of values carefully selected in order to minimize the average distortion introduced by this approximation. A quantizer achieves compression by mapping multiple inputs onto the same index; being many-to-one, this mapping is of course irreversible (lossy). Which quantizer fits best a given input source depends both on the input statistics and on the distortion measure being minimized.

A formal definition of a scalar quantizer is the following: let x be a random point on the real line $\mathfrak{R}$; an N-level scalar quantizer (or SQ) of $\mathfrak{R}$ is a triple $Q = (A, F, P)$ where:

- $A = \{y_1, y_2, ..., y_N\}$ is a finite indexed subset of $\mathfrak{R}$ consisting of quantization levels;
- $P = \{S_1, S_2, ..., S_N\}$ is a partition of $\mathfrak{R}$. Equivalence classes (or *cells*) S_j of P satisfy:

$$\bigcup_{j=1}^{N} S_j = \mathfrak{R},$$

$$S_j \cap S_k = \emptyset \text{ for } j \neq k;$$

- $F : \mathfrak{R} \mapsto A$ is a mapping that defines the relationship between the quantization levels and the partitions:

$$F(x) = y_j \text{ if and only if } x \in S_j.$$

The encoder function $E(x)$ mentioned earlier maps x to the integer index i such that $F(x) = y_i$ and the decoder $D(i)$ maps the index to the i-th quantization level y_i. Quantization is carried out by composing the two functions E and D as:

$$D(E(x)) = y_i = \hat{x}$$

where $\hat{x}$ is the quantized representation of x.

The distortion introduced by the process is frequently measured by means of the squared quantization error, a measure chosen for both its relevance and mathematical tractability:

$$d(x,\hat{x})=(x-\hat{x})^2.$$

With this choice, the total distortion expressed in term of *mean squared (quantization) error* (MSE) equals to:

$$D_{MSE} = \sum_{j=1}^{N} \int_{x_{j-1}}^{x_j} (x-y_j)^2 f(x)d(x)$$

where $f(x)$ is the density function of the input X and x_{j-1} and x_j are the boundaries of the partition S_j corresponding to the quantization level y_j.

Given the number of quantization levels and the distribution of the input, by minimizing D_{MSE} it is possible to derive two necessary conditions for the optimality of a non-uniform scalar quantizer. A quantizer that satisfies both conditions is called Lloyd-Max quantizer since the conditions were first derived in an unpublished paper by Lloyd [16] and later by Max [17].

The partitions of an N-level scalar quantizer that minimizes the mean squared error must have boundaries satisfying:

$$x_j = \frac{y_j + y_{j+1}}{2} \text{ for } 1 \le j \le N-1,$$

$$x_0 = -\infty, \quad x_N = \infty.$$

Its quantization levels must necessarily satisfy:

$$y_j = \frac{\int_{x_{j-1}}^{x_j} x f(x)d(x)}{\int_{x_{j-1}}^{x_j} f(x)d(x)} \text{ for } 1 \le j \le N.$$

Since the scalar quantizer encodes input symbols one by one, unless the input source is stationary and memoryless its compression performance will be limited by the fact that it has no means to exploit inter-symbol or time dependence.

A possible way of exploiting symbol dependence is by grouping a number of input symbols together and treating this block (or *vector*) as a single coding unit. This approach results in the so-called vector quantizer; a vector quantizer clusters source symbols and encodes vectors instead of scalars. Each vector is independently encoded by searching the closest match in a *dictionary* (sometimes called *codebook*) of representative vectors. The codebook is shared by both encoder and decoder and can be hard-wired, sent as side information or determined adaptively on the statistics of previously encoded vectors.

The formal definition of a *vector quantizer* is very similar to the definition given for the scalar quantizer: if $\mathbf{x}$ is a d-dimensional random vector in $\mathfrak{R}^d$, an N-levels Vector Quantizer of $\mathfrak{R}^d$ is a triple $Q = (A, F, P)$ where:

- $A = \{\mathbf{y}_1, \mathbf{y}_2, ..., \mathbf{y}_N\}$ is a finite indexed subset of $\mathfrak{R}^d$ called codebook. Its elements $\mathbf{y}_i$ are called code vectors;

- $P = \{S_1, S_2, ..., S_N\}$ is a partition of $\mathfrak{R}^d$ where the equivalence classes S_i in P satisfy:

$$\bigcup_{i=i}^{N} S_i = \mathfrak{R}^d \text{ and } S_i \cap S_j = \varnothing \text{ for } i \neq j;$$

- $F : \mathfrak{R}^d \to A$ is a function that defines the relation between the codebook and the partition as:

$$F(\mathbf{x}) = \mathbf{y}_i \text{ if and only if } \mathbf{x} \in S_i.$$

With the dimension of the vectors growing asymptotically, a VQ is able to capture more and more inter-symbol dependency and converge to a theoretically optimal coding in the sense that, for any given distortion, it is capable to achieve the lowest possible rate.

Shannon's theorem proves the existence of asymptotically optimal vector quantizers by using a probabilistic proof that demonstrates existence without suggesting a method to construct an optimal VQ. In practice, as Lin [18] has demonstrated, the design of an optimal vector quantizer is an NP-complete problem.

A locally optimal algorithm for the design of the codebook was introduced by Linde, Buzo and Gray [19]. This method, known as *generalized Lloyd algorithm* (GLA or LBG, from the authors' names) uses a generalization of the Lloyd-Max optimality conditions previously described to design a locally optimal codebook with no natural order or structure. LBG algorithm also extends the Lloyd-Max conditions in two important ways:

- It designs the codebook from a set of sample vectors and not from the input distribution that could be not available or analytically hard to express;
- It solves the problem of specifying partition boundaries (very hard in a

high-dimensional space) by observing that the nearest-neighbor encoding rule always generates a Voronoi (or Dirichlet) partition of the space.

The LBG algorithm takes as input a training set $T = \{\mathbf{x}_1, \mathbf{x}_2, \ldots, \mathbf{x}_L\}$ of d-dimensional sample vectors generated by the information source that must be represented. N random vectors are generated and, by using these vectors as codewords, the corresponding Voronoi partition is determined. For each cell of the partition, a centroid is calculated by averaging all vectors in the cell; the newly determined centroids replace the original codewords. This operation reduces the total distortion. The generation of the Voronoi partition and the determination of new codewords are iterated until there is no further improvement or until the improvement falls below a threshold.

When the quantizer is seen as a composition of the two functions $E(\cdot)$ and $D(\cdot)$, the computation of the Voronoi partition has the property of reducing the encoding error and the computation of the new set of centroids improves the decoder error. In practice, LBG can be seen as an algorithm that optimizes in turn encoder and decoder until no further improvement is possible.

A VQ generated by LBG is locally optimal and has no structure. As a consequence of this lack of structure, the memory needed to store the codebook grows exponentially with the dimension of the vectors. Also, since the partition boundaries are not explicitly specified, encoding a source vector requires an exhaustive search to locate the codeword that minimizes the distortion. In the following, this quantizer will be called *exhaustive search vector quantizer* (or ESVQ). The performance of an ESVQ provides an upper bound on the performance achievable in practice.

Encoding an information source with a vector quantizer is an asymmetrical process; encoder and decoder have computational complexities that typically differ by orders of magnitude. Once a suitable codebook has been determined by means of LBG or similar algorithm, in order to represent a vector, the encoder must perform an exhaustive search in the codebook, locate the closest code vector and send its index to the decoder. The decoder, which shares with the encoder the knowledge of the codebook, simply retrieves the code word associated to that index. In synthesis, codebook design for an ESVQ is an extremely expensive procedure that is usually performed off-line and, due to the search, the encoding process is typically much more expensive than the decoding one.

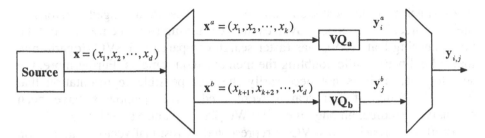

Figure 1: Partitioned Vector Quantizer.

Even if conventional ESVQs require exponentially growing computational power and memory, the quality achieved by this VQ is frequently desirable in applications where only a limited amount of resources is available.

Several authors have proposed techniques to speed up codebook design, such as constraining the search of the closest codeword [20], or seeding the dictionary with vectors having special properties [21]. One of the most recent and interesting methods is due to Kaukoranta, Franti and Nevalainen [22]. The proposed algorithm monitors the activity of the clusters during the LBG execution and performs updates only on the active clusters. Qian [23] applies similar ideas to the vector quantization of hyperspectral data.

An alternative to off-line codebook construction has been proposed in the work of Constantinescu [24]. With a method similar to dictionary compression, the codebook starts from a default configuration and it is adaptively changed while the data are compressed. This method, called *adaptive vector quantization* (AVQ), adjusts dynamically the dimension of the vectors in the codebook. Improvements, extensions and theoretical assessments of the AVQ algorithm are described in Rizzo et alii [25, 26].

When off-line construction is possible or desirable, imposing a structure to the codebook has been suggested to be a practical method to both simplify the LBG and speed up the nearest-neighbor search. Careful design of structured VQs allows the use of fast search algorithms while marginally compromising compression [27].

The most immediate way of simplifying the design of a VQ is to divide input vectors into subvectors of lower dimensionality. This approach is called *partitioned* or *product VQ* (PVQ) because the output codewords are obtained by composing the codebooks associated to the individual partitions by mean of a Cartesian product (Figure 1). This quantizer is described in more detail in the next section.

One of the most-used alternatives to ESVQ is *tree-structured VQ* (TSVQ).

In its simplest implementation, intermediate nodes are averaged versions of their sub-tree. The encoder traverses the tree starting from the root to find the best matching leaf. TSVQ has faster search compared to ESVQ (logarithmic instead of linear) while doubling the memory requirements. Furthermore, the selected leaf node is not necessarily the best possible representation that would be found if full search were used. Tree quantizers have been extensively studied, among others, by Wu [28], Lin and Storer [29, 30].

Another approach to fast VQ is represented by residual vector quantization which encodes input vectors in stages by using a cascade of small-sized quantizers. At each stage the best match is subtracted from the input vector and the residual vector is fed to the next stage. *Residual vector quantizers have been* described by Barnes [31] and Barnes and Frost [32]. Besides faster quantization speed, tree and residual structured VQs allow for progressive encoding: decoding can be stopped at an earlier stage in order to obtain a coarser approximation of the input vector. Riskin [33] and Kossentini, Smith and Barnes [34] show some applications of progressive VQ.

Finally, it is worth mentioning the use of trellises to structure the quantization process. Works by Viterbi and Omura [35], Colm Stewart [36] and Ungerboeck [37] pioneered the use of trellises in source coding and proved that trellises can be effectively used to take advantage of inter-symbol dependencies. Trellis structured quantizers were first introduced and studied by Fischer, Marcellin and Wang [38], Marcellin [39], and Marcellin and Fischer [40]. A combination of residual and trellis quantization has been described by Motta and alii [41]. An application of trellis quantizers to the encoding of hyperspectral imagery has been described by Aboulesman [3].

III. LOCALLY OPTIMAL PARTITIONED VQ

The three-dimensional data cube generated by a hyperspectral imager can be modeled by a discrete-time, discrete-values, bi-dimensional random source $\bar{\mathbf{I}}(x,y)$ emitting d-dimensional pixels vectors $\mathbf{I}(x,y)$. Each vector component $I_i(x,y)$, $0 \leq i \leq d-1$, is drawn from a finite alphabet $\mathfrak{X}_i$ and is distributed according to a space variant probability distribution that may depend on other components. In the following, it is assumed that the alphabet has the canonical form $\mathfrak{X}_i = \{0, 1, \ldots, \mathfrak{M}_i\}$.

Vector quantization is particularly appealing to the coding of hyperspectral imagery because pixel vectors have components that are naturally highly correlated. Furthermore, pixel-based compression simplifies some operations like browsing, classification and target detection. Unfortunately, the dimension of the pixel vectors in the current imagers is typically large and the next generation promises even higher spectral resolution.

A solution is to use a Partitioned Vector Quantizer (or PVQ): divide the pixel vectors into non-overlapping subvectors and encode each of them with an independent vector quantizer of reduced dimensionality. In the following a PVQ for the pixel vectors will consist of W independent, N-levels, d_w-dimensional exhaustive search vector quantizers $Q_w = (A_w, F_w, P_w)$, such that $\sum_{1 \leq w \leq W} d_w = d$ and:

- $A_w = \{\mathbf{y}_1^w, \mathbf{y}_2^w, ..., \mathbf{y}_N^w\}$ is a finite indexed subset of $\mathfrak{R}^{d_w}$ called codebook. Its elements $\mathbf{y}_j^w$ are the code vectors.

- $P_w = \{S_1^w, S_2^w, ..., S_N^w\}$ is a partition of $\mathfrak{R}^{d_w}$ and its equivalence classes S_j^w satisfy:

$$\bigcup_{j=1}^{N} S_j^w = \mathfrak{R}^{d_w} \text{ and } S_h^w \cap S_k^w = \varnothing \text{ for } h \neq k.$$

- $F_w : \mathfrak{R}^{d_w} \rightarrow A_w$ is a function defining the relation between the codebook and the partition as $F_w(\mathbf{x}) = \mathbf{y}_j^w$ if and only if $\mathbf{x} \in S_j^w$.

The index j of the codeword $\mathbf{y}_j^w$, resulting from the quantization of the d_w-dimensional subvector $\mathbf{x}$, is the information actually sent to the decoder.

With reference to the previously defined W vector quantizers $Q_w = (A_w, F_w, P_w)$, a *partitioned vector quantizer* (PVQ) can be formally described by a triple $\overline{\mathbf{Q}} = (\overline{\mathbf{A}}, \overline{\mathbf{P}}, \overline{\mathbf{F}})$ where:

- $\overline{\mathbf{A}} = A_1 \times A_2 \times ... \times A_W$ is a codebook in $\mathfrak{R}^d$;
- $\overline{\mathbf{P}} = P_1 \times P_2 \times ... \times P_W$ is a partition of $\mathfrak{R}^d$;
- $\overline{\mathbf{F}} : \mathfrak{R}^d \rightarrow \overline{\mathbf{A}}$ is computed on an input vector $\mathbf{x} \in \mathfrak{R}^d$ as the concatenation of the independent quantization of the W subvectors of $\mathbf{x}$. Similarly, the index vector sent to the decoder is obtained as a concatenation of the W indices.

The choice of a partitioned vector quantizer over other structured quantizers is motivated by the fact that the efficiency of a VQ decreases with its dimensionality [42, 43]. Since in a PVQ the subvectors are encoded independently, the design of the quantizer is simpler and coding and decoding present a number of advantages in terms of speed, memory requirements and exploitable parallelism.

If each quantizer is required to have the same number N of levels, the non-uniform nature of the distribution of the components of $\mathbf{I}(x, y)$ excludes the possibility of an efficient encoding based on equally sized partitions. So the design of a Partitioned VQ has to aim at the joint determination of the $W + 1$ partition boundaries $b_0 = 0 \leq b_1 \leq \ldots \leq b_W = d$ and at the design of the W independent vector quantizers having dimension $d_w = b_w - b_{w-1}$, $1 \leq w \leq W$.

Given the number of partitions W and the number of codebook levels N, it is possible to find the partition boundaries achieving minimum distortion with a brute-force approach: first determine, for every $0 \leq i \leq j < d$, the distortion $Dist(i, j)$ that an N-levels vector quantizer achieves on the subvectors of boundaries i and j. Then, by means of a dynamic program, traverse the matrix $Dist(i, j)$ and find the W costs corresponding to the input partition of boundaries $b_0 = 0 \leq b_1 \leq \ldots \leq b_W = d$ and whose sum is minimal. A more sophisticated approach discussed by Matsuyama [44] uses dynamic programming at each step to decide the current optimal partition, instead of designing one vector quantizer for each possible partition configuration first and then applying dynamic programming. Nevertheless, even this approach is computationally intensive.

The locally optimal partitioning algorithm proposed by Motta et alii [13] provides an efficient alternative to dynamic programming, while performing comparably in practical applications. This partitioning algorithm is based on an extension of the LBG. The key observation is that, once the partition boundaries are kept fixed, distortion measures that are additive with respect to the vector components, like the MSE, can be minimized independently for each partition by applying the optimality conditions on the centroids and on the cells. Similarly, when the centroids and the cells are held fixed, the (locally optimal) partitions boundaries can be determined in a greedy fashion.

Before describing the details of this algorithm, the necessary notation is introduced. Given a source vector $\mathbf{I}(x, y)$, the symbol $\mathbf{I}_{b_{w-1}}^{b_w - 1}$ indicates the wth subvector of boundaries b_{w-1} and $b_w - 1$ (for simplicity, the x and y spatial coordinates are omitted when clear from the context).

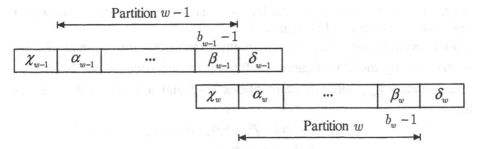

Figure 2: Error contributions for adjacent partitions.

The MSE between the input vector $\mathbf{I}$ and its quantized representation $\hat{\mathbf{I}}$ is equal to

$$\left(\mathbf{I}-\hat{\mathbf{I}}\right)^2 = \sum_{w=1}^{W}\left(\mathbf{I}_{b_{w-1}}^{b_w-1}-\hat{\mathbf{I}}_{b_{w-1}}^{b_w-1}\right)^2$$

$$= \sum_{w=1}^{W}\left(\mathbf{I}_{b_{w-1}}^{b_w-1}-\mathbf{y}_{J_w}^{w}\right)^2 = \sum_{w=1}^{W}\sum_{h=b_{w-1}}^{b_w-1}\left(I_h-y_{J_w,h-b_{w-1}}^{w}\right)^2$$

where $\mathbf{y}_{J_w}^{w}=\left(y_{J_w,0}^{w},\ldots,y_{J_w,d_w-1}^{w}\right)$ is the codeword of the wth codebook minimizing the reconstruction error on $\mathbf{I}_{b_{w-1}}^{b_w-1}$, and

$$J_w = \operatorname*{argmin}_{1\le n\le N} MSE\left(\mathbf{I}_{b_{w-1}}^{b_w-1},\mathbf{y}_n^{w}\right).$$

The LBG step is applied independently to each partition. The equivalence classes are determined as usual, except that the new centroids are computed in a (d_w+2)-dimensional space $((d_1+1)$ and (d_W+1) for the first and last partition respectively) by including the components $I_{b_{w-1}-1}$ and I_{b_w}.

As shown in Figure 2, the computation keeps explicit record of the contribution of the leftmost and rightmost components of each partition to the quantization error:

$$\alpha_w = \sum_{x,y}\left(I_{b_{w-1}}(x,y)-\hat{I}_{b_{w-1}}(x,y)\right)^2 \text{ and } \beta_w = \sum_{x,y}\left(I_{b_w-1}(x,y)-\hat{I}_{b_w-1}(x,y)\right)^2.$$

Two extra components

$$\chi_w = \sum_{x,y}\left(I_{b_{w-1}-1}(x,y)-\hat{I}_{b_{w-1}-1}(x,y)\right)^2 \text{ and } \delta_w = \sum_{x,y}\left(I_{b_w}(x,y)-\hat{I}_{b_w}(x,y)\right)^2$$

are also computed, except for the leftmost and rightmost partition for which only one component will be available.

The reconstruction values used in the expressions for χ_w and δ_w are determined by the classification performed on the components $b_{w-1},...,b_w$. The boundary b_{w-1} between the partitions $w-1$ and w is changed according to:

$$M_w = \min(\beta_{w-1} + \alpha_w, \beta_{w-1} + \delta_{w-1}, \chi_w + \alpha_w)$$
$$\text{if } (M_w = \chi_w + \alpha_w)$$
$$b_{w-1} = b_{w-1} - 1$$
$$\text{else if } (M_w = \beta_{w-1} + \delta_{w-1})$$
$$b_{w-1} = b_{w-1} + 1$$

This design converges to locally optimal centroids and vector boundaries. The resulting quantizer is called *locally optimal PVQ* (or LPVQ). While LPVQ is optimized with respect MSE, it is important to notice that the mean squared error is not a fidelity criterion that can be used to lossy compress hyperspectral images. Due to its statistical nature, minimizing this distortion will penalize atypical vectors that are often the main focus of the analysis. However, a MSE optimal LPVQ can be effectively used as a dimensionality reduction tool for efficient lossless (and near-lossless) compression of hyperspectral data. The lossy part of the proposed method also preserves the original statistical properties of the data and partition indices can be used for fast (remote) browsing and classification.

The index vectors $\mathbf{J}(x, y)$ and the codewords $\mathbf{y}_n^w = \left(y_{n,b_{w-1}}^w, ..., y_{n,b_w-1}^w \right)$, with $1 \le w \le W$ and $1 \le n \le N$, are sufficient to a lossy reconstruction of the data.

For higher accuracy, the compressed data stream can be augmented by the quantization error

$$\mathbf{E}(x, y) = \left(\mathbf{E}_{b_0}^{b_1-1}(x, y), \mathbf{E}_{b_1}^{b_2-1}(x, y), ..., \mathbf{E}_{b_{W-1}}^{b_W-1}(x, y) \right)$$

where

$$\mathbf{E}_{b_{w-1}}^{b_w-1}(x, y) = \mathbf{I}_{b_{w-1}}^{b_w-1}(x, y) - \hat{\mathbf{I}}_{b_{w-1}}^{b_w-1}(x, y).$$

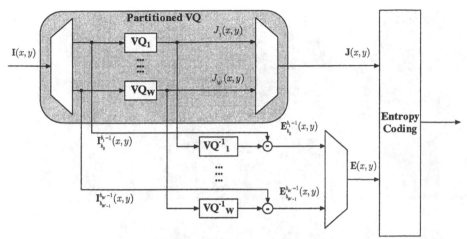

Figure 3: LPVQ encoder.

The unconstrained quantizers operate independently from each other and independently on each source vector, so a suitable entropy encoder must be used to exploit any residual redundancy. For example, each VQ index $J_w(x, y)$ can be encoded by conditioning its probability with respect to a set of causal indices spatially and spectrally adjacent and the components of the residual vector $\mathbf{E}_{b_{w-1}}^{b_w-1}(x, y)$ can be entropy coded with their probability conditioned on the VQ index $J_w(x, y)$. In near-lossless applications, a small, controlled error could be introduced at this stage. Figure 3 shows a diagram of a LPVQ-based encoder.

A straightforward implementation of LPVQ requires $O(L \cdot N \cdot d)$ time for a single iteration, where L is the size of the training set. Most of the experiments presented later in this chapter assume that one codebook is designed for each hyperspectral data cube, which limits the applicability of LPVQ to an off-line tool. Nevertheless, as mentioned earlier, there are many techniques in the literature to speedup the design process of a vector quantizer. All these improvements, as well as many other, clearly apply to our method as well; furthermore, practical scenarios arise in which our algorithm can be applied as is, without the computational complexity being an obstacle.

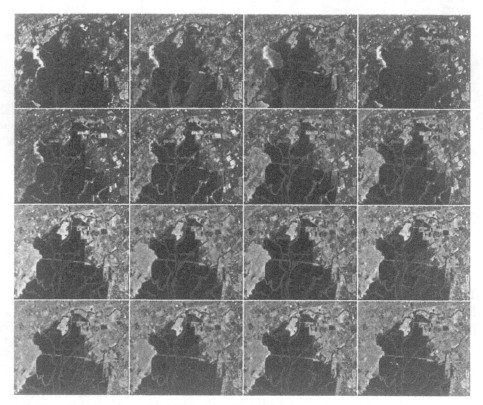

Figure 4: Index planes for second scene of the image "Moffet Field".

IV. ENTROPY CODING

LPVQ has been tested on a set of five images generated by the *airborne visible/infrared imaging spectrometer* (AVIRIS). AVIRIS images are obtained by flying the spectrometer over the target area; they are 614 pixels wide and have a height depending on the duration of the flight, typically on the order of 2,000 pixels. Each pixel represents the light reflected by a 20 x 20 meters area (high altitude) or 4 x 4 meters area (low altitude). The spectral response of the reflected light is decomposed into 224 contiguous bands (or channels), approximately 10nm wide, spanning from visible to near infrared light (400nm to 2500nm). Each of these vectors provides a *spectral signature* of the area. Spectral components are acquired in floating point 12-bit precision and then scaled and packed into signed 16 bit integers. After acquisition, AVIRIS images are processed to correct various physical effects (geometrical distortion due to the flight trajectory, time of day, etc.) and stored in *scenes* of 614 by 512 pixels each (when the image height is not a multiple of 512, the last scene will be smaller). All files for each of the 5 test images can be downloaded from the NASA JPL web site [45] and the scenes belonging to the same flight can be merged together in order to form a complete image. JPL provides *radiance* (on which all experiments were performed) and *reflectance* measurements for all AVIRIS datasets. Reflectance is the ratio of the measured radiance against the radiance of a *standard 100% reflecting body* (i.e., whose radiance is known).

As in natural graylevel and color images, pixels in hyperspectral images exhibit spatial correlation. Spectral components in each pixel are typically correlated as well. When quantizing a given pixel, the partitioned VQ is able to decorrelate the spectral components in each subvector. In general, residual correlation will be present between subvectors of the same pixel. If the number of quantization levels N is small, the index planes generated by LPVQ can be entropy compressed as if they were W correlated graylevel images by using techniques derived from the image coding domain. It has been observed in Motta et alii [14] that if the indices are sorted according to the energy of the subvectors they represent, each index plane retains the spatial features of the imaged area and it can be used to select regions of interest. Figure 4 shows the $W = 16$ planes generated by LPVQ for scene 2 of Moffett Field when the codebook size is $N = 256$. This phenomenon is remarkable in LPVQ, but it has been observed in standard VQ as well. For example, see Nasrabadi and Feng [46], Wu et alii [47], and Gong et alii [48].

A. *Index planes coding*

Since the VQ indices resemble a grayscale image, an algorithm based on LOCO-I [49], the core of the ISO/JPEG standard for lossless coding of natural images JPEG-LS, seems to be a natural choice to compress index planes. LOCO-I is a low complexity predictive coder with a context-driven error-feedback technique. After the prediction, the encoder classifies the prediction context and adds the mean prediction error for such class to the current prediction. The prediction residual is then computed and coded, while the statistics of the prediction context are updated. Because errors in different contexts have different probability distributions, the net effect of prediction and context-modeling is a spatial decorrelation of the input data.

If $N = 256$ and $W = 16$, quantization indices alone give a $28:1$ lossy compression. The use of LOCO-I improves this result by more than 40%.

```
Input:
  J ;  // LPVQ quantization indices

Local variables:
  entropy_coder EC[N+1];

Main Loop:
  // encode indices of bin 1 using EC[0]
  For each spatial location (x,y)
     Encode J₁(x,y) with EC[0];

  For each bin w with 2≤w≤W
     For each spatial location (x,y)
          Encode Jw(x,y) using EC[Jw(x,y)];
```

Figure 5: Entropy coding of LPVQ quantization indices.

```
Input:
  E ;  // LPVQ quantization residuals
  τ ;  // Thresholds vector

Local variables:
  entropy_coder EC[N];        // for residuals <τ
  entropy_coder EC_Tail[W];   // for residuals ≥τ

Main Loop:
  For each bin w with 1≤w≤W
     For each spatial location (x,y)
        For each band i with bw ≤i<bw+1
           If  Ei(x,y)<τw
              Encode  Ei(x,y) using EC[Jw(x,y)];
           Else
              Encode  τw using EC[Jw(x,y)];
              Encode  Ei(x,y)-τw using EC_Tail[w];
```

Figure 6: Entropy coding of LPVQ quantization residual.

The three-dimensional nature of the LPVQ index planes, though, suggests the use of a 3-D causal context, which LOCO-I/JPEG-LS does not have. The statistics of the index planes show that the inter-plane correlation is much stronger than the spatial correlation.

As described in the next section, by conditioning the entropy coding of the indices with corresponding indices in adjacent planes, it is possible to achieve more than 95% improvement upon the independent coding (i.e., more than 30% better than LOCO-I). Figure 5 shows the pseudo-code of the entropy coding structure used for LPVQ quantization indices.

B. Quantization residual coding

Both lossless and near-lossless entropy coding can be applied to the residual error. Near-losslessness is achieved by quantizing the quantization error prior to entropy coding. An additional feature of this compression method is the possibility of tightly bounding the error on a pixel-by-pixel-basis.

In the experimental results reported in the next section the quantization error of each bin is classified according to the respective quantization index, with the assumption that errors in different bins and different classes have different probability distributions.

To take care of distributions with long tails, it is possible to introduce a threshold mechanism: If the error is above a given threshold, an escape symbol is encoded and an alternative entropy coder is used for the current error. Pseudo-code of this procedure is shown in Figure 6.

The threshold could be set to $\tau_w = \infty$ (i.e., quantization error is encoded as is), dynamically determined by an on-line, adaptive procedure (90th quantile seem to work well in practice), or computed off-line for optimal results. All experiments reported in the next section will assume the latest option.

V. DATA COMPRESSION WITH LPVQ

Experiments have been performed by changing the number of partitions and the size of the codebook. The results reported here were obtained for $W = 16$ partitions and $N = 256$ codebook levels. The particular choice of the number of levels makes also practical the use of off-the-shelf image compression tools that are fine-tuned for 8 bit data. The LPVQ codebook is trained on each image independently and it is sent to the decoder as side information. The size of the codebook is negligible with respect the size of the compressed data (256 x 224 x 2 bytes = 112 KB uncompressed) and its cost is included in the results reported here.

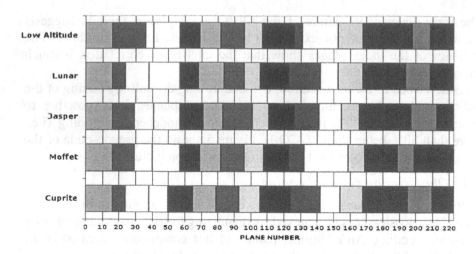

Figure 7: Partition sizes and alignment.

The partition boundaries for each of the five images are depicted in Figure 7. While similarities exist, the algorithm converges to different locally optimal boundaries on different input images showing that LPVQ adapts the partition to input statistics. It has been verified that a uniformly partitioned codebook populated by random image pixels adapts fairly quickly, with the partition boundaries converging to their definitive values in less than one hundred iterations. If LPVQ is bootstrapped with the method described by Katsavounidis et alii [21], the algorithm exhibits an even faster convergence. Furthermore, this procedure speeds up by a factor of 2 the constrained search for the closest codeword. This method populates the dictionary incrementally: the first vector to enter the dictionary is the one having the highest norm; as long as the dictionary is not full, the vector having the largest minimum distance from the current dictionary is added.

LPVQ performances are analyzed in terms of compression ratio (defined as the size of the original file divided by the size of the compressed one), signal to quantization noise ratio, maximum absolute error and percentage maximum absolute error.

The *signal to quantization noise ratio* (SQNR) is defined here as:

$$SQNR\ (dB) = \frac{10}{d} \sum_{i=0}^{d-1} \log_{10} \left(\frac{\sigma_{I_i}^2}{\sigma_{E_i}^2 + \frac{1}{12}} \right).$$

AVIRIS	gzip	bzip2	JPEG-LS	JPEG 2K	CDPCM	LPVQ
Cuprite	1.35	2.25	2.09	1.91	3.42	3.27
Jasper Ridge	1.39	2.05	1.91	1.78	3.46	3.12
Low Altitude	1.38	2.13	2.00	1.80	N.A.	2.97
Lunar Lake	1.36	2.30	2.14	1.96	3.37	3.31
Moffett Field	1.41	2.10	1.99	1.82	3.46	3.01
Average	1.38	2.17	2.03	1.85	3.43	3.14

Table 1: Compression ratio for lossless mode.

The constant correction factor added to the denominator is introduced to take into account the error introduced by the 12 bit analog-to-digital converter used by the AVIRIS spectrometer. This solution also avoids unbounded values in the case of a band perfectly reconstructed.

The *maximum absolute error* (MAE) is defined in terms of the MAE for the ith band as:

$$MAE = \max_i MAE_i = \max_i \left(\max_{x,y} \left| \mathbf{I}_i(x,y) - \hat{\mathbf{I}}_i(x,y) \right| \right)$$

The *average percentage maximum absolute error* (PMAE) for the ith band having canonical alphabet $\mathfrak{X}_i = \{0,1,\ldots,\mathfrak{M}_i\}$ is defined as:

$$PMAE\ (\%) = \frac{1}{d} \sum_{i=0}^{d-1} \frac{MAE_i}{\mathfrak{M}_i} \times 100$$

Table 1 shows that LPVQ achieves on these five images an average compression of 3.14:1. This improves by 45% the 1-D lossless compressor bzip2 applied to the plane–interleaved images (worse results are achieved by bzip2 on the original, pixel–interleaved, image format) and by 55% the standard lossless image compressor JPEG-LS. Results for *differential* JPEG-LS and *differential* JPEG2000 are also reported here, where "differential" means that, for better spectral decorrelation, the compression is applied to the difference between bands. This pre-preprocessing improves the two standard algorithms by 40% and 53% respectively; still 11% better compression is achieved by LPVQ. Finally, LPVQ has been compared to the clustered DPCM method (here addressed as CDPRM) presented by Mielikäinen and Toivanen [11], even though experiments were performed only on a subset of our data set. CDPCM uses LBG to cluster data. An optimized predictor is computed for each cluster and for each band.

AVIRIS	CR	SQNR
Cuprite	53.44	24.15
Jasper Ridge	51.08	24.44
Low Altitude	54.32	25.50
Lunar Lake	59.17	26.91
Moffett Field	58.03	25.32
Average	**55.21**	**25.27**

Table 2: Compression ratio for lossy mode.

	Constant MAE				
Δ	CR	RMSE	SQNR	MAE	PMAE
1	4.64	0.82	42.06	1,00	0.45
2	5.62	1.41	37.65	2,00	0.89
3	6.54	1.98	34.82	3,00	1.34
4	7.48	2.52	32.81	4,00	1.79
5	8.48	3.01	31.33	5,00	2.23
6	9.53	3.46	30.21	6,00	2.68
7	10.57	3.87	29.35	7,00	3.12
8	11.57	4.25	28.66	8,00	3.54
9	12.54	4.62	28.10	8,98	3.86
10	13.47	4.97	27.63	9,95	4.13

Table 3: Average compression ratio (CR), root mean squared error (RMSE), signal to quantization noise ratio (SQNR), average maximum absolute error (MAE) and percentage maximum absolute error (PMAE) as a function of Δ achieved by the constant MAE near-lossless LPVQ.

Prediction error is computed and entropy coded, along with side information regarding the optimized predictors. The resulting method outperforms LPVQ, while sharing time complexity similar to the design stage of LPVQ and lacking any extra feature provided by the latter, like lossy and near-lossless mode, fast browsing and classification, et cetera.

Table 2 reports, as a reference, the compression and the SQNR when only the indices are encoded; in this configuration LPVQ achieves an average compression ratio of 55:1 with 25.27dB of SQNR.

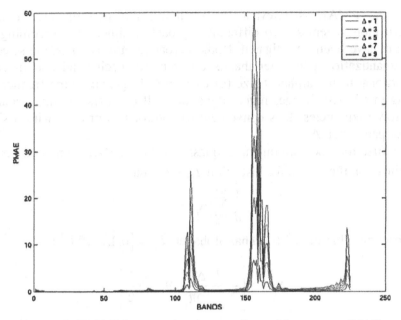

Figure 8: PMAE for near-lossless coding with constant MAE.

A. Near-lossless coding

More interesting and practical are the results obtained with the near-lossless settings, shown in Table 3. At first, the introduction of a small and constant quantization error across each dimension is considered; that is, before entropy coding, each residual value x is quantized by dividing x adjusted to the center of the range by the size of the range:

$$q(x) = \left\lfloor \frac{x + \Delta}{2\Delta + 1} \right\rfloor.$$

This is the classical approach to the near-lossless compression of image data and results into a constant MAE across all bands. With this setting, it is possible to obtain an average compression ratio ranging from $4.64 : 1$ with the introduction of an error $\Delta = \pm 1$ and a $MAE = 1$ to $13.47 : 1$ with and error of $\Delta = \pm 10$ and $MAE = 9.95$. While the performance in this setting seems to be acceptable for most applications and the SQNR is relatively high even at high compression, the contribution to the PMAE of some bands shows artifacts that might be unacceptable. In particular, while the average PMAE measured across the 224 bands of the AVIRIS cube is low, the percentage error peaks well over 50% on several bands (see Figure 8).

Since the PMAE is relevant in predicting the performance of many classification schemes, two different approaches aimed at overcoming this problem have been investigated. Both approaches are based on the selection of a quantization parameter that is different for each band and inversely proportional to the alphabet size (or dynamic). In general, high frequencies, having in AVIRIS images higher dynamic, will be quantized more coarsely than low frequencies. It is convenient to control this process with a single integer parameter Δ.

The first method, aiming at a quasi–constant PMAE across all bands, introduces on the ith band a distortion Δ_i such that:

$$\frac{1}{d}\sum_{i=0}^{d-1}\left|\Delta_i\right| \approx \Delta .$$

By observing that the ith band has alphabet $\mathcal{X}_i = \left\{0, 1, \ldots, \mathfrak{M}_i\right\}$:

$$\Delta_i = \pm\left|\frac{d\cdot\Delta}{\sum_{i=0}^{d-1}\mathfrak{M}_i}\cdot\mathfrak{M}_i + \frac{1}{2}\right|.$$

The alternative approach, aims at a quasi–constant SQNR across the bands. If a maximum absolute error $\left|\Delta_i\right|$ is allowed on the ith band, it is reasonable to assume that the average absolute error on that band will be $\left|\Delta_i/2\right|$.

If ξ_i indicates the average energy of that band and Δ represents the target average maximum absolute error, then the absolute quantization error allowed on each band is obtained by rounding to the nearest integer the solution of this system of equations:

$$\begin{cases} 10\log_{10}\dfrac{\xi_i^2}{\left|\Delta_i/2\right|^2} \approx 10\log_{10}\dfrac{\xi_j^2}{\left|\Delta_j/2\right|^2} & i,j \in [0,\ldots,d-1],\ i \neq j \\[4mm] \dfrac{1}{n}\sum_{i=0}^{d-1}\left|\Delta_i\right| \approx \Delta \end{cases}.$$

Δ	Quasi-Constant PMAE				
	CR	RMSE	SQNR	MAE	PMAE
1	3.92	0.81	46.82	0.65	0.01
2	4.44	1.64	43.15	1.61	0.03
3	4.99	2.44	40.43	2.58	0.06
4	5.51	3.25	38.35	3.57	0.09
5	6.00	4.04	36.71	4.54	0.12
6	6.50	4.86	35.27	5.54	0.15
7	6.92	5.68	34.18	6.54	0.18
8	7.39	6.49	33.15	7.56	0.21
9	7.86	7.22	32.34	8.53	0.24
10	8.43	7.91	31.50	9.57	0.27

Table 4: Statistics achieved by the quasi-constant near-lossless LPVQ.

Δ	Quasi-Constant SQNR				
	CR	RMSE	SQNR	MAE	PMAE
1	3.91	0.79	46.90	0.63	0.01
2	4.43	1.60	43.18	1.58	0.03
3	5.05	2.40	40.16	2.58	0.06
4	5.58	3.19	38.12	3.54	0.09
5	6.12	3.99	36.35	4.55	0.12
6	6.56	4.78	35.09	5.52	0.15
7	7.04	5.61	33.91	6.56	0.18
8	7.49	6.37	33.01	7.50	0.21
9	8.06	7.10	32.03	8.53	0.25
10	8.58	7.77	31.32	9.55	0.28

Table 5: Statistics achieved by the quasi-constant near-lossless LPVQ.

Tables 4 and 5 report respectively results for quasi-constant PMAE and quasi-constant SQNR near-lossless compression. The three methods for near-lossless coding of AVIRIS data are roughly equivalent in terms of average SQNR at the same compression.

The small variations are due to the lossless compression of some bands and the rounding used in the equations. The average SQNR is not compromised as well.

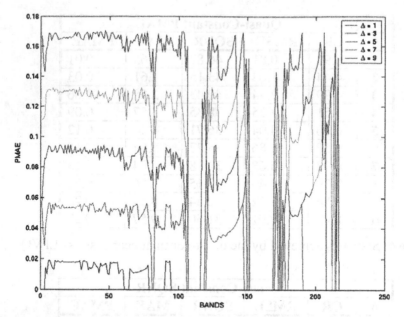

Figure 9: PMAE for near-lossless coding with quasi-constant PMAE.

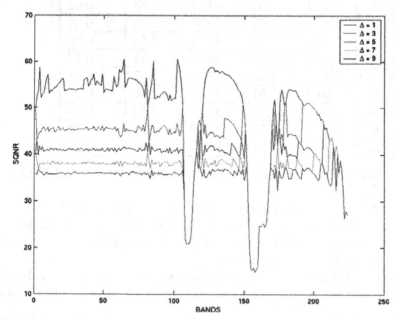

Figure 10: SQNR for near-lossless coding with quasi-constant SQNR.

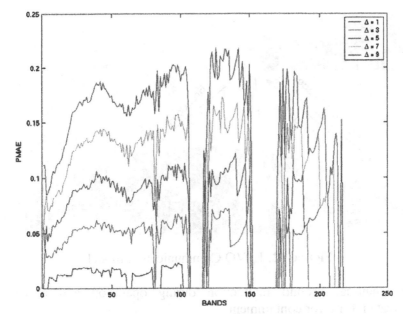

Figure 11: PMAE for near-lossless coding with quasi-constant SQNR.

Figure 9 shows that the quasi-constant PMAE method is indeed able to stabilize the PMAE across each band, while the SQNR for the quasi-constant SQNR approach is almost flat (Figure 10), except for those bands that are losslessly encoded and those with small dynamic. Furthermore, Figure 11 shows that the PMAE achieved by the quasi-constant SQNR method is also more stable than the one of constant MAE method (Figure 8).

VI. APPLICATIONS

A. *Space-borne Compression/Broadcasting*

In a scenario anticipated by the NOOA for the next generation of GOES satellites [50], a remote acquisition platform should be able to acquire, compress in real time and broadcast processed data to final users. According to the requirements addressed by the Consultative Committee for Space Data Systems (CCSDS) Sub-panel 1A, an implementation of a compression system suitable for space applications should be able to process frame- and non-frame-based input source data, offer adjustable data rate, work with data quantized at 16 bit, offer real-time processing at limited power consumption,

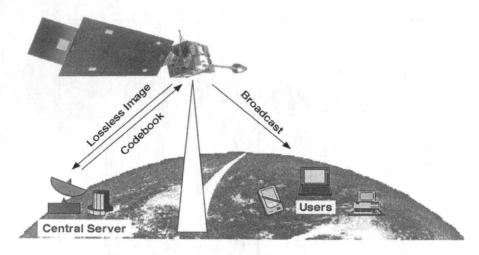

Figure 12: LPVQ Communication model.

require minimal ground interaction during operation and allow data packetization for error containment.

Like most vector quantizers, LPVQ is a highly asymmetrical algorithm, where the complexity of the codebook design is orders of magnitude larger than the complexity of the encoding and the encoding is more complex than the decoding. The amount of resources and the limited computational power available on a remote acquisition platform preclude the possibility of an on-board design of the codebook. However, once the codebook has been designed (for example by a central server on the ground), the encoding can be easily sped up and implemented on the remote platform because of its intrinsic parallel structure. The decoding, typically implemented via look up tables, is anyway extremely fast.

LPVQ can be easily adapted in order to fit this paradigm (see Figure 12). The assumption is that a remote platform acquires at regular intervals an image of a designated area, for example while tracking a meteorological event. The data is compressed on board with hardware of limited computational power by using a codebook and partitions previously determined. Due to the lossless nature of the codec, a mismatched codebook will influence only the compression ratio while leaving the image quality unaffected. The ground server, which has higher computational power, receives an image, decodes it, refines the codebook and the partitions, and sends this new information back to the remote platform that will use the newly determined codebook and partitions for future acquisitions.

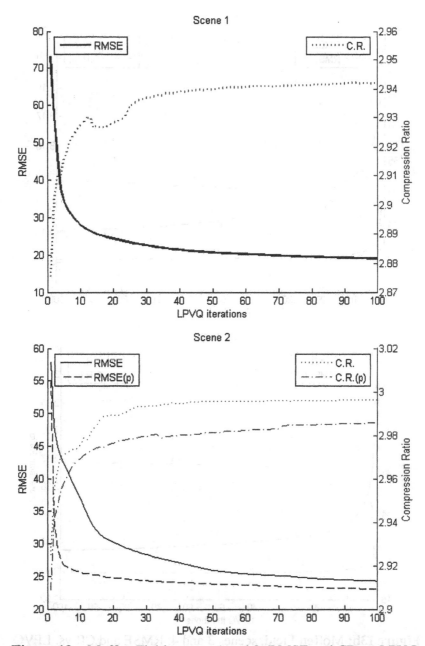

Figure 13a: Moffett Field, scenes 1 and 2. RMSE and CR vs. LPVQ iterations. RMSE(p) and CR (p) are obtained by initializing the dictionary with the optimal dictionary used for the previous scene.

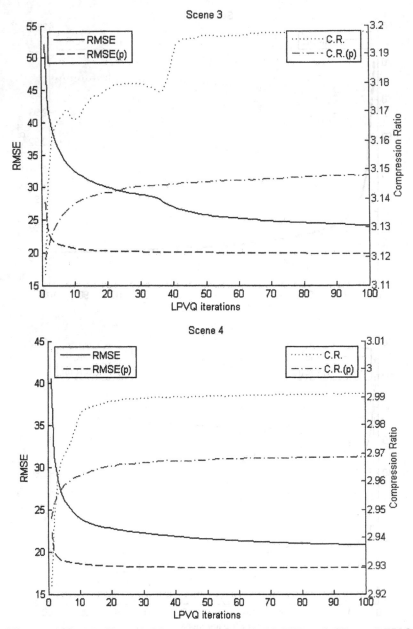

Figure 13b: Moffett Field, scenes 3 and 4. RMSE and CR vs. LPVQ iterations. RMSE(p) and CR (p) are obtained by initializing the dictionary with the optimal dictionary used for the previous scene.

In general, if the scenes have similar characteristics, only a few iterations will be necessary to refine the codebook, adjust the partition boundaries and maximize compression.

As mentioned earlier, the size of the new codebook is negligible even when uncompressed and its transmission represents the only interaction that the remote platform has with the ground. The selection of the bootstrapping codebook affects only the compression of the very first image transmitted. It has been experimentally verified that a mismatched codebook, if carefully selected, has a limited impact on the compression.

LPVQ and Mismatched Dictionaries

In order to evaluate the proposed approach in the described framework, the following experiments have been performed on each scene of the Moffett Field image:

1) the compression ratio and RMSE have been recorded at each step of the LPVQ algorithm, when starting with a random dictionary;

2) same except that the starting dictionary is the locally optimal dictionary used for the previous scene.

Figures 13a and 13b show how compression stabilizes after 50 iterations. Initializing LPVQ with the locally optimal dictionary used for the previous scene improves the RMSE greatly, while slightly penalizing the compression ratio. This suggests that the entropy coder needs to be tuned-up for this case and that lossy compression is slightly better when only a few iterations are allowed.

Experiments with different schemes to generate and use random dictionaries to quantize data suggest that a careful sampling of the input data may be sufficient to achieve compression reasonably close (10% lower at most) to the locally optimal solution produced by the full fledged LPVQ design, and that the non-uniform partitioning gains effectiveness at high compression rates.

B. Fast Nearest Neighbor Classification

An additional feature of the LPVQ compressor is the possibility to tightly bound the quantization error on a pixel-by-pixel basis. Due to the hierarchical structure of the data compressed by this algorithm, it is possible to perform pure-pixel classification and target detection directly in the compressed domain, with considerable speed-up and memory savings.

Given a pure pixel representing a target vector $\mathbf{T} = (t_0, t_1, \cdots, t_{d-1})$, a similarity measure $\mathbf{D}(\mathbf{I},\mathbf{T})$ and a classification threshold Δ, a classifier must determine, for each image pixel $\mathbf{I}(x,y)$, whether $\mathbf{D}(\mathbf{I}(x,y),\mathbf{T}) < \Delta$. When this condition is satisfied, the pixel $\mathbf{I}(x,y)$ is said to be similar to (or a member of the class) $\mathbf{T}$. This simplified pure-pixel classification is based on the nearest neighbor search and does not take into account mixed pixels issues and sub-pixel classification that are also common applications of hyperspectral imagery. Instead, it is meant to simplify tracking of known objects and selection of regions of interest.

When the similarity measure is the *Euclidean distance*, here defined as:

$$ED(\mathbf{I},\mathbf{T}) = \sqrt{\sum_{i=0}^{d-1}(I_i - t_i)^2}$$

the problem of the nearest neighbor pure-pixel classification can be solved for most pixels directly in the LPVQ compressed domain using solely index information. For only a few pixels, a partial decompression of the residual is necessary to decide the classification.

This simple algorithm is based on the observation that LPVQ indices retain most of the information necessary to classify the pixels, and that it is possible to bound the minimum and maximum quantization error for each vector component. Bounds on the quantization error are available at design time or can be inferred from the encoded image. This algorithm has two main advantages. First: since the number of partitions and the number of centroids are typically small, pre-computed values can be arranged into a lookup table indexed by the VQ indices. If most vectors can be classified without the need of the error, this will result into a substantial speed-up. Second: it is possible to imagine a user browsing and trying different classifications on the LPVQ indices instead of the whole image. Then, when a parameterization of interest is found, the user can query the server for the error vectors necessary to resolve any classification ambiguity.

Given a threshold Δ, a pure pixel $\mathbf{T}$ and a similarity measure $\mathbf{D}(\mathbf{I}(x,y),\mathbf{T})$, it is possible to determine, from the quantization indices of a pixel $\mathbf{I}(x,y)$, two quantities $\mathbf{D}_{min}(\mathbf{I}(x,y),\mathbf{T})$ and $\mathbf{D}_{max}(\mathbf{I}(x,y),\mathbf{T})$, respectively lower and upper bounding the distance $\mathbf{D}(\mathbf{I}(x,y),\mathbf{T})$.

Since $\mathbf{I}(x,y)$ belongs to the class $\mathbf{T}$ only if $\mathbf{D}(\mathbf{I}(x,y),\mathbf{T}) < \Delta$, it is possible to observe that:

- If $\mathbf{D}_{min}(\mathbf{I}(x,y),\mathbf{T}) \geq \Delta$, the pixel $\mathbf{I}(x,y)$ clearly does not belong to the class $\mathbf{T}$;

- If $D_{\max}(I(x,y),T) < \Delta$, the pixel $I(x,y)$ trivially belongs to the class T;
- If $D_{\min}(I(x,y),T) < \Delta \leq D_{\max}(I(x,y),T)$ then the quantization indices and the bounds on the error are not sufficient to decide the classification. In this case, and only in this case, it is necessary to access the error vector and compute $D(I(x,y),T) < \Delta$.

The main assumption is that the quantities $D_{\min}(I(x,y),T)$ and $D_{\max}(I(x,y),T)$ can be computed by adding up the individual contributions of each vector component i, upper and lower bounded by the minimum and maximum of the quantization residuals $\min(E_{i,n})$ and $\max(E_{i,n})$. This is clearly the case for the Euclidean distance.

By changing the threshold Δ into Δ^2, it is possible to focus on the contribution of $\min(E_{i,n})$ and $\max(E_{i,n})$ to the individual terms of the sum.

For a given component i, $0 \leq i < d$, in the partition w, $0 \leq w < W$:

$$\left(I_i - t_i\right)^2 = \left(\left(\hat{I}_i + E_i\right) - t_i\right)^2.$$

If I_i has been quantized with the centroid $w, 0 \leq n < N$:

$$\min\left\{\left(\left(\hat{I}_i + \min(E_{i,n})\right) - t_i\right)^2, \left(\left(\hat{I}_i + \max(E_{i,n})\right) - t_i\right)^2\right\} \leq \left(I_i - t_i\right)^2$$

and

$$\max\left\{\left(\left(\hat{I}_i + \min(E_{i,n})\right) - t_i\right)^2, \left(\left(\hat{I}_i + \max(E_{i,n})\right) - t_i\right)^2\right\} \geq \left(I_i - t_i\right)^2.$$

The quantities $D_{\min}(C_{n,w},T)$ and $D_{\max}(C_{n,w},T)$ are derived by summing these bounds over all components of the partition w. These terms can be pre-computed and, since there are only $2 \cdot N \cdot W$ possible values and N and W are typically small ($N = 256$ and $W = 16$ for example), $D_{\min}(C_{n,w},T)$ and $D_{\max}(C_{n,w},T)$ can be stored into a lookup table indexed by n and w. The computation of $D_{\min}(I(x,y),T)$ and $D_{\max}(I(x,y),T)$ requires a total of $2 \cdot W$ lookups and $2 \cdot (W-1)$ sums.

```
Input:
    T = [t₀  ···  t_{d-1}]ᵀ = [t₀  ···  t_{W-1}]ᵀ ;    // Target vector
    I(x,y) = J(x,y) + E(x,y) ;        // LPVQ quantized image
    min(E_{i,n}) ;                     // Error bounds for
    max(E_{i,n}) ;                     // component i, centroid n

Output:
    Class(I(x,y)) : (x,y) ↦ {0,1}       // Classification

Pre computation:
    For each centroid n with 0 ≤ n < N
        For each partition w with 0 ≤ w < W
                Compute D_min(C_{n,w}, T) from min(E_{i,n})
                Compute D_max(C_{n,w}, T) from max(E_{i,n})

Main loop:
    For each pixel I(x,y)
```

$$D_{\min}(I(x,y),T) = \sum_{w=0}^{W-1} D_{\min}\left(C_{J_w,w},T\right)$$

$$D_{\max}(I(x,y),T) = \sum_{w=0}^{W-1} D_{\max}\left(C_{J_w,w},T\right)$$

```
    If  D_min(I(x,y),T) ≥ Δ
            Class(I(x,y)) = 0 ;                // Not in T
        Else if  D_max(I(x,y),T) < Δ
            Class(I(x,y)) = 1 ;                // In class T
    Else
            Class(I(x,y)) = D(I(x,y),T) < Δ ; // Use error
```

Figure 14: Fast classification algorithm.

If one of the two comparisons $D_{\min}(I(x,y),T) \geq \Delta$ and $D_{\max}(I(x,y),T) < \Delta$ succeeds, then the pixel $I(x,y)$ is classified from its indices only, with a number of operations proportional to W. Otherwise, the error vector $E(x,y)$ must be retrieved, $I(x,y)$ exactly reconstructed as $I(x,y) = J(x,y) + E(x,y)$

and finally $\mathbf{D}(\mathbf{I}(x, y), \mathbf{T}) < \Delta$ computed. This requires a sum, a subtraction, and a product for each component and $d - 1$ sums to accumulate the result, i.e., a total of d subtractions, $2 \cdot d - 1$ sums, and d products; a number of operations proportional to d (for AVIRIS images, $d = 224$). Figure 14 summarizes the algorithm described above.

The speed of the new classification algorithm depends on the probability that the two tests fail and that the error vector is necessary to decide the classification. Let this probability be:

$$\Pr\left(\mathbf{D}_{\min}(\mathbf{I}(x, y), \mathbf{T}) < \Delta \leq \mathbf{D}_{\max}(\mathbf{I}(x, y), \mathbf{T})\right).$$

If τ_{sub}, τ_{add} and τ_{mul} are respectively the times to perform a subtraction, a sum and a multiplication on a given computing platform, the total running time of the new classification is:

$$2 \cdot (W - 1) \cdot \tau_{add} \quad + \quad (d \cdot (\tau_{sub} + \tau_{mult}) + (2 \cdot d - 1) \cdot \tau_{add})$$
$$\cdot \quad \Pr\left(\mathbf{D}_{\min}(\mathbf{I}(x, y), \mathbf{T}) < \Delta \leq \mathbf{D}_{\max}(\mathbf{I}(x, y), \mathbf{T})\right).$$

The experimental assessment of $\Pr\left(\mathbf{D}_{\min}(\mathbf{I}(x, y), \mathbf{T}) < \Delta \leq \mathbf{D}_{\max}(\mathbf{I}(x, y), \mathbf{T})\right)$ on the images in our test set shows that the percentage of vectors on which the simplified test fails to classify the points reaches a maximum between 7.5% and 11% for a 1024 levels quantizer and 12% to 18% for a 256 level quantizer. Practical figures are typically better since, in the regions of interest, the percentages are usually much lower than the maxima.

These results can be used in two ways. Given an image encoded with LPVQ, it is possible to speed up the measurement of the Euclidean distance between a target vector and the image pixels by using a lookup table. Alternatively, this method can be used as a criterion to determine the number of quantization levels necessary to match a desired average classification speed.

VII. CCSDS ENTROPY CODER

The Consultative Committee on Space Data Systems (CCSDS) has adopted the extended-Rice algorithm as the recommendation for international standards for space applications [51, 52]. This technique was developed specifically for science instruments data and based on requirements of high speed for real-time processing, low complexity, and quick adaptation to statistics. The core algorithm uses a Rice encoder [53] of parameter $m = 2^k$, and encodes a positive integer n with a unary representation of $\lfloor n/m \rfloor$, followed by a stop bit and finally by a binary representation of $\mathrm{mod}(n,m)$.

The particular choice of the code parameter simplifies encoder hardware because the modulus operation can be computed by masking all but the k least significant bits of the input n. These codes achieve optimality (in the Huffman sense) for geometric distributions [54] of non-negative integers and, with an appropriate mapping, can be used to encode sequences of integers having two-sided geometric distributions, as in the case of prediction error. Furthermore, due to the regularity of their construction, Rice codes apply to large or even infinite alphabets of symbols.

The CCSDS Rice encoder groups the prediction errors in blocks of 8 or 16 samples and tries on the block all possible choices of k. Special options are available to deal with highly compressible blocks (all zeros, for example) as well as with uncompressible data. The option that achieves shortest encoding is used and signaled to the decoder. Because blocks of samples are encoded independently, no side information is carried across packet boundaries, and the performance of the algorithm is independent of packet size and error-resilient.

The compression of the LPVQ algorithm has been analyzed by using a two-dimensional predictor for the compression of the VQ indices and an arithmetic encoder, conditioned on the indices, for the entropy coding of the residual. While the partitioned VQ is fast enough to be implemented in real time, even on general purpose hardware, the arithmetic encoder is too slow and too complicated for a low-power hardware implementation. A viable alternative is to sacrifice some compression and use the CCSDS encoder for the entropy coding of the residual.

The experiments described here have been performed by using our own software implementation of the CCSDS encoder. For simplicity the implementation focused on the encoding and did not include the full transmission protocol. Data were encoded with two separate buffers: one for the LPVQ index information (8 bit data in the case of a codebook having $N = 256$ levels) and the other for the quantization error (16 bit signed data). Each buffer employs the *unit delay predictor* to pre-process each block and uses no *reference value* [51, 52].

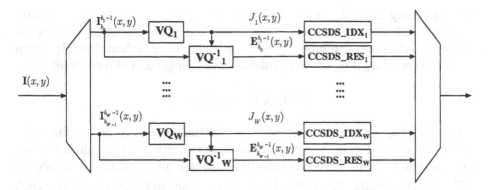

Figure 15: LPVQ with CCSDS entropy coder.

	Differential JPEG-LS	Differential JPEG2000	LPVQ		
			AC	CCSDS	PRED + CCSDS
Cuprite	2.91	2.92	3.27	2.77	2.84
Jasper Ridge	2.81	2.82	3.12	2.74	2.80
Low Altitude	2.70	2.69	2.97	2.64	2.70
Lunar Lake	2.93	2.94	3.31	2.75	2.84
Moffett Field	2.84	2.83	3.01	2.72	2.79
AVERAGE	**2.84**	**2.84**	**3.14**	**2.72**	**2.79**

Table 6: Comparison of compression achieved by LPVQ with three different entropy encoders.

The results refer to a block size of 16 samples. A second experiment exploits the two-dimensional nature of the VQ indices by applying to them a median predictor and by encoding the prediction error with the CCSDS entropy coder. A block diagram of LPVQ+CCSDS is described in Figure 15.

Compression results are reported in Table 6. For reference, the table also reports compression figures that JPEG-LS and JPEG2000 achieve when applied to the difference between consecutive planes. The baseline CCSDS is on average 13% worse than arithmetic encoding. The former, on the other hand, has the advantage of being extremely fast and practically real-time even when implemented in software. Furthermore, it is possible to use a radiation hardened VLSI chip implementing the CCSDS lossless data encoder, which has been successfully deployed in several space missions [55] as a flexible module for on-board applications.

The encoding algorithm of LPVQ is so straightforward that can be easily implemented in hardware, with a very high degree of parallelism. The use of a small dictionary combined with a full-search equivalent fast algorithm achieves encoding time close to real-time even on general purpose hardware.

VIII. CONCLUSIONS

The foregoing discussion describes in details an extension of the LBG algorithm to the locally optimal design of a partitioned vector quantizer for the encoding of source vectors drawn from a high dimensional source on $\Re^d$. LPVQ breaks down the input space into subspaces and, for each subspace, designs a minimal-distortion vector quantizer. The partition is adaptively determined while building the quantizers in order to minimize the total distortion. Experiments on lossless and near-lossless compression of publicly available AVIRIS images show the effectiveness of the proposed method. The peculiar statistics of this class of data requires a suitable entropy coder for both quantization indices and residuals. Off-the-shelf lossless image compressors perform reasonably well on quantization indices, but it is shown how careful conditioning allows for faster and more efficient compression of the quantization indices. Applications of LPVQ to real-time compression and broadcasting, fast browsing pure-pixel classification, and real-time compression on general-purpose hardware are described in detail.

ACKNOWLEDGEMENTS

The authors thank the *NSF* and *BAE Systems* (Information Systems Sector, Center for Transformation) for their support of this work.

REFERENCES

[1]   G. P. Abousleman. "Compression of Hyperspectral Imagery Using Hybrid DPCM/DCT and Entropy Constrained Trellis Coded Quantization," *Proceedings Data Compression Conference*, IEEE Computer Society Press, 322-331, 1995.

[2]   B. Aiazzi, L. Alparone, and S. Baronti. "Near-lossless Compression of 3-D Optical Data," *IEEE Transactions on Geoscience and Remote Sensing* 39:11, 2547-2557, November 2001.

[3]   G. P. Abousleman, T. T. Lam, and L. J. Karam. "Robust Hyperspectral Image Coding with Channel-Optimized Trellis-Coded

Quantization," *IEEE Transaction on Geoscience and Remote Sensing* 40:4, 820-830, April 2002.

[4]   M. J. Ryan and J. F. Arnold. "The Lossless Compression of AVIRIS Images By Vector Quantization," *IEEE Transactions on Geoscience and Remote Sensing* 35:3, 546-550, May 1997.

[5]   M. Manohar and J. C. Tilton. "Browse Level Compression of AVIRIS Data Using Vector Quantization on a Massively Parallel Machine," *Proceedings AVIRIS Airborne Geosciences Workshop*, 2000.

[6]   M. Pickering and M. Ryan. "Efficient Spatial-Spectral Compression of Hyperspectral Data," *IEEE Transaction on Geoscience and Remote Sensing* 39:7, 1536-1539, 2001.

[7]   J. Mielikäinen and P. Toivanen. "Improved Vector Quantization for Lossless Compression of AVIRIS Images," *Proceedings of the XI European Signal Processing Conference*, EUSIPCO-2002, EURASIP, September 2002.

[8]   S. Subramanian, N. Gat, A. Ratcliff, and M. Eismann. "Real-Time Hyperspectral Data Compression Using Principal Component Transform," *Proceedings AVIRIS Airborne Geosciences Workshop*, 1992.

[9]   M. H. Sharp. "Noise-Constrained Hyperspectral Data Compression," SPIE Optical Engineering 41:9, 1-10, 2002.

[10]   J. Mielikäinen, A. Kaarna, and P. Toivanen. "Lossless Hyperspectral Image Compression via Linear Prediction," *Proceedings SPIE* 4725:8, 600-608, 2002.

[11]   J. Mielikäinen and P. Toivanen. "Clustered DPCM for the Lossless Compression of Hyperspectral Images," *IEEE Transactions on Geoscience and Remote Sensing*, vol. 41, no. 12, 2943-2946, December 2003.

[12]   F. Rizzo, B. Carpentieri, G. Motta, and J. A. Storer. "Low-Complexity Lossless Compression of Hyperspectral Imagery via Linear Prediction," *IEEE Signal Processing Letters*, vol. 12, n. 2, February 2005.

[13]   G. Motta, F. Rizzo, and J.A. Storer. "Compression of Hyperspectral Imagery," *Proceedings Data Compression Conference*, IEEE Computer Society Press, 333-342, March 2003.

[14]   F. Rizzo, B. Carpentieri, G. Motta, and J. A. Storer. "High Performance Compression of Hyperspectral Imagery with Reduced Search Complexity in the Compressed Domain," *Proceedings Data*

Compression Conference, IEEE Computer Society Press, 479-488, March 2004.

[15]   C. Shannon. "A Mathematical Theory of Communication," Bell Systems Technical Journal 27, 1948. Also in "The Mathematical Theory of Communication," C. Shannon and W. Weaver, University of Illinois Press, Urbana, IL, 1949.

[16]   S. Lloyd. "Least Squares Quantization in PCM," *IEEE Transactions on Information Theory* IT-28, 1982.

[17]   J. Max. "Quantizing for Minimum Distortion," *IEEE Transactions on Information Theory* IT-6:2, 1960.

[18]   J. Lin. *Vector Quantization for Image Compression*, Ph.D. Dissertation, Computer Science Department, Brandeis University, Waltham, MA, 1992.

[19]   Y. Linde, A. Buzo, and R. Gray. "An Algorithm for Vector Quantizer Design," *IEEE Transactions on Communications* 28, 84-95, 1980.

[20]   C.M. Huang, Q. Bi, G.S. Stiles, and R.W. Harris. "Fast Full Search Equivalent Encoding Algorithm for Image Compression Using Vector Quantization," *IEEE Transactions on Image Processing*, 413-416, July 1992.

[21]   I. Katsavounidis, C.-C.J. Kuo, and Z. Zhang. "A New Initialization Technique for Generalized Lloyd Iteration," *IEEE Signal Processing Letters*, vol. 1, no. 10, 144-146, October 1994.

[22]   T. Kaukoranta, P. Franti, and O. Nevalainen. "Reduced Comparison Search for the Exact GLA," *Proceedings Data Compression Conference*, IEEE Computer Society Press, 33-41, March 1999.

[23]   Shen-En Qian. "Hyperspectral Data Compression Using a Fast Vector Quantization Algorithm," *IEEE Transactions on Geoscience and Remote Sensing*, vol. 42, no. 8, August 2004.

[24]   C. Constantinescu. *Single-Pass Adaptive Vector Quantization*, Ph.D. Dissertation, Computer Science Department, Brandeis University, Waltham, MA, 1995.

[25]   F. Rizzo, J. A. Storer, and B. Carpentieri. "LZ-based Image Compression," *Information Sciences*, vol. 135, issues 1-2, Jun 2001.

[26]   F. Rizzo, J. A. Storer, and B. Carpentieri. "Overlap and Channel Errors in Adaptive Vector Quantization for Image Coding," *Information Sciences*, vol. 171, issues 1-3, Mar 2005.

[27]   A. Gersho and R. M. Gray. *Vector Quantization and Signal Compression*. Kluwer Academic Press, 1991.

[28]   X. Wu. "A Tree-Structured Locally Optimal Vector Quantizer," *Proceedings Tenth International Conference on Pattern Recognition*, Atlantic City, NJ, 1990.

[29]   J. Lin and J. Storer. "Improving Search for Tree-Structured Vector Quantization," *Proceedings Data Compression Conference*, IEEE Computer Society Press, 339-348, 1992.

[30]   J. Lin and J. Storer. "Design and Performance of Tree-Structured Vector Quantizers," *Proceedings Data Compression Conference,* IEEE Computer Society Press, 1993.

[31]   C. Barnes. *Residual Vector Quantizers*, Ph.D. Dissertation, Brigham Young University, 1989.

[32]   C. Barnes and R. Frost. "Necessary Conditions for the Optimality of Residual Vector Quantizers," *Proceedings IEEE International Symposium on Information Theory*, 1990.

[33]   E. Riskin. *Variable Rate Vector Quantization of Images*, Ph.D. Dissertation, Stanford University, 1990.

[34]   F. Kossentini, M. Smith, and C. Barnes. "Image Coding with Variable Rate RVQ," *Proceedings IEEE ICASSP Conference*, San Francisco, CA, 1992.

[35]   A. Viterbi and J. Omura. "Trellis Encoding of Memoryless Discrete-Time Sources with a Fidelity Criterion," *IEEE Transactions on Information Theory* IT-20, 1974.

[36]   L. Colm Stewart. *Trellis Data Compression*, Xerox, Palo Alto Research Center, 1981.

[37]   G. Ungerboeck. "Channel Coding with Multilevel/Phase Signals," *IEEE Transactions on Information Theory* IT-28, 1982.

[38]   T. Fischer, M. W. Marcellin, and M. Wang. "Trellis Coded Vector Quantization," *IEEE Transactions on Information Theory* IT-37, 1991.

[39]   M. Marcellin. "Transform Coding of Images using Trellis Coded Quantization," *Proceedings International Conference on Acoustics, Speech and Signal Processing*, 1990.

[40]   M. Marcellin and T. Fischer. "Trellis Coded Quantization of Memoryless and Gauss-Markov Sources," *IEEE Transactions on Communications* COM-38, 1990.

[41]   G. Motta and B. Carpentieri. "A New Trellis Vector Residual Quantizer: Applications to Image Coding," *Proceedings IEEE International Conference on Acoustics, Speech, and Signal Processing,* Munich, Germany, 1997.

[42]   D. Landgrebe. "Hyperspectral Image Data Analysis," *IEEE Signal Processing Magazine*, 17–28, January 2002

[43]   M. G. Kendall. *A course in the Geometry of n-Dimensions*. New York: Hafner, 1961.

[44]   Y. Matsuyama. "Image Compression Via Vector Quantization with Variable Dimension," *TENCON 87: IEEE Region 10 Conference Computers and Communications Technology Toward 2000*, Seoul, South Korea, August 1987.

[45]   JPL NASA URL: http://popo.jpl.nasa.gov/html/aviris.freedata.html.

[46]   N. M. Nasrabadi and U. Feng. "Image Compression Using Address-Vector Quantization," *IEEE Transactions on Communications*, vol. 38, 2166-2173, December 1990.

[47]   X. Wu, J. Wen, and W. H. Wong. "Conditional Entropy Coding of VQ Indexes for Image Compression," *Proceedings Data Compression Conference*, IEEE Computer Society Press, 347-356, March 1997.

[48]   Y. Gong, M. K. H. Fan, and C. M. Huang. "Image Compression Using Lossless Coding on VQ Indexes," *Proceedings Data Compression Conference*, IEEE Computer Society Press 583, March 2000.

[49]   M. J. Weinberger, G. Seroussi, and G. Sapiro, "The LOCO-I Lossless Image Compression Algorithm: Principles and Standardization into JPEG-LS," *IEEE Transactions on Image Processing*, vol. 9, no. 8, 1309-1324, August 2000.

[50]   NESDIS GOES R. Satellite Series Hyperspectral Sounder Data Compression Meeting, May 22, 2003.

[51]   Consulting Committee for Space Data Systems. *Lossless Data Compression, Report Concerning Space Data System Standards*, CCSDS 121.0-G-1, Green Book, May 1997.

[52]   Consulting Committee for Space Data Systems. *Lossless Data Compression, Recommendation for Space Data Systems Standards*, CCSDS 121.0-B-1, Blue Book, May 1997.

[53]   R. F. Rice, Pen-Shu Yeh, and W. H. Miller. "Algorithms for High-Speed Universal Noiseless Coding," *Proceedings AIAA Computing in Aerospace 9 Conference*, San Diego, CA, October 1993.

[54]   Pen-Shu Yeh, R. F. Rice, and W. H. Miller. "On the Optimality of a Universal Noiseless Coder," *Proceedings AIAA Computing in Aerospace 9 Conference*, San Diego, CA, October 1993.

[55]   Pen-Shu Yeh and W. H. Miller. "A Real Time Lossless Data Compression Technology for Remote Sensing and Other Applications," *Proceedings of ISCAS-95*, 1995.

Near-Lossless Compression of Hyperspectral Imagery Through Crisp/Fuzzy Adaptive DPCM

Bruno Aiazzi[1], Luciano Alparone[2], Stefano Baronti[1],
Cinzia Lastri[1], and Leonardo Santurri[1]

[1] Institute of Applied Physics "Nello Carrara", National Research Council,
Via Panciatichi, 64, 50127 Florence, Italy
[2] Department of Electronics and Telecommunications, University of Florence,
Via Santa Marta, 3, 50139 Florence, Italy

1 Introduction

It is a widespread belief that the new generation of spaceborne imaging spectrometers (NASA/JPL's MODIS on Terra and Aqua, NASA/GSFC's Hyperion on EO-1, and ESA's MERIS on EnviSat) will create several problems, on one side for on-board compression and transmission to ground stations, on the other side for an efficient dissemination and utilization of the outcome hyperspectral images. In fact, the huge amount of data due to moderate ground resolution, but extremely high spectral resolution (around 10 nm), together with the high radiometric resolution (typically 12 bit wordlength of the raw, i.e., uncalibrated, data from the digital counter) originates an amount of data of approximately 300 bytes/pixel. Therefore, the use of advanced compression techniques and of suitable analysis/processing procedures for dissemination to users of thematic information is mandatory.

Data compression consists of a decorrelation, aimed at generating a memoryless version of the correlated information source, possibly followed by quantization, which introduces a distortion to allow a reduction in the information rate to be achieved, and entropy coding. If the decorrelation is achieved by means of an orthonormal transformation, e.g., the discrete cosine transform (DCT) or the discrete wavelet transform (DWT), the variance of quantization errors in the transformed domain is preserved when the data are transformed back into the original domain. Thus, the mean square error (MSE) can be easily controlled through the step sizes of quantizers. However, quantization errors in the transformed domain, which are likely to be uniformly distributed and upper bounded in modulus by half of the step size, are propagated by the inverse transformation and yield broad-tailed distributions, whose maximum absolute amplitude cannot be generally set a "priori". Therefore lossy compression methods, e.g., those proposed by the Joint Photographic Expert Group, the current standard JPEG [1] and the new standard JPEG 2000 [2], are not capable of controlling the reconstruction error but in the MSE sense; hence, apart from the lossless case, relevant image features may be locally distorted by an unpredictable and unquantifiable extent.

Compression algorithms are said to be fully reversible (lossless) when the data that are reconstructed from the compressed bit stream are identical to the original, or lossy otherwise. The difference in performance expressed by the compression ratio (CR) between lossy and lossless algorithms can be of one order of magnitude without a significant visual degradation. For this reason lossy algorithms are extremely interesting and are used in all those application in which a certain distortions may be tolerated. Actually these algorithms are more and more popular and their use is becoming widespread also in such remote sensing applications as those in which it was rightly believed that the data had to exactly retain their original values for further processing and quantitative evaluations [3]. This aspect is crucial for transmission from satellite to Earth receiving stations [4]; in fact, once the data were lossy compressed, they would not be available as they were acquired for the user community. The distortions introduced might influence such research activities as modeling, classification and postprocessing in general. As a matter of fact, however, the intrinsic noisiness of sensors prevents from adopting strictly lossless techniques in order to obtain a considerable bandwidth reduction [5, 6]. In this light, error-bounded near-lossless algorithms [7, 8] are growing in importance since they are capable of guaranteing that at every pixel of the reconstructed image the error is bounded and user-defined.

In the medical field objective measurements, like MSE, maximum absolute distortion (MAD), widely known as *peak error*, and percentage MAD (PMAD) may be integrated with qualitative judgements of skilled experts, e.g., expressed in terms of Receiver Operating Characteristic (ROC) curves [9]. In remote sensing applications, however, photoanalysis is not the sole concern. The data are often postprocessed to extract information that may not be immediately available by user inspection. In this perspective, if the MAD error is constrained to be, e.g., one half of the standard deviation of the background noise, assumed to be additive, Gaussian, and independent of the signal, the decoded image will be *virtually lossless*. This term indicates not only visual indistinguishability from the original, but also that possible outcomes of postprocessing are likely to be practically the same as if they were calculated from the original data. The price of compression becomes a small and uniform increment in noisiness.

When higher compression ratios are demanded, a PMAD-constrained approach may be rewarding in terms of scientific quality preservation of the decompressed data [10]. The rationale is that automatic analysis and processing algorithms may be more sensitive to *relative* errors on pixels, than to *absolute* errors. For best performance, however, relative error-constrained compression requires logarithmic quantization [8], which is penalized with respect to linear quantization in the Rate Distortion (RD) sense, with an MSE distortion measure [11].

When multispectral or better hyperspectral data are being dealt with, *spectral* distortion becomes a primary concern, besides spatial and radiometric distortions. Spectral distortion is a measurement of how a pixel vector (i.e., a vector having as many components as spectral bands) changes because of an irreversible compression of its components. A widely used measurement is the angle between the two spectral vectors. More sophisticated measurements based on information-theoretic criteria have recently been introduced for discriminating spectral classes [12].

Goal of this chapter is to investigate two different strategies of adaptive 3D prediction (i.e., jointly spatial and spectral) for the compression of hyperspectral image data through differential pulse code modulation (DPCM). The former consists of selecting the mean square error (MSE) minimizing predictor for each block of pixels in each spectral band from a dictionary of precalculated predictors. According to the latter, an adaptive predictor is obtained at each pixel by linearly combining the output of the predictors in the dictionary through adaptive weights measuring the fuzzy membership of that predictor to that pixel. The two methods are also compared from the viewpoint of both spectral and radiometric distortions introduced in hyperspectral pixel vectors, once they are decompressed. The main result of this analysis is that, for a given compression ratio, near-lossless methods, having constrained pixel error, either absolute or relative, are suitable for preserving the spectral discrimination capability among pixel vectors, which is the principal source of spectral information. Therefore, whenever a lossless compression is not practicable, the use of near-lossless compression is recommended in such application where spectral quality is a crucial point.

2   Lossless/Near-Lossless Image Compression Algorithms

Considerable research efforts have been recently spent in the development of lossless image compression techniques. The first specific standard has been the lossless version of JPEG [13, 1], which may use either Huffman or arithmetic coding. More interestingly, a new standard, which provides also near-lossless compression, has been recently released under the name JPEG-LS [14]. It is based on an adaptive nonlinear prediction and exploits context modeling followed by Golomb-Rice entropy coding. A similar context-based algorithm named CALIC has also been recently proposed [15]. The simple adaptive predictors used by JPEG-LS and CALIC, however, the *median adaptive predictor* (MAP) and the *gradient adjusted predictor* (GAP), are empirical. Thorough comparisons with more advanced methods [16] have revealed that their performance is limited and still far from the entropy bounds. It is noteworthy that, unlike a locally MMSE linear prediction, a nonlinear prediction, like GAP of CALIC and MAP of JPEG-LS, that may occur to minimize the *mean absolute error* (MAE), does not ensure local entropy minimization [17]. Therefore only linear prediction, yet adaptive, will be concerned for a 3D extension suitable for multi/hyperspectral data.

A number of integer-to-integer transforms, e.g., [18–21], are capable of ensuring a perfect reconstruction with integer arithmetics. Their extension to multiband data is straightforward, if a spectral decorrelation is preliminarily performed [22]. However, the drawback of all critically-subsampled multiresolution transform, is that they are suitable for L_2-constrained compression. Thanks to Parceval's theorem, if the transformation is orthogonal, the MSE, or its square root (RMSE), namely the L_2 distortion between original and decoded data, is controlled by the user, up to possibly yield lossless compression, by resorting to the aforementioned integer-to-integer transforms. However, L_∞-constrained, i.e., near-lossless, compression is not trivial and, whenever feasible [23] is not rewarding in terms of L_∞-bitrate plots with respect to DPCM. Indeed, DPCM schemes, either *causal* (prediction-based) or *noncausal*, i.e., interpolation-based or *hierarchical* [24], are suitable for L_∞-constrained compression, that is either lossless or near-lossless. The latter is recommended for lower quality compression (i.e., higher CR), the former for higher-quality, which is the primary concern in remote sensing applications.

Eventually, it is worth mentioning that Part I of the JPEG2000 image coding standard [2] incorporates a lossless mode, based on reversible integer wavelets, and capable of providing a scalable bit stream, that can be decoded from the lossy (not near-lossless) up to the lossless level. However, image coding standards are not suitable for the compression of 3D data sets: in spite of their complexity, they are not capable of exploiting the 3D signal redundancy featured, e.g., by multi/hyperspectral imagery.

2.1   Adaptive Prediction

DPCM basically consists of a decorrelation followed by entropy coding of the outcome prediction errors. Fig. 1 outlines the flowchart of the encoder, featuring context modeling for entropy coding, and the decoder. The quantization noise feedback loop at the encoder allows the L_∞ error to be constrained, by letting prediction at the encoder be carried out from the same distorted samples that will be available at the decoder.

The simplest way to design a predictor, once a *causal* neighborhood is set, is to take a linear combination of pixel values within such a neighborhood, with coefficients optimized in order to yield *minimum mean square error* (MMSE) over the whole image. Such a prediction, however, is optimum only for stationary signals. To overcome this drawback, two variations have been proposed:

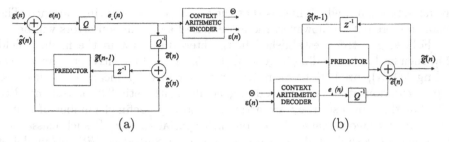

Figure 1: Flowchart of DPCM with quantization noise feedback loop at the encoder, suitable for near-lossless compression: (a) encoder; (b) decoder

adaptive DPCM (ADPCM) [1], in which the coefficients of predictors are continuously recalculated from the incoming new data at each pixel location, and *classified* DPCM [25], in which a preliminary training phase is aimed at recognizing some statistical classes of pixels and at calculating an optimized predictor for each class. Once such predictors are available, the most performing (in the MMSE sense) on a block of pixels may be *selected* to encode the current block [26]. Alternatively, predictors may be adaptively combined [27], also based on a fuzzy-logic concepts [16], to attain an MMSE space-varying prediction. The two strategies of classified prediction will be referred to as *adaptive selection/combination of adaptive predictors* (ASAP/ACAP). In the ACAP case, the linearity of prediction makes it possible to formulate the problem as an approximation of the optimum space-varying linear predictor at each pixel through its projection onto a set of nonorthogonal prototype predictors capable of embodying the statistical properties of the data.

To enhance the entropy coding performance, both ASAP and ACAP schemes may use context modeling (see Sect. 2.2) of prediction errors followed by arithmetic coding. It is noteworthy that the original 2D encoder following the ACAP paradigm [16] achieves lossless compression ratios 5 % better than CALIC and 10 % than JPEG-LS, on an average. Although 2D ASAP encoder [26] is slightly less performing than the former, its feature of real-time decoding is highly valuable in application contexts, since an image is usually encoded only once, but decoded many times.

2.2 Context Modeling for Entropy Coding

A notable feature of all advanced image compression methods [28] is statistical context modeling for entropy coding. The underlying rationale is that prediction errors should be similar to stationary white noise as much as possible. As a matter of fact, they are still spatially correlated to a small extent and especially are non-stationary, which means that they exhibit space-varying variance. The better the prediction, however, the more noise-like prediction errors will be.

Following a trend established in the literature, first in the medical field [29], then for lossless coding in general [19, 15, 14], and recently for *near-lossless* coding [30, 31], prediction errors are entropy coded by means of a classified implementation of an entropy coder, generally arithmetic [32] or Golomb-Rice [33]. For this purpose, they are arranged into a predefined number of statistically homogeneous classes based on their spatial *context*. If such classes are statistically discriminated, then the entropy of a *context-conditioned* model of prediction errors will be lower than that derived from a stationary memoryless model of the decorrelated source [34].

A context function may be defined and measured on prediction errors lying within a causal neighborhood, possibly larger than the prediction support, as the RMS value of prediction errors (RMSPE). The context function should capture the non-stationarity of prediction errors, regardless of their spatial correlation. Again, causality of neighborhood is necessary in order to make the same information available both at the encoder and at the decoder. At the former, the probability density function (PDF) of RMSPE is calculated and partitioned into a number of intervals chosen as equally populated; thus, contexts are equiprobable as well. This choice is motivated by the use of adaptive arithmetic coding for encoding the errors belonging to each class. Adaptive entropy coding, in general, does not require previous knowledge of the statistics of the source, but benefits from a number of data large enough for training, which happens simultaneously with coding. The source given by each class is further split into sign bit and magnitude. The former is strictly random and is coded as it stands, the latter exhibits a reduced variance in each class, –null if the context (RMSPE) of the current pixel is always equal its magnitude; thus, it may be coded with fewer bits than the original residue. It is noteworthy that such a context-coding procedure is independent of the particular method used to decorrelate the data. Unlike other schemes, e.g., CALIC [15], in which context-modeling is embedded in the decorrelation procedure, the method [30] can be applied to any DPCM scheme, either lossless or near-lossless, without adjustments in the near-lossless case, as it happens to other methods [31].

3   Hyperspectral Data Compression Through 3D DPCM

Whenever multiband images are to be compressed, advantage may be taken from the spectral correlation of the data for designing a prediction that is both *spatial* and *spectral*, from a causal neighborhood of pixels [35, 36]. Causal means that only previously scanned pixels on the current and previously encoded bands may be used for predicting the current pixel value. This strategy is as more effective as the data are more spectrally correlated, as in the case of hyperspectral data. If the *interband* correlation of the data is weak, as it usually occurs for data with few and sparse spectral bands, a 3D prediction may lead to negligible coding benefits, unless the available bands are reordered in such a way that the average correlation between two consecutive bands is maximized [37]. In this case, however, advantage may be taken from a *bidirectional* spectral prediction [38], in which once the $(k-1)$st band is available, first the kth band is skipped and the $(k+1)$st band is predicted from the $(k-1)$st one; then, both these two bands are used to predict the kth band in a spatially causal but spectrally non-causal fashion. In practice, the bidirectional prediction is achieved by applying a causal prediction to a permutation of the sequence of bands. This strategy, however, is not rewarding when hyperspectral data are concerned [8].

When hyperspectral data are concerned, the non-stationarity characteristics of the data in both spatial and spectral domains, together with computational constraints, make the jointly spatial and spectral prediction to take negligible extra advantage from a number of previous bands greater than two. In this case the original hyperspectral pixel vectors may be classified into spatially homogeneous classes, whose map must be transmitted as side information. Then a purely spectral prediction is carried out on pixel spectra belonging to each class, by means of a large set of linear spectral predictors of length up to twenty, i.e., spanning up to twenty previous bands. This original approach was introduced very recently for lossless compression [39, 40], and provides compression ratios among the very best in the literature. The obvious drawbacks are the computational effort for pre-classifying the data, as well as a crucial adjustment of such parameters as number of classes and length of predictors (one for each wavelength of each class), which determine a large coding overhead. Furthermore, since the cost of overhead (classification map and set of spectral predictors) is independent of the target compression ratio, the method seems to be not recommendable for near-lossless compression, even if it might be achieved in principle.

Another interesting approach specific to hyperspectral images is the extension of 3D CALIC [41], originally conceived for color images, having few spectral bands, to image data having a larger number of highly correlated bands. The novel algorithm, referred to as M-CALIC [42] significantly outperforms 3D CALIC, to which it largely sticks, with a moderately increased computational complexity and absence of setup parameters crucial for performances.

The 3D ACAP encoder has been extended by the authors to 3D data [43], same as the 3D ASAP encoder [8], by simply changing the 2D neighborhood into a 3D one spanning up to three previous bands. The two algorithms will be reviewed in the following Subsects. 3.1 and 3.1. Eventually, we wish to remind that a forerunner of the ACAP paradigm is the fuzzy 3D DPCM [44], in which the prototype MMSE spatial/spectral linear predictors constituting the dictionary were calculated on *clustered* data, analogously to [40].

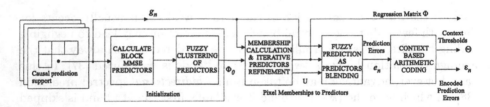

Figure 2: Flowchart of Fuzzy-Matching-Pursuit 3D DPCM Lossless Encoder

Eventually, it is important to remind that in satellite on-board compression computing power is is limited and coding benefits must be traded off with computational complexity [42, 45].

3.1   3D Fuzzy-Matching-Pursuit DPCM Encoder

Matching pursuit (MP) is an iterative method to expand a signal by using an over-complete dictionary of nonorthogonal functions [46]. Although MP was recently employed mostly for video coding [47], its original formulation is quite general. In this light, we assume that the MMSE adaptive predictor at the current pixel position, may be expressed as a series expansion of a "dictionary" made of a number of predictors that are fitting the different classes of features occurring throughout the image. Given the ambiguous or "fuzzy" nature of the problem, the coefficients of the expansion are found out not as scalar products, as for the conventional formulation of MP, but as the degrees of membership of that pixel to the predictors of the dictionary.

Images are first partitioned into blocks and a linear MMSE predictor is calculated for each block. From the large number of predictors, a fuzzy clustering algorithm produces an initial guess of a user-specified number of prototype predictors that are given as input to an iterative procedure, in which pixels are given degrees of membership to each predictor, measuring prediction fitness. Then predictors are recalculated from pixels depending on their memberships.

The overall prediction will be fuzzy, being given by the sum of the outputs of each predictor weighted by the memberships of the current pixel to that predictor. The linearity of prediction makes it possible to formulate the above approach as a problem of approximating the optimum space-varying predictor at each pixel by projecting it onto a set of nonorthogonal *prototype* predictors capable of embodying the statistical properties of the image data. Coding performances rely also on the use of a context-based entropy coding strategy: advantage is taken both of the non-stationarity and of the residual correlation of prediction errors. Fig. 2 shows the overall flowchart of the encoder. All the blocks except the last one exploit fuzzy-logic concepts, as well as fuzzy techniques for computation.

Bruno Aiazzi, Luciano Alparone, Stefano Baronti,
Cinzia Lastri, and Leonardo Santurri

Basic Definitions A discrete grey scale image $\{g(i,j)\}$ may be scanned left to right and top to bottom by successive lines, so as to yield a 1D set of coordinates $\{n\}$. Let us define $\mathcal{N}_p^W(n)$, *causal* neighborhood of the current pixel $n \equiv (i,j)$, a circle of radius $W \in \mathbb{Z}^+$ in L_p (p-norm), in which the causality constraint leads to discarding all pixels that have not been encountered along the raster scan before n. It is possible to sort the kth sample $\in \mathcal{N}_p^W(n)$ by its Euclidean distance from n, δ_k. Fig. 3 depicts examples of 2D causal neighborhoods of radius $W = 3$ of the current pixel n, i.e., ($\bullet$). Pixels are labeled for increasing Euclidean distance from n.

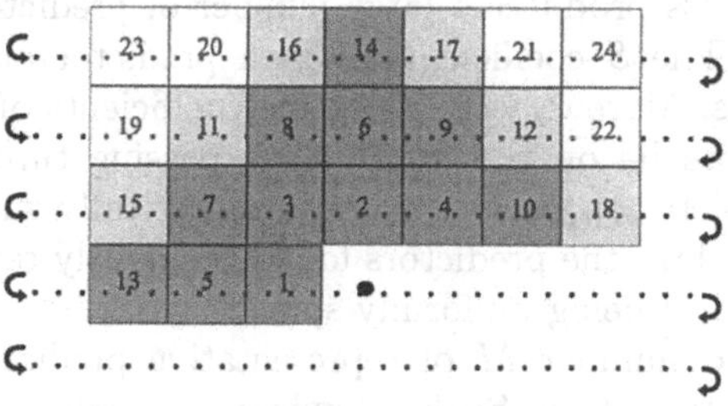

Figure 3: 2D causal neighborhoods with radius $R = 3$. Pixels are labeled for increasing Euclidean distance from the current pixel n ($\bullet$): 1 through 10 plus 13 and 14 define an L_1 neighborhood (diamond shaped), 1 through 18 an L_2 neighborhood (circular), 1 through 24 an L_∞ neighborhood (square)

Prediction is usually based on a linear combination of surrounding pixels lying in $\mathcal{N}_p^W(n)$. Let us define as *prediction support* of size S centered on n, $\mathcal{P}_S(n)$, a subset of $\mathcal{N}_p^W(n)$. Let $\psi(n)$ denote the vector containing the grey levels of the K samples lying within $\mathcal{P}_S(n)$ sorted by increasing Euclidean distance from the pixel n. Let also $\phi = \{\phi_k \in \mathbb{R}, \ k = 1, \cdots, S\}^T$, with $\sum_{k=1}^{S} \phi_k = 1$, denote the vector comprising the S coefficients of a linear predictor operating on $\mathcal{P}_S$. Thus, a linear prediction for $g(n)$ is defined as $\hat{g}(n) = \sum_{k=1}^{S} \phi_k \cdot \psi_k(n)$, in which $< \cdot, \cdot >$ indicates scalar (inner) product.

Pixels both on the current band and on previously encoded bands may be used for a jointly spatial and spectral prediction. A causal 3D neighborhood for the pixel n in the kth band comprises a causal 2D neighborhood on the kth band and one or more *non-causal* 2D neighborhoods on *previous* bands, according to the band scan order. The order of prediction still denotes the overall number of pixels belonging to the union of the 2D neighborhoods.

Initialization The determination of the dictionary of predictors for the MP-DPCM is the key to the success of the coding process. It starts from observing that patterns of pixel values occurring within $\mathcal{P}_S(n)$, $n = 1, \cdots, N-1$ ($\mathcal{P}_S(0) = \emptyset$), reflect local spatial features of the image, e.g., edges, textures, and shadings. An efficient prediction should be capable of reflecting such features as much as possible. After preliminarily partitioning the input image into square blocks, e.g., 16×16, a causal prediction support of size S is set, and the S coefficients of an MMSE linear predictor are calculated for each block by means of a standard least squares (LS) algorithm. Specifically, if B denotes one block of the partition, the LS algorithm is fed by the pairs $\{(\psi(n), g(n)) \mid n \in B\}$ to yield the related predictor ϕ_B.

The above process produces a large number of predictors, each optimized for a single block. The S coefficients of each predictor are arranged into an S-dimensional space. More exactly, since the coefficients of any predictor sum to one, all predictors lie on the hyper-plane passing through the versors of the coordinate axes. It can be noticed that statistically similar blocks exhibit similar predictors. Thus, the predictors found previously tend to cluster on the hyper-plane, instead of being uniformly spread.

A user provided number M of representative predictors is identified by a fuzzy clustering procedure. Such "dominant" predictors are calculated as *centroids* of as many clusters in the predictors' space, according to a vector Euclidean metrics. Although a variety of fuzzy clustering algorithms exists [48], the widespread Bezdek's *Fuzzy C Means* (FCM) algorithm [49] was used (with exponent $m = 1.1$) because it yields centroids that speed-up convergence of the following training, as experimentally noticed. Thus, an $S \times M$ matrix $\Phi^{(0)} = \{\phi_m^{(0)}, \ m = 1, \cdots, M\}$ containing the coefficients of the M predictors is produced. The superscript $^{(0)}$ highlights that such predictors are start-up values of the iterative refinement procedure which will yield the "dictionary" of predictors for the MP. Fig. 4 illustrates a number of block MMSE predictors and eight "dominant" predictors found out by the FCM algorithm.

Membership Function and Training of Predictors The M predictors found out through fuzzy clustering are used to initialize a training procedure in which firstly pixels are given degrees of membership to predictors. Then, each predictor is recalculated based only on pixels whose membership to it exceeds a threshold μ. The procedure is analogous to a *relaxation labelling*, in which the labelling is not *crisp* but *fuzzy*.

The choice of the fuzzy-membership function is extremely crucial for performances of a DPCM encoder. On one side, such a function should reflect the ability of a predictor to yield a $\hat{g}(n)$ as close as possible to $g(n)$. On the other side, it must be calculated from a *causal* subset of pixels, not necessarily identical to the prediction support. A suitable fuzzy membership function of the nth

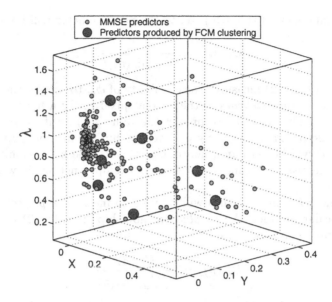

Figure 4: Example of eight spatial-spectral predictors produced by the Fuzzy C-means clustering algorithm starting from a large number of MMSE predictors

pixel to the mth predictor was devised as the reciprocal of the weighted squared prediction error, produced by the mth predictor on a causal neighborhood of n, raised to an empirical exponent γ, and incremented by one to avoid divisions by zero.

The causal neighborhood adopted is square and, thus, uniquely defined by its radius R as $\mathcal{N}_\infty^R(n)$. Although a more general definition (any p-norm) might seem more appropriate, this choice was validated empirically. $\mathcal{M}_R \triangleq \mathcal{N}_\infty^R$ will be referred to as *membership support* in the following.

The *weighted* squared prediction error produced by the mth predictor on the nth pixel is defined as

$$\bar{d}_m^2(n) \;=\; \frac{\displaystyle\sum_{k \in \mathcal{M}_R(n)} \delta_k^{-1} \cdot [g(k) - \, < \phi_m , \psi(k) >]^2}{\displaystyle\sum_{k \in \mathcal{M}_R} \delta_k^{-1}}. \tag{1}$$

The weight of each squared prediction error is taken to be inversely proportional to the distance δ_k from the current pixel n. Thus, closer neighbors will contribute more than farther ones. The weighted squared error (1) is normalized to the sum of its weights. Thus, its magnitude is roughly independent of the neighborhood size.

The membership of the nth pixel to the mth predictor will be

$$U_m(n) = \frac{1}{1 + [\bar{d}_m^2(n)]^\gamma}. \tag{2}$$

As a matter of fact, (2) measures the capability of ϕ_m to predict the grey levels of the closest *causal neighbors* of the current pixel n. By a fuzzy inference, it also reflects the ability of ϕ_m to predict the value $g(n)$ itself. If the outputs of the mth predictor exactly fit the grey levels within the membership support of n, then $\bar{d}_m^2(n)$ will be zero and, hence, $U_m(n) = 1$. The membership exponent γ rules the degree of fuzziness of the membership function; it was adjusted empirically.

Since the fuzzy membership will be used to measure a *projection pursuit*, same as a scalar product, the *absolute* membership given by (2) is normalized to yield a *relative* membership

$$\tilde{U}_m(n) = \frac{U_m(n)}{\sum_{m=1}^M U_m(n)} \tag{3}$$

suitable for a *probabilistic* clustering.

Iterative Refinement of Predictors With reference to the flowchart of Fig. 2, the iterative procedure is outlined in the following steps:

- **Step 0:** for each pixel n, $n \geq 1$, calculate the initial membership array, $\tilde{U}_m^{(0)}(n)$, $m = 1, \cdots, M$, from the initial set of predictors $\Phi^{(0)} = \{\phi_m^{(0)}, m = 1, \cdots, M\}$ by using (1), (2) and (3); set the iteration step $h = 0$ and a membership threshold μ.
- **Step 1:** recalculate predictors $\{\phi_m^{(h+1)}, m = 1, \cdots, M\}$ from those pixels whose membership $\tilde{U}_m^{(h)}(n)$ exceeds μ; weight by $\tilde{U}_m^{(h)}(n)$ the contribution of the pair $(\psi(n), g(n))$ to $\phi_m^{(h+1)}$ in the LS algorithm.
- **Step 2:** recalculate memberships to the new predictors, $\tilde{U}_m^{(h+1)}(n)$, $m = 1, \cdots, M$, $n = 1, \cdots, N - 1$.
- **Step 3:** check convergence; if realized, stop; otherwise, increment h by one and go to **Step 1**.

Convergence can be checked by thresholding the decrement in cumulative *mean square prediction error* (MSPE) associated to the current iteration. Another iteration is executed if such an amount exceeds a preset threshold. Such an *open loop* check is ruled by thresholds that can be calculated once through a *closed loop* procedure, in which the coder of Fig. 2 is enabled to produce code bits at each iteration. The threshold values corresponding to negligible, if not zero, further code benefits are found out accordingly.

Notice that the standard LS algorithm has been modified to account for the memberships of pixels to predictors at the previous iteration. Pixels having larger degrees of memberships to one predictor will contribute to the determination of that predictor more than pixels having smaller degrees. Furthermore, depending on the threshold μ, a pixel may contribute, though with different extents, to more predictors, in the fuzzy-logic spirit. The membership threshold μ is non-crucial for coding performances.

Eventually, an $S \times M$ matrix $\Phi = \{\phi_m, \ m = 1, \cdots, M\}$, containing the coefficients of the M predictors after the last iteration stage is produced and stored in the file header.

Fuzzy Matching-Pursuit Prediction Although the concept of *fuzzy* prediction, as opposed to a classified or *crisp* prediction is not novel, the use of *linear* predictions makes it possible, besides an LS adjustment of predictors, to formulate the fuzzy prediction as a problem of MP.

In fact, by the linearity of prediction, a *weighted sum* of the outputs of predictors is equal to the output of a linear combination of the same predictors with the same weights, that is to calculate an adaptive predictor at every pixel:

$$\phi(n) \triangleq \sum_{m=1}^{M} \tilde{U}_m(n) \cdot \phi_m \tag{4}$$

in which the weights are still provided by $\tilde{U}_m(n)$, i.e., (3), with (1) calculated from the predictors $\{\phi_m, \ m = 1, \cdots, M\}$ after the last iteration stage. The predictor (4) will yield the adaptive linear prediction as $\hat{g}(n) = < \phi(n), \psi(n) >$.

Equivalently, each pixel value $g(n)$ can be predicted as a *fuzzy switching*, i.e., a *blending*, of the outputs of all the predictors, which are defined as

$$\hat{g}_m(n) = < \phi_m, \psi(n) > \tag{5}$$

with the *fuzzy* prediction, $\hat{g}(n)$, given by

$$\hat{g}(n) = \text{round} \left[\sum_{m=1}^{M} \tilde{U}_m(n) \cdot \hat{g}_m(n) \right] \tag{6}$$

The right term of (6) is rounded to integer to yield integer valued prediction errors, i.e., $e(n) = g(n) - \hat{g}(n)$, that are sent to the entropy coding section.

Context-Based Arithmetic Coding A context function was defined on prediction errors lying within the 2D causal neighborhood comprising the 2D prediction support on the current band, as the *Root Mean Square* (RMS) of decoded prediction errors weighted by the reciprocal of the Euclidean distance from n [30]:

$$c(n) \triangleq \sqrt{\frac{\sum\limits_{h \in \mathcal{N}_\infty^W (n)} \delta_h^{-1} \cdot \tilde{e}^2(h)}{\sum\limits_{h \in \mathcal{N}_\infty^W} \delta_h^{-1}}} \tag{7}$$

Again, causality of the neighborhood is necessary in order to make the same information available both at the encoder and at the decoder. At the former, the probability density function (PDF) of $c(n)$ is calculated and partitioned into a number L of intervals chosen so as to be equally populated. From such a PDF, $L - 1$ thresholds, $\Theta = \{\theta_l \in \mathbb{R}^+, \ l = 1, \cdots, L - 1\}$, are calculated so as to define the decision intervals of each class.

3.2   3D Relaxation-Labeled-Prediction DPCM Encoder

The second DPCM encoder, which will be reviewed and assessed in this work, whose flowchart is shown in Fig. 5 follows the ASAP paradigm, being based on a classified linear-regression prediction followed by context-based arithmetic coding of the outcome residues. Images are partitioned into blocks and an MMSE linear predictor is calculated for each block. Given a preset number of classes, a Fuzzy-C-Means algorithm [49] produces an initial guess of classified predictors to be delivered to an iterative labelling procedure which classifies pixel blocks simultaneously refining the associated predictors. All the predictors are transmitted along with the label of each block. For sake of clarity the procedure method is presented in its 2D form. The extension to 3D data coding is simply obtained by changing the dimension of the neighborhood.

Iterative Block Labelling and Predictors Estimation Once M predictors have been found out through fuzzy clustering, they are used to initialize an iterative procedure in which image blocks are assigned to M classes, and an optimized predictor is obtained for each class.

   Step 0: classify blocks based on their *mean squared prediction error* (MSPE). The label of the predictor minimizing MSPE for a block is assigned to the block itself. This operation has the effect of partitioning the set of blocks into M classes that are best matched by the predictors previously found out.

   Step 1: recalculate each of the M predictors from the data belonging to the blocks of each class. The new set of predictors is thus designed so as to minimize MSPE for the current block partition into M classes.

   Step 2: reclassify blocks: the label of the new predictor minimizing MSPE for a block is assigned to the block itself. This operation has the effect of moving

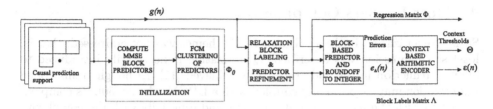

Figure 5: Flowchart of Relaxation-Labeled-Prediction 3D Lossless Encoder

some blocks from one class to another, thus repartitioning the set of blocks into M new classes that are best matched by the current predictors.

Step 3: check convergence; if found, stop; otherwise, go to **Step 1**.

Block-Based Data Prediction Once blocks have been classified and labeled, together with the attached optimized predictor, each band is raster scanned and predictors are *activated* based on the classes of crossed blocks. Thus, each pixel belonging to one block of the original partition, $g(i,j)$, is predicted as a $\hat{g}(i,j)$ by using the one out of the M predictors that was found to better fit the statistics of that class of data block in the MMSE sense. The integer valued prediction errors, viz., $e(i,j) = g(i,j) - \text{round}[\hat{g}(i,j)]$, are delivered to the *context-coding* section, identical to to that of FMP.

Decoder Some overhead information is required by the decoder: $S \times M$ coefficients of predictors, $L-1$ thresholds for context decoding, and a label identifying one out of the M prediction classes for each block ($\log_2 M$ bits per label, on an average, if labels are not further compressed).

The decoder can be summarized by the following steps:

- Retrieve predictors Φ, block labels Λ, and context thresholds Θ from the file header, as well as image dimensions and word-length (e.g., 8 $b/pixel$), and the first image sample $g(0) \equiv g(i = 0, j = 0)$ which is PCM coded.
- Calculate context $c(n)$ by using (7) from the previously decoded pixel values within $\mathcal{N}_\infty^W(n)$.
- Decode the encoded prediction error $\epsilon(n)$, after labelling its context class by thresholding $c(n)$ through $\{\theta_l, \ l = 1, \cdots, L-1\}$, to yield $e(n)$.
- Calculate the output of the mth predictor at the nth pixel, $\hat{g}_m(n)$, from decoded pixels lying on $\mathcal{P}_S(n)$.
- Add $\hat{g}(n)$ to the previously decoded $e(n)$ to yield $g(n)$.

Decoding is simpler than encoding, due to the absence of training, and is feasible in real-time.

4   Near-Lossless Compression

So far, quantization in the FMP and RLP schemes was not addressed; that is, lossless compression was described. Quantization is necessarily introduced to allow a reduction in the code rate to be achieved [11]. Although trellis coded quantization may be optimally coupled with a DPCM scheme [50], its complexity grows with the number of output levels and especially with the complexity of predictors. Therefore, in the following only linear and logarithmic quantization will be concerned. The latter is used to yield relative error bounded compression.

4.1   Distortion Measurements

Before discussing quantization in DPCM schemes, let us review the most widely used distortion measurements suitable for single-band image data (2D) and multiband image data (3D), either multispectral or hyperspectral.

Radiometric Distortion Let $0 \le g(i,j) \le g_{fs}$ denote an N-pixel digital image and let $\tilde{g}(i,j)$ be its possibly distorted version achieved by compressing $g(i,j)$ and decompressing the outcome bit stream. Widely used distortion measurements are the following.
Mean absolute error (MAE), or L_1 (norm),

$$\text{MAE} = \frac{1}{N} \sum_i \sum_j |g(i,j) - \tilde{g}(i,j)|; \tag{8}$$

Mean Squared Error (MSE), or L_2^2,

$$\text{MSE} = \frac{1}{N} \sum_i \sum_j [g(i,j) - \tilde{g}(i,j)]^2; \tag{9}$$

Root MSE (RMSE), or L_2,

$$\text{RMSE} = \sqrt{\text{MSE}}; \tag{10}$$

Signal to Noise Ratio (SNR)

$$\text{SNR}_{(\text{dB})} = 10 \cdot \log_{10} \frac{\bar{g}^2}{\text{MSE} + \frac{1}{12}}; \tag{11}$$

Peak SNR (PSNR)

$$\text{PSNR}_{(\text{dB})} = 10 \cdot \log_{10} \frac{g_{fs}^2}{\text{MSE} + \frac{1}{12}}; \tag{12}$$

Bruno Aiazzi, Luciano Alparone, Stefano Baronti,
Cinzia Lastri, and Leonardo Santurri

Maximum absolute distortion (MAD), or *peak error*, or L_∞,

$$\text{MAD} = \max_{i,j}\{|g(i,j) - \tilde{g}(i,j)|\}; \tag{13}$$

Percentage maximum absolute distortion (PMAD)

$$\text{PMAD} = \max_{i,j}\left\{\frac{|g(i,j) - \tilde{g}(i,j)|}{g(i,j)}\right\} \times 100. \tag{14}$$

In both (11) and (12) the MSE is incremented by the variance of the integer roundoff error, to handle the limit lossless case, when MSE=0. Thus, SNR and PSNR will be upper bounded by $10 \cdot \log_{10}(12 \cdot \bar{g}^2)$ and $10 \cdot \log_{10}(12 \cdot g_{fs}^2)$, respectively.

When multiband data are concerned, let $v_l \triangleq g_l(i,j)$, $l = 1, \cdots, L$ denote the lth component of the original multispectral pixel vector **v** and $\tilde{v}_l \triangleq \tilde{g}_l(i,j)$, $l = 1, \cdots, L$ its distorted version. Some of the radiometric distortion measurements (8)-(14) may be extended to vector data.

Average vector RMSE (VRMSE), or $L_1(L_2)$ (the innermost norm L_2 refers to vector space (l), the outer one to pixel space (i,j))

$$\text{VRMSE}_{\text{avg}} = \frac{1}{N}\sum_{i,j}\sqrt{\sum_l [g_l(i,j) - \tilde{g}_l(i,j)]^2}; \tag{15}$$

Peak VRMSE, or $L_\infty(L_2)$,

$$\text{VRMSE}_{\text{max}} = \max_{i,j}\sqrt{\sum_l [g_l(i,j) - \tilde{g}_l(i,j)]^2}; \tag{16}$$

$$\text{SNR} = 10 \cdot \log_{10}\frac{\sum_{i,j,l}g_l^2(i,j)}{\sum_{i,j,l}[g_l(i,j) - \tilde{g}_l(i,j)]^2}; \tag{17}$$

$$\text{PSNR} = 10 \cdot \log_{10}\frac{N \cdot L \cdot g_{fs}^2}{\sum_{i,j,l}[g_l(i,j) - \tilde{g}_l(i,j)]^2}; \tag{18}$$

MAD, or $L_\infty(L_\infty)$,

$$\text{MAD} = \max_{i,j,l}\{|g_l(i,j) - \tilde{g}_l(i,j)|\}; \tag{19}$$

PMAD

$$\text{PMAD} = \max_{i,j,l}\left\{\frac{|g_l(i,j) - \tilde{g}_l(i,j)|}{g_l(i,j)}\right\} \times 100. \tag{20}$$

In practice, (15) and (16) are respectively the average and maximum of the Euclidean norm of the distortion vector. SNR (17) is the extension of (11) to the 3D data cube. PSNR is the maximum SNR, given the full-scales of each vector component. MAD (19) is the maximum over the pixel set of the maximum absolute component of the distortion vector. PMAD (20) is the maximum percentage error over each vector component of the data cube.

Spectral Distortion Given two spectral vectors $\mathbf{v}$ and $\tilde{\mathbf{v}}$ both having L components, let $\mathbf{v} = \{v_1, v_2, \cdots, v_L\}$ be the original spectral pixel vector $v_l = g_l(i,j)$ and $\tilde{\mathbf{v}} = \{\tilde{v}_1, \tilde{v}_2, \cdots, \tilde{v}_L\}$ its distorted version obtained after lossy compression and decompression, i.e., $\tilde{v}_l = \tilde{g}_l(i,j)$. Analogously to the *radiometric* distortion measurements, *spectral* distortion measurement may be defined.

The spectral angle mapper (SAM) denotes the absolute value of the spectral angle between the couple of vectors:

$$\text{SAM}(\mathbf{v}, \tilde{\mathbf{v}}) \triangleq \arccos\left(\frac{<\mathbf{v}, \tilde{\mathbf{v}}>}{||\mathbf{v}||_2 \cdot ||\tilde{\mathbf{v}}||_2}\right) \tag{21}$$

in which $< \cdot, \cdot >$ stands for scalar product. SAM can be measured in either degrees or radians. Another measurement especially suitable for hyperspectral data (i.e., for data with large number of components) is the spectral information divergence (SID) [12] derived from information-theoretic concepts:

$$\text{SID}(\mathbf{v}, \tilde{\mathbf{v}}) = D(\mathbf{v}||\tilde{\mathbf{v}}) + D(\tilde{\mathbf{v}}||\mathbf{v}) \tag{22}$$

with $D(\mathbf{v}||\tilde{\mathbf{v}})$ being the Kullback-Leibler distance (KLD), or entropy divergence, or *discrimination* [11], defined as

$$D(\mathbf{v}||\tilde{\mathbf{v}}) \triangleq \sum_{l=1}^{L} p_l \log\left(\frac{p_l}{q_l}\right) \tag{23}$$

in which

$$p_l \triangleq \frac{v_l}{||\mathbf{v}||_1} \quad \text{and} \quad q_l \triangleq \frac{\tilde{v}_l}{||\tilde{\mathbf{v}}||_1} \tag{24}$$

In practice SID is equal to the symmetric KLD and can be compactly written as

$$\text{SID}(\mathbf{v}, \tilde{\mathbf{v}}) = \sum_{l=1}^{L} (p_l - q_l) \log\left(\frac{p_l}{q_l}\right) \tag{25}$$

which turns out to be symmetric, as one can easily verify. It can be proven as well that SID is always nonnegative, being zero iff. $p_l \equiv q_l$, $\forall l$, i.e., if $\mathbf{v}$ is parallel to $\tilde{\mathbf{v}}$. The measure unit of SID depends on the base of logarithm: *nat/vector* with natural logarithms and *bit/vector* with logarithms in base two.

Both SAM (21) and SID (25) may be either averaged on pixel vectors, or the maximum may be taken instead, as more representative of spectral quality.

Note that radiometric distortion does not necessarily imply spectral distortion. Conversely, spectral distortion is always accompanied by a radiometric distortion, that is minimal when the couple of vectors have either the same Euclidean length (L_2) for SAM, or the same city-block length (L_1), for SID.

4.2   Linear and Logarithmic Quantization

Linear quantization In order to achieve reduction in bit rate within the constraint of a near-lossless compression, prediction errors are quantized, with a quantization noise feedback loop embedded into the encoder, so that the current pixel prediction is formulated from the same "noisy" data that will be available at the decoder, as shown in Fig. 1(a). Prediction errors, $e(n) \triangleq g(n) - \hat{g}(n)$, may be linearly quantized with a step size Δ as $e_\Delta(n) = \text{round}[e(n)/\Delta]$ and delivered to the *context-coding* section, as shown in Fig. 1(a). The operation of inverse quantization, $\tilde{e}(i,j) = e_\Delta(i,j) \cdot \Delta$ introduces an error, whose variance and maximum modulus are $\Delta^2/12$ and $\lfloor \Delta/2 \rfloor$, respectively. Since the MSE distortion is a quadratic function of the Δ, an odd-valued step size yields a lower L_∞ distortion for a given L_2 than an even size does; thus, odd step sizes are preferred for near-lossless compression. The relationship between the target peak error, i.e., $\epsilon \in \mathbb{Z}^+$, and the step size to be used is $\Delta = 2\epsilon + 1$.

Logarithmic Quantization For the case of a relative-error bounded compression a rational version of prediction error must be envisaged. Let us define the *relative prediction error* (RPE) as ratio of original to predicted pixel value:

$$r(n) \triangleq \frac{g(n)}{\hat{g}(n)} \tag{26}$$

The *rational* nature of RPE, however, makes linear quantization unable to guarantee a strictly user-defined relative-error bounded performance.

Given a step size $\Delta \in \mathbb{R}$ ($\Delta > 0$, $\Delta \neq 1$), define direct and inverse *logarithmic* quantization (Log-Q) of $t \in \mathbb{R}$, $t > 0$, as

$$\mathcal{Q}_\Delta(t) \triangleq \text{round}\left[\log_\Delta(t)\right] = \text{round}\left[\log(t)/\log(\Delta)\right]$$

$$\mathcal{Q}_\Delta^{-1}(l) = \Delta^l \tag{27}$$

Applying (27) to (26) yields

$$\mathcal{Q}_\Delta[r(n)] = \text{round}\left[\frac{\log(g(n)) - \log(\hat{g}(n))}{\log \Delta}\right] \tag{28}$$

Hence, Log-Q of RPE is identical to Lin-Q of $\log(g(n)) - \log(\hat{g}(n))$ with a step size $\log \Delta$. If a Log-Q with a step size Δ is used to encode pixel RPE's (26), it can be proven that the ratio of original to decoded pixel value is strictly bounded around one

$$\min\left\{\sqrt{\Delta}, \frac{1}{\sqrt{\Delta}}\right\} \leq \frac{g(n)}{\tilde{g}(n)} \leq \max\left\{\sqrt{\Delta}, \frac{1}{\sqrt{\Delta}}\right\} \tag{29}$$

From (29) and (26) it stems that the percentage pixel distortion is upper bounded

$$PMAD = \max\left\{\sqrt{\Delta} - 1, 1 - \frac{1}{\sqrt{\Delta}}\right\} \times 100 \tag{30}$$

depending on whether $\Delta > 1$, or $0 < \Delta < 1$. Hence, the relationship between the target percentage peak error, ρ, and the step size will be, e.g., for $\Delta > 0$, $\Delta = (1 + \rho/100)^2$.

Quantized prediction errors are then arranged into activity classes based on the spatial *context*, which are entropy coded by means of arithmetic coding. The refined predictors are transmitted along with the label of each block and the set of thresholds defining the context classes for entropy coding.

5 Experimental Results

5.1 Data Set

The data set comprises four sequences of hyperspectral images collected in 1997 by the *Airborne Visible InfraRed Imaging Spectrometer* (AVIRIS), operated by NASA/JPL. The four test sites are *Cuprite Mine* and *Lunar Lake* in Nevada, *Moffett Field* and *Jasper Ridge* in California. All the sequences are constituted by 224 bands recorded at different wave-lengths in the range $380 \div 2500$ nm, with a nominal spectral separation between two bands of 10 nm.

Each raw sequence was acquired by the 12 *bit* analog-to-digital converter (ADC) with which the sensor was equipped in 1995, in place of the former 10-bit ADC. The raw data from the digital counter have been radiometrically calibrated by multiplying by a gain and adding an offset (both varying with wavelengths), and are expressed as radiance values, rounded to integers, and packed in a 16-bit wordlength, including a sign bit. The size of each hyperspectral image is 2048 rows × 614 columns × 224 bands × 2 bytes/sample for a total of $563,347,456$ bytes. Due to the huge data volume, only a subset of 256 rows per image, for a total of $70,418,432$ bytes per image has been compressed. The subsets of AVIRIS images will be referred to as: *Cuprite, Moffett Field, Jasper Ridge*, and *Lunar Lake*. Sample bands are displayed in Fig. 6.

The second spectrometer, covering the near-infrared (NIR) spectrum, was analyzed in a recent work by the authors [6]. It was found that the noise is somewhat correlated spectrally and across track, due to the "whisk-broom" scan mechanism, as well as to postprocessing.

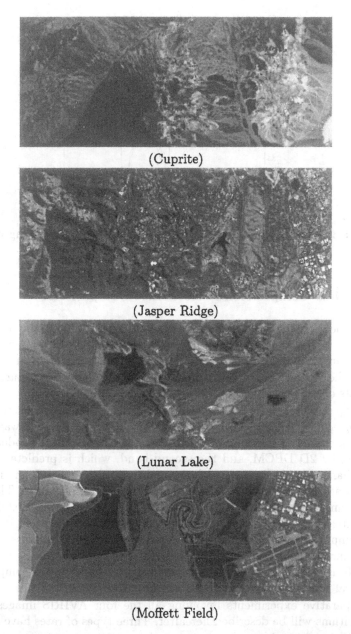

(Cuprite)

(Jasper Ridge)

(Lunar Lake)

(Moffett Field)

Figure 6: AVIRIS '97 hyperspectral images: 256 × 614 details used for tests

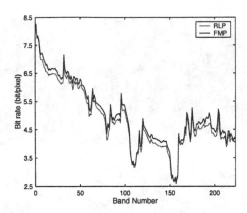

Figure 7: Bit-rates produced by FMP and RLP on *Cuprite* varying with band
number

5.2   Lossless Compression Performance Comparisons

The 256-lines subset from the 224 bands of *Cuprite* was reversibly compressed
by means of both the methods described. The resulting bit rates, in bit per pixel
per band, are shown in Fig. 7 for the FMP and RLP encoders. Here and in the
following the bit rates reported do include all coding overhead, in particular the
coefficients of predictors and block labels (for RLP only).

Work parameters have been selected for each encoder to exhibit comparable
processing times, regardless of the bit rate. 3D prediction is always carried
out from a couple of previous bands, except for the first band, coded in intra
mode, i.e., by 2D DPCM, and the second band, which is predicted from one
previous band only. As it appears, the two schemes, although different in the way
predictors are generated and used, are very similar in performances. The bit rate
profile against band number reflects the typical spectral energy distribution of
a desert area containing geological features. The performance of RLP cannot be
sensibly improved by increasing the number and length of predictors, because of
overhead increasing as well, mainly labels. The FMP encoder, being not labeled,
benefits from 12 predictors of length 24 for each band, with a computational
cost several times greater than that relative to the plot in Fig. 7.

Comparative experiments involving all the four AVIRIS images and the
two algorithms will be described hereafter. Three types of rates have been considered: first-order entropy, i.e., entropy of a stationary memoryless model of
prediction residues; context entropy, i.e., entropy of residues conditioned to the
surrounding causal spatial context; true bit rates on disk achieved by applying
the context-based arithmetic coding to residues.

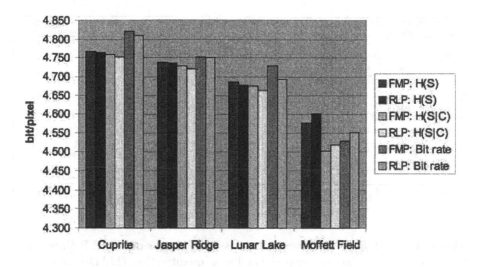

Figure 8: Average rates (in bit/pixel) produced by FMP and RLP on the four 1997 AVIRIS images: first-order entropy, context-conditioned entropy, and true bit-rate on disk of both schemes grouped by test image

Fig. 8 reports average rates (in bit/pixel) produced by FMP and RLP on the four test AVIRIS images. Rates are grouped by test image to highlight differences between the two algorithms as well as possible benefits of context modeling for entropy coding. There is a discrepancy of about five hundredths of bit between theoretical and true bit rates, which is due to imperfect convergence of the adaptive arithmetic encoders, as many as are the context classes. This effect is missing in the case of absence of context modelling, whose bit rates on disk differ from the theoretical entropy by less than one hundredth of bit. Nevertheless, it appears that the advantages of context modelling before entropy coding are negligible for the case of 3D DPCM coding of hyperspectral bands. The explanation is obvious when one considers that context modelling takes advantages for entropy coding of the residual correlation and especially of the non-stationarity of residues [30]. Both the methods attain a decorrelation performance close to yield stationary uncorrelated residues; hence, the theoretical bounds given by the entropy rate of the source are likely to have been approached. It is easily noticed that *Cuprite* is the least compressible out of the four images; *Moffett Field* the most. The difference between the two boundary cases, however, is less than 5%, mainly because all the data have been gathered by the same sensor and processed, i.e., calibrated, in the same manner.

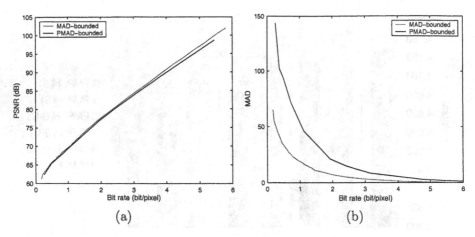

Figure 9: Band # 48 of *Cuprite* compressed by means of 3D RLP (interband) from two previous bands, with either linear quantization (MAD-bounded), or logarithmic quantization (PMAD-bounded): (a) PSNR vs. bit rate; (b) MAD vs. bit rate

It is worth noticing that RLP outperforms FMP on the first three images; FMP is better than RLP on the last one. On *Jasper Ridge* the two methods are almost identical, even if the performances shown in Fig. 8 have been obtained by stressing the setup parameters of FMP. Performances of RLP quickly saturate; so, there is no need of stressing its parameters.

The conclusion that RLP wins the comparison is not surprising, notwithstanding 2D FMP is superior to 2D RLP [16]. In fact RLP is particularly effective for little noisy data (the X-ray image reported in [16]), as hyperspectral data are. Conversely, FMP seems to take advantage from the intrinsical noisiness of the data.

5.3   Near-Lossless Compression Performance Comparisons

Rate-distortion (RD) plots are reported in Fig. 9(a) for the RLP scheme operating with $M = 12$ predictors of length 24 coefficients spanning two previous bands, besides the current one. Due to the sign bit, the full scale g_{fs} in (12) was set equal to $2^{15}-1 = 32767$ instead of 65535, since negative values possibly introduced by calibration never occur in the sample band. Hence, the PSNR attains a value of $10 \cdot \log_{10}(12 \cdot g_{fs}^2) \approx 102 \; dB$, due to integer roundoff noise only, when the reversibility is reached. Quantization was either linear, for MAD-constrained compression, or logarithmic, for PMAD-constrained compression. According to RD theory [11], when a uniform threshold quantizer (UTQ) is employed, all the

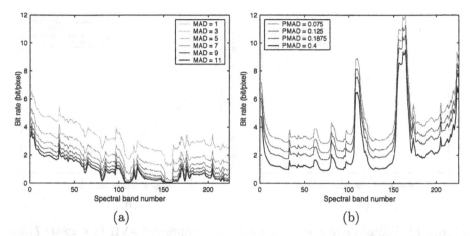

Figure 10: Bit rates produced by 3D RLP on the *Cuprite* sequence of bands: (a) linear quantization to yield user-defined MAD values; (b) logarithmic quantization to yield user-defined PMAD values

SNR/PSNR-bit rate plots are straight lines with slope $\approx$ 6 dB/bit, for rates larger than, say, 1 bit/pel. This does not happen for logarithmic quantization, which loses about 1 dB and deviates from the theoretical line as the lossless case is approached.

The near-lossless performance is shown in the peak error vs. bit rate plots of Fig. 9(b). Values of MAD are extremely large, because the full scale is 32767, instead of 255, typical of 8-bit data. The overall trends are in accordance with those of PSNR; however, the logarithmic quantizer attains a performance much poorer than that of the UTQ.

All bands have been compressed in both MAD-constrained mode (linear quantization) and PMAD constrained mode (logarithmic quantization). Bit rates varying with band number, together with the related distortion parameters are shown in Fig. 10. The bit rate plots follow similar trends varying with the amount of distortion, but quite different trends for the two types of distortion (i.e., either MAD or PMAD). For example, around the water vapor absorption wavelengths ($\approx$ Band 80) the MAD-bounded plots exhibit pronounced valleys, that can be explained because the intrinsic SNR of the data becomes lower; thus the linear quantizer dramatically abates the *noisy* prediction errors. On the other hand the PMAD-bounded encoder tends to quantize the noisy residuals more finely when the signal is lower. Therefore bit rate peaks are generated instead of valleys. More generally speaking, bit rate peaks from the PMAD-bounded encoder are associated with low responses from the spectrom-

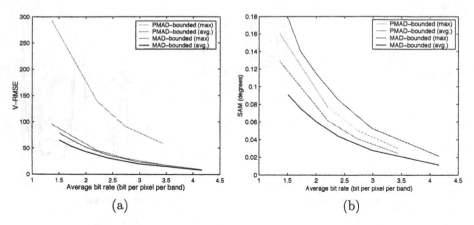

(a)   (b)

Figure 11: Vector distortions vs bit rate for compressed AVIRIS *Cuprite Mine '97* data. Radiometric distortion (a) VRMSE; spectral distortion (b) SAM

eter. This explains why the bit rate plots of Fig. 10(b) never fall below one bit per pixel per band.

Some of the radiometric distortion measures defined in Subsect. 4.1 have been calculated on the distorted hyperspectral pixel vectors achieved by decompressing the bit streams generated by the near-lossless RLP encoder, both MAD- and PMAD-bounded. VRMSEs of the vector data, both *average* (15) and *maximum* (16), are plotted in Fig. 11(a) as a function of the bit rate from the encoder.

The MAD-bounded encoder obviously minimizes both the average and maximum of VRMSE, that is the Euclidean norm of the pixel error vector. A further advantage is that average and maximum VRMSE are very close to each other for all bit rates. The PMAD-bounded encoder is somewhat poorer: average VRMSE is comparable with that of the former, but peak VRMSE is far larger, due to the high-signal components that are coarsely quantized in order to minimize PMAD. Trivial results, not reported in the plots, are that MAD of the data cube (19) is exactly equal to the desired value, whereas the PMAD, being unconstrained, is higher. Symmetric results have been found by measuring PMAD on MAD-bounded and PMAD-bounded decoded data.

As far as *radiometric* distortion is concerned, results are not surprising. Radiometric distortions measured on vectors are straightforwardly derived from those measured on scalar pixel values. The introduction of such *spectral* measurements as SAM (21) and SID (25) may overcome the rationale of *distortion*, as established in the signal/image processing community. Fig. 11(b) shows spectral distortions between original and decompressed hyperspectral pixel vectors. The PMAD-bounded algorithm yields plots that lie in the middle between the corresponding ones produced by the MAD-bounded algorithm and are very close to each other too. Since the *maximum* SAM is a better clue of spectral quality of the decoded data than the *average SAM* may be, a likely conclusion would be that PMAD-bounded compression optimizes the *spectral* quality of the data, while MAD-bounded is superior in terms of *radiometric* quality. Furthermore, the maximum SAM introduced by the P-MAD bounded logarithmic quantizer is lower than 0.2 degrees for an average rate of 1 bit/pixel per vector component, i.e., CR=16. Extensive results of spectral discrimination from compressed hyperspectral data have demonstrated that a SAM distortion lower than 0.5 degrees has negligible impact on the capability of automated classifiers of identifying spectral signatures of materials [51].

6 Conclusions

This work has demonstrated the potential usefulness of *near-lossless* compression, i.e., with bounded pixel error, either *absolute* or *relative*, for data produced by imaging spectrometers. Unlike lossless compression achieving typical CRs between three and four, near-lossless compression can be adjusted to allow a *virtually lossless* compression with CR equal to ten, or more, for hyperspectral data. The main reason of that is the *quantization noise-shaping* effect achieved by L_∞-bounded image encoders, like those based on DPCM.

The term *virtually-lossless* compression, which was briefly explained in the introduction, indicates that the distortion introduced by compression should appear as an additional amount of noise, being uncorrelated and having space-invariant first order statistics such that the overall probability density function (PDF) of the noise corrupting the decompressed data, i.e., intrinsic noise plus compression-induced noise, matches the noise PDF of the original data as much as possible. This requirement is trivially fulfilled if compression is lossless, but may also hold if the difference between uncompressed and decompressed data exhibits a peaked and narrow PDF without tails, as it happens for near-lossless techniques, whenever the user defined peak error is sufficiently smaller than the standard deviation of the background noise. Therefore, noise modeling and estimation from the uncompressed data becomes a major task to accomplish a virtually-lossless compression [52].

This analysis was recently carried out by the authors on remote-sensing multispectral image data [8, 53]. It was found that for some spectral bands in the visible wavelengths (green and red) the estimated standard deviation of the noise is lower than one (0.70 and 0.61, respectively); hence, compression of integer valued data with peak error $\epsilon = 1$ (and quantization step size $\Delta = 2\epsilon + 1 = 3$) would yield an RMSE distortion equal to $\sqrt{2/3} \approx 0.82$, slightly greater than the RMS value of the intrinsic noise, which would be more than doubled after decompression. In that case, virtually-lossless compression would better coincide with lossless compression.

The main result of the present analysis concerning hyperspectral data compression is that, for a given CR, near-lossless methods, either MAD- or PMAD-constrained, are more suitable for preserving the spectral discrimination capability among pixel vectors, which is the principal source of spectral information. Therefore, whenever a strictly lossless compression is not practicable, near-lossless compression is recommended in such application where spectral quality is a crucial point. Furthermore, since the maximum reconstruction error is defined by the user before compression, whenever higher CR's are required, the loss of performance expected on application tasks can be accurately modeled and predicted.

Acknowledgments

This work has been carried out under grants of the *Italian Space Agency* (ASI).

References

[1] Rao, K.K., Hwang, J.J.: Techniques and Standards for Image, Video, and Audio Coding. Prentice Hall, Engl. Cliffs, NJ (1996)

[2] Taubman, D.S., Marcellin, M.W.: JPEG2000: Image compression fundamentals, standards and practice. Kluwer Academic Publishers, Dordrecht, The Netherlands (2001)

[3] Vaughn, V.D., Wilkinson, T.S.: System considerations for multispectral image compression design. IEEE Signal Processing Magazine **12** (1995) 19–31

[4] ISO TC 20/SC 13/ICS 49.140: 15887-2000: Space data and information transfer systems – Data systems – Lossless data compression. (12-10-2000)

[5] Roger, R.E., Arnold, J.F.: Reversible image compression bounded by noise. IEEE Trans. Geosci. Remote Sensing **32** (1994) 19–24

[6] Aiazzi, B., Alparone, L., Barducci, A., Baronti, S., Pippi, I.: Information-theoretic assessment of sampled hyperspectral imagers. IEEE Trans. Geosci. Remote Sensing **39** (2001) 1447–1458

[7] Chen, K., Ramabadran, T.V.: Near-lossless compression of medical images through entropy-coded DPCM. IEEE Trans. Medical Imaging **13** (1994) 538–548

[8] Aiazzi, B., Alparone, L., Baronti, S.: Near-lossless compression of 3-D optical data. IEEE Trans. Geosci. Remote Sensing **39** (2001) 2547–2557

[9] Aiazzi, B., Alparone, L., Baronti, S., Chirò, G., Lotti, F., Moroni, M.: A pyramid-based error-bounded encoder: An evaluation on X-ray chest images. Signal Processing **59** (1997) 173–187

[10] Ryan, M.J., Arnold, J.F.: Lossy compression of hyperspectral data using vector quantization. Remote Sens. Environ. **61** (1997) 419–436

[11] Jayant, N.S., Noll, P.: Digital Coding of Waveforms: Principles and Applications to Speech and Video. Prentice Hall, Englewood Cliffs, NJ (1984)

[12] Chang, C.I.: An information-theoretic approach to spectral variability, similarity, and discrimination for hyperspectral image analysis. IEEE Trans. Inform. Theory **46** (2000) 1927–1932

[13] Pennebaker, W.B., Mitchell, J.L.: JPEG: Still Image Compression Standard. Van Nostrand Reinhold, New York (1993)

[14] Weinberger, M.J., Seroussi, G., Sapiro, G.: The LOCO-I lossless image compression algorithm: principles and standardization into JPEG-LS. IEEE Trans. Image Processing **9** (2000) 1309–1324

[15] Wu, X., Memon, N.: Context-based, adaptive, lossless image coding. IEEE Trans. Commun. **45** (1997) 437–444

[16] Aiazzi, B., Alparone, L., Baronti, S.: Fuzzy logic-based matching pursuits for lossless predictive coding of still images. IEEE Trans. Fuzzy Systems **10** (2002) 473–483

[17] Matsuda, I., Mori, H., Itoh, S.: Lossless coding of still images using minimum-rate predictors. In: Proc. IEEE Int. Conf. on Image Processing. Volume I/III. (2000) 132–135

[18] Aiazzi, B., Alparone, L., Baronti, S.: A reduced Laplacian pyramid for lossless and progressive image communication. IEEE Trans. Commun. **44** (1996) 18–22

[19] Said, A., Pearlman, W.A.: An image multiresolution representation for lossless and lossy compression. IEEE Trans. Image Processing **5** (1996) 1303–1310

[20] Abrardo, A., Alparone, L., Bartolini, F.: Encoding-interleaved hierarchical interpolation for lossless image compression. Signal Processing **56** (1997) 321–328

[21] Reichel, J., Menegaz, G., Nadenau, M.J., Kunt, M.: Integer wavelet transform for embedded lossy to lossless image compression. IEEE Trans. Image Processing **10** (2001) 383–392

[22] Benazza-Benyahia, A., Pesquet, J.C., Hamdi, M.: Vector-lifting schemes for lossless coding and progressive archival of multispectral images. IEEE Trans. Geosci. Remote Sensing **40** (2002) 2011–2024

[23] Alecu, A., Munteanu, A., Cornelis, J., Dewitte, S., Schelkens, P.: On the optimality of embedded deadzone scalar-quantizers for wavelet-based L-infinite-constrained image coding. IEEE Signal Processing Lett. **11** (2004) 367–370

[24] Aiazzi, B., Alparone, L., Baronti, S., Lotti, F.: Lossless image compression by quantization feedback in a content-driven enhanced Laplacian pyramid. IEEE Trans. Image Processing **6** (1997) 831–843

[25] Golchin, F., Paliwal, K.K.: Classified adaptive prediction and entropy coding for lossless coding of images. In: Proc. IEEE Int. Conf. on Image Processing. Volume III/III. (1997) 110–113

[26] Aiazzi, B., Alparone, L., Baronti, S.: Near-lossless image compression by relaxation-labelled prediction. Signal Processing **82** (2002) 1619–1631

[27] Deng, G., Ye, H., Cahill, L.W.: Adaptive combination of linear predictors for lossless image compression. IEE Proc.-Sci. Meas. Technol. **147** (2000) 414–419

[28] Carpentieri, B., Weinberger, M.J., Seroussi, G.: Lossless compression of continuous-tone images. Proc. of the IEEE **88** (2000) 1797–1809

[29] Ramabadran, T.V., Chen, K.: The use of contextual information in the reversible compression of medical images. IEEE Trans. Medical Imaging **11** (1992) 185–195

[30] Aiazzi, B., Alparone, L., Baronti, S.: Context modeling for near-lossless image coding. IEEE Signal Processing Lett. **9** (2002) 77–80

[31] Wu, X., Bao, P.: L_∞ constrained high-fidelity image compression via adaptive context modeling. IEEE Trans. Image Processing **9** (2000) 536–542

[32] Witten, I.H., Neal, R.M., Cleary, J.G.: Arithmetic coding for data compression. Commun. ACM **30** (1987) 520–540

[33] Rice, R.F., Plaunt, J.R.: Adaptive variable-length coding for efficient compression of spacecraft television data. IEEE Trans. Commun. Technol. **COM-19** (1971) 889–897

[34] Weinberger, M.J., Rissanen, J.J., Arps, R.B.: Applications of universal context modeling to lossless compression of gray-scale images. IEEE Trans. Image Processing **5** (1996) 575–586

[35] Wang, J., Zhang, K., Tang, S.: Spectral and spatial decorrelation of Landsat-TM data for lossless compression. IEEE Trans. Geosci. Remote Sensing **33** (1995) 1277–1285

[36] Roger, R.E., Cavenor, M.C.: Lossless compression of AVIRIS images. IEEE Trans. Image Processing **5** (1996) 713–719

[37] Tate, S.R.: Band ordering in lossless compression of multispectral images. IEEE Trans. Comput. **46** (1997) 477–483

[38] Rao, A.K., Bhargava, S.: Multispectral data compression using bidirectional interband prediction. IEEE Trans. Geosci. Remote Sensing **34** (1996) 385–397

[39] Mielikainen, J., Toivanen, P., Kaarna, A.: Linear prediction in lossless compression of hyperspectral images. J. Optical Engin. **42** (2003) 1013–1017

[40] Mielikainen, J., Toivanen, P.: Clustered DPCM for the lossless compression of hyperspectral images. IEEE Trans. Geosci. Remote Sensing **41** (2003) 2943–2946

[41] Wu, X., Memon, N.: Context-based lossless interband compression–Extending CALIC. IEEE Trans. Image Processing **9** (2000) 994–1001

[42] Magli, E., Olmo, G., Quacchio, E.: Optimized onboard lossless and near-lossless compression of hyperspectral data using CALIC. IEEE Geosci. Remote Sensing Lett. **1** (2004) 21–25

[43] Aiazzi, B., Alparone, L., Baronti, S., Santurri, L.: Near-lossless compression of multi/hyperspectral images based on a fuzzy-matching-pursuits interband prediction. In Serpico, S.B., ed.: Image and Signal Processing for Remote Sensing VII. Volume 4541. (2002) 252–263

[44] Aiazzi, B., Alba, P., Alparone, L., Baronti, S.: Lossless compression of multi/hyper-spectral imagery based on a 3-D fuzzy prediction. IEEE Trans. Geosci. Remote Sensing **37** (1999) 2287–2294

[45] Rizzo, F., Carpentieri, B., Motta, G., Storer, J.A.: Low-complexity lossless compression of hyperspectral imagery via linear prediction. IEEE Signal Processing Lett. **12** (2005) 138–141

[46] Mallat, S., Zhang, Z.: Matching pursuits with time-frequency dictionaries. IEEE Trans. Signal Processing **41** (1993) 3397–3415

[47] Neff, R., Zakhor, A.: Very low bit-rate video coding based on matching pursuits. IEEE Trans. Circuits Syst. Video Technol. **7** (1997) 158–171

[48] Baraldi, A., Blonda, P.: A survey of fuzzy clustering algorithms for pattern recognition–Parts I and II. IEEE Trans. Syst. Man Cybern.–B **29** (1999) 778–800

[49] Bezdek, J.C.: Pattern Recognition with Fuzzy Objective Function Algorithm. Plenum Press, New York (1981)

[50] Ke, L., Marcellin, M.W.: Near-lossless image compression: minimum entropy, constrained-error DPCM. IEEE Trans. Image Processing **7** (1998) 225–228

[51] Keshava, N.: Distance metrics and band selection in hyperspectral processing with applications to material identification and spectral libraries. IEEE Trans. Geosci. Remote Sensing **42** (2004) 1552–1565

[52] Aiazzi, B., Alparone, L., Barducci, A., Baronti, S., Marcoionni, P., Pippi, I., Selva, M.: Noise modelling and estimation of hyperspectral data from airborne imaging spectrometers. Annals of Geophysics **48** (2005) in press

[53] Aiazzi, B., Alparone, L., Barducci, A., Baronti, S., Pippi, I.: Estimating noise and information of multispectral imagery. J. Optical Engin. **41** (2002) 656–668

Joint Classification and Compression of Hyperspectral Images

Grégoire MERCIER* and Marc LENNON[†]

* GET - ENST Bretagne, dpt ITI,
CNRS FRE 2658 TAMCIC, team TIME.
Technopole Brest-Iroise, CS 83818; 29238 Brest cedex - France
Email: gregoire.mercier@enst-bretagne.fr

[†] SAS ActiMar
24 Quai de la Douane, 29200 Brest - France
Email: marc.lennon@actimar.fr

I. INTRODUCTION

In this chapter, the problem of compressing hyperspectral images using a classification point of view is addressed. The goal is to compress with loss a hyperspectral data cube in order to obtain interesting compression ratio with the constraint to be near lossless from a classification point of view.

We focus the analysis on three strategies for hyperspectral image classification: the first with a physical meaning, the second based on spectral unmixing and the last as a hard-classifier. From a compression point of view, these strategies may be seen as three designs of Vector Quantization (VQ) as: a VQ with a particular distortion measure, a product code VQ and a Classified VQ.

Joint compression and classification VQ does not optimize distortion-rate constraint but minimizes the mis-classification rate. We present typical example of oil slick detection and characterization in an operational use. Airborne hyperspectral images may be compressed at 70 : 1 while still remaining of sufficient quality for operational monitoring. In fact, this kind of compression optimizes the transmission delay and decision making constraint.

There are applications for lossless compression, that allow data transmission and storage without distortion so that no data is discarded before it reaches the end-user. Nevertheless, lossy compression may be considered once is known what images have been acquired for. Then, on the one hand, lossy compression can achieve very high compression ratio, and on the other hand, significant information — essential for image interpretation — is given by the context.

In hyperspectral data processing, classification procedures are mainly interested in the spectral information instead of the spatial. Also, efficient tools, that may characterize texture from a hyperspectral point of view, still have to be defined! Spectral signature remains the main concept as input of classification procedure. From target detection, from land-use application, from precision agriculture topics point of view, the process is based on the information yielded by spectral signatures.

When the compression of a hyperspectral data cube intends to perform high compression ratio, the induced distortion may be hidden by considering tolerance of classification procedures. Then, a distortion measure may replace the widely used Mean Square Error and be carefully defined taking into consideration the classification point of view.

Several classification strategies are studied in order to understand how information is processed. Then a compression algorithm that follows the same consideration on spectral signatures is proposed.

II. Classification Point of view

Hyperspectral image analysis is essentially achieved by spectral signature analysis. Each type of ground is characterized by its spectral signature, moreover similar pieces of ground have similar spectral response. The relationship between type of ground and spectral response means that a hyperspectral image can be considered as a group of reflectance vectors. Thus, in order to detect a known type of ground in a hyperspectral image, it is relevant to find its spectral signature in the image.

To perform classification or target detection, several algorithms may be used. We propose to take into consideration 3 different points of view:

- Spectral Angle Mapper (SAM) to introduce physical meaning,
- Spectral Unmixing,
- Support Vector Machines (SVM) as a hard-classifier,

for their ability to be integrated into a compression scheme.

A. Spectral Angle Mapper

The SAM algorithm is a spectral classification algorithm that detects spectral signatures close to a given input, according to a threshold value and a distance measure, while spectral signatures are considered as vectors of dimension N (N being the number of spectral bands in the image). The spectral angle is more appropriate for spectral signature compression since it takes into consideration the shape of the spectra instead of the overall energy.

The spectral angle (SA) between two spectral signatures x and y is defined by:

$$\text{SA}(x, y) = \arccos\left(\frac{< x, y >}{\|x\|\,\|y\|}\right), \tag{1}$$

where $< \cdot, \cdot >$ is the dot-product and $\|\cdot\|$ the norm: $< x, y >= \sum_{n=1}^{N} x(n)y(n)$ and $\|x\| = \sqrt{\sum_{n=1}^{N} x(n)^2}$.

It is of interest to take a geometrical point of view to interpret the value of the spectral angle from one spectral signature x and a given threshold, and to compare with the quadratic distance that is defined by:

$$d_{\mathcal{L}^2}(x, y) = \|x - y\|. \tag{2}$$

Figure 1 shows two wavelength of x (components i and j from $\{1, \ldots, N\}$). From a geometrical point of view, it appears that the spectral angle may be

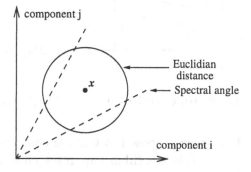

Figure 1: Comparison between spectral angle and Euclidian distance.

view as a cone while the Euclidian distance, as a ball of center x.

Then, the classification procedure may be written as follows.

Let $\{y_1, y_2, \ldots, y_L\}$ be a set of spectral signatures characterizing class centers,

$$\forall x, \qquad x \approx y_\ell \qquad \text{if } \forall k \neq \ell \quad \text{SA}(x, y_\ell) \leqslant \text{SA}(x, y_k), \tag{3}$$

which seems so closely to a vector quantization point of view associated to a spectral angle distortion measure!

B. Spectral Unmixing

Due to the spatial resolution of hyperspectral sensors (from meter to tens of meters) it is reasonnable to consider that each pixel is constituted by several components. Then, each pixel may be characterized by a mixture of *endmembers* (*e*). When considering a linear mixture of endmembers, each spectral signature x may be decomposed into:

$$x = \sum_{\ell=0}^{L} \omega_\ell e_\ell + n, \quad \text{with} \quad \forall \ell, \omega_\ell \geqslant 0 \text{ and } \sum_{\ell=0}^{L} \omega_\ell = 1. \quad (4)$$

where ω_ℓ is the weight of endmember e_ℓ and n a random noise.

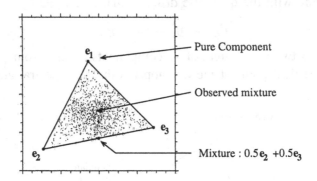

Figure 2:   Linear mixture model for observed spectral signatures.

Several techniques have been proposed to find the endmembers:

1) Pixel Purity Index: This algorithm requires a known number of endmembers and will find spectral signatures from the input hyperspectral data cube that maximize a purity criteria [1].

In the N-D space, a line is generated randomly and each observation x is projected onto this line. The purity index is incremented for the x when their projections are located at the extremum of the overall projected point. This process is iterated several times with randomly generated lines.

2) N-FindR: Instead of considering lines, N-FindR maximizes the volume of a simplex. First, the simplex is set by choosing vertex randomly from the observations. Then, each vertex is subtituted one by one, by all the spectral signature of the image. The vertex is replaced by the spectral signature that maximizes the volume of the simplex [2].

3) Iterative Error Analysis: At each step, a spectral signature from the hyperspectral data cube is considered as new endmember when it induces the maximum error from its characterization with the endmembers already founded. The algorithm begins with the spectral signature farest from the mean value of the image and stops when the error of unmixing remains below a threshold [3].

4) Automated Morphological Endmember Extraction: The process of endmembers estimation is performed locally through sliding windows of increasing size. A *"purity indice"* is defined by using the spectral angle between the local mean spectrum and each pixel, normalized by the farest (d_+) and the closest (d_-) indice [4].

5) Convex Cone Analysis: By considering irradiance or reflectance observation as vectors of positive components, the overall data set may be characterized by a convex cone into a N-D space. The eigen vectors of the correlation matrix are used to estimate endmembers as a linear combination of the eigen vectors associated to the highest values [5].

6) Independant Component Analysis: While all the previous methods are mostly geometrical, and consider endmembers as part of observations, ICA gives endmembers by means of independence criterium. The drawback of this statistical point of view is that independent *"sources"* may not correspond to any physical meaning [6].

Once the endmembers e_ℓ have been estimated, each spectral signature of the image is decomposed into components ω_ℓ of the basis formed by those endmembers in the N-D space. A least square method gives the components ω_ℓ of the spectral signatures into this basis which is not orthogonal.

All those unmixing methods may substitute any observation x to a mixture of endmembers so that:

$$\forall x, \qquad x = \sum_{\ell=1}^{L} \omega_\ell\, e_\ell, \tag{5}$$

which may be though of as a product code vector quantizer!

C. Support Vector Machines

Support Vector Machines (SVM) [7] have been recently introduced in the statistical learning theory domain [8] for regression and classification problems, and applied to the classification of multispectral [9] and hyperspectral [10–12] images. The main advantage of this technique is to perform good classification with a limited number of training sample. Furthermore, Kernel methods are of interest in hypespectral processing for their ability to prevent the Hughes'phenomenon [13]. In fact, usual classification methods, such as the Maximum Likelihood, are limited by the estimation of the covariance matrix of a hyperspectral data cube in a space of high dimension (as high as the number of spectral bands) with a limited number of training samples.

The complete mathematical formulation of SVM can be found in [7, 8]. We just give a brief description of the classification process.

1) SVM basis: A two-class classification problem can be stated the following way: T_s training sample are available and can be represented by the set of pairs $\{(y_i, x_i), i = 1, 2, \ldots, T_s\}$ with y_i a class label of value ± 1 and $x_i \in \mathbb{R}^N$ feature vector with N components. The classifier is represented by the function $f(x; \alpha) \longrightarrow y$, α being the parameters of the classifier.

The SVM method consist in finding the optimum separating hyperplane so that:

1) Samples with labels $y = \pm 1$ are located on each side of the hyperplane;
2) The distance of the closest vectors to the hyperplane in each side is maximum. These closest vectors are called support vectors and the distance is the optimal margin (see Fig. 3-a-).

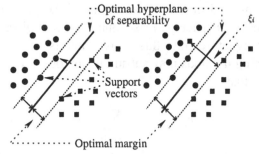

(a) Linear separability   (b) Non-linear separability

Figure 3: SVM classifier.

The hyperplane is defined by $< w, x > + b = 0$ where (w, b) are the parameters of the hyperplane. The vectors that are not on this hyperplane lead to $< w, x > + b \geqslant 0$ and allow the classifier to be defined as: $f(x; \alpha) = \text{sgn}\,(< w, x > + b)$. The support vectors lie on two hyperplanes, which are parallel to the optimal hyperplane, of equation: $< w, x > + b = \pm 1$.

The maximization of the margin with the equations of the two support vector hyperplanes leads to the following constrained optimization problem:

$$\min\left\{\tfrac{1}{2}\|w\|^2\right\} \text{ with } y_i\,(< w, x > + b) \geqslant 1,\ i = 1, \ldots, N. \qquad (6)$$

2) Non-linear separability: If the training samples are not linearly separable (see Fig. 3-b-), a regularization parameter C and error variables ε_i are introduced in (6) in order to reduce the weightening of misclassified vectors. This optimization problem can be solved using Lagrange multipliers and then becomes:

$$\begin{cases} \min\left\{\displaystyle\sum_{i=1}^{T_s}\lambda_i - \tfrac{1}{2}\sum_{i,j=1}^{T_s}\lambda_i\lambda_j\,y_iy_j < x_i, x_j >\right\}, \\[2mm] 0 \leqslant \lambda_i \leqslant C, \quad \forall i = 1, 2, \ldots, T_s, \\[2mm] \displaystyle\sum_{i=1}^{T_s}\lambda_i y_i = 0, \quad \forall i = 1, 2, \ldots, T_s, \end{cases} \qquad (7)$$

where the λ_i are the Lagrangian multipliers and are non-zero only for the support vectors. Thus, hyperplane parameters (w, b) and the classifier function $f\,(x; w, b)$ can be computed by optimization process.

3) Non-linear classifier with kernels: SVM can be generalized to compute nonlinear decision surfaces in $\mathbb{R}^n$. The method consists in projecting the data into a higher dimension space where they are becoming linearly separable. SVM, applied in this space, lead to the determination of nonlinear surfaces in the original space. In fact, the projection can be simulated using a kernel method.

It can be noticed that only dot products $< x_i, x_j >$ are involved in (7). If $x \in \mathbb{R}^N$ is projected into a higher-dimension space $\mathcal{H}$ with a non-linear function $\Phi : \mathbb{R}^N \longrightarrow \mathcal{H}$, then $< x_i, x_j >$ is replaced by $< \Phi\,(x_i), \Phi\,(x_j) >$ into the feature space. The kernel function $K(x_i, x_j) = < \Phi\,(x_i), \Phi\,(x_j) >$ is introduced in (7) and do not require explicit knowledge of $\Phi(\cdot)$ anymore.

Then, the non-linear classifier can be expressed as:

$$f(x; \alpha) = \text{sgn}\left(\sum_{i=1}^{N_s}\lambda_i\,y_i\,K(s_i, x) + b\right), \qquad (8)$$

where the s_i are the N_S support vectors.

Every function $K(\cdot, \cdot)$ that satisfies Mercer's conditions may be considered as an eligible kernel. The Mercer's conditions state that:

$$\forall g(\cdot) \in \mathcal{L}^2(\mathbb{R}^N) \quad \text{so that} \quad \int g(x)^2 dx \text{ is finite,}$$

$$\text{if} \quad \int K(x, y) \, g(x) \, g(y) \, dx dy \geqslant 0,$$

$$\text{then} \quad K(\cdot, \cdot) \quad \text{is an eligible kernel.} \quad (9)$$

A great number of kernels exist and it is difficult to explain their individual characteristics. As shown in [14], two kinds of kernels may be defined:

- *Global kernels.* Samples that are far away from each others still have an influence on the kernel value. All kernels based on the dot-product are global:

$$\text{Linear: } K(x, x_i) = <x, x_i>,$$

$$\text{Polynomial: } K(x, x_i) = (<x, x_i> + 1)^p,$$

$$\text{Sigmoid: } K(x, x_i) = \tanh(<x, x_i> + 1).$$

- *Local kernels.* Only the data that are close or in the proximity of each others have an influence on the kernel values. Basically, all kernels that are based on a distance function are local kernels. Examples of typical local kernels are:

$$\text{Radial basis: } K(x, x_i) = \exp\left(-\|x - x_i\|^2\right),$$

$$\text{KMOD: } K(x, x_i) = \exp\left(\frac{1}{1 + \|x - x_i\|^2}\right) - 1,$$

$$\text{Inverse multiquadric: } K(x, x_i) = \frac{1}{\sqrt{(\|x - x_i\|^2 + 1)}}.$$

The local kernels are based on a quadratic distance evaluation between two samples. In order to fit hyperspectral point of view, it is of interest to consider new criteria that take into consideration spectral signature concept [15]. Spectral angle $SA(x, x_i)$ is defined in order to measure the spectral difference between x and x_i while being robust to differences of the overall energy (*e.g.* illumination, shadows...). Then, the *spectral kernel* is defined as:

$$K(x, x_i) = \exp\left(-SA(x, x_i)\right) = \exp\left(-\arccos\left(\frac{<x, x_i>}{\|x\| \|x_i\|}\right)\right).$$

The local kernels listed earlier that are based on quatratic distance (Radial basis function, KMOD, Inverse multiquadric) may be defined with SA distance. Since $|\mathrm{SA}(x, x_i)|$ is bounded and positive, spectral angle based kernels satisfy the Mercer's conditions (9).

SVM classifications, shown on section IV, are based on a mixture of kernels defined by:

$$K(x, x_i) = s \exp\left(-\|x - x_i\|^2\right) + (1-s) \exp\left(-\mathrm{SA}(x, x_i)\right), \qquad 0 < s < 1. \tag{10}$$

4) Multiple class separation: SVM are designed to solve two-class problems. Two approaches can be used for a M-class problem:

- so called *one against all*: M classifiers are iteratively applied on each class against all the others.
- so called *one against one*: $\frac{M(M-1)}{2}$ classifiers are applied on each pair of classes, the most often computed label is kept for each vector.

We have used the second approach, although needing more SVM to be applied, that allows the computing time to be decreased because the complexity of the algorithm strongly depends on the number of training samples.

Lets have a look at the hyperplane separations induced by several SVM to perform multiple class separation (Fig. 4). With compression in mind, it is easy to think about Voronoi cells defined by the hyperplanes. Then SVM can be used for the design of vector quantization for compressing spectral signatures.

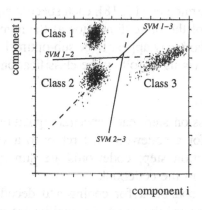

Figure 4: Multiple class separation with "one against one" SVMs.

III. Compression Point of View

In order to adopt the same strategy as the classification algorithms and to keep the physical meaning of each spectral signature into the compressed code, it appears that the Vector Quantization (VQ) strategy is the most appropriate [16]. As we have seen in the previous section, it is possible to link classification strategy (and its care of spectral signature) to a vector quantization associated to a distortion mesure. Then, the compression strategy is based on the VQ of each spectral signature (pixels of the image). This strategy could be called spectral quantization, as it is mentioned in Fig. 5. On

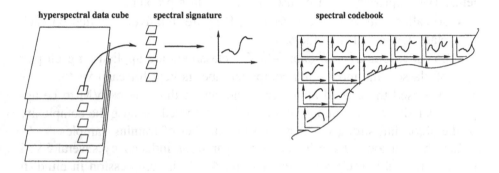

Figure 5:   Spectral Quantization.

the contrary of some strategies [17, 18], each spectral signature is considered to be a unique vector of the same dimension as the number of spectral bands in the image. Our method may appear to be sub-optimal from a rate-distortion point of view, but allows us to follow the classification strategy.

A. Vector Quantization

During the compression step, each spectral signature of the hyperspectral image is substituted for a codeword that refers to a vector in a codebook. During the reconstruction step, codewords are simply substituted for the corresponding vectors in the codebook.

Thus, knowing the codebook for coding and decoding, it is possible to associate to each codeword the semantic significance of the referred vector. Then, the compression achieved by VQ appears to act as a pre-classification of the original image.

B. *Vector Quantization Design*

VQ is based on the knowledge of a codebook. This codebook is generated by a clustering technique and can be thought of a set of the most representative spectral signatures of the training data. Several approaches may be investigated for codebook generation: classical VQ from a spectral point of view, unmixing-based VQ and SVM-based classified VQ. Lets begin with the last two that have been already defined in the previous section.

1) Unmixing-based VQ

 The unmixing methods substitute each spectral signature x for a mixture of endmembers e_ℓ. Lets re-write eq. (5) from product code point of view:

$$x = \sum_{\ell=1}^{L} \omega_\ell \, e_\ell = (\omega_1, \omega_2, \dots, \omega_L)_{\{e_1, e_2, \dots, e_L\}}.$$

 The set $(\omega_1, \omega_2, \dots, \omega_L)$ may then be called *feature scalars* since it characterizes the *partial description* of x through e_ℓ. It may be compressed with L independent scalar quantizers or by a vector quantization approach and x may be reconstructed with:

$$\widehat{x} = \sum_{\ell=1}^{L} \widehat{\omega}_\ell \, e_\ell \approx x.$$

 Unfortunately, a product code quantizer may not be optimal because of its structural constraint. Moreover, the set of endmembers e_ℓ is not representative to the observations x since endmembers do not integrate any distortion point of view but *purity* which is worse for compression. Then, the compression will be mostly helped by a classification instead of unmixing procedure.

2) SVM-based Classified VQ (CVQ)

 Instead of a test codebook that characterizes the overall N-D space, a classifier may be used to select a particular subset of the codebook to be searched.

 Many possibilities exist for the choice of classifier. When using SVM approach for hyperspectral data cube, the CVQ uses subsets of the codebook that are partitioned into *meta*-Voronoi cells defined by the set of hyperplanes.

Then, when the quantization of the support vectors does not modify their relative positions to the hyperplanes, CVQ does not interfere with the overall classification results.

3) Codebook generation

Several strategies may be used for generating codebook (retricted by a classification domain or not). The state of the art recommends the use of Linde-Buzo-Gray (LBG) procedure to buid an optimal set of vectors with a rate-distortion constraint. Nevertheless, the Kohonen's Self Organizing Map (SOM) is used to generate the codebook [19]. The convergence performances are the same as the K-means method, but the SOM leads to an index assignment. In fact, vectors that represent equivalent spectral signatures in the hyperspectral image are encoded with codewords that refer to vectors that are close to each other in the codebook, as drawn on Fig. 5.

The Self-Organizing Map is a neural network algorithm proposed by T. Kohonen [20] that forms a two-dimensional presentation of multi-dimensional data. Typically, SOM networks have two layers of nodes: the input layer and the Kohonen layer (see Fig. 6). The input layer

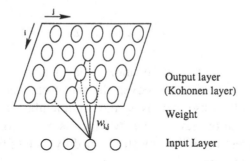

Figure 6:   A Kohonen map with 4×5 neurons.

is fully connected to the Kohonen layer which is of two dimensions. During the training process, input data are fed to the network through the nodes in the input layer. As the training process proceeds, the nodes adjust their weight values according to the topological relations in the input data and also the neighborhood relations in the Kohonen layer. The node with the minimum distance is called the *winner* and adjusts its weights to be closer to the value of the input pattern.

Euclidian distance is the most common way of measuring the distance between vectors. Here, we can take the spectral angle distance criteria or a combination of Euclidian and angular distances. During the iterative training, each neuron to be modified (the so-called winning neuron as it is the closest neuron to the input x) of position (i_0, j_0) has its weight $w_t(i_0, j_0)$ modified in order to minimize the cost function as follows:

$$w_{t+1}(i,j) = w_t(i,j) - \alpha(t)\beta_t(i_0 - i, j_0 - j)E\left(w_t(i_0, j_0) - x\right),$$

where $\alpha(t)$ modifies the weighting of the neurons and ensures convergence over iterations t; $\beta_t(\cdot)$ modifies the weighting of the neighborhood $\mathcal{B}_0$ of the winning neuron of position (i_0, j_0).
$\alpha(t)$ takes its expression as:

$$\alpha(t) = \begin{cases} \frac{1-e^{-(1+t)}}{1+t} & \text{if } 0 \leqslant t \leqslant t_0 = T\left(1 - \frac{1}{\sqrt{\mathcal{B}_0}}\right), \\ \frac{1}{t-t_0} & \text{if } t_0 < t < T. \end{cases}$$

Here, $e^{-(1+t)}$ avoids losing the local minima location at the beginning of the training since it retains $\alpha(t)$ of limited value. In addition, convergence of the map is ensured since $\sum_t \alpha(t) \xrightarrow[t\to+\infty]{} \infty$ while $\lim_{t\to+\infty} \sum_t \alpha(t)^2 \in \mathbb{R}$.
$\beta_t(\cdot)$ is dedicated to the neighborhood influence with:

$$\beta_t(i_0 - i, j_0 - j) = \begin{cases} \frac{1}{1+(i-i_0)^2+(j-j_0)^2} & \text{if } (i,j) \in \mathcal{B}_t(i_0, j_0), \\ 0 & \text{if not.} \end{cases}$$

Furthermore, the neighborhood itself is defined over iterations through:

$$\mathcal{B}_t(i_0, j_0) = \mathcal{B}_0(i_0, j_0)\left(1 - \frac{t}{T}\right)^2.$$

The distance $E\left(w_t(i_0, j_0) - x\right)$ is usually evaluated with the Euclidian distance as $\|w_t(i_0, j_0) - x\|$ for distortion minimization but for spectral application, spectral angle SA $\left(w_t(i_0, j_0) - x\right)$ is more appropriate. A compromise may be found when using a mixture of these two measures as:

$$E\left(w_t(i_0, j_0) - x\right) = \|w_t(i_0, j_0) - x\| \times \text{SA}\left(w_t(i_0, j_0) - x\right). \quad (11)$$

Furthermore, this training is integrated into a CVQ procedure such that the Kohonen map is divided in subsets dedicated to each class characterized by the SVM classification.

C. Entropy Coding

When using a codebook generated by a Kohonen map, similar spectral signatures are substituted for closed codewords. Thus, the high spatial correlation of the spectral signature is converted to codeword redundancies into the codeword stream. It is possible to compress this stream with an entropy encoding (e.g. Lempel-Ziv-Welch — LZW —) that performs a lossless compression based on the stream redundancies.

IV. APPLICATION TO CASI IMAGES

The proposed algorithm has been applied on images acquired by a Compact Airborne Spectrographic Imager (CASI) over a maritime oil spill. Fig. 7 shows two CASI images including 32 spectral bands and 2 meters ground spatial resolution pixels. Oil slicks and surrounding water can be easily

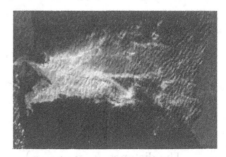

Figure 7: CASI images including 32 spectral bands showing oil slicks on the sea surface (the visualisation of those images has been adapted to the specificity of oil slick detection).

distinguished. Spectral signatures have been acquired between 423.0 and

952.5 nm with a spectral resolution of 17 nm and encoded with 16 bits per pixel. Those hyperspectral images fit in files as high as 15 and 23 Mb respectively, for a spatial coverage of approximately 1 km^2 each only. A large amount of images has been acquired for oil slicks detection, mapping and monitoring usages. In this paper, analysis is focused on two main topics:

- Discrimination between water and oil in order to estimate the spatial coverage of the slicks and to produce geographical maps of the slicks,
- Evaluation of different oil states within the slicks in order to determine the best monitoring schemes. The spectral variability within the slicks is representative of those different states and should be segmented into different classes.

Those information are of very high importance in an accidental oil spill where hot decisions have to be taken in near real time by people responsible for determining the best pollution fighting strategies. In that kind of applications, images have to be forwarded quickly to decision headquarters, thus leading to the need for high rate compressions with low distortions from a further classification point of view.

The SAM algorithm has been used to achieve the segmentation between water and oil and to determine 3 different oil states classes within the slicks. Fig. 8 shows classifications of the two CASI images over the oil spills into those 4 different classes.

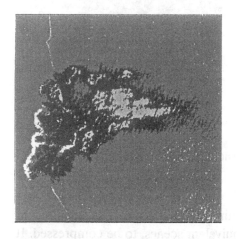
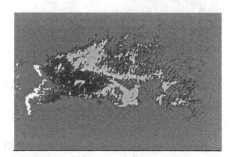

Figure 8:   Classification of the CASI images within 3 different oil states classes and non-polluted water.

The images have been compressed with a spectral-based CVQ. After the compression and reconstruction steps, the reconstructed image has been classified with the same algorithm. In order to limit classification errors, VQ has been achieved with a 16×16 Kohonen's map. The quantifiaction step uses a distortion measure shown on eq. (11). It induces limited distortion and classification artifacts. At this point (without entropy encoding stage), the compression ratio is $\eta = 64 : 1$ with a Mean Square Error of MSE = 269 (PSNR = 48.6 dB with a maximum value of 4435). In addition, a LZW entropy encoding raises the compression ratio up to $\eta = 70 : 1$.

Fig. 9 shows that the SVM classification yields the same results as the Fig. 8. In fact, the codebook can be viewed as a classification stage that defines cluster centers inside *meta*-Voronoi cells defined by a SVM classification. Then, a classification applied on reconstructed data yields the same accuracy. In that sense, the spectral quantization yields a near lossless compression scheme; where *lossless* refers to the evolution of the classification accuracy when applied to the original or the reconstructed image.

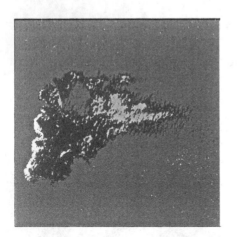

Figure 9:   Classification of the reconstructed CASI image, after a compression of 70:1.

Usually a codebook allows a set of images, that have been acquired in the same condition and that represent equivalent scenes, to be compressed. It makes sense in a monitoring usage where our problem is focused on oil slicks estimation and characterization. Nevertheless, a codebook used to compress a large amount of images may not be relevant to characterize sea states which were unexpected during the codebook generation. In that case, it is possible to include the codebook itself into the compressed code. This stand alone spectral VQ would be achieved with a similar compression ratio since the codebook can be represented with only 16384 bytes.

V. CONCLUSION

This paper introduced an original approach to hyperspectral image compression based on a joint classification and compression technique, in order to achieved high compression ratio with limited loss of critical information, according to the classification point of view. VQ was a good candidate to compress those images using the same point of view as the SAM classification algorithm. The VQ has been implemented with the Kohonen's SOM that preserves spatial correlation of the image. Finally an entropy coding, implemented with the LZW algorithm, yields an interesting compression ratio (up to 70 : 1).

In fact, classified Vector Quantization, implemented with SVM proved to be powerful in this context. Both classification and compression have been implemented with a mixture of Euclidian distance and spectral angle for optimizing hyperplane definition — eq. (10) — and codebook generation — eq. (11) —.

A typical example has been shown with CASI images dedicated to oil slicks detection and characterization. Here an efficient compression has to be performed for efficient data management. Nevertheless, decision making has to be performed with no consideration on the transmission nor on the compression. That is why joint compression and classification is more appropriate than a distortion-rate optimization when lossless compression is not conceivable.

REFERENCES

[1] W. Boardman, F. Kruse, and R. Green, "Mapping target signatures via partial unmixing of AVIRIS data," in *VI JPL airborne Earth Science Workshop*, Pasadena, CA, 1995.

[2] M. Winter, "N-FINDR: An algorithm for fast autonomous spectral end-member determination in hyperspectral data," in *Proc. SPIE*, vol. 3753, 1999, pp. 266–275.

[3] R. Neville, K. Staenz, T. Szeredi, and P. Hauff, "Automatic endmember extraction from hyperspectral data for mineral exploration," in *21st Can. Symp. Remote Sensing*, Ottawa, ON, Canada, 1999.

[4] A. Plaza, P. Martinez, R. Perez, and J. Plaza, "Spatial/spectral endmember extraction by multidimensional morphological operations," *IEEE transactions on geoscience and remote sensing*, vol. 40, pp. 2025–2041, Sept. 2002.

[5] A. Ifarraguerri and C.-I. Chang, "Multispectral and hyperspectral image analysis with convex cones," *IEEE transactions on geoscience and remote sensing*, vol. 37, pp. 756–770, Mar. 1999.

[6] M. Lennon, G. Mercier, M.-C. Mouchot, and L. Hubert-Moy, "Spectral unmixing of hyperspectral images with the Independent Component Analysis and wavelet packets," in *IGARSS*, vol. 6, July 1999, pp. 2896–2898.

[7] C. J. Burges, "A tutorial on support vector machines for pattern recognition," in *Data mining and knowledge discovery*, U. Fayyad, Ed. Kluwer Academic, 1998, pp. 1–43.

[8] V. N. Vapnick, *Statistical Learning Theory*. John Wiley and Sons Inc., 1998.

[9] C. Huang, L. S. Davis, and J. R. G. Townshend, "An assessement of support vector machines for land cover classifiocation," *Int. J. Remote sensing*, vol. 23, no. 4, pp. 725–749, 2002.

[10] J. A. Gualtieri and R. F. Cromp, "Support vector machines for hyperspectral remote sensing classification," in *Proceedings of the SPIE*, vol. 3584, 1999, pp. 221–232.

[11] F. Melgani and L. Bruzzone, "Support vector machines for classification of hyperspectral remote sensing images," in *IGARSS*, 2002.

[12] M. Lennon, G. Mercier, and L. Hubert-Moy, "Classification of hyperspectral images with nonlinear filtering and support vector machines," in *IGARSS*, 2002.

[13] G. Hughes, "On the mean accuracy of statistical pattern recognition," *IEEE transactions on information theory*, vol. 14, no. 1, pp. 55–63, 1968.

[14] G. Smits and E. Jordaan, "Improved SVM regression using mixtures of kernels," in *IJCNN*, 2002.

[15] G. Mercier and M. Lennon, "Support Vector Machines for hyperspectral image classification with spectral-based kernels," in *IGARSS*, 2003.

[16] A. Gersho and R. Gray, *Vector Quantization and Signal Compression*. Klower Academic Publisher, 1992.

[17] M. Ryan and J. Arnold, "The lossless compression of AVIRIS images by vector quantization," *IEEE transactions on geoscience and remote sensing*, vol. 35, no. 3, pp. 546–550, May 1997.

[18] S.-E. Qian, A. Hollinger, D. Williams, and D. Manak, "3D data compression of hyperspectral imagery using vector quantization with NDVI-based multiple codebooks," in *IGARSS*, 1998.

[19] A. Czihò, B. Solaiman, G. Cazuguel, C. Roux, and I. Loványi, "Kohonen's self organizing feature maps with variable learning rate. application to image compression," in 3rd *international workshop on Image and Signal Processing*, Santorini, Greece, 1997.

[20] T. Kohonen, "The self-organizing map," *Proceedings of the IEEE*, vol. 78, no. 9, pp. 1464–1480, September 1990.

Predictive Coding of Hyperspectral Images [*]

Agnieszka C. Miguel[*]   Richard E. Ladner[‡]

Eve A. Riskin[†]   Scott Hauck[†]   Dane K. Barney[‡]

Amanda R. Askew[‡]

Alexander Chang[‡]

[*] Dept. of Electrical and Computer Engineering, Box 222000,
Seattle University, Seattle, WA 98122-1090

[†] Dept. of Electrical Engineering, Box 352500,
University of Washington, Seattle, WA 98195-2500

[‡] Dept. of Computer Science and Engineering, Box 352350,
University of Washington, Seattle, WA 98195-2350

1   Introduction

Every day, NASA and other agencies collect large amounts of hyperspectral data. For example, one Airborne Visible InfraRed Imaging Spectrometer (AVIRIS) alone can produce data that require up to 16 Gbytes

---

[*]This work appeared in part in the Proceedings of the NASA Earth Science Technology Conference, 2003, and in the Proceedings of the Data Compression Conference, 2004. Research supported by NASA Contract NAS5-00213 and National Science Foundation grant number CCR-0104800. Scott Hauck was supported in part by an NSF CAREER Award and an Alfred P. Sloan Research Fellowship. Contact information: Professor Richard Ladner, University of Washington, Box 352500, Seattle, WA 98195-2500, (206) 543-9347, ladner@cs.washington.edu.

of storage per day. The hyperspectral images are used to identify, measure, and monitor constituents of the Earth's surface and atmosphere [1].

This huge amount of data presents a compression challenge. In this research, we propose algorithms to code the hyperspectral data. To reduce the bit rate required to code hyperspectral images, we use linear prediction between the bands. Each band, except the first one, is predicted by previously transmitted band. Once the prediction is formed, it is subtracted from the original band, and the residual (difference image) is compressed using a standard compression algorithm.

To optimize the prediction algorithm we study several methods of ordering the bands for prediction. To rearrange the bands into a particular ordering, we define a measure of prediction quality, the prediction mean squared error. We compute the optimal ordering using this measure as well as two restricted orderings in which each band can be predicted by the best predictor among all of the previous or future bands in the standard band numbering. In addition, we define two simple orderings in which each band is predicted by its immediate previous or future neighbor. We use the prediction mean squared error to compare those orderings.

The first proposed algorithm is lossless, that is the decompressed images are exact replicas of the original data. The difference images are encoded using bzip2 data compression algorithm [2]. We use bzip2 because it is a state-of-the-art open-source lossless data coding algorithm. We compare our results for five standard hyperspectral images with recently published results and conclude that our algorithm achieves comparable compression ratios.

The second algorithm is lossy and therefore, the decompressed image is an approximation of the original image. In this case we encode the difference image using the Set Partitioning in Hierarchical Trees (SPIHT) algorithm [3], which is a wavelet-based lossy compression technique that codes images with both high compression ratio and high fidelity. SPIHT was originally designed as a sequential algorithm; however, with some modifications, it can be parallelized for implementation on field programmable gate arrays (FPGAs) [4] and therefore has great potential for applications where the compression is performed in hardware on the aircraft and satellite platforms. Note that we compress all bands to the same fidelity.

To compute the exact difference between a band and its prediction, the encoder must have access to the decoded version of the band used for prediction; however, such a closed loop system requires a full implementation of the decoder at the transmitter, which increases its complexity. In this chapter we present a new prediction technique, *bit plane-synchronized closed loop prediction*, that significantly reduces the complexity of the encoder [5]. Instead of requiring the encoder to fully reconstruct the compressed band from which the current band is predicted, the encoder and the decoder simply use the same integral number of full bit planes of the wavelet-coded difference image of the band used for prediction. This enables the transmitter to be less complex because, while it must still do an inverse wavelet transform, full decompression is avoided. The proposed prediction method is very promising in that for the same target fidelity, the average bit rate is only slightly higher than for traditional predictive coding.

The chapter is organized as follows. In Section 2, we review related background material. In Sections 3 and 4, we describe our prediction methodology. The algorithm for lossless predictive coding of hyperspectral images is presented in Section 5. In Section 6, we introduce our new reduced complexity lossy encoder. Finally, we conclude in Section 7.

2 Background

In this section, we present related work. We first review hyperspectral images, the bzip2 and SPIHT algorithms, and predictive coding. Then, we discuss prior work in lossless and lossy hyperspectral image compression.

2.1 Hyperspectral Images

Hyperspectral images are obtained using imaging spectrometers. Such hyperspectral sensors obtain a continuous spectrum of electromagnetic radiation reflected from the surface of the Earth. Hyperspectral image can be viewed as a 3D data cube, with the X and Y dimensions representing different coordinates on the Earth's surface, while the third dimension is the band, representing the frequency being imaged. The actual data values are the intensity of the light at one wavelength from the particular location on the Earth. The upper layers in the image cube (higher number bands) correspond to the data collected in the longest wavelengths and the bottom layers (lower number bands) correspond to the shortest wavelengths. A hyperspectral image contains several hundred narrow and contiguous wavelength bands.

Applications of hyperspectral imaging include mineral exploration, environmental monitoring, and military surveillance. Image processing tools are used to extract detailed information from hyperspectral images. Most often the objective of those algorithms involves target detection, material mapping and identification, and mapping details of surface properties [6]. After adjustments for sensor, atmospheric, and terrain effects are applied, the reflected spectral data are compared, and matched, to spectral data of known absorption features stored in libraries. Because hyperspectral data are spectrally overdetermined, it is possible to identify and distinguish between spectrally similar materials, for example, between different types and even conditions of vegetation.

Most imaging spectrometers are used aboard air-based platforms. The NASA's Airborne Visible InfraRed Imaging Spectrometer (AVIRIS) is flown on the ER-2 jet at 20km above the ground or on the Twin Otter turboprop at 4km above the ground. It produces 224 bands with wavelengths from 400 to 2500 nanometers (nm) at a resolution of 20×20 meters (ER-2) and 4×4 meters (Twin Otter). The images are 614 pixels wide and about 2000 pixels high. The output of the spectrometer consists of 12-bit floating point values which are later on scaled and rounded into signed 16-bit integers [1]. The 16-bit images are stored in scenes of 614×512 each. Typically, there are five scenes for each image. In this chapter we test our algorithms on the five AVIRIS images available for download at NASA's JPL [1]. The 3-8 scenes in each image were concatenated to form the test data.

The Hyperspectral Digital Imagery Collection Experiment (HYDICE) operated by the Naval Research Lab is an imaging spectrometer that performs measurements in the same 400-2500 nm range but in 210 bands. It is capable of achieving resolution of 0.8 to 4 meters if flown at an altitude in the range from 5,000 to 25,000 feet [7]. The Probe-1 sensor is operated by Earth Search Sciences, Inc. and measures 128 wavelengths in the same 400-2500 nm range at a spatial resolution of 5-10 meters [8]. ITRES Research developed two hyperspectral sensors. The CASI-2 is capable of measuring up to 228 bands in the range of 400 to 1000 nm at a spatial resolution of 0.5-10 m. The CASI-3 sensor measures up to 288 bands in the range of 400 to 1050nm at a spatial resolution of 0.5-10 m [9]. The HyMap sensor from Integrated Spectronics measures 100-200 wavelengths in the visible to infrared spectral range [10]. The Group for Environmental Research Earth Resources Exploration Consortium operates a variety of hyperspectral sensors capable of imaging up to 76 bands in the range from 400 to 12500 nm [11]. Finally, the AISA sensors from Spectral Imaging measure up to 244 bands in the range 400-2400 nm [12].

There are only a few spaceborne hyperspectral sensors. The Hyperion sensor on-board the EO-1 satellite launched by the NASA Goddard Space Center is capable of resolving 220 spectral bands (from 0.4 to 2.5 m) with a 30-meter resolution [13]. The FTHSI sensor on the MightySat II satellite from Air Force Research Lab measures 256 wavelengths in the range of 350 to 1050 nm.

There is a trade-off between spatial and spectral resolution in all of the hyperspectral sensors: as the number of bands increases there is a corresponding decrease in spatial resolution. Therefore, most pixels are mixed pixels, i.e. they contain spectral contribution from neighboring pixels, and the size of most targets of interest is sub-pixel.

2.2   Lossless Image Compression

Lossless compression guarantees the recovery of an exact replica of the original data and can only provide limited compression ratios, usually on the order of 2:1 to 3:1 for natural images.

2.2.1   Bzip2

Bzip2 is a recently developed state-of-the-art lossless data compression algorithm [2]. It encodes files using a block-sorting text compression algorithm based on the Burrows-Wheeler transform [14] followed by Huffman coding.

2.3   Lossy Image Compression

In lossy compression algorithms, the original image cannot be perfectly recovered. Instead, the decompressed image is an approximation of the original image. Lossy compression algorithms provide a mechanism for a controlled loss of information to ensure that the quality of the reconstructed image is adequate for the particular application. Typical compression ratios for gray scale natural images with no noticeable difference to the eye between the original and recovered images are on the order of 10:1 to 20:1.

2.3.1   Set Partitioning in Hierarchical Trees

SPIHT is a progressive lossy image coder, which first approximates an image with a few bits of data, and then improves the quality of approximation as more information is encoded [3]. As shown in Figure 1, the encoder first performs a wavelet transform on the image pixels. Then, the wavelet coefficients are encoded one bit plane at a time. The embedded bit stream, in which the later bits refine the earlier bits, can be truncated at any time (see Figure 2). Bit plane encoding and decoding take significantly more time than the wavelet transform.

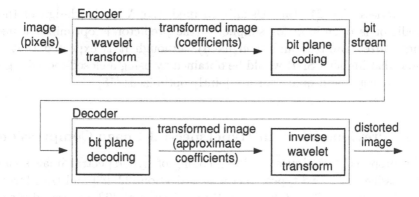

Figure 1: Block diagram of SPIHT.

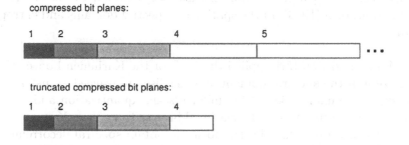

Figure 2: Bit plane coding.

2.4 Predictive Coding

Predictive coding has been a popular data compression technique for years. Prediction exploits the correlation in spatial or temporal dimensions, or context, to improve compression performance over independent coding. It is used in both lossy and lossless coding. For example, differential pulse code modulation (DPCM) [15] uses prediction to improve performance over standard PCM. The MPEG video coding standard [16] uses temporal prediction to significantly improve compression ratios over independent coding of video frames. Predictive vector quantization (VQ) [17, 18, 19, 20] exploits spatial correlation over a larger region of an input image or speech signal to give improvements over memoryless VQ [21, 19]. Usually in predictive VQ, the design of the predictor is open-loop for simplicity (the predictor is optimized using unquantized samples and then fixed), although it is expected that a somewhat higher PSNR would be obtained by using a closed-loop design (the predictor and quantizer are jointly optimized) [18].

2.5   Previous Work in Hyperspectral Image Compression

The proposed techniques for lossy coding of hyperspectral images can be classified into two types: vector quantization [22, 23] and transform-based [24, 25, 26, 27, 28, 29] algorithms. Qian et al. [22] generated separate subcodebooks for regions with similar spectral characteristics. Ryan and Pickering [23] used mean-normalized VQ followed by the discrete-cosine transform (DCT) in the spatial and spectral domains and entropy coding.

Markas and Reif [27] applied the DCT or the Karhunen-Loeve (KL) transform in the spectral domain and the discrete wavelet transform in the spatial domain, followed by uniform scalar quantization and block-based encoding using multidemensional bitmap trees. Lee, Younan, and King [25] used different 1-D transforms to obtain spectral decorrelation (KL, DCT, and the difference pulse-coded modulation (DPCM)) and applied JPEG2000 to the resulting data. Abousleman, Marcellin, and Hunt in [28] proposed using DPCM for spectral decorrelation and 2D DCT for spatial decorrelation combined with entropy-constrained trellis coded quantization (ECTCQ).

Tang, Cho, and Pearlman compared the performance of several 3D versions of SPIHT on hyperspectral data with the performance of the JPEG2000 algorithm [26]. The methods included the original 3D-SPIHT, 3D-SPIHT with asymmetric trees (AT-3DSPIHT), and the 3D Set Partitioned Embedded Block method. AT-3DSPIHT outperformed the other algorithms by 0.2-0.9 dB. All of the SPIHT-based algorithms were significantly better then JPEG2000 applied to each band separately. Dragotti, Poggi, and Ragozini [29] modified the 3D-SPIHT algorithm to better compress multispectral images. In the first method, they performed a

3D transform which consisted of the wavelet transform in the spatial domain and the KL transform in the spectral domain. The 3D transform was followed by 3D-SPIHT coding. In the second method, 2D wavelet transform was first taken in the spatial domain. Then, spectral vectors of pixels were vector quantized and gain-driven SPIHT was used.

Linear prediction as a method to reduce inter-band correlation was investigated by Memon in [30] who proposed adaptive reordering of the spectral components of each pixel followed by a piecewise linear function at a specified error tolerance. Rao and Bhargava [31] used simple block-based linear inter-band prediction followed by a block-based DCT. To take advantage of linear prediction between bands, Tate in [32] explored unconstrained optimal reordering of the multispectral bands followed by linear prediction, which uses spatial neighborhoods to predict each pixel and arithmetic coding.

An appropriate distortion measure for compressed hyperspectral data was investigated by Ryan and Arnold in [33]. Their goal was to find a measure that is a suitable error metric for decompressed data used in various scientific algorithms instead of viewed by humans. The proposed distortion measure was the Percentage Maximum Absolute Distortion which guarantees that each pixel in the reconstructed image is within a maximum percentage distance of its original value.

In addition to lossy compression, lossless hyperspectral image coding has been also widely investigated. Motta, Rizzo, and Storer [34] designed a product VQ with an algorithm to determine how to form subvectors across bands. In [35], Rizzo, Carpentieri, Motta, and Storer modified this method to include a low-complexity encoder. Pickering and Ryan proposed a method based on joint optimization of a mean-normalized vector quantization (proposed by Ryan and Arnold in [36]) applied in the spatial domain and a DCT in the spectral domain [37]. Aiazzi, Alba, Alparone, and Baronti compressed multi- and hyperspectral data using a 3D fuzzy prediction [38]. Qian, Hollinger, and Hamiaux applied the Consulatative Committee for Space Data System (CCSDS) compression algorithm as an entropy coder to the results of several different prediction methods [39]. Adaptive DPCM with linear prediction was investigated by Roger and Cavenor [40].

3   Prediction Methodology

Because each band of a hyperspectral image corresponds to the same location on Earth, there is a high level of correlation between the bands (see Figure 3 for an example). However, bands corresponding to different wavelengths have different dynamic ranges, and thus, do not lend themselves easily to simple difference coding. For example, in Figure 3, Bands 30 and 200 of a 224-band image of the Cuprite geology site are highly correlated, yet a simple difference between the two would contain significant energy. It has been suggested in the literature that the pixel values across different bands are linearly related [32, 41] and simple linear prediction has been successfully used to remove the spectral correlation between bands [28].

We also use linear prediction to take advantage of correlation between bands. Assume there are m bands B_i for $0 \leq i < m$. We define an additional *root band* B_m in which each pixel is the constant 1. This band will be the only band that is not predicted by another band. Each band B_i ($0 \leq i < m$) can be linearly predicted from another band B_j ($0 \leq j \leq m$), including the root band as described in Equations (1). The values a_{ij} and c_{ij} are the *prediction coefficients* and P_{ij} is the prediction of the current band B_i from a previously transmitted band B_j. The difference D_{ij} between B_i and P_{ij} is a residual and can usually be compressed well. Once D_{ij} is transmitted, band B_i can be recovered by adding D_{ij} to the prediction P_{ij}.

$$
\begin{aligned}
P_{ij} &= a_{ij}B_j + c_{ij}B_m \\
D_{ij} &= B_i - P_{ij} \\
B_i &= P_{ij} + D_{ij}.
\end{aligned}
\tag{1}
$$

Figure 4 visually shows the advantage of linear prediction over direct difference coding for the first scene of the Cuprite image. Figure 4 (a) is the simple difference of Bands 77 and Band 78 ($B_{77} - B_{78}$), whereas Figure 4 (b) is the result of solving Equation 1 when predicting Band 77 from Band 78. Notice that the difference corresponding to the linearly predicted band (right) contains a great deal less energy than the simple

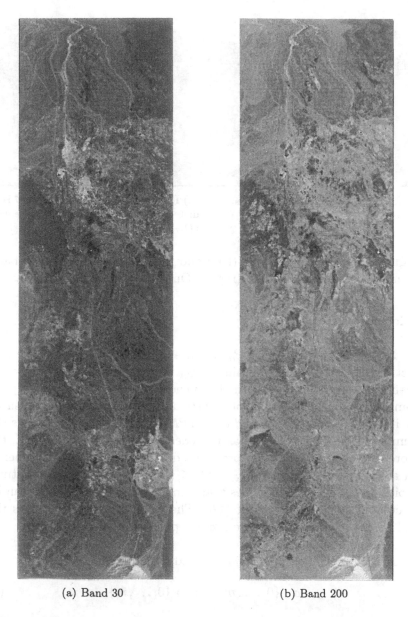

(a) Band 30   (b) Band 200

Figure 3: Sample bands 30 and 200 of a 224-band image of the Cuprite geology site.

 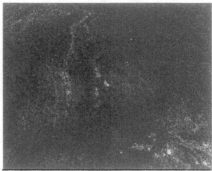

(a) Difference band $B_{77} - B_{78}$.   (b) Difference band 77 when band 77 is pre-
                                              dicted from band 78 using linear prediction
                                              ($D_{77\ 78}$).

Figure 4: Band 77 - Band 78 (left) and the difference band when band 77 is predicted from band 78 (right). Only the first scene is shown.

difference (left).

Note that the prediction P_{im} requires that $a_{im} = 0$ so that the prediction only depends on the value of c_{im}. We assume that the prediction coefficients are known to both the encoder and decoder by some prior communication. The quality of a particular prediction can be measured by its *prediction mean squared error (PMSE)*, $\|D_{ij}\|^2/n$, where n is the number of pixels in a single band. Generally, the larger the PMSE, the more bits are needed to compress the difference. The PMSE depends on a good choice of a_{ij} and c_{ij}. If $0 \le i, j < m$, $i \ne j$, then a natural choice for a_{ij} and c_{ij} are values that minimize the PMSE. These can be calculated by least squares fit [42]. The value c_{im} that minimizes the PMSE $\|D_{im}\|^2/n$ is simply the average pixel value of the band B_i.

A *band prediction ordering* is defined by a function

$$\sigma : \{0, \ldots, m-1\} \rightarrow \{0, \ldots, m\}. \tag{2}$$

That is, except for band B_m, band B_i is predicted by band $B_{\sigma(i)}$. The function σ must satisfy the following property: For each i such that $0 \le$

$i < m$, there is a sequence $i = i_1, i_2, \ldots, i_k = m$ such that $i_{j+1} = \sigma(i_j)$ for $1 \leq j < k$. An alternative definition is that a prediction order is a tree with nodes labeled uniquely from $\{0, 1, \ldots, m\}$ with root labeled m. For $0 \leq i < m$, i's parent in the tree is $\sigma(i)$.

We measure the quality of the prediction ordering σ as the *average PMSE*:

$$\frac{1}{mn} \sum_{i=0}^{m-1} \|D_{i,\sigma(i)}\|^2. \tag{3}$$

4   Band Prediction Ordering Solutions

The simplest band ordering is the *forward monotonic ordering* where $\sigma(0) = m$ and $\sigma(i) = i - 1$ for $1 \leq i < m$, and the *reverse monotonic ordering* where $\sigma(i) = i + 1$ for $0 \leq i < m$. There are two relatively easy-to-compute alternatives that are significantly better than the monotonic orderings. These alternatives are based on examining the $m \times (m + 1)$ *prediction matrix*, where the (i, j)-th entry is $\|D_{ij}\|^2 / n$, the PMSE.

Figure 5 is an example of a prediction matrix. The horizontal axis represents the predictor band numbers and the vertical axis represents the predicted band numbers. The darker color represents larger values, which is where the prediction does not perform well. Clearly, some bands do not perform well as predictors, while other bands are very easily predicted. For example, bands 110 and 160 do not predict others well, whereas bands 110 and 158 are well predicted by any other band.

To take advantage of the fact that some bands are better predictors than others we define the *best forward ordering* by choosing $\sigma(i) < i$ or $\sigma(i) = m$ that minimizes $\|D_{i,\sigma(i)}\|^2 / n$ for $0 \leq i < m$. That is, the bands are predicted smallest to largest, and a particular band is predicted by the best band with a smaller number, with the exception of the root band. Similarly, we can define the *best reverse ordering* by choosing $\sigma(i) > i$ that minimizes $\|D_{i,\sigma(i)}\|^2 / n$ for $1 \leq i < m$. That is, the bands are predicted largest to smallest, and a particular band is predicted by the best band with a larger number. Both best orderings can be computed in $O(m^2)$ time once the prediction matrix is constructed.

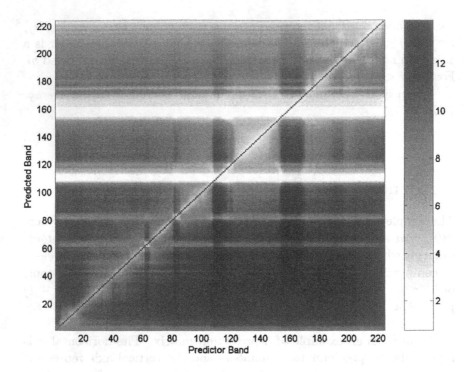

Figure 5: Prediction matrix for the Cuprite image (log scale).

We also consider the *optimal ordering* in which there is no constraint on which band can predict other bands. We formulate the problem of determining the best ordering as a graph problem — more specifically, the problem of finding the minimum weight rooted spanning tree on a directed graph. The directed graph has $m+1$ vertices representing the m bands and the root band. The root band is the root of the spanning tree. The directed graph has a directed edge from j to i if, $i \neq j$, $0 \leq i < m$ and $0 \leq j \leq m$. The weight of the edge from j to i is $\|D_{ij}\|^2/n$, a value in the prediction matrix. A minimum spanning tree is a spanning tree that minimizes the sum of all the weights of the edges in the spanning tree. A minimum spanning tree T defines a prediction ordering σ_T as follows. If (j, i) is a directed edge in T, then $\sigma_T(i) = j$. That is, band B_i is predicted from band B_j if (j, i) is an edge in the spanning tree. The fact that T has a minimum sum of weights ensures that Equation (3) is minimized.

The algorithm for finding the minimum spanning tree in a directed graph was first developed in the 1960s [43]. It was then applied in the 1970s [44] to solve network flow problems and its implementation was further improved in [45]. The best complexity bound for finding the minimum spanning tree in a directed graph is $O(n^2)$ [44, 45], but these algorithms are significantly more complex than computing the other orderings. The minimum spanning tree technique was also used by Tate [32] to find an optimal band ordering for lossless compression of multispectral images and by Kopylov and Fränti [46] to find an optimal layer ordering for lossless compression of multilayered maps. In both these works the weight on the edge from j to i was the size of the losslessly compressed difference D_{ij}. We use the PMSE because it approximately represents the size of the lossy compressed difference regardless of the amount of loss required.

Examples of the five possible orderings are shown in Fig. 6. Table 1 lists the average PMSE over five 224-band images: Cuprite (C), Jasper Ridge (JR), Low Altitude (LA), Lunar Lake (LL), and Moffett Field (MF). These images were downloaded from the NASA's JPL AVIRIS site at [1]. The test images are all stored as 16-bit signed integers. As can be seen, the best reverse ordering is actually very close to the optimal ordering (within 19%).

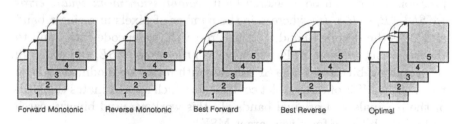

Figure 6: Examples of prediction band orderings.

Ordering	C	JR	LA	LL	MF
Forward Monotonic	367.6	1100.5	3121.1	550.2	2529.6
Best Forward	359.4	1096.9	3118.0	530.5	2443.3
Reverse Monotonic	296.4	1007.9	2609.8	424.5	2401.2
Best Reverse	264.7	1001.4	2606.4	335.0	2311.3
Optimal	263.8	875.6	2187.7	332.2	2005.9

Table 1: Average PMSE for five different band orderings.

4.1 Compression Quality Measures

In this Section we discuss the various metrics that we used to quantify
the quality of the proposed lossless and lossy compression algorithms.

Average Compression Ratio The quality of a particular lossless
compression scheme is measured by its average compression ratio computed by dividing the sum of all of the original file sizes by the sum of
all of the compressed file sizes.

Bit Rate A common measure of compression is the bit rate, which is
defined to be the file size in bits divided by the total number of pixels.
For example, for the uncompressed Cuprite image, which is 16 bits per
pixel (bpp), a compressed file bit rate of 2 bpp is equivalent to an 8:1
compression ratio.

Target MSE For each band i, the quality of a particular lossy compression scheme can be measured by its *compression mean square error
(MSE)*, $\|B_i - \hat{B}_i\|^2/n$, where n is the number of pixels in a single band
and $\hat{B}_i$ is the decoded band i. In this research, we encode each band to
the same compression MSE, which we call the *target MSE*, and compare
the resulting bit rates. The SPIHT algorithm can be modified to keep
track of the MSE of the wavelet coefficients which approximates the MSE
of the residuals and original bands. In this work we used binary search
to find the bit rate for given target MSE.

Spectral MSE To evaluate the effects of our lossy compression algorithm on the shape of the spectral profile of each image pixel, we compute

the spectral MSE defined as

$$\text{SMSE}(x,y) = \frac{1}{m} \sum_{i=0}^{m-1} \left(B_i(x,y) - \hat{B}_i(x,y) \right)^2 \tag{4}$$

where m is the number of bands. Its purpose is to show the extent to which the target MSE is satisfied in the spectral direction. Note that the proposed algorithm was designed to deliver the target MSE for each band but not for each spectral profile. However, we feel that it is important to test the performance of our method in the spectral domain.

Maximum Scaled Difference Error We introduce the Maximum Scaled Difference Error (MaxSDE) to facilitate direct comparison between spectral signatures of pixels in the original and decompressed images. Such comparison is important because classification of hyperspectral images is based on matching the spectral profile of each pixel with predefined spectral signatures stored in a library. If the compression algorithms modify the shape of spectral curves, some pixels may not be classified correctly. The MaxSDE of a pixel (x,y) is computed as a ratio of the maximum absolute difference between the original and decompressed pixel values and the average absolute spectrum of that pixel. The MaxSDE is defined as

$$\text{MaxSDE}(x,y) = \max_{i} \left\{ \frac{m \left| B_i(x,y) - \hat{B}_i(x,y) \right|}{\sum_{i=0}^{m-1} |B_i(x,y)|} \right\}. \tag{5}$$

Mean Scaled Difference Error To further evaluate the quality of our lossy compression algorithm, we also study the Mean Scaled Difference Error (MSDE). MSDE of a pixel (x,y) is defined as a ratio of the average absolute difference between the original and decompressed pixel values and the average spectrum of that pixel:

$$\text{MSDE}(x,y) = \frac{\sum_{i=0}^{m-1} \left| B_i(x,y) - \hat{B}_i(x,y) \right|}{\sum_{i=0}^{m-1} |B_i(x,y)|}. \tag{6}$$

Note that because some hyperspectral bands have very different range of pixel values, in both cases (MaxSDE and MSDE), we scale the absolute difference errors by the average value of each spectrum.

5 Lossless Coding Using Prediction

In this section we examine the benefit of using prediction for lossless compression of hyperspectral images. Previous work of Tate [32] has shown that prediction works very well for lossless compression of multispectral images. The same holds true for hyperspectral images.

5.1 Algorithms

As noted in the previous section there are several band orderings that can be used based on the PMSE metric. We saw that the best reverse ordering achieved almost the same PMSE as the optimal ordering. With lossless compression one can choose an ordering that is based on compressed file size (CFS), rather than PMSE. Unlike in the lossy setting, in the lossless setting the decoder has available for prediction any *original* band that it has already received. To compute the best forward, best reverse, and optimal orderings we first compute an $m \times (m + 1)$ matrix F where F_{ij} is the compressed file size in bytes of D_{ij} (cf. equations (1)). The difference images D_{ij} are computed using a_{ij} and c_{ij} that minimize $\|D_{i,\sigma(i)}\|^2 = \|B_{ij} - (a_{ij}B_j + c_{ij}B_m)\|^2$. We then use the same algorithms as described in Section 4 substituting the file size F_{ij} for PMSE $\|D_{i,\sigma(i)}\|^2/n$. Naturally, the forward and reverse monotonic algorithms do not change because they do not depend on PMSE.

5.2 Results

To compare the PMSE and CFS metrics and the different ordering algorithms we used the five hyperspectral images and compressed them using the different methods. All difference images were compressed using bzip2. We tested several data compression algorithms (bzip2 version 1.0.2 [2], lzp version 1 [47], shcodec version 1.0.1 [48], gzip version 1.1.3 as included with Linux ppmz [49], bwtzip version 1.0.2 [50], szip version 1.12a [51], and zzip version 0.36b [52]) and found that bzip2 performed as well as any of them. In addition, bzip2 is readily available and free on many platforms. We measure the performance of a method using compression ratio. As can be seen in Table 2, results for the compression based on CFS are consistently slightly better than those based on PMSE. As expected the optimal ordering gives the best compression ratios for the CFS metric. Somewhat surprising is that in the PMSE metric, all orderings we considered performed about the same. In fact, the best forward algorithm slightly outperforms the optimal algorithm. This can happen because in the optimal PMSE algorithm, optimality is based on finding the minimum PMSE over all orderings, not on finding the minimum file size over all orderings. From Table 1 the best reverse ordering has PMSE almost the same as the optimal ordering, while the best forward has significantly larger PMSE. However, as seen in Table 2, this difference does not translate to better lossless compression for the best reverse algorithm in either the PMSE or CFS metrics.

	Fwd	Rev	BestRev		BestFwd		Optimal	
			PMSE	CFS	PMSE	CFS	PMSE	CFS
Cuprite	3.09	3.08	3.10	3.22	3.09	3.21	3.10	3.23
Jasper Ridge	3.07	3.06	3.08	3.17	3.07	3.16	3.07	3.18
Low Altitude	2.88	2.87	2.90	3.02	2.89	3.01	2.88	3.03
Lunar Lake	3.08	3.06	3.09	3.20	3.07	3.20	3.08	3.21
Moffett Field	3.02	3.01	3.03	3.12	3.01	3.11	3.01	3.13

Table 2: Compression ratios based on PMSE and CFS metrics.

Table 3 compares using bzip2 with no prediction, with the best reverse, best forward, and optimal orderings using the CFS metric. The last column contains the results for SLSQ-OPT, which is the best algorithm of Rizzo et al [35]. Clearly, using prediction is significantly better than using no prediction. The best forward, best reverse, and optimal algorithms perform about the same, but slightly worse than SLSQ-OPT.

5.3   Universality

We investigated the problem of how sensitive the compression ratio is to the particular prediction coefficients and band ordering. We hypothesize that the prediction coefficients and band orderings are similar for a given instrument and only vary a moderate amount from image to image. If

	No Pred	BestRev	BestFwd	Optimal	SLSQ-OPT
Cuprite	2.30	3.21	3.22	3.23	3.24
Jasper Ridge	2.12	3.16	3.17	3.18	3.23
Low Altitude	2.15	3.01	3.02	3.03	3.04
Lunar Lake	2.35	3.20	3.20	3.21	3.23
Moffett Field	2.13	3.11	3.12	3.13	3.21
Average	2.21	3.14	3.15	3.16	3.19

Table 3: Compression ratios for various band orderings using bzip2 and CFS metric.

this were true then one could define a single set of prediction coefficients and a band ordering that would work well for a wide variety of images. That is, we could define *universal* prediction coefficients and band ordering. Table 4 gives the results of how sensitive the compression ratio is when varying the prediction coefficients and band ordering. In this chapter, for each image I, we computed the optimal prediction coefficients a_{ij}^I and c_{ij}^I minimizing $\|D_{ij}^I\|^2/n$. We then computed the optimal ordering using the CFS metric. For every two images I and J, we used the prediction coefficients and optimal ordering for J to compress image I using bzip2 on the difference images. Thus, the image J is the training image for compressing image I. As can be seen from the table, using a training image other than the image to be compressed always yields a worse compression ratio, but not remarkably worse. The worst training image is Low Altitude. In the worst case (compressing Jasper Ridge image using Low Altitude as a training image), the compression ratio reduces from 3.027 to 2.802, which is still quite close.

	Training Image				
	C	JR	LA	LL	MF
Cuprite	**3.231**	-0.107	-0.158	-0.059	-0.068
Jasper Ridge	-0.158	**3.179**	-0.225	-0.094	-0.080
Low Altitude	-0.152	-0.178	**3.027**	-0.178	-0.138
Lunar Lake	-0.067	-0.055	-0.187	**3.212**	-0.086
Moffett Field	-0.057	-0.060	-0.151	-0.082	**3.127**

Table 4: Compression sensitivity to prediction coefficients and orderings. Compression ratios are shown.

6   Wavelet-Based Lossy Coding Using Prediction

In this section we examine the benefit of using prediction for lossy compression of hyperspectral images. We also investigate a low complexity implementation of the wavelet-based lossy coding algorithm. In all of the following experiments we use best forward ordering of the bands because it achieved the best compression ratios compared to the other orderings.

Prediction significantly improves the results of lossy compression. For example, as shown in Figure 7, for the Cuprite image, when all of the bands are encoded to a target MSE of 100 per band, using prediction increases the compression ratio from 8:1 to 33:1.

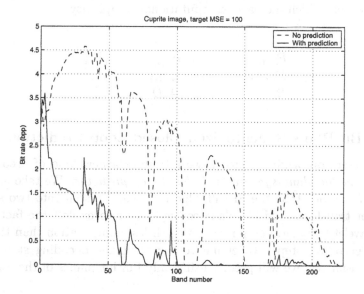

Figure 7: Comparison of bit rates in bits per pixel (bpp) required to code the Cuprite image to MSE=100 with and without prediction for best forward ordering.

6.1   Standard Closed Loop Prediction

To predict the current band, a previous band is needed. In *closed loop prediction*, shown in Figure 8, the decompressed version of a previously encoded band is used for prediction by both the transmitter and receiver.

Let σ be a prediction ordering. As described in Equations (7), the transmitter uses a decompressed previous band $\hat{B}_{\sigma(i)}$ to form $P_{i,\sigma(i)}$, the prediction of original band B_i. Next, $P_{i,\sigma(i)}$ is subtracted from B_i to obtain the difference $D_{i,\sigma(i)}$, which is then coded with SPIHT to the bit rate which yields the target MSE. The decompressed difference band $\hat{D}_{i,\sigma(i)}$ is summed with $P_{i,\sigma(i)}$ to obtain $\hat{B}_i$. Finally, $\hat{B}_i$ is stored in the encoder and decoder so that it can be used to predict some other band, if necessary. Note that this method requires the transmitter to implement the decoder, which increases computational complexity.

$$
\begin{aligned}
P_{i,\sigma(i)} &= a_{i,\sigma(i)}\hat{B}_{\sigma(i)} + c_{i,\sigma(i)}B_m \\
D_{i,\sigma(i)} &= B_i - P_{i,\sigma(i)} \\
\hat{B}_i &= P_{i,\sigma(i)} + \hat{D}_{i,\sigma(i)}
\end{aligned}
\tag{7}
$$

6.2   Bit Plane-Synchronized Closed Loop Prediction

As a lower complexity solution, we introduce a new kind of predictive coder, the *bit plane-synchronized closed loop predictor*. We take advantage of the fact that the SPIHT algorithm can be split into two steps: wavelet transform and bit plane coding. We also exploit the fact that the wavelet transform step requires much less computation than the bit plane encoding step. To eliminate the bit plane decoding step from the transmitter, we will predict using only full bit planes of the wavelet transform.

6.2.1   The Algorithm

The transmitter first performs the wavelet transform on the difference band $D_{i,\sigma(i)}$ to obtain $W_{i,\sigma(i)}$. Let $R(W_{i,\sigma(i)})$ be the bit rate required to encode $W_{i,\sigma(i)}$ to the target MSE. This corresponds to stopping the encoder mid-bit-plane, for example, in bit plane number $k+1$. Let $W^k_{i,\sigma(i)}$

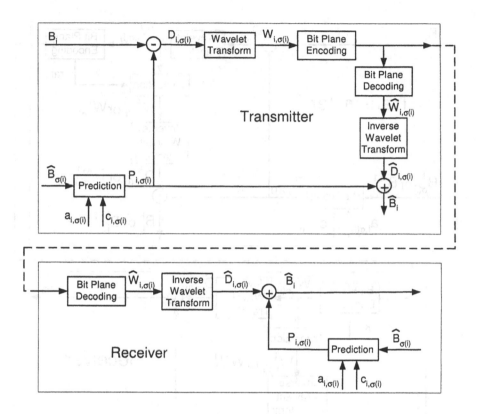

Figure 8: Standard closed loop prediction.

and $W_{i,\sigma(i)}^{k+1}$ be the wavelet coefficients truncated to k or $k+1$ bit planes, respectively. Also, let $R(W_{i,\sigma(i)}^{k})$ and $R(W_{i,\sigma(i)}^{k+1})$ be the bit rates required to code $W_{i,\sigma(i)}^{k}$ and $W_{i,\sigma(i)}^{k+1}$ losslessly. Note that

$$R(W_{i,\sigma(i)}^{k}) \leq R(W_{i,\sigma(i)}) < R(W_{i,\sigma(i)}^{k+1}). \tag{8}$$

The basic idea of our algorithm is to only use complete bit planes for prediction. Thus, if we reach our target MSE mid-bit plane, we now have to decide whether to trim our prediction back to the last full bit plane. Alternatively, if we are close enough to the end of the current bit

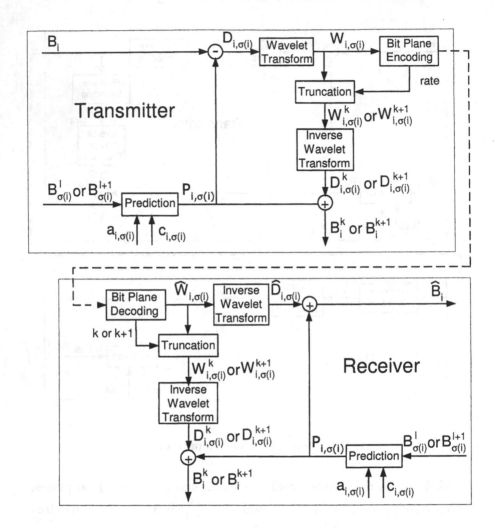

Figure 9: Bit plane-synchronized closed loop prediction.

plane, we can decide to transmit the remaining portion of the bit plane in order to have a better predictor.

In our algorithm, if Equation (9) is satisfied, k complete bit planes are selected for prediction, and the bit rate at which we transmit $W_{i,\sigma(i)}$, $R(W_{i,\sigma(i)})$, does not change. Otherwise, $k+1$ complete bit planes are used for *both prediction and coding*. The bit rate at which we transmit $W_{i,\sigma(i)}$ must be increased to $R(W_{i,\sigma(i)}^{k+1})$. In both cases, the transmitter and receiver use the same number of complete bit planes (either k or $k+1$) for prediction. In Equation (9), T is a threshold with typical values on the order of $0.1 - 1.0$. Note that to reduce the computational complexity, we do not look ahead to see how the prediction results propagate into the future.

$$R(W_{i,\sigma(i)}) - R(W_{i,\sigma(i)}^{k}) \leq T(R(W_{i,\sigma(i)}^{k+1}) - R(W_{i,\sigma(i)}^{k})) \qquad (9)$$

For example, the bit rate required to code the difference band 35 of the Cuprite image to the target MSE of 100 is 1.5 bpp. This corresponds to stopping mid-bit-plane in bit plane number 13. The bit rates required to code this difference band to 12 and 13 bit planes are 0.64 bpp and 1.89 bpp, respectively. If our threshold in Equation (9) is $T = 0.2$, we use 13 bit planes for prediction and encode the difference band to 13 bit planes for transmission (1.89 bpp).

However, in the case of the difference band 69, the bit rate required to code it to the target MSE of 100 is 0.16 bpp. This corresponds to stopping mid-bit-plane in bit plane number 6. The bit rates required to code this difference band to 5 and 6 bit planes are 0.04 bpp and 0.73 bpp, respectively. For the same threshold $T = 0.2$ in Equation 9, we use 5 bit planes for prediction and encode the difference band to 0.16 bpp for transmission.

Figure 9 further describes the prediction and encoding processes. If k bit planes are used for prediction, the transmitter sends $W_{i,\sigma(i)}$ at bit rate $R(W_{i,\sigma(i)})$. The receiver decodes to $\hat{W}_{i,\sigma(i)}$, takes the inverse wavelet transform to obtain $\hat{D}_{i,\sigma(i)}$ and adds to $P_{i,\sigma(i)}$, the prediction of the current band, to compute the decompressed band $\hat{B}_i$. However, to form the prediction of the current band for possible later use, both the transmitter and receiver truncate $W_{i,\sigma(i)}$ and $\hat{W}_{i,\sigma(i)}$ to $W_{i,\sigma(i)}^{k}$, take the inverse wavelet transform to obtain $D_{i,\sigma(i)}^{k}$, and then add $D_{i,\sigma(i)}^{k}$ to $P_{i,\sigma(i)}$ to compute the decompressed truncated band B_i^k which is stored.

If $k + 1$ bit planes are used for prediction, the encoder transmits $W_{i,\sigma(i)}^{k+1}$ at bit rate $R(W_{i,\sigma(i)}^{k+1})$. The receiver decodes to $\hat{W}_{i,\sigma(i)} = W_{i,\sigma(i)}^{k+1}$, takes the inverse wavelet transform to obtain $\hat{D}_{i,\sigma(i)} = D_{i,\sigma(i)}^{k+1}$ and adds to $P_{i,\sigma(i)}$, the prediction of the current band, to compute the decompressed band $\hat{B}_i$. What differs from the previous case of using k bit planes for prediction is that to form the prediction of B_i for possible later use, here, both the encoder and receiver simply inverse transform $W_{i,\sigma(i)}^{k+1}$ to obtain $D_{i,\sigma(i)}^{k+1}$ which is added to $P_{i,\sigma(i)}$ to compute B_i^{k+1}.

Note that in a software implementation of SPIHT we can imagine an easy alternative to the bit plane-synchronized approach. As we compress the image, we maintain an array, one location per wavelet coefficient, containing information about how much of that coefficient has been transmitted. Each time the SPIHT algorithm encodes a bit, the corresponding coefficient locations are updated to the current bit plane. Then, once we have emitted the desired number of bits to meet a maximum file size, we stop. The coefficient array then holds the information about the data that have been transmitted, and we can quickly create a prediction frame from the original frame and the coefficient array we have maintained. However, similarly to the standard closed loop, this method would have higher computational complexity compared to the bit-plane synchronized closed loop solution. For every wavelet coefficient in every bit plane, we would have to execute one additional operation of counter increment. Therefore, the proposed bit plane synchronized algorithm is more feasible than this approach since it is easier to implement and has a lower computational complexity.

6.2.2   Results

In this section we present results. We first study the effects of compression on the spectral profiles of image pixels. Then, we compare the bit plane-synchronized closed loop prediction with the standard closed loop. Finally, we comment on the universality of the prediction coefficients and band ordering.

Effects of Lossy Compression on the Shape of Spectral Profiles
For some applications, it may be important to preserve the shape of the
spectral profiles of image pixels. For example, during classification, the
decompressed spectral profiles may be compared to a standard spectrum
shape stored in a spectral library. Our lossy compression algorithm has
not been designed with this goal in mind, instead we concentrated on
optimizing the rate-distortion performance using the MSE of each band
as the distortion measure. However, to study the effects of lossy compression on the spectral profiles, we computed the Spectral MSE for each
pixel in the five test images after they were encoded to a target MSE of
100 using the closed loop algorithm with best forward band ordering. In
Table 5 we show the percentage of pixels with a spectral MSE below 50,
100, 150, 200, and 500. Note that not all pixels have their spectral MSE
lower than the target MSE of 100. However, a large number of pixels
(89-95%) is within 1.5 times the target MSE.

	Spectral MSE lower than				
	50	100	150	200	500
Cuprite	7.15%	69.45%	91.62%	97.16%	99.93%
Low Altitude	2.86%	70.97%	95.26%	99.04%	99.95%
Jasper Ridge	4.49%	68.54%	93.76%	98.54%	99.94%
Lunar Lake	5.89%	66.98%	89.17%	95.67%	99.88%
Moffett Field	9.09%	65.00%	91.65%	97.81%	99.93%

Table 5: Percentage of pixels with a spectral MSE below given value
when all bands are encoded to a target MSE of 100.

Next we calculate the Maximum Scaled Difference Error (MaxSDE)
to find out how similar the shape of the decompressed spectrum is to the
shape of the original spectrum. In Table 6 we show the percentage of
pixels with a spectrum such that for each band the absolute difference
between the original and decompressed pixel values is below 0.01, 0.015,
0.02, and 0.05. Note that about 90-100% of all pixels have their MaxSDE
lower than 0.05. This leads us to believe that our algorithm preserves
the spectral profile shape for most image pixels.

Finally, we compute the Mean Scaled Difference Error (MSDE) and

	MaxSDE lower than			
	0.01	0.015	0.02	0.05
Cuprite	1.39%	39.59%	83.59%	99.98%
Low Altitude	0.07%	3.50%	20.53%	96.35%
Jasper Ridge	0.00%	0.70%	13.36%	97.18%
Lunar Lake	7.11%	42.94%	73.14%	99.85%
Moffett Field	0.05%	2.98%	22.61%	89.71%

Table 6: Percentage of pixels such that the Maximum Scaled Difference Error is below a given value.

calculate the number of pixels that have their MSDE below 0.0025, 0.005, 0.0075, 0.01, and 0.02. As shown in Table 7, at least 87% of pixels have an average absolute difference error less than 0.01. In summary, our lossy compression algorithm, although not designed to preserve the shape of the spectral profiles exhibits satisfactory performance in that area.

	MSDE lower than				
	0.0025	0.005	0.0075	0.01	0.02
Cuprite	0.83%	85.16%	99.19%	99.94%	100.00%
Low Altitude	0.03%	19.93%	73.84%	92.77%	98.65%
Jasper Ridge	0.00%	9.66%	69.20%	92.25%	97.56%
Lunar Lake	5.45%	71.58%	94.48%	98.93%	99.99%
Moffett Field	0.05%	20.45%	71.21%	87.11%	99.60%

Table 7: Percentage of pixels such that their MSDE is below a certain value.

Compression Results: Bit Plane-Synchronized Closed Loop vs. Standard Closed Loop Prediction In Figure 10, we compare the standard closed and new bit plane-synchronized predictive coders. Over a range of target MSEs from 50 to 500, the bit rate of the bit plane-synchronized coder is only slightly higher than the bit rate of the standard closed loop technique. For a target MSE of 100, the average bit rate for the proposed method is 0.51 bpp, which is an 13.3% increase in bit rate over the 0.45 bit rate for the closed loop prediction. However, for a target MSE of 200, the bit rates are very close. Hence, the bit plane-synchronized loop is a very promising method to code hyperspectral data. It achieves a very good compression ratio with a low MSE and has a much lower computational complexity compared to the original closed loop prediction.

In Table 8, we test our algorithm on five different image sets to verify that our results are consistent across different images. As the table shows, across the five image sets, the compression ratio for the synchronized closed-loop is never less than 13.8% lower than standard closed loop for a target MSE of 100.

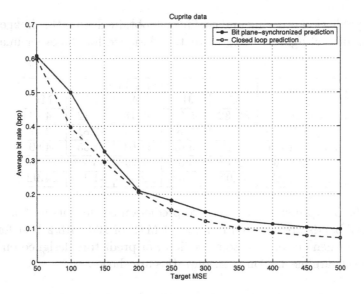

Figure 10: Average bit rate vs. target MSE for bit plane-synchronized closed loop prediction and standard closed loop prediction.

Universality Next, we investigated the universality of the prediction ordering and of the prediction coefficients (the a_{ij}s and c_{ij}s). We designed five best forward predictors using images from the Cuprite, Low Altitude, Jasper Ridge, Lunar Lake, and Moffett Field sites. For each of these five images, we compared the compression performance when

Image Data	No Prediction	Closed Loop	Bit Plane-Synchronized Closed Loop
Cuprite	7.63	35.32	31.05
Jasper Ridge	5.77	25.58	24.13
Low Altitude	6.55	24.61	22.78
Lunar Lake	8.35	35.79	31.79
Moffett Field	6.16	24.93	23.92

Table 8: Compression ratio when all bands are encoded to a target MSE of 100. Best forward ordering was used for the closed and the bit plane-synchronized loop simulations.

using prediction ordering and coefficients obtained from this image (custom predictor) against using predictors designed for the other images.

	Training Image				
	C	JR	LA	LL	MF
Cuprite	**35.32**	-5.60	-6.37	-2.12	-4.73
Jasper Ridge	-4.09	**25.58**	-6.02	-2.81	-3.17
Low Altitude	-4.19	-5.62	**24.61**	-5.35	-4.60
Lunar Lake	-2.72	-3.67	-7.79	**35.79**	-5.35
Moffett Field	-0.03	-1.43	-2.52	-1.48	**24.93**

Table 9: Compression sensitivity to prediction coefficients and orderings when all bands are encoded to a target MSE of 100 with a best forward ordering when either a custom predictor or predictors designed on other image sets are used. Compression ratios are shown.

Table 9 shows the compression ratio when the five data sets are encoded to a target MSE of 100 using different predictors. Best forward ordering and the closed loop algorithm were used for this experiment. As expected, the best performance is obtained when an image is compressed using a custom predictor. When a predictor designed on a different image set is used, the performance may be affected quite severely. The decrease in compression ratio when a non-custom predictor is used is on the order of 0 - 25%. Nonetheless, using any image as the predictor yields large compression ratios for the target MSE of 100.

Agnieszka C. Miguel, Richard E. Ladner, Eve A. Riskin, Scott Hauch,
Dane K. Barney, Amanda R. Askew, and Alexander Chang

We also compared the prediction ordering. When the Cuprite image was compressed using predictors designed using the Jasper Ridge, Low Altitude, Lunar Lake and Moffett Field data, only 31-42 out of the 224 bands were predicted from different previous bands compared to the custom predictor. Thus we believe that good hyperspectral image compression can be obtained with a fixed band ordering and set of prediction coefficients.

7 Conclusion

In this research, we have investigated different methods of using prediction to code hyperspectral data. As expected, combining prediction with a state-of-the-art image compression algorithm significantly improves the compression ratio (from 8:1 to 33:1 for the Cuprite image and lossy compression with a target MSE of 100 and from 2.3:1 to 3.2:1 for the same image and lossless compression).

We studied the impact of different band orderings on the compression ratios. We found that the lossless compression performance for both best forward and best reverse ordering is very close to that for optimal ordering. We also considered two measures of prediction quality: compressed file size (CFS) and the prediction MSE (PMSE), and analyzed their impact on the compression performance. We discovered that lossless compression ratios based on the CFS metric were consistently better than those based on the PMSE, however, the difference was very small. We concluded that the resulting lossless compression algorithm displays performance that is comparable with other recently published results.

To reduce the complexity of the lossy predictive encoder, we proposed a bit plane-synchronized closed loop predictor that does not require full decompression of a previous band at the encoder. The new technique achieves similar compression ratios to that of standard closed loop predictive coding and has a simpler implementation.

References

[1] J. P. Laboratory, "AVIRIS (airborne visible/infrared imaging spectrometer) homepage." http://aviris.jpl.nasa.gov/.

[2] J. Seward, "The bzip2 and libbzip2 official home page." http://sources.redhat.com/bzip2/.

[3] A. Said and W. A. Pearlman, "A new, fast, and efficient image codec based on set partitioning in hierarchical trees," *IEEE Transactions on Circuits and Systems for Video Technology*, vol. 6, pp. 243–250, June 1996.

[4] T. W. Fry and S. Hauck, "Hyperspectral image compression on reconfigurable platforms," in *IEEE Symposium on Field-Programmable Custom Computing Machines*, pp. 251–260, 2002.

[5] A. Miguel, A. Askew, A. Chang, S. Hauck, R. Ladner, and E. Riskin, "Reduced complexity wavelet-based predictive coding of hyperspectral images for FPGA implementation," in *Proceedings Data Compression Conference*, pp. 469–478, 2004.

[6] P. Shippert, "Why use hyperspectral imagery?," *Photogrammetric Engineering & Remote Sensing, Journal Of The American Society For Photogrammetry And Remote Sensing*, vol. 70, pp. 377–380, April 2004.

[7] R. W. Basedow, M. Kappus, L. J. Rickard, and M. E. Anderson, "HYDICE: Operational system status." http://ltpwww.gsfc.nasa.gov/ISSSR-95/hydiceop.htm.

[8] Earth Search Sciences, Inc., "Probe-1." http://www.earthsearch.com/index.htm.

[9] ITRES Research, Inc., "CASI-2 and CASI-3." http://www.earthsearch.com/index.htm.

[10] Integrated Spectronics, "HyMap." http://www.intspec.com/.

[11] Group for Environmental Research Earth Resources Exploration Consortium, "Airborne hyperspectral and multispectral imaging systems." http://www.ger.com/ie.html.

[12] Spectral Imaging, "AISA." http://www.specim.fi/index.html.

[13] U.S. Geological Survey EROS Data Center, "USGS EO-1 website." http://eo1.usgs.gov/hyperion.php.

[14] M. Burrows and D. J. Wheeler, "A block-sorting lossless data compression algorithm," Tech. Rep. 124, Digital Equipment Corporation, 1994.

[15] N. S. Jayant and P. Noll, *Digital Coding of Waveforms*. Englewood Cliffs, N. J.: Prentice-Hall, 1984.

[16] J. L. Mitchell, W. B. Pennebaker, C. E. Fogg, and D. J. LeGall, *MPEG Video Compression Standard*. New York: Chapman & Hall, 1996.

[17] V. Cuperman and A. Gersho, "Adaptive differential vector coding of speech," in *Conference Record GlobeCom 82*, pp. 1092–1096, Dec. 1982.

[18] P.-C. Chang and R. M. Gray, "Gradient algorithms for designing predictive vector quantizers," *IEEE Transactions on Acoustics Speech and Signal Processing*, vol. 34, pp. 679–690, Aug. 1986.

[19] A. Gersho and R. M. Gray, *Vector Quantization and Signal Compression*. Norwell, MA: Kluwer Academic Publishers, 1992.

[20] H.-M. Hang and J. W. Woods, "Predictive vector quantization of images," *IEEE Transactions on Acoustics Speech and Signal Processing*, vol. 33, pp. 1208–1219, Nov. 1985.

[21] R. M. Gray, "Vector quantization," *IEEE ASSP Magazine*, vol. 1, pp. 4–29, Apr. 1984.

[22] S.-E. Qian, A.-B. Hollinger, D. Williams, and D. Manak, "Vector quantization using spectral index-based multiple subcodebooks for hyperspectral data compression," *IEEE Transactions on Geoscience and Remote Sensing*, vol. 38, no. 3, pp. 1183–1190, 2000.

[23] M. J. Ryan and M. R. Pickering, "An improved M-NVQ algorithm for the compression of hyperspectral data," in *Proceedings of the IEEE International Geoscience and Remote Sensing Symposium (IGARSS)*, vol. 2, pp. 600–602, 2000.

[24] G. P. Abousleman, T.-T. Lam, and L. J. Karam, "Robust hyperspectral image coding with channel-optimized trellis-coded quantization," *IEEE Transactions on Geoscience and Remote Sensing*, vol. 40, no. 4, pp. 820–830, 2002.

[25] H. S. Lee, N.-H. Younan, and R. L. King, "Hyperspectral image cube compression combining JPEG 2000 and spectral decorrelation," in *Proceedings of the IEEE International Geoscience and Remote Sensing Symposium (IGARSS)*, vol. 6, pp. 3317–3319, 2000.

[26] X. Tang, S. Cho, and W. A. Pearlman, "Comparison of 3D set partitioning methods in hyperspectral image compression featuring an improved 3D-SPIHT," in *Proceedings of the Data Compression Conference*, p. 449, 2003.

[27] T. Markas and J. Reif, "Multispectral image compression algorithms," in *Proceedings of the Data Compression Conference*, vol. 3, pp. 391–400, 1993.

[28] G. P. Abousleman, M. W. Marcellin, and B. R. Hunt, "Hyperspectral image compression using using entropy-constrained predictive trellis coded quantization," *IEEE Transactions on Image Processing*, vol. 6, no. 7, pp. 566–573, 1997.

[29] P.-L. Dragotti, G. Poggi, and R. P. Ragozini, "Compression of multispectral images by three-dimensional SPIHT algorithm," *IEEE Transactions on Geoscience and Remote Sensing*, vol. 38, no. 1, pp. 416–428, 2000.

[30] N. D. Memon, "A bounded distortion compression scheme for hyper-spectral data," in *Proceedings of the IEEE International Geoscience and Remote Sensing Symposium (IGARSS)*, vol. 2, pp. 1039–1041, 1996.

[31] A. Rao and S. Bhargava, "Multispectral data compression using bidirectional interband prediction," *IEEE Trans. on Geoscience and Remote Sensing*, vol. 34, no. 2, pp. 385–397, 1996.

[32] S. R. Tate, "Band ordering in lossless compression of multispectral images," *IEEE Transactions on Computers*, vol. 46, pp. 477–483, Apr. 1997.

[33] M. J. Ryan and J. F. Arnold, "A suitable distortion measure for the lossy compression of hyperspectral data," in *Proceedings of the IEEE International Geoscience and Remote Sensing Symposium (IGARSS)*, vol. 4, pp. 2056–2058, 1998.

[34] G. Motta, F. Rizzo, and J. A. Storer, "Compression of hyperspectral imagery," in *Proceedings Data Compression Conference*, pp. 333–342, Mar. 2003.

[35] F. Rizzo, B. Carpentieri, G. Motta, and J. A. Storer, "High performance compression of hyperspectral imagery with reduced search complexity in the compressed domain," in *Proceedings Data Compression Conference*, pp. 479–488, 2004.

[36] M. J. Ryan and J. F. Arnold, "The lossless compression of AVIRIS images by vector quantization," *IEEE Transactions on Geoscience and Remote Sensing*, vol. 35, pp. 546 –550, May 1997.

[37] M. R. Pickering and M. J. Ryan, "Efficient spatial-spectral compression of hyperspectral data," *IEEE Transactions on Geoscience and Remote Sensing*, vol. 39, no. 7, pp. 1536–1539, 2001.

[38] B. Aiazzi, P. Alba, L. Alparone, and S. Baronti, "Lossless compression of multi/hyper-spectral imagery based on a 3-D fuzzy prediction," *IEEE Transactions on Geoscience and Remote Sensing*, vol. 37, no. 5, pp. 2287–2294, 1999.

[39] S.-E. Qian, A. B. Hollinger, and Y. Hamiaux, "Study of real-time lossless data compression for hyperspectral imagery," in *Proceedings of the IEEE International Geoscience and Remote Sensing Symposium (IGARSS)*, vol. 4, pp. 2038–2042, 1999.

[40] R. E. Roger and M. C. Cavenor, "Lossless compression of AVIRIS images," *IEEE Transactions on Image Processing*, vol. 5, no. 5, pp. 713–719, 1996.

[41] V. D. Vaughn and T. S. Wilkinson, "System considerations for multispectral image compression designs," *IEEE Signal Processing Magazine*, vol. 12, pp. 19–31, January 1995.

[42] T. H. Cormen, C. E. Leiserson, R. L. Rivest, and C. Stein, *Introduction to Algorithms*. 2001. Second edition.

[43] J. Edmonds, "Optimum branchings," *Journal of Research of the National Bureau of Standards*, vol. 71B, pp. 233–240, 1967.

[44] R. E. Tarjan, "Finding optimum branchings," *Networks*, vol. 7, pp. 2–35, 1977.

[45] H. N. Gabow, Z. Galil, T. Spencer, and R. E. Tarjan, "Efficient algorithms for finding minimum spanning trees in undirected and directed graphs," *Combinatorica*, vol. 6, no. 2, pp. 109–122, 1986.

[46] P. Kopylov and P. Fränti, "Optimal layer ordering in the compression of map images," in *Proceedings of the Data Compression Conference*, pp. 323–332, 2003.

[47] C. Bloom, "Dictionary coders (lzp)." http://www.cbloom.com/src/index_lz.html.

[48] A. Simakov, "Shcodec home page." http://webcenter.ru/~xander/.

[49] H. Peltola and J. Tarhio, "Ppmz for Linux." http://www.cs.hut.fi/u/tarhio/ppmz/.

[50] S. T. Lavavej, "bwtzip." http://nuwen.net/bwtzip.html.

[51] M. Schindler, "Szip homepage." http://www.compressconsult.com/szip/.

[52] D. Debin, "Zzip homepage." http://debin.org/zzip/.

Coding of Hyperspectral Imagery with Trellis-Coded Quantization

Glen P. Abousleman

General Dynamics C4 Systems
8201 E. McDowell Road
Scottsdale, AZ 85257
glen.abousleman@gdc4s.com

1 Introduction

The common operating mode for strategic and tactical reconnaissance sensors has been, from the earliest days of photography, panchromatic. That is, the usual form of focal plane sensors integrate a wide range of data wavelengths into a single response. This single response is then usually displayed as a gray-scale image in which the integrated wavelength response at a given spatial point is given a gray-scale range between pure white (maximum response) and pure black (zero response). The choice of panchromatic sensing has been purely pragmatic in motivation. Although it is known that some narrow-band responses are of interest, such as in infrared, there have been few problems of reconnaissance significance that were driven by the need to couple wavelength sensitivity to spatial resolution.

The preferability of only panchromatic sensing has begun to wane in recent years. A variety of questions are now important that can only be answered by the ability to perform precise recording of sensed energy in a number of narrow wavelength slices. For example, various types of camouflage and concealment techniques are revealed by narrow-band spectral sensing. The effluents of various manufacturing facilities, as sensed by fine spectral resolution, can be a critical clue to the type of processes employed in the facility. The agricultural yield and health of crops can be predicted from quantitative analysis of fine resolution spectral images [1]. The development and utilization of fine resolution spectral sensors is becoming of prominent interest for these and many other applications.

The Landsat series of earth satellites conclusively established the value of employing image sensors with multiple wavelength sensitivity [2]. Landsat images represent a rather course slicing of the optical wavelength spectrum, however, being only 4 to 6 overlapping bands through the visible and near infrared wavelengths, with each band having a width of 100 to 200 nm. Given that many surface materials have absorption features that are only 20 to 40 nm wide [1], it is apparent that this class of "multispectral" sensor cannot record the narrow wavelength absorption features that are indicative of specific materials in laboratory-based spectroscopy [3].

The limitation associated with multispectral scanners has led to imaging spectrometers which register many narrow waveband images of a scene and allow the assemblage of a contiguous reflectance spectrum for each pixel in the scene. An early example of such a sensor is the Airborne Imaging Spectrometer (AIS) [4]. AIS was developed by the NASA Jet Propulsion Laboratory (JPL) for civil environmental applications. AIS could simultaneously record 128 near-infrared wavebands (each being 9.3 nm wide) with a 365 to 787 m swath.

A more complex JPL sensor is the Airborne Visible/Infrared Imaging Spectrometer (AVIRIS) [5, 6]. ARIRIS can collect 209 visible and near-infrared wavebands, each of width 10 nm, with an 11-km swath. The radiometric quantization of AVIRIS is 10 bits for each spectral band.

Because of the enhanced spectral and spatial resolution of modern hyperspectral scanners, tremendous amounts of raw data are produced. In fact, high-resolution hyperspectral scanners can expel on the order of 512 megabits/second in their operational state. With satellite-based systems, transmission of the complete data record to an earth receiving station is difficult since current satellite downlink channels are capable of only 300 megabits/second, and must service all on-board experiments, not just the hyperspectral scanner [7].

Once the sensor information is down-loaded to an earth receiving station, processing and handling of the data is very problematic. For example, a satellite hyperspectral sensor platform could expel terabytes of data per day [8], with the total data collected being on the order of 10^{16} bytes over a typical 15-year mission. Moreover, data handling expenses alone could amount to hundreds of millions of dollars over the life of the system [9]. Ground-based operations include archival, browsing, dissemination, and rapid delivery and analysis of the hyperspectral data.

In uncoded form, storage of the data is feasible (although expensive) with the use of optical disk technology, but transmission from site to site places undue demands on the communications link, and browsing as a prelude to analysis is nearly impossible. It may be advantageous to have browse-quality data online to facilitate rapid viewing of several hyperspectral images. Fewer bytes on the disk equate to much faster read times, and transmission costs for the data are reduced significantly [9].

AVIRIS is exemplary of the characteristics of fine-spectral-resolution image sensors. The volume of data in such images requires fundamental rethinking of many image processing operations that have been developed for panchromatic and even low-dimensional multispectral data. A property of fine-spectral-resolution imagery is interband correlation. It is easy to observe in even coarse-band imagery, such as Landsat multispectral or three-primary color images, that many features of edge definition, contrast, texture, gray-level, etc., remain substantially the same from spectral band to spectral band. The interband correlation facilitates substantial reduction of the data required for the storage and transmission of the imagery. However, a careless approach to reducing the correlation could lead to disastrous loss of the information differences between bands that are the critical value of multispectral imagery. An improper reduction of correlation redundancy could make it impossible to exploit the imagery for significant utility.

Compression of hyperspectral imagery can manifest itself in sensor-based and/or ground-based systems. The former requires fast, efficient algorithms, implementable with existing low complexity (low power consumption) hardware in near-real-time. The requirements of the latter are somewhat relaxed in that hardware of greater complexity can be utilized, and speed may not be of paramount importance. However, for uses such as rapid browsing, decoding should be fast enough to handle data rates in real time. Also, savings in transmission and storage should not be negated by the computational costs associated with decoding. Accordingly, much attention has been focused recently on the compression of hyperspectral imagery, and a broad sampling of techniques can be found in [10–18].

In this chapter, we present several image coding systems for the lossy compression of hyperspectral imagery, where each system employs a form of trellis-coded quantization (TCQ). The chapter is organized as follows. Section 2 outlines several version of TCQ that are used in the various hyperspectral image coders that are presented throughout the chapter. These include fixed-rate TCQ (FRTCQ), entropy-constrained TCQ (ECTCQ), entropy-constrained predictive TCQ (ECPTCQ) [16], and channel-optimized TCQ (COTCQ) [10]. Section 3 presents a hyperspectral image coder that combines the discrete cosine transform (DCT) with ECPTCQ [16]. In Section 4, a coder is presented where the 3-D DCT is used in conjunction with ECTCQ [18]. Section 5 discusses two adaptive coders that utilize differential pulse code modulation (DPCM), adaptive classification, and ECTCQ. The first coder is based on the discrete wavelet transform (DWT) [19], while the second is based on the DCT [20]. For noisy channels, Section 6 presents a wavelet-based coder that uses COTCQ, which is resilient to channel errors [10]. Coding results and comparisons are presented in Section 7, and a conclusion is given in Section 8.

2   Trellis-Coded Quantization

Trellis-coded quantization (TCQ) is an effective and computationally tractable
method for encoding memoryless sources as well as sources with memory [21].
The mean-squared-error (MSE) performance of TCQ is excellent with modest
complexity when compared with other fixed-rate quantization schemes.

For memoryless sources, entropy-constrained TCQ (ECTCQ) was introduced in [22]. This version of ECTCQ cascades a specially designed TCQ system with entropy coding (e.g., Huffman or arithmetic) to provide the best MSE
performance seen to date for encoding memoryless sources at rates above 1.0
bits per sample. In [23], that same excellent performance was extended to *all*
non-negative encoding rates by introducing the notion of superset entropy. In
what follows, we briefly review the concepts of FRTCQ and ECTCQ, and then
proceed with a detailed discussion of ECPTCQ and COTCQ.

2.1   Fixed-Rate Trellis-Coded Quantization

Trellis-coded quantization was originally developed in [21]. For encoding a memoryless source at R bits per sample, a codebook of size 2^{R+1} is partitioned into
four subsets, each containing 2^{R-1} codewords. These subsets are labeled D_0,
D_1, D_2, and D_3, and are used as labels for the branches of a suitably chosen
trellis. An example is shown in Figure 1 for R = 2.

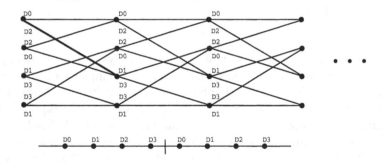

Figure 1: A 4-state trellis with subset labeling and codebook.

Sequences of codewords that are produced by the TCQ system are those
that result from "walks" along the trellis from left to right. For example, if
beginning in the top left state of the trellis in Figure 1, the first codeword must
be chosen from either D_0 or D_2. If a codeword from D_2 is chosen, then we walk
along the lower branch (shown with a heavy line) to the second state from the
bottom, at which we must choose a codeword from either D_1 or D_3.

Given an input data sequence, $x_1, x_2, \ldots$, the best (minimum mean-squared-error) allowable sequence of codewords is determined as follows. For the ith stage in the trellis (corresponding to x_i), the best codeword in the jth subset ($j = 0, 1, 2, 3$), say c_j, is chosen, and the associated cost, $\rho_j = (x_i - c_j)^2$, is calculated. Each branch in the ith stage of the trellis that is labeled with subset, D_j, is assigned cost, ρ_j. The Viterbi algorithm [24] is then used to find the path through the trellis with the lowest overall cost.

Two methods are commonly used to map the codeword sequence specified by the selected trellis path into a bit sequence suitable for digital transmission. The first scheme [21] uses 1 bit/sample to specify the path through the trellis, and hence the subset, while the remaining $R - 1$ bits/sample are used to specify the chosen codeword from the particular subset (the initial trellis state is assumed to be known). The resulting bit sequence is then transmitted through the channel to the decoder. The second method [23] results by noting that at each step in the encoding, the codeword must be chosen from either $A_0 = D_0 \cup D_2$ or $A_1 = D_1 \cup D_3$. Each of these "supersets" contains 2^R codewords and hence, given an initial trellis state, the sequence of selected codewords can be transmitted using one R-bit label for each sample.

2.2 Entropy-Constrained Trellis-Coded Quantization

To improve the performance of TCQ for sources with non-uniform densities, an entropy-constrained TCQ (ECTCQ) system was developed in [22]. That system was based on the first method of assigning a bit sequence to a codeword sequence (as discussed in the previous section). Specifically, 1 bit/sample was used to specify a path through the trellis, while an estimate of the rate required to entropy-code the specific element from the chosen subset is specified by the conditional entropy of the codebook, given the subset. The overall average encoding rate is then given by $1 + H(C|D)$, where

$$H(C|D) = \sum_{i=0}^{3} \sum_{c \in D_i} P(c|D_i)P(D_i) \log_2 P(c|D_i), \qquad (1)$$

and $P(c|D_i)$ is the probability of choosing the codeword, c, given the subset, D_i. It is apparent that the minimum achievable encoding rate is 1 bit/sample (when using scalar codebooks).

It was shown in [23] that by using the second method of constructing the bit sequence (as discussed above), it is possible to encode a source at all non-negative rates. In that system, the codeword labels were noiselessly compressed using one variable length code for each superset. The encoding rate achievable by this process is the conditional entropy of the codebook, C, given the superset:

$$H(C|A) = -\sum_{i=0}^{1}\sum_{c\in A_i} P(c|A_i)P(A_i)\log_2 P(c|A_i). \tag{2}$$

For a codebook of size 2^{R+1} (as discussed above), this noiseless compression causes the encoding rate to fall below R bits/sample, thus requiring that the size of the codebook be increased.

For the systems in [22] and [23], optimum codebooks (in terms of both the number and values of codewords) were designed using a generalized version of the Lloyd algorithm for vector quantizer design [25]. This algorithm chooses the "best" codeword by considering both the MSE and the number of bits required to represent a particular codeword. This is facilitated by minimizing the cost functional,

$$J = E[\rho(x,c)] + \lambda E[l(c)], \tag{3}$$

where x is the data, c is the encoded version of x, $\rho(x,c)$ is the cost of representing x by c, λ is a Lagrange multiplier, and $l(c) \approx -\log_2 P(c|D_i)$ or $l(c) \approx -\log_2 P(c|A_i)$ is the number of bits used by the variable length code to represent c, for the subset and superset entropy calculations, respectively. It is shown in [23] that for encoding a memoryless Gaussian source with an 8-state trellis (based on superset entropy), performance within 0.5 dB of the rate-distortion function is obtained at all non-negative rates.

2.3 Entropy-Constrained Predictive Trellis-Coded Quantization

For sources with memory, a predictive TCQ (PTCQ) system was developed in [21]. In that system, each path through the trellis corresponds to a potential output sequence of PTCQ. Predictions of the data sample, x_i, are made at each state using the potential output sequences leading into that state. The prediction residual for state k, say, d_i^k, is calculated by subtracting the prediction from the current data sample. The codeword closest to the prediction residual in each subset corresponding to a branch exiting state k is chosen, and the branch cost is calculated as the squared error between that codeword and the prediction residual at state k. The quantized value of the current data sample (for each branch) is formed by adding the chosen codeword (quantized prediction residual) to the prediction. As in the memoryless case, the Viterbi algorithm is used to choose a path through the trellis.

Three *entropy-constrained* versions of PTCQ were introduced in [22]. In the first system, unconstrained codebooks were designed for autoregressive sources using a slightly modified version of the generalized Lloyd algorithm as discussed above. Recall that for the predictive case, the cost associated with a particular branch is given by the squared error between the codeword and the prediction residual at state k. The design algorithm then minimizes the functional,

$$J = E[\rho(d,c)] + \lambda E[l(c)],$$ (4)

where d is the prediction residual, and c is the encoded version of d. In the second version, the codewords were constrained to be uniform. That is, the codewords, c_i, were selected as a scaled version of a finite subset of an integer lattice. The design and encoding rule are as in (4), with the scale factor (for the uniform codebook) and codeword lengths being updated at each iteration. The third version uses optimal codebooks designed for the memoryless Gaussian source. Recall that for a Pth-order linear predictor, if the prediction of x_j is $\hat{x}_j$, and $\hat{x}_j \approx x_j$, then the prediction error is $x_j - \hat{x}_{j|j-1} \approx w_j$. Since w_j is a Gaussian random variable, use of Gaussian-optimized codebooks are a reasonable choice for moderate to high encoding rates.

The performance of the three systems as outlined in [22] were shown to be nearly identical for first- and second-order autoregressive sources at rates greater than 1.5 bits/sample. Since the entropy was calculated using (1), performance comparisons at rates less than 1 bit/sample were not possible.

Motivation for the ECPTCQ system discussed here lies in previous work on entropy-constrained scalar quantization (ECSQ) [26] and entropy-constrained differential pulse code modulation (ECDPCM) [27]. It is shown in [26] that for ECSQ, the optimum reconstruction levels are computed using

$$Q_l = \frac{1}{P_l} \int_{T_{l-1}}^{T_l} x f_X(x) dx,$$ (5)

where $f_X(x)$ is the probability density function (pdf) of the source, and P_l is the probability that the source output assumes a value in the lth partition:

$$P_l \equiv \text{prob}(T_{l-1} < X \leq T_l) = \int_{T_{l-1}}^{T_l} f_X(x) dx.$$ (6)

The optimum threshold levels (for a given output entropy) are computed using

$$T_l = \frac{Q_{l+1} + Q_l}{2} - \frac{\lambda}{2(Q_{l+1} - Q_l)} \ln(P_{l+1}/P_l).$$ (7)

It can be shown that the output entropy depends only on the threshold levels, T_l, and is independent of the Q_l. Also, it is shown in [26] that nearly equal performance can be obtained by using *uniform thresholds*. That is, rather than designing the threshold levels according to (7), it suffices to simply choose the T_l uniformly, with spacing, Δ, and calculate the Q_l using (5). The choice of Δ

determines the output entropy, and hence, the design of the quantizer is greatly simplified.

Consider now a TCQ codebook with separate decision and reconstruction codewords. The codeword chosen for each branch is that which minimizes the distance between the prediction residual (of the state from which the branch emanates) and a decision codeword, t_j. However, the quantized prediction residual is represented by the corresponding reconstruction codeword, c_j. The cost associated with each branch (for use in the Viterbi search) is set to $\rho_i^k = (d_i^k - t_j)^2$. The decision codewords, t_j, are formed by taking a uniform scalar codebook with stepsize, Δ, and assigning its codewords (from left-to-right) to subsets D_0, D_1, D_2, D_3, D_0, D_1, D_2, D_3,.... It is important that a "midtread" codebook be used, and that the "zero" codeword is included in the D_0 subset [23]. By partitioning the decision codewords in this fashion, four codebooks are created, each corresponding to a uniform threshold scalar quantizer with stepsize 4Δ. The reconstruction codewords, c_j, are the *centroids* of support regions defined by $t_j \pm 2\Delta$.

Philosophically, this process is a generalization (to a trellis-based structure) of that employed in [27]. In that system, the codewords used for reconstruction are computed as centroids (based on the probability density function (pdf) of prediction residuals), while the decisions of which codewords to use are based on uniform thresholds. From the point of view of minimizing a cost function, this is equivalent to making codeword decisions based on minimizing the distance between prediction residuals and the codewords of a uniform codebook. This is exactly what is done by the ECPTCQ system discussed here. In fact, finding the best t_j in each subset can be accomplished by performing a uniform threshold quantization.

Design of the reconstruction codewords is facilitated with the following algorithm:

1. For a given stepsize, Δ, and integer, N, let $c_j^{(0)} = t_j, j = 1, \ldots, N$, be the codewords of a midtread uniform scalar quantizer with stepsize Δ. Partition these codewords into subsets and set $i = 0$.

2. Set $i = i + 1$; quantize the training data and assign the prediction residual, d, at each stage (of the surviving path) to one of the sets, $S_1, \ldots, S_N$, corresponding to the codeword selected for that residual.

3. For each S_j, compute a reconstruction codeword as $c_j^{(i)} = \frac{1}{|S_j|} \sum_{d \in S_j} d$, where $|S_j|$ is the number of elements belonging to S_j.

4. If the difference in quantizer structure, $\frac{1}{N} \sum_{j=1}^{N} |c_j^{(i)} - c_j^{(i-1)}|$, is greater than some small $\epsilon > 0$, go to Step 2. Otherwise, stop with codebook C.

Experiments using different codebook sizes at various rates were performed to determine the appropriate codebook size, N. It was found that excellent performance can be obtained when N is at least $2^{(R+5)}$, where R is the desired entropy. It should be noted that the ECPTCQ training algorithm is not guaranteed to converge. However, suitable codebooks can typically be obtained in less than five iterations with N = 512 and $\epsilon = 0.0001$.

Performance of ECPTCQ The performance curve for an 8-state ECPTCQ system is shown in Figure 2. For comparison, Figure 2 also shows the performance of an entropy-constrained DPCM system obtained by applying the same training algorithm to a scalar-quantizer-based system. In each case, the codebooks were trained using 50,000 data samples from a unity-variance, first-order Gauss-Markov source with correlation coefficient $\rho = 0.8$. The results of Figure 2 were then obtained by encoding 50,000 samples from outside the training sequence. Each curve was produced parametrically by varying the value of the step size, Δ (i.e., each point on a particular curve was obtained by applying the algorithm with a different choice of Δ). Although not shown here, experiments with different values of ρ provide similar results.

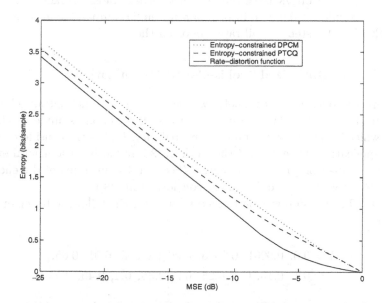

Figure 2: MSE performance of ECPTCQ.

At rates above 2.0 bits/sample, the performance of the DPCM system in Figure 2 is equivalent to that obtained in [27]. At rates below 2.0 bits/sample, the DPCM results reported here are superior to those in [27]. Apparently, at low rates, the polynomial model of the prediction residual pdf used there is not sufficiently accurate, and the training-sequence-based approach yields superior performance. The ECPTCQ system provides a further performance increase over both scalar-quantizer-based schemes for all rates above 0.25 bits/sample. For example, at 1.0 bits/sample, ECPTCQ is roughly 1.1 dB and 1.75 dB better than the ECDPCM results reported here and in [27], respectively.

Asymptotically, as the rate is increased and the quantization becomes very fine, the residual pdf should approach that of the memoryless Gaussian source, and the performance of ECPTCQ (and ECDPCM) should approach that of entropy-constrained TCQ (and entropy-constrained scalar quantization) operating on the memoryless Gaussian source. This is in fact what occurs. At high rates, the performance of the ECDPCM system is within 1.53 dB of the rate-distortion function (as expected from [26, 27]) and the ECPTCQ system is within 0.5 dB of the rate-distortion function (as expected from [22, 23]). It should be pointed out that this convergence is markedly faster for the scalar system than for the trellis-based system. The asymptotic result is nearly achieved for the DPCM systems at about 2.0 bits/sample, while the ECPTCQ system requires rates as high as 5 bits/sample. For the first-order Gauss-Markov source with correlation coefficient 0.9 used in [22], our system is comparable in performance to the ECPTCQ systems at all rates reported there.

2.4   Channel-Optimized Trellis-Coded Quantization

For operation over noisy channels, we designed a channel-optimized trellis-coded quantization (COTCQ) system for use with the binary symmetric channel (BSC), which is defined by the bit error probability, P_b. For the considered image coding application, we extended the work in [28] by deriving a general expression of the transition probability matrix (Section 2.4) in terms of the encoding bit rate R (only $R = 1$ and $R = 2$ are considered in [28]).

The COTCQ design was performed to support the following bit error probabilities:

$$P_b = 0.0,\ 0.0001,\ 0.0005,\ 0.001,\ 0.005,\ 0.01,\ 0.05,$$
$$0.1,\ 0.15,\ 0.2,\ 0.25,\ 0.3,\ 0.35,\ 0.4,\ 0.45,\ 0.5. \qquad (8)$$

For each P_b, fixed-rate COTCQ codebooks were designed in one-bit increments from $R = 1$ to 8 bits per sample.

In what follows, let R denote the encoding bit rate (corresponding to one COTCQ quantizer), P_b the bit error probability of the transmission channel, and N_1 the number of TCQ subsets. In our case, since we consider a 4-state trellis, $N_1 = 4$. The COTCQ codebook used to encode a sequence at R bits/sample contains 2^{R+1} codewords. Each of the four subsets then contains $N_2 = 2^{R-1}$ codewords.

Consider an input sequence, $X = \{x_j\}_{j=1}^{\|x\|}$, where $\|x\|$ denotes the number of elements in the sequence, X. Let $Y = \{y_{k,l}\}$ be the set of reconstructed levels, or codewords. $y_{k,l}$, $0 < k < 4$, $0 \le l \le 2^{R-1}$, denotes the codeword corresponding to the lth level of the kth subset, D_k. We define the distortion measure between x_j and $y_{k,l}$ as

$$d(x_j, y_{k,l}) = \sum_{i=0}^{N_1-1} \sum_{n=0}^{N_2-1} P_{i,n/k,l}(x_j - y_{i,n})^2, \tag{9}$$

where $P_{i,n/k,l} = \text{Prob}\{y_{i,n} \text{ received} / y_{k,l} \text{ is sent}\}$, and is given by the transition probability matrix derived in Section 2.4. We define the overall distortion as

$$D = \frac{1}{\|x\|} \sum_{x_j \in X} d(x_j, y_{k,l}), \tag{10}$$

where x_j has been encoded as $y_{k,l}$, after the COTCQ has found its path through the trellis to minimize the overall distortion, D.

For a given bit error probability, P_b, and an encoding rate, R, the quantization codebook is designed using the K-means algorithm [29] and the defined distortion metric (10). At each iteration, a training sequence is encoded using the metric above and clustered. The cluster centroids are then used to encode the training sequence and to update the old centroids until the algorithm converges to a local optimum.

Let m be an iteration index. Let $Y^{(m)} = \{y_{k,l}^{(m)}\}$ be the set of reconstruction levels at the mth iteration, $D^{(m)}$ be the overall distortion at the mth iteration, and $Q_{k,l}^{(m)} = \{x_j : x_j \in X \text{ is encoded as } y_{k,l}^{(m)}\}$. The algorithm used to design the optimum codebooks is described as follows [28]:

1. Initialization: Set $m = 0$, and the overall distortion measure, $D^{(-1)} = \infty$. The training sequence, the convergence threshold, ϵ, and the initial reproduction codebook are given.

2. Reproduction Codebook Update: Encode the training sequence using the Viterbi algorithm and the codebook, $\{y_{k,l}^{(m)}\}$, to obtain $\{Q_{k,l}^{(m)}\}$ and $D^{(m)}$, as given by (10). If $(D^{(m-1)} - D^{(m)})/D^{(m)} < \epsilon$, stop; otherwise, update the centroids as follows:

$$y_{i,n}^{(m+1)} = \frac{\sum_{x_j \in Q_{k,l}^{(m)}} x_j}{\sum_{k=0}^{N_1-1} \sum_{l=0}^{N_2-1} P_{i,n/k,l} \|Q_{k,l}\|^{(m)}}. \tag{11}$$

3. Set $m = m + 1$, and go to Step 2.

For the hyperspectral image coder discussed in Section 6, we designed a set of channel-optimized trellis-coded quantizers for values of R ranging from 1 to 8 bits per sample, and the values of P_b as indicated in (8). For $P_b = 0.0$ (which corresponds to ordinary TCQ, since no noise is present), the initial codebook in Step 0 is chosen to contain the reconstruction levels of a scalar quantizer. For the subsequent P_b values, we follow the method described in [30], which consists of using, as the initial codebook, the optimum codebook that was found for the preceding P_b value.

Transition probability matrix The entries of the transition probability matrix consist of the transition probabilities, $P_{i,n/k,l} = \mathrm{Prob}\{y_{i,n}$ received $/$ $y_{k,l}$ sent$\}$, where $y_{k,l}$ is generated by the encoder and sent through the binary symmetric channel. i, k correspond to the selected subsets, and n, l to the codewords chosen from subsets i and k, respectively. The transition probability matrix is characterized by the channel bit error probability, P_b.

The transition probability matrix for $R = 1$ is [28]

$$
\begin{bmatrix}
a & b & c & d \\
b & a & d & c \\
c & d & a & b \\
d & c & b & a
\end{bmatrix},
\tag{12}
$$

where

$$
\begin{aligned}
a &= P_{0,0/0,0} = (1 - P_b)^3 + (1 - P_b)P_b^2 \\
b &= P_{1,0/0,0} = (1 - P_b)^2 P_b + P_b^3 \\
c &= P_{2,0/0,0} = 2(1 - P_b)^2 P_b \\
d &= P_{3,0/0,0} = 2(1 - P_b)P_b^2.
\end{aligned}
\tag{13}
$$

This matrix is symmetric with respect to its two axes, due to the structure of the trellis.

Let $b_{(i,n)}$ and $b_{(k,l)}$ denote the $(R - 1)$-bit binary code of codeword n of subset i, and codeword l of subset k, respectively. For higher bit rates, it can be shown that the transition probability, $P_{i,n/k,l}$, is proportional to $P_{i,0/k,0}^{(R=1)}$, and that for any bit rate, R, it is given by

$$
P_{i,n/k,l} = P_{i,0/k,0}^{(R=1)} (1 - P_b)^{\#same} P_b^{\#different}.
\tag{14}
$$

$\#different$ and $\#same$ in (14) are given by

$$
\begin{cases}
\#different = \|b_{(i,n)} \ xor \ b_{(k,l)}\|_{\mathrm{Hamming}} \\
\#same \quad\ \ = R - 1 - \#different,
\end{cases}
\tag{15}
$$

where $\|.\|_{\text{Hamming}}$ is the Hamming distance.

For example, with a, b, c, and d as defined in (13), (14) gives the following transition probability matrix for $R = 2$:

$$
\begin{array}{c}
\\
P_{0,0} \\
P_{0,1} \\
P_{1,0} \\
P_{1,1} \\
P_{2,0} \\
P_{2,1} \\
P_{3,0} \\
P_{3,1}
\end{array}
\begin{array}{cccccccc}
P_{0,0} & P_{0,1} & P_{1,0} & P_{1,1} & P_{2,0} & P_{2,1} & P_{3,0} & P_{3,1} \\
\left[a\overline{P_b} \right. & aP_b & b\overline{P_b} & bP_b & c\overline{P_b} & cP_b & d\overline{P_b} & dP_b \\
aP_b & a\overline{P_b} & bP_b & b\overline{P_b} & cP_b & c\overline{P_b} & dP_b & d\overline{P_b} \\
b\overline{P_b} & bP_b & a\overline{P_b} & aP_b & d\overline{P_b} & dP_b & c\overline{P_b} & cP_b \\
bP_b & b\overline{P_b} & aP_b & a\overline{P_b} & dP_b & d\overline{P_b} & cP_b & c\overline{P_b} \\
c\overline{P_b} & cP_b & d\overline{P_b} & dP_b & a\overline{P_b} & aP_b & b\overline{P_b} & bP_b \\
cP_b & c\overline{P_b} & dP_b & d\overline{P_b} & aP_b & a\overline{P_b} & bP_b & b\overline{P_b} \\
d\overline{P_b} & dP_b & c\overline{P_b} & cP_b & b\overline{P_b} & bP_b & a\overline{P_b} & aP_b \\
dP_b & d\overline{P_b} & cP_b & c\overline{P_b} & bP_b & b\overline{P_b} & aP_b & \left. a\overline{P_b} \right]
\end{array}
\tag{16}
$$

where $\overline{P_b}=1-P_b$. It can be seen that the transition probability matrix (16) follows the pattern given by the transition matrix for $R = 1$. Using (14), the transition probability matrix can be derived in a similar way for other values of R.

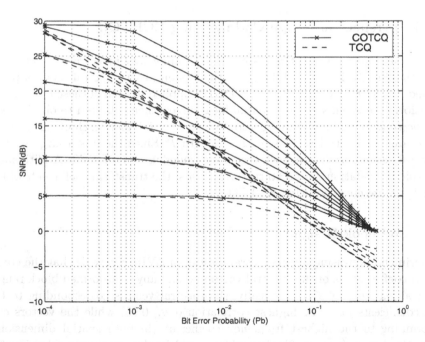

Figure 3: Performance of COTCQ vs. TCQ for Gaussian sources at encoding rates $R = 1$ to 8 bits/sample.

Simulation results for COTCQ The performance of COTCQ relative to TCQ is illustrated in Figure 3 for Gaussian sources. Figure 3 shows the signal-to-noise Ratio (SNR) for COTCQ (solid lines) and TCQ (dashed lines) as a function of P_b, for $R = 1$ (bottom solid and dashed plots) to 8 (top solid and dashed plots), in one-bit increments. A training sequence of 100,000 samples was used for designing the COTCQ and TCQ codebooks. The plots of Figure 3 were generated by encoding a Gaussian sequence of 100,000 samples (different from the training sequence) using the designed quantization codebooks.

At $P_b = 0$ (not shown in Figure 3), COTCQ and TCQ have identical performance (the COTCQ and TCQ curves intersect at $P_b = 0$). However, as P_b increases, the performance of TCQ degrades at a significantly faster rate as compared to COTCQ. Also, as R increases, the relative degradation rate of TCQ increases, and the TCQ performance curves diverge significantly from the COTCQ curves even at values of P_b as low as 10^{-4}. Note that for $R = 1$ to 4, the TCQ and COTCQ performance curves are almost identical for low values of P_b, but diverge as P_b increases, with TCQ degrading at a faster rate than COTCQ.

3   Hyperspectral Image Coding using ECPTCQ

In this section, we present a system for encoding hyperspectral imagery that uses the 2-D DCT and ECPTCQ. In this system, each spectral band is partitioned into 8×8 blocks, and the 2-D DCT is applied to each of these blocks. The transform coefficients at each spatial location are then collected to obtain *spectral vectors*. Thus, for a hyperspectral image with L bands, each of size $N \times N$, there are N^2 spectral vectors, each of length L. Since there is a large within-spectral-vector correlation, each vector is encoded using ECPTCQ. Additionally, to avoid degradation due to startup transients, the transform coefficients of the first band are encoded using ECTCQ.

3.1   Codebook Design

Experimentation using hyperspectral data from AVIRIS reveals that the correlation coefficient, ρ, of the spectral vectors within any transformed block ranges from about 0.6 to 0.95. Specifically, the spectral vectors corresponding to the DC coefficients have the highest correlation (e.g., 0.95) while the vectors corresponding to the highest frequency coefficient (in both spatial dimensions) have the lowest (e.g., 0.60). Accordingly, codebooks were designed using the ECPTCQ training algorithm for correlation coefficient values ranging from 0.60 to 0.95, in 0.05 increments. For each allowable value of ρ, twenty-one codebooks were designed with rates ranging from 0.25 bits/sample to 5.25 bits/sample, in quarter-bit increments. Each training sequence consisted of 50,000 samples from a first-order Gauss-Markov pseudo random number generator with the appropriate value of ρ (as discussed above). In each case, first-order linear prediction was used with a coefficient value equal to ρ.

The first spectral band in the hyperspectral sequence must also be encoded, with each quantized coefficient being used as the initial condition to encode the corresponding spectral vector using ECPTCQ. Coefficients corresponding to the same position within each block ("like-coefficients") are collected into sequences to be encoded using ECTCQ. Codebooks were designed using the algorithm in [23]. This algorithm uses a modified version of the generalized Lloyd algorithm [25] to minimize the MSE of an encoding, subject to an entropy constraint.

It was shown in [23] that for rates greater than 2.5 bpp, optimum codebooks do not yield increased performance over uniform codebooks. Thus, optimum codebooks with 256 elements were designed in one-tenth bit increments for rates up to 2.4 bpp, with uniform codebooks used thereafter.

The sequence corresponding to the DC coefficients is assumed to have Gaussian statistics, while the remaining high-frequency sequences are assumed to have Laplacian statistics [31]. Therefore, training sequences consisted of 100,000 samples derived from Gaussian and Laplacian pseudo random number generators, respectively.

3.2   Side Information and Rate Allocation

The side information required for this algorithm is substantial. In principle, the mean, standard deviation, and correlation coefficient for each spectral vector must be transmitted. Additionally, the transform coefficients of the first band must be transmitted, along with the initial states for the trellises used to encode the spectral vectors having nonzero rates (assuming 4-state trellises, each initial state requires 2 bits).

Fortunately, for a given spatial frequency, the variance of the correlation coefficients is extremely small. That is, if a sequence is formed by collecting the spectral correlation coefficients from each block at a given frequency, the variance of the sequence is negligible compared to its mean or average value. Thus, only the average correlation coefficients (quantized using 16 bit uniform scalar quantizers) are transmitted as side information and used for encoding and rate allocation. Since for an 8 × 8 DCT, there are 64 spatial frequencies, only 64 average correlation coefficients need to be transmitted.

Similarly, the variance of the spectral standard deviations is quite small for all spatial frequencies except DC. Thus, the average spectral standard deviations (again, quantized to 16 bits) are used in encoding and transmitted as side information for each of the 63 non-DC spatial frequencies. The DC spectral standard deviations change considerably throughout the image, but are highly correlated in neighboring blocks. Thus, the DC spectral standard deviations are quantized using ECPTCQ with raster scan (back and forth) at 5.25 bits/sample[1]. The "extra" side information required for encoding this sequence is 66 bits (16 bits each for the initial value, mean, standard deviation, and correlation coefficient of the sequence, and 2 bits for the initial trellis state).

Unfortunately, the means of the spectral vectors are quite random in nature, except for the DC spectral means, which exhibit a very high degree of correlation (typically 0.99) if scanned in an order similar to that of the DC spectral standard deviations. Hence, ECPTCQ is also used to encode this sequence at 5.25 bits/sample (plus an additional 66 bits, as in the case of the DC spectral standard deviations).

Since the remaining spectral means exhibit no significant correlation, EC-TCQ is used to encode the 63 sequences formed by grouping all spectral means for a given (non-DC) spatial frequency ("like-means"). These sequences are encoded at an average rate chosen so that the rate required for all spectral means (including the DC means) is R_μ bits/pixel. The first spectral band, which is encoded in the same manner as the non-DC spectral means, is assigned an average rate of R_1 bits/pixel.

Rate allocation is performed using the algorithm described in [32]. This scheme uses the rate-distortion performance of different quantizers to provide a near-optimal allocation of bits, given an overall bit quota. The overall MSE incurred by encoding the N^2 spectral vectors using ECPTCQ at an average rate of R_s bits/coefficient is represented by

$$E_s = \sum_{i=1}^{N^2} \sigma_i^2 E_{ij}(r_i), \qquad (17)$$

where σ_i^2 is the variance of sequence i, and $E_{ij}(r_i)$ denotes the rate-distortion performance of the jth quantizer (i.e., $\rho = 0.6$ to 0.95 in 0.05 increments) at r_i bits/sample.

The rate allocation vector, $B = (r_1, r_2, \ldots, r_{N^2})$, is chosen such that E_s is minimized, subject to an average rate constraint:

$$\sum_{i=1}^{N^2} r_i \leq R_s \text{ bits/coefficient.} \qquad (18)$$

It is shown in [32] that the solution, $B^*(r_1^*, r_2^*, \ldots, r_{N^2}^*)$, to the unconstrained problem,

$$\min_{B,} \left\{ \sum_{i=1}^{N^2} (\sigma_i^2 E_{ij}(r_i) + \lambda r_i) \right\} \qquad (19)$$

---

[1] The highest rate codebook available was used to ensure accurate representation of these values.

minimizes E_s subject to $\sum_{i=1}^{N^2} r_i \leq \sum_{i=1}^{N^2} r_i^*$. Thus, to find a solution to the constrained problem of equations (17) and (18), it suffices to find λ such that the solution to equation (19) yields $\sum_{i=1}^{N^2} r_i^* \leq R_s$. Procedures for finding the appropriate λ are given in [32].

For a given λ, the solution to the unconstrained problem is obtained by minimizing each term of the sum in (19) separately. If $S_j = \{p_j, \ldots, q_j\}$ is the set of allowable rates for the jth quantizer, and r_i^* is the ith component of the solution vector, B^*, then r_i^* solves

$$\min_{r_i \in S_j} \{\sigma_i^2 E_{ij}(r_i) + \lambda r_i\}. \tag{20}$$

Testing revealed that equal performance was obtained whether globally allocating bits using all N^2 spectral variances, or by using the 64 average spectral variances (as discussed above). The latter approach was adopted since the rate allocation algorithm need only take into account 64 spectral variances (rather than N^2), thus resulting in far fewer computations. Also, this results in all blocks having identical spectral bit maps. All spectral variances are quantized prior to being used in the spectral rate allocation algorithm.

As in the case of the spectral vectors themselves, rate allocation for the spectral means and the first spectral band is accomplished using the algorithm in [32]. The scalar-quantized variances of the "like-coefficient" and "like-mean" sequences are used in the rate allocation algorithms for the first band and spectral means, respectively. It should be noted that the rate allocation for the spectral vectors is used to constrain the spatial rate allocation of the first spectral band. Thus, if any spectral vector is assigned zero rate, the corresponding transform coefficient in the first spectral band is also assigned zero rate. Finally, any spectral vector that is assigned zero rate is set to (the quantized value of) its corresponding spectral mean.

The total side information required for encoding an $N \times N$ hyperspectral image at an average rate of R_s bits/coefficient consists of the spectral correlation coefficients ($64 \cdot 16$ bits), spectral standard deviations ($63 \cdot 16 + 5.25(N^2/8^2) + 66$ bits), the spectral means ($R_\mu N^2$ bits), the first spectral band ($R_1 N^2$ bits), and the initial trellis states ($2n$ bits, where $n \leq N^2$ is the number of spectral vectors assigned a non-zero encoding rate). Combining these quantities yields $(2098 + 2n + (R_\mu + R_1 + 0.082)N^2)$ bits. The overall encoding rate for the system operating on a hyperspectral image with L bands is then $(R_s(L-1) + R_\mu + R_1 + 0.082 + (2098 + 2n)/N^2)/L$ bits/pixel/band (b/p/b).

Figure 4 shows the overall encoding rate of a hyperspectral sequence as a function of the number of spectral bands. In this particular case, the asymptotic rate, R_s, is 0.10 bits/coefficient, and the encoding rates of the first band, R_1, and the spectral means, R_μ, are 1.0 and 2.0 bits/pixel (bpp), respectively. Note that for small sequences (e.g., less than ten bands), the side information dominates the overall rate.

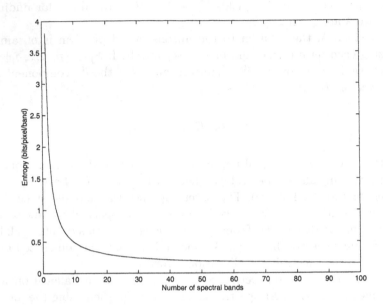

Figure 4: Overall rate versus number of spectral bands for the ECPTCQ coder.

4   3-D DCT Hyperspectral Image Coder

A hyperspectral coding system using the 3-D DCT and ECTCQ is shown in Figure 5. The image sequence is partitioned into $8 \times 8 \times 8$ cubes and transformed using the 3-D DCT. Coefficients corresponding to the same position within each cube ("like-coefficients") are collected into sequences to be encoded using ECTCQ. For a hyperspectral sequence with L bands, each of size $N \times N$, the total number of sequences to be encoded is $8^3 = 512$, each of length $LN^2/512$.

4.1   Codebook Design

Codebooks optimized for Gaussian and Laplacian distributions were used for the DC and non-DC sequences, respectively. Codebooks were designed for these distributions by employing the algorithm in [23]. This algorithm uses a modified version of the generalized Lloyd algorithm [25] to minimize the cost function

$$J = E[\rho(x, c)] + \lambda E[l(c)].\qquad(21)$$

Here, x is the data, c is the encoded version of x, $\rho(x, c)$ is the cost (usually MSE) of representing x by c, λ is a Lagrange multiplier, and $l(c) \approx -\log_2 P(x|A_i)$ is the number of bits used by the variable-length code to represent c. This algorithm chooses the "best" codeword by considering both the MSE and the number of bits required to represent the particular codeword.

It was shown in [23] that for the Gaussian distribution, optimum codebooks do not yield significant MSE improvement over uniform codebooks at rates greater than 2.5 bits/sample. Accordingly, optimum codebooks were designed in one-tenth bit increments up to 2.5 bits/sample. Thereafter, uniform codebooks were designed in one-tenth bit increments up to 12 bits/sample. Training sequences consisted of 100,000 samples derived from Gaussian and Laplacian pseudo random number generators.

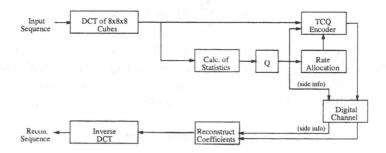

Figure 5: Hyperspectral image coder using the 3-D DCT and ECTCQ.

4.2   Side Information and Rate Allocation

Given the three-dimensional frequency space in the transform domain, where the x and y axes represent the spatial dimensions, and the z axis represents the spectral dimension, all like-coefficient sequences should (theoretically) be zero mean except the DC sequence (i.e., $x, y, z = 0$). In fact, the sample means of the like-coefficient sequences drop off very rapidly in any frequency direction relative to DC, with the mean of the DC sequence typically being two orders of magnitude greater than the means of those sequences corresponding to frequencies one position higher along any axis (i.e., $(x, y, z) = (1,0,0)$, $(0,1,0)$, and $(0,0,1)$). Thus, only the DC mean should need to be transmitted as side information. Experiments confirm this for the $(x, 0, 0)$ and $(0, y, 0)$ sequences, which have sample standard deviations at least an order of magnitude larger than their corresponding sample means. On the other hand, the extremely high correlation along the z-axis (spectral dimension) causes a sharp drop in standard deviation along that axis. As a result, the sample means along this axis are within an order of magnitude of their respective standard deviations. For this reason, we chose to transmit all eight sample means for the sequences with coordinates of the form $(0, 0, z)$.

The side information then consists of 512 standard deviations and 8 spatial means. These quantities are quantized using 16 bit uniform scalar quantizers, resulting in a total of $(520)(16) = 8320$ bits. The initial trellis states are also transmitted which (for 4-state trellises) total $(512)(2) = 1024$ bits. Combining these quantities yields 9344 bits of side information per hyperspectral sequence.

As in the Section 3, rate allocation is performed by using the algorithm described in [32]. In this case, the overall MSE incurred by encoding the like-coefficient sequences using ECTCQ at an average rate of R_s bits/coefficient is represented by

$$E_s = \sum_{i=1}^{512} \sigma_i^2 E_{ij}(r_i),\tag{22}$$

where σ_i^2 is the variance of sequence i, and $E_{ij}(r_i)$ denotes the rate-distortion performance of the jth quantizer (i.e., Gaussian or Laplacian) at r_i bits/sample.

The rate allocation vector, $B = (r_1, r_2, \ldots, r_{512})$, is chosen such that E_s is minimized, subject to an average rate constraint:

$$\sum_{i=1}^{512} r_i \leq R_s \text{ bits/coefficient}.\tag{23}$$

5   DPCM-Based Hyperspectral Image Coding

In this section, we present two coder configurations that are based on differential pulse code modulation (DPCM). The first coder is a wavelet-based design, while the second coder utilizes the DCT. Both coders incorporate adaptive classification and ECTCQ.

DPCM is a simple and well-known method of achieving moderate compression of correlated sequences [33–35]. Given a pixel, x_{i-1}, the next pixel in the sequence, x_i, is predicted. If $\tilde{x}_{i|i-1}$ is the predicted value of x_i, then the difference, $\epsilon_i = x_i - \tilde{x}_{i|i-1}$, will, on average, be significantly smaller in magnitude than x_i. Accordingly, fewer quantization bins, and thus, fewer bits are required to encode the error sequence than would be required to encode the original sequence of pixels. It can be shown that for a nonzero-mean input sequence, the optimum (minimum MSE) first-order linear predictor is given by

$$\tilde{x}_{i|i-1} = \rho x_{i-1} + \mu(1 - \rho),\tag{24}$$

where μ and ρ are the mean and correlation coefficient of the sequence, respectively, and $\tilde{x}_{i|i-1}$ is the predicted value of x_i. It is apparent that the input sequence must be normalized to zero mean or the sequence mean must be included in (24). In either case, for applying DPCM to a nonzero-mean sequence, the mean must be transmitted as side information.

The utilization of DPCM to exploit the spectral correlation of hyperspectral imagery is straightforward. For an L-band image of size $N \times N$, an ordinary DPCM loop could be employed to encode each of the N^2 sequences that result from treating each hyperspectral pixel as a sequence of length L. Unfortunately, while this scheme exploits spectral correlation, it does not exploit the spatial correlation inherent to the data, and requires the transmission of N^2 spectral means.

Consider now the encoder configuration shown in Figure 6. Here, the DPCM loop operates on entire images rather than on individual sequences. Given an image, $\mathbf{x}_{n-1}$, the next image in the hyperspectral sequence can be estimated, and an "error image" can be formed from the difference, $\epsilon_n = \mathbf{x}_n - \tilde{\mathbf{x}}_{n|n-1}$. The error image (at each instant in time) is spatially correlated and can be quantized using any image coding scheme. Note that the error image must be decoded within the encoder loop so that the quantized image, $\hat{\mathbf{x}}_n$, can be constructed and used to predict the next image.

The prediction error images have much lower energy than the original bands and can be subjected to very coarse quantization. The bit rate chosen to encode each error image will be the asymptotic bit rate for the system. The first spectral band is encoded and transmitted (as the initial conditions for DPCM) at a total rate (including side information) of R_1 bits/pixel (bpp).

Testing of data obtained by AVIRIS revealed that the spectral correlation coefficient, ρ, for any pixel in the hyperspectral image is approximately 0.95. Accordingly, this value of ρ was used in the DPCM loop.

Each error image is encoded using the coder configuration shown in Figure 7. In the wavelet-based system, each error image is encoded using a scheme similar to that in [36]. The image is transformed using the 2-D DWT in a 10-band octave decomposition. The block size used for classification within each subband is adjusted so as to correspond to 16×16 blocks in the error image. Each subband is classified into J classes by maximizing the classification gain as discussed below. All $10J$ sequences are normalized by dividing by their respective standard deviations. The mean is subtracted from the lowest-frequency subband.

The total side information to be transmitted consists of the mean of the lowest-frequency subband, and the standard deviations of all $10J$ coefficient sequences. These quantities are quantized using 16-bit uniform scalar quantizers for a total of $(10J + 1) \times 16$ bits. The initial trellis state for each sequence must also be transmitted, which (for 4-state trellises) equals $20J$ bits. For $J = 4$, the total side information consists of 736 bits. This corresponds to ≈ 0.0112 bpp for a 256×256 image, and ≈ 0.0028 bpp for a 512×512 image. In addition,

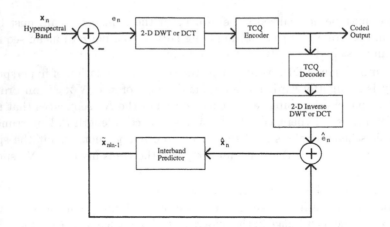

Figure 6: Adaptive hyperspectral image encoder.

the classification maps for the entire hyperspectral sequence are derived from the first spectral band and thus contribute only ≈ 0.00195 bits/pixel/band for a 40-band sequence. The first spectral band is encoded and transmitted (as the initial conditions for DPCM) at a total rate (including side information) of R_1 bpp.

In the DCT-based system, each image is divided into non-overlapping 8×8 blocks and transformed using the 2-D DCT. Prior to application of the DCT, each block is assigned to one of J classes by maximizing the classification gain. For each class, DCT coefficients corresponding to the same frequency within each block are grouped into sequences to be encoded using ECTCQ. All DCT coefficients are normalized by subtracting their mean (only the sequences corresponding to the DC transform coefficients have non-zero mean) and dividing by their respective standard deviations. Since each class contains 64 DCT coefficient sequences, the total number of sequences to be encoded would then be $64J$.

The side information required to encode each error image (and the first spectral band) consists of the means of the J DC sequences and the standard deviations of all $64J$ sequences. These quantities are quantized using 8-bit uniform scalar quantizers to yield $(64J + J) \times 8$ bits. In addition, the initial trellis state of each sequence requires 2 bits (for a 4-state trellis), which yields $128J$ bits. The total side information is then $648J$ bits, which corresponds to $1296/(256)^2 = 0.0198$ bpp for a 256×256 image and $J = 2$, or $2592/(256)^2 = 0.0396$ bpp for $J = 4$. The first spectral band is encoded and transmitted (as the initial condition for DPCM) at a total rate (including side information) of R_1 bits/pixel. In addition, the classification maps for the hyperspectral sequence must also be

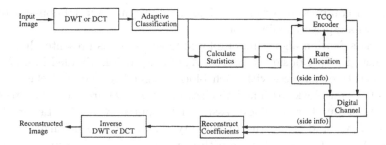

Figure 7: Block diagram of the adaptive-DWT/adaptive-DCT image coder.

transmitted. One map is used for every ten spectral bands. Each map requires 1024 bits for $J = 2$, or 2048 bits for $J = 4$. Averaged over ten spectral bands, this corresponds to 0.00156 bpp and 0.00313 bpp for $J = 2$ and $J = 4$, respectively.

The DWT or DCT coefficient sequences are assumed to have various generalized Gaussian statistics. Accordingly, codebooks were designed using sample sequences derived from generalized Gaussian pseudo random number generators as discussed below. Additionally, rate allocation is performed by using the algorithm in [32].

5.1   Adaptive Classification

The statistical nature of digital imagery is inherently non-stationary. That is, different regions of the source image contain varying amounts of image detail. Regions with significant detail must be coded at higher bit rates than those with less detail, thus achieving equivalent fidelity in the coded image. Accordingly, the efficiency of image coding algorithms can be increased substantially by exploiting the non-stationary nature of the source imagery. Previous attempts to track the local characteristics of the source imagery include spatial adaptation of the transform used to decorrelate the image, and spatial adaptation of the quantizer.

In the case of subband decomposition, it can be shown that the statistical properties of the lowest frequency subband (LFS) are similar to those of the original image, and therefore, well-established techniques for image compression are suitable for encoding the LFS. The remaining high-frequency subbands (HFSs) have small intraband correlation. Thus, subband-coding systems that use a particular decorrelating technique, such as transform or prediction for the LFS, and treat the HFSs as memoryless sources, can achieve excellent performance. However, inspection of the high-frequency subbands reveals that the majority of the subband energy is concentrated in regions corresponding to high edge content in the original image. Consequently, these regions of high-energy concentration can be coded with more bits than areas with lower concentrations, resulting in much higher compression efficiency. The exploitation of spatial non-stationarity is known as adaptive classification.

The classification algorithm employed in the systems presented here is similar to that in [36]. Consider a source, X, of length, NL, divided into N blocks of L consecutive samples, with each block assigned to one of J classes. If the samples from all blocks assigned to class i $(1 \leq i \leq J)$ are grouped into source X_i, the total number of blocks assigned to source X_i is N_i. Let σ_i^2 be the variance of X_i, and p_i be the probability that a sample belongs to X_i (i.e., $p_i = N_i/N, 1 \leq i \leq J$). The algorithm in [36] is a pairwise maximization of classification gain and is repeated here for convenience:

1. Initialize $N_1, N_2, \ldots, N_J$ to satisfy $\sum_{i=1}^{J} N_i = N, N_i > 0$ for $1 \leq i \leq J$. Let $j = 1$ and $\underline{N}_{prev} = [N_1, N_2, \ldots, N_J]'$.
2. Find N_j' and N_{j+1}' such that $N_j' + N_{j+1}' = N_j + N_{j+1}$ and $(\sigma_j^2)^{p_j'}(\sigma_{j+1}^2)^{p_j'}$ is minimized.
3. $N_j = N_j'$ and $N_{j+1} = N_{j+1}'$.
4. $j = j + 1$. If $j < J$, go to Step 2.
5. Let $\underline{N} = [N_1, N_2, \ldots, N_J]'$. If $\underline{N}$ is equal to $\underline{N}_{prev}$, then stop. Otherwise, $j = 1$. $\underline{N}_{prev} = \underline{N}$. Go to Step 2.

Here, the average mean-squared energy of a block (i.e., $E = (\sum_{i=1}^{L} x_i^2)/L$) is the criterion for classification.

5.2   Codebook Design

The probability distribution of each sequence to be encoded is modeled by the so-called *Generalized Gaussian Distribution* (GGD), whose probability density function (pdf) is given by

$$f_X(x) = \left[\frac{\alpha\eta(\alpha,\sigma)}{2\Gamma(1/\alpha)}\right] \exp\{-[\eta(\alpha,\sigma)|x|]^\alpha\}, \tag{25}$$

where

$$\eta(\alpha,\sigma) \equiv \sigma^{-1}\left[\frac{\Gamma(3/\alpha)}{\Gamma(1/\alpha)}\right]^{1/2}. \tag{26}$$

The shape parameter, α, describes the exponential rate of decay, and σ is the standard deviation of the associated random variable [26]. The gamma function, $\Gamma(\cdot)$, is defined as

$$\Gamma(n) = \int_0^\infty e^{-x}x^{n-1}dx. \tag{27}$$

Distributions corresponding to $\alpha = 1.0$ and 2.0 are Laplacian and Gaussian, respectively. Figure 8 shows generalized Gaussian pdfs corresponding to $\alpha = 0.5, 1.0, 1.5, 2.0$, and 2.5.

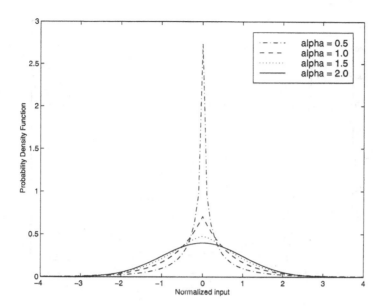

Figure 8: Probability density functions for generalized Gaussian distributions with alpha values of 0.5, 1.0, 1.5, and 2.0.

It can be shown that

$$E[X^4] = \int_{-\infty}^{\infty} x^4 f_X(x)dx = K\sigma^4 , \qquad (28)$$

or

$$K = \frac{E[X^4]}{\sigma^4} = \frac{\Gamma(5/\alpha)\Gamma(1/\alpha)}{\Gamma(3/\alpha)^2} , \qquad (29)$$

where K is the fourth central moment, or Kurtosis. Recall that the Kurtosis is a measure of the peakedness of a given distribution. If a pdf is symmetric about its mean and is very flat in the vicinity of its mean, the coefficient of Kurtosis is relatively small. Similarly, a pdf that is peaked about its mean has a large Kurtosis value.

The sample Kurtosis of any sequence can be calculated easily and used as a measure by which the distribution of the sequence can be determined. Figure 9 shows the relationship between the shape parameter, α, and the Kurtosis, K. Once the Kurtosis for a particular sequence is calculated, this graph is used to select the appropriate generalized Gaussian codebook.

ECTCQ codebooks were designed for generalized Gaussian distributions with α values of 0.5, 0.75, 1.0, 1.5, and 2.0, using the algorithm in [23]. It was shown in [23] that for the Gaussian distribution, optimum codebooks do

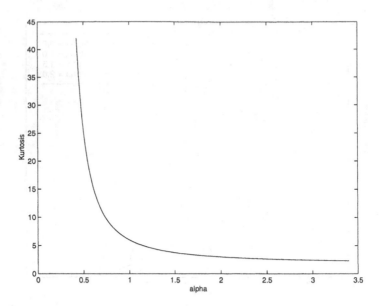

Figure 9: Kurtosis vs. alpha.

not yield significant MSE improvement over uniform codebooks at rates greater than 2.5 bits/sample. Experimentation revealed that this is also true for $\alpha = 1.5$ and $\alpha = 1.0$. However, for $\alpha = 0.75$, optimum codebooks are superior up to 3.0 bits/sample, while for $\alpha = 0.5$, optimum codebooks should be used up to 3.5 bits/sample. Accordingly, for α values of 2.0, 1.5, and 1.0, optimum codebooks were designed in one-tenth bit increments up to 2.5 bits/sample, while for $\alpha = 0.75$ and $\alpha = 0.5$, optimum codebooks were designed in one-tenth bit increments up to 3.0 and 3.5 bits/sample, respectively. Thereafter, uniform codebooks were designed in one-tenth bit increments up to 12 bits/sample. Training sequences consisted of 100,000 samples derived from generalized Gaussian pseudo-random number generators, each tuned to the appropriate α value.

5.3   Rate Allocation

As before, rate allocation is performed by using the algorithm presented in [32]. The overall MSE incurred by encoding the coefficient sequences using ECTCQ at an average rate of R_s bits/coefficient is represented by

$$E_s = \sum_{i=1}^{K} \alpha_i \sigma_i^2 E_{ij}(r_i), \tag{30}$$

where σ_i^2 is the variance of sequence i, $E_{ij}(r_i)$ denotes the rate-distortion performance of the jth quantizer (i.e., the quantizer corresponding to the Kurtosis of sequence i) at r_i bits/sample, K is the number of data sequences, and α_i is a weighting coefficient to account for the variability in sequence length. For a 10-band decomposition and J classes, $K = 10J$. For 8×8 blocks and J classes, $K = 64J$.

6 Robust Channel-Optimized Hyperspectral Image Coder

The hyperspectral image compression algorithms presented in the previous sections were developed under the ideal assumption of reliable, noise-free transport. Consequently, if the transmitted data is corrupted by channel noise, the quality of the reconstructed data may be degraded substantially unless redundant information or error-correcting methods are added. Although channel coding can be quite effective in protecting the images from channel noise, error-correcting methods can add significant complexity and delay to the image coder. Moreover, adding redundancy to the compressed data results in a significantly lower overall compression efficiency.

In this section, we present a hyperspectral coder that is designed to operate in noisy environments. The developed algorithm is based on DPCM used in conjunction with the discrete wavelet transform (DWT). In this algorithm, DPCM is used for spectral decorrelation, with each "error image" being encoded with a robust 2-D DWT coder and channel-optimized trellis-coded quantization (COTCQ). The error image is first decomposed into 22 subbands using a modified Mallat tree configuration. Each subband is then all-pass filtered by employing a phase scrambling operation, and all resulting sequences are quantized using fixed-rate COTCQ.

The overall coder configuration is shown in Figure 10, and is similar to the configuration of the adaptive DWT and adaptive DCT coders presented in Section 5. As before, the first spectral band is encoded and transmitted (as the initial conditions for DPCM) at a total rate (including side information) of R_1 bits per pixel (bpp).

Each error image is encoded using the robust COTCQ-based wavelet image coder shown in Figure 11. The input image is first decomposed using a 9-7 biorthogonal 2-D DWT into 22 subbands as in [37]. The statistics of each subband are computed, and all subbands are normalized by subtracting their mean (only the sequence corresponding to the lowest-frequency subband is assumed to have a nonzero mean) and dividing by their respective standard deviations. Each normalized subband is then all-pass filtered using a phase scrambling operation. The filtered subbands are encoded using a fixed-rate COTCQ system designed for the memoryless (zero mean and unit-variance) Gaussian source. In addition, an optimal (in the MSE sense) rate allocation scheme is utilized.

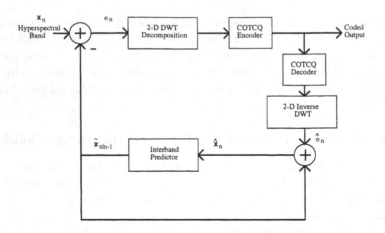

Figure 10: Robust wavelet hyperspectral image encoder.

The encoder transmits the mean of the lowest-frequency subband and the standard deviations of all 22 subbands as side information. These quantities are quantized with 16-bit uniform scalar quantizers using a total of 368 bits. The initial trellis state for each encoded subband and the target compression ratio must also be transmitted, and are allotted 2 bits per subband (for a 4-state trellis) and 10 bits, respectively. Therefore, the total side information consists of 422 bits per image. The decoder performs the inverse operations and consists of a COTCQ decoder, a phase descrambler, and a wavelet synthesis stage.

The wavelet decomposition, all-pass filtering, COTCQ, and rate allocation stages are discussed below.

6.1   Wavelet Decomposition

The input image is transformed using a 9-7 biorthogonal 2-D DWT [38] into 22 subbands in a modified Mallat tree configuration. That is, the image is initially decomposed into 16 equal-sized subbands, with two additional levels of decomposition being applied to the lowest-frequency subband.

6.2   All-Pass Filtering

It was shown in [39] that Lloyd-Max quantization (LMQ) achieves the best possible SNR performance when encoding the memoryless Gaussian source, and degraded performance when encoding generalized Gaussian sources with exponential shape parameters, α, of less than two. Figure 12 shows the obtained signal-to-noise ratios of Lloyd-Max quantization when encoding the memoryless

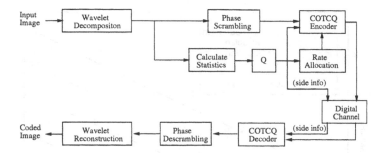

Figure 11: Block diagram of the wavelet image coder using robust COTCQ.

Gaussian, Laplacian, and generalized Gaussian ($\alpha = 0.5$) sources at bit rates of 1-4 bits/sample. Also shown are the respective rate-distortion functions. From the graph, it is evident that the performance of LMQ is opposite in order to that theoretically possible as seen from the rate-distortion functions. That is, LMQ achieves the best possible SNR performance when encoding the memoryless Gaussian source, and degraded performance when encoding all other generalized Gaussian sources with shape parameters of less than two. Note that these same general performance characteristics hold true when TCQ is employed.

To address this issue, a robust quantization method has been developed whereby the signal to be quantized is all-pass filtered to produce a signal with Gaussian statistics [40]. Since fixed-rate channel-optimized trellis-coded quantization is used, the performance curves obtained by quantizing the memoryless Laplacian source or any generalized Gaussian source (with shape parameter of $\alpha < 2$) will be elevated to the performance of the encoded Gaussian source. The all-pass filter is implemented by using a phase scrambling operation. The input sequence, x(n), is transformed using the fast Fourier transform (FFT), and separated into its magnitude and phase components. The phase spectrum of an appropriate reference function is then added to the phase spectrum of the input sequence. An inverse FFT is performed, with the resulting sequence, y(n), being (nearly) Gaussian distributed. In this way, the performance curve of a Gaussian-optimized quantizer can be achieved with a broad range of source distributions. Thus, a fixed (Gaussian) rate-distortion performance is guaranteed, independent of the source distribution. In addition, the phase scrambling operation provides a more secure bit stream between the encoder and decoder.

A convenient reference function for the phase scrambling operation is the binary pseudo-noise (PN) sequence, also known as the m-sequence. The m-sequence is chosen because of its ease of generation and its autocorrelation

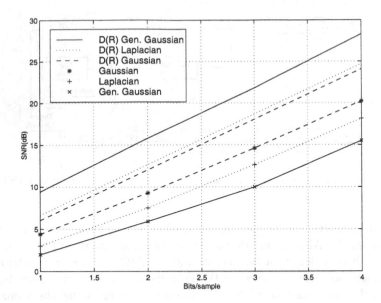

Figure 12: SNR performance of Lloyd-Max quantization for generalized Gaussian sources.

properties. The sequence utilized in the system discussed herein is generated from a feedback shift register corresponding to the 16th-order primitive polynomial, $x^{16} + x^5 + x^3 + x + 1$ [41]. The sequence is then truncated to the length of the considered subband prior to Fourier transformation, thus guaranteeing frequency-domain phase symmetry.

6.3 Rate Allocation

As before, rate allocation is performed by using the algorithm in [32]. The overall MSE incurred by encoding the coefficient sequences using COTCQ at an average rate of R_s bits/coefficient is represented by

$$E_s = \sum_{i=1}^{K} \alpha_i \sigma_i^2 E_i(r_i), \tag{31}$$

where σ_i^2 is the variance of sequence i, $E_i(r_i)$ denotes the rate-distortion performance of the quantizer at r_i bits/sample, K is the number of data sequences, and α_i is a weighting coefficient to account for the variability in sequence length. For a 22-band decomposition, $K = 22$.

7   Coding Results

Coding simulations were performed using a 140-band, 8-bit hyperspectral image sequence of Cuprite, Nevada, obtained by the AVIRIS system. The bands were 256×256 pixels and were extracted from larger images (for computational simplicity). The performance of each encoding system is reported using the peak signal-to-noise ratio (PSNR), which is defined as

$$10\log_{10} \frac{(255)^2}{\frac{1}{N^2}\sum_{u=0}^{N-1}\sum_{v=0}^{N-1}|I(u,v) - \hat{I}(u,v)|^2}, \qquad (32)$$

where $\hat{I}(u,v)$ is the coded version of the original band, $I(u,v)$.

For the DPCM-based systems (i.e., adaptive DWT, adaptive DCT, and robust COTCQ), the first band in the sequence was encoded at $R_1 = 0.75$ bits/pixel, and was used as the initial condition for the spectral DPCM. This rate was chosen so that the PSNR of the coded first band did not significantly deviate from the average PSNR of the sequence when encoded at an asymptotic rate, R_s, of 0.10 bits/pixel/band (b/p/b).

7.1   Channels Without Noise

Figure 13 shows the PSNRs obtained by encoding bands 30 through 69 of the hyperspectral sequence using the ECPTCQ coder (Section 3) [16], the 3-D DCT (Section 4) and DPCM/DCT hybrid coders [18], the adaptive DWT-based system with $J = 4$ classes (Section 5) [19], the adaptive DCT-based system with $J = 2$ classes (Section 5) [20], and the robust wavelet coder (Section 6) [10]. Note that the DPCM/DCT hybrid coder in [18] is simply the adaptive DCT coder presented in Section 5 without the adaptive classification stage. All coders were operated at an asymptotic bit rate[2] of $R_s = 0.1$ b/p/b. The average PSNR of the ECTPTQ, 3-D DCT, hybrid, adaptive DWT, adaptive DCT, and robust wavelet systems are 43.10 dB, 40.75 dB, 40.29 dB, 41.24 dB, 40.72 dB, and 40.13 dB, respectively. The dip in PSNR around bands 56 and 57 is indicative of high sensor noise that is clearly evident upon visual examination.

Figure 14 shows the original image from band 50 of the hyperspectral sequence, while Figures 15(a), (b), (c), & (d) show the coded versions derived from the ECPTCQ, 3-D DCT, adaptive DWT, and adaptive DCT systems, respectively. As seen in Figure 15, the ECPTCQ-based coder exhibits slightly better subjective performance than the other systems, preserving slightly more

---

[2] It should be noted that the asymptotic rates of the hybrid, adaptive DWT, adaptive DCT, and robust wavelet coders include the side information required to encode each error image, since the contribution of the side information to the overall rate will remain constant regardless of sequence length.

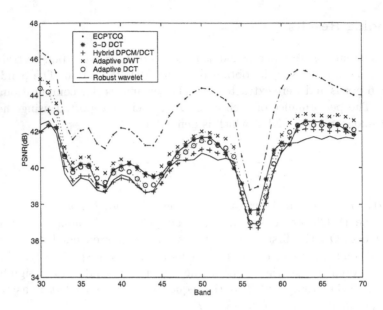

Figure 13: Performance of encoding hyperspectral sequence at $R_s = 0.10$ b/p/b.

detail, while the remaining coders provide subjective results that are remarkably similar to one another. It should be noted that in all cases, the coded images are virtually indistinguishable from the original, with no artifacts or contrast variations. This subjective performance is indicative of the entire hyperspectral sequence.

Despite having lower PSNR performance, the adaptive DCT system gains advantages over the adaptive DWT coder in terms of computational simplicity, and over the ECPTCQ system in terms of memory requirements. The adaptive coders require only two bands at once to encode an image sequence, while the ECPTCQ system uses the entire transformed sequence. When compared to the 3-D DCT coder, the adaptive DCT coder achieves comparable PSNR performance, while offering lower complexity and memory requirements. Both adaptive coders outperform the DCT-based hybrid system and the robust wavelet system. However, the robust wavelet system is a non-entropy-coded design, which gives it several advantages as outlined in [10] and [37].

Figure 16 shows the overall encoding rate (including all side information) of each system as a function of sequence length. Note that for encoding short subsequences (e.g., less than 10 bands), the overall rate of the DPCM-based systems is dominated by the rate required to code the first spectral band. For example, the overall rate for encoding the 40-band sequence using either the adaptive DWT or the adaptive DCT system is ≈ 0.118 b/p/b when $R_s = 0.1$ b/p/b. If all 140 bands were coded, the overall rate would be 0.106 b/p/b. It is evident that at least 73 bands are required such that the overall rate is within 10% of the asymptotic rate (when $R_1 = 0.75$ bpp). For the ECPTCQ system, the side infomation dominates the overall rate, especially for shorter sequences. Thus, the increased performance of the ECPTCQ system as compared to the other systems (for a given asymptotic rate) is largely attributable to this large amount of side information. Methods to reduce the side information are given in [42]. Since the 3-D DCT system requires very little side information, excellent performance is obtained with very short sequences.

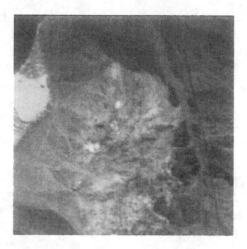

Figure 14: Original 8-bit band 50 image.

7.2   Noisy Channels

For noiseless channels (i.e., $P_b = 0.0$), the robust COTCQ-based coder achieves an average PSNR of 40.13 dB at an asymptotic encoding rate of $R_s = 0.1$ b/p/b, as shown in the previous section.

For channels with noise, Figure 17 shows the average PSNR performance of the coder as a function of bit error probability, P_b, for encoding the 40-band sequence at $R_s = 0.1$ b/p/b. For comparison, Figure 17 also shows the performance of the non-robust (no all-pass filtering) versions of the TCQ-based and COTCQ-based hyperspectral image coders. As seen from the plot, the robust COTCQ coder outperforms the non-robust version by about 0.7 dB up to $P_b = 0.01$. Beyond that point, the performance disparity increases rapidly.

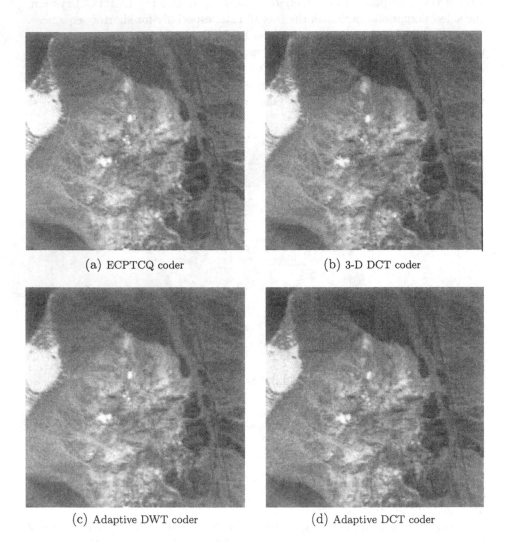

(a) ECPTCQ coder   (b) 3-D DCT coder

(c) Adaptive DWT coder   (d) Adaptive DCT coder

Figure 15: 256×256 band 50 image encoded at $R_s = 0.1$ b/p/b.

Additionally, the robust COTCQ coder outperforms the TCQ-based coder by about 4 dB at $P_b = 0.01$, with the TCQ-based coder exhibiting unstable behavior beyond that point due to its predictive nature and non-channel-optimized design.

To illustrate the subjective performance of the robust COTCQ-based image coder, Figures 18(b), (c), & (d) show band 50 of the hyperspectral image sequence encoded at $R_s = 0.1$ b/p/b, and a bit error probability, $P_b = 0.01$, using the TCQ-based image coder, the COTCQ-based image coder, and the robust COTCQ-based image coder, respectively. For comparison, Figure 18(a) shows the original 8-bit image. The Peak SNR is 39.62 dB using the robust COTCQ scheme (Figure 18(d)), and decreases to 37.52 dB and 27.79 dB for non-robust COTCQ (Figure 18(c)) and non-robust TCQ (Figure 18(b)), respectively. It is evident that the noisy channel introduces severe impulsive artifacts in the reconstructed image using TCQ. Replacing the TCQ stage by the COTCQ stage removes most of these artifacts. However, using all-pass filtering in conjunction with COTCQ completely removes all impulsive artifacts. These artifacts have been effectively "spread" throughout the image by the all-pass filtering operation. Additionally, details in the image are much more apparent in the all-pass-filtered version.

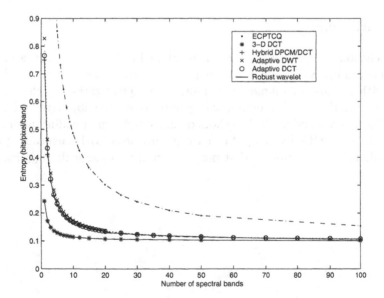

Figure 16: Overall encoding rate versus number of spectral bands.

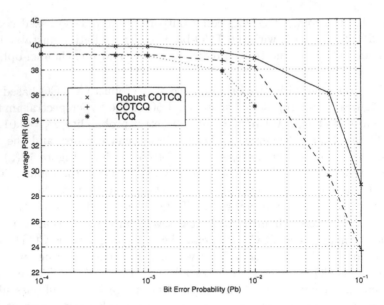

Figure 17: Performance of the robust (all-pass filtered) COTCQ-based coder at various bit error probabilities, P_b.

8 Conclusions

In this chapter, we presented several algorithms for the lossy compression of hyperspectral imagery. The algorithms employ a variety of decorrelation techniques along with various embodiments of trellis-coded quantization. Each coder configuration was described in detail, and quantitative and subjective performance evaluations were conducted. We showed that outstanding coding performance can be obtained with a variety of coder configurations, with each coder possessing a unique set of attributes that may be suited to a particular application.

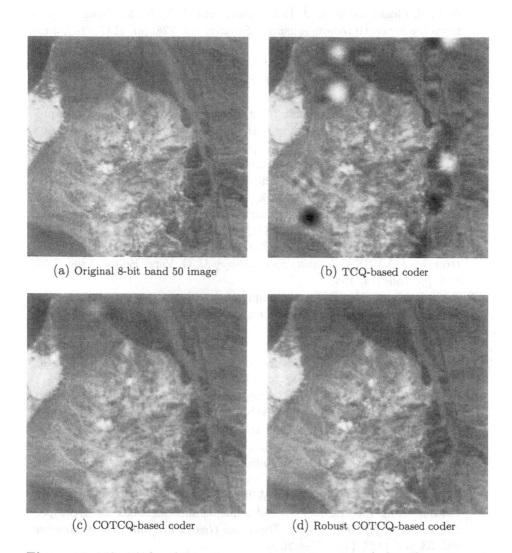

(a) Original 8-bit band 50 image   (b) TCQ-based coder

(c) COTCQ-based coder   (d) Robust COTCQ-based coder

Figure 18: 256×256 band 50 image encoded at $R_s = 0.1$ b/p/b with a channel bit error probability, $P_b = 0.01$.

References

[1] A. F. H. Goetz, G. Vane, J. E. Solomon, and B. N. Rock, "Imaging spectrometry for earth remote sensing," *Science*, vol. 228, pp. 1147–1153, June 1985.

[2] L. Blanchard and O. Weinstein, "Design challenges of the Thermatic Mapper," *IEEE Trans. Geosci. Remote Sensing*, vol. GE-18, pp. 146–160, Apr. 1980.

[3] P. J. Curran and J. L. Dungan, "Estimation of signal-to-noise: a new procedure applied to AVIRIS data," *IEEE Trans. Geosci. Remote Sensing*, vol. 27, pp. 620–628, Sept. 1989.

[4] G. Vane and A. F. H. Goetz, "Terrestrial imaging spectrometry," *Remote Sensing Environ.*, vol. 24, pp. 1–29, 1988.

[5] W. M. Porter and H. T. Enmark, "A system overview of the Airborne Visible/Infrared Imaging Spectrometer (AVIRIS)," *Imaging Spectroscopy II*, G. Vane, Editor, Proc. SPIE 834, pp. 22–29, 1987.

[6] G. Vane, "First results from the Airborne Visible/Infrared Imaging Spectrometer (AVIRIS)," *Imaging Spectroscopy II*, G. Vane, Editor, Proc. SPIE 834, pp. 166–174, 1987.

[7] R. L. Baker and Y. T. Tze, "Compression of high spectral resolution imagery," *Applications of Digital Image Processing XI*, A. G. Tescher, Editor, Proc. SPIE 974, pp. 255–264, 1988.

[8] B. R. Epstein, R. Hingorani, J. M. Shapiro, and M. Czigler, "Multispectral KLT-wavelet data compression for Landsat thermatic mapper images," *Proc. Data Compression Conf.*, pp. 200–208, Apr. 1992.

[9] M. Manohar and J. C. Tilton, "Progressive vector quantization of multispectral image data using a massively parallel SIMD machine," *Proc. Data Compression Conf.*, pp. 181–190, Apr. 1992.

[10] G. P. Abousleman, T.-T. Lam, and L. J. Karam, "Robust hyperspectral image coding with channel-optimized trellis-coded quantization," *IEEE Trans. on Geoscience and Remote Sensing*, vol. 40, pp. 820–830, Apr. 2002.

[11] S.-E. Qian, A. B. Hollinger, D. Williams, and D. Manak, "Vector quantization using spectral index-based multiple subcodebooks for hyperspectral data compression," *IEEE Trans. on Geoscience and Remote Sensing*, vol. 38, pp. 1183–1190, May 2000.

[12] C.-I. Chang, Q. Du, T.-L. Sun, and M. Althouse, "A joint band prioritization and band-decorrelation approach to band selection for hyperspectral image classification," *IEEE Trans. on Geoscience and Remote Sensing*, vol. 37, pp. 2631–2641, Nov. 1999.

[13] B. Aiazzi, P. Alba, L. Alparone, and S. Baronti, "Lossless compression of multi/hyper-spectral imagery based on a 3-d fuzzy prediction," *IEEE*

Trans. on Geoscience and Remote Sensing, vol. 37, pp. 2287–2294, Sep. 1999.

[14] G. Canta and G. Poggi, "Kronecker-product gain-shape vector quantization for multispectral and hyperspectral image coding," *IEEE Trans. on Image Processing*, vol. 7, pp. 668–678, May 1998.

[15] M. J. Ryan and J. F. Arnold, "The lossless compression of AVIRIS images by vector quantization," *IEEE Trans. on Geoscience and Remote Sensing*, vol. 35, pp. 546–550, May 1997.

[16] G. P. Abousleman, M. W. Marcellin, and B. R. Hunt, "Hyperspectral image compression using entropy-constrained predictive trellis coded quantization," *IEEE Trans. Image Processing*, vol. IP-6, pp. 566–573, Apr. 1997.

[17] R. E. Roger and M. C. Cavenor, "Lossless compression of AVIRIS images," *IEEE Trans. on Image Processing*, vol. 5, pp. 713–719, May 1996.

[18] G. P. Abousleman, M. W. Marcellin, and B. R. Hunt, "Compression of hyperspectral imagery using the 3-D DCT and hybrid DPCM/DCT," *IEEE Trans. Geoscience and Remote Sensing*, vol. 33, pp. 26–34, Jan. 1995.

[19] G. P. Abousleman, "Adaptive wavelet coding of hyperspectral imagery," *Proceedings of the SPIE*, vol. 2762, pp. 545–556, 1996.

[20] G. P. Abousleman, "Coding of hyperspectral imagery using adaptive classification and trellis-coded quantization," *Proceedings of the SPIE*, vol. 3071, pp. 203–213, 1997.

[21] M. W. Marcellin and T. R. Fischer, "Trellis coded quantization of memoryless and Gauss-Markov sources," *IEEE Trans. Commun.*, vol. COM-38, pp. 82–93, Jan. 1990.

[22] T. R. Fischer and M. Wang, "Entropy-constrained trellis coded quantization," *IEEE Trans. Inform. Th.*, vol. 38, pp. 415–425, Mar. 1992.

[23] M. W. Marcellin, "On entropy-constrained trellis coded quantization," *IEEE Trans. Commun.*, vol. 42, pp. 14–16, Jan. 1994.

[24] G. D. Forney, Jr., "The Viterbi algorithm," *Proc. IEEE*, vol. 61, pp. 268–278, Mar. 1973.

[25] P. Chou, T. Lookabaugh, and R. M. Gray, "Entropy-constrained vector quantization," *IEEE Trans. Acoust., Speech, and Signal Proc.*, vol. ASSP-37, pp. 31–42, Jan. 1989.

[26] N. Farvardin and J. W. Modestino, "Optimum quantizer performance for a class of non-gaussian memoryless sources," *IEEE Trans. Inform. Th.*, vol. 30, pp. 485–497, May 1984.

[27] N. Farvardin and J. W. Modestino, "Rate-distortion performance of DPCM schemes for autoregressive sources," *IEEE Trans. Inform. Th.*, vol. 31, pp. 402–418, May 1985.

[28] M. Wang and T. R. Fischer, "Trellis coded quantization designed for noisy channels," *IEEE Trans. Information Theory*, vol. 40, pp. 1792–1801, 1994.

[29] J. Tou and R. Gonzalez, *Pattern Recognition Principles*, vol. 1, ch. 3. 1974. Pattern Classification by Distance Functions.

[30] E. Ayanoglu and R. M. Gray, "The design of joint source and channel trellis waveform coders," *IEEE Trans. Information Theory*, vol. 33, pp. 855–865, 1987.

[31] R. C. Reininger and J. D. Gibson, "Distributions of the two-dimensional DCT coefficients for images," *IEEE Trans. Commun.*, vol. COM-31, pp. 835–839, June 1983.

[32] Y. Shoham and A. Gersho, "Efficient bit allocation for an arbitrary set of quantizers," *IEEE Trans. Acoust., Speech, and Signal Proc.*, vol. 36, pp. 1445–1453, Sept. 1988.

[33] A. K. Jain, *Fundamentals of Digital Image Processing*. Englewood Cliffs, NJ: Prentice-Hall, 1989.

[34] R. C. Gonzalez and P. Wintz, *Digital Image Processing*. Reading, MA: Addison Wesley, 1989.

[35] N. S. Jayant and P. Noll, *Digital Coding of Waveforms*. Englewood Cliffs, NJ: Prentice-Hall, 1984.

[36] R. L. Joshi, T. R. Fischer, and R. H. Bamberger, "Optimum classification in subband coding of images," *Proc. International Conference on Image Processing*, pp. 883–887, Nov. 1994.

[37] G. P. Abousleman, "Wavelet-based hyperspectral image coding using robust fixed-rate trellis coded quantization," *Proceedings of the SPIE*, vol. 3372, pp. 74–85, 1998.

[38] M. Antonini, M. Barlaud, P. Mathieu, and I. Daubechies, "Image coding using wavelet transforms," *IEEE Trans. on Image Processing*, vol. 1, pp. 205–220, Apr. 1992.

[39] Q. Chen and T. R. Fischer, "Robust quantization for image coding and noisy digital transmission," *Proc. Data Compression Conf.*, pp. 3–12, Mar. 1996.

[40] C. J. Kuo and C. S. Huang, "Robust coding technique - transform encryption coding for noisy communications," *Opt. Engr.*, vol. 32, pp. 150–156, Jan. 1993.

[41] F. J. MacWilliams and N. J. A. Sloane, "Pseudo-random sequences and arrays," *Proc. IEEE*, vol. 64, pp. 1715–1730, Dec. 1976.

[42] G. P. Abousleman, "Entropy-constrained predictive trellis-coded quantization and compression of hyperspectral imagery," Ph.D. dissertation, The University of Arizona, Tucson, AZ, May 1994.

Three-Dimensional Wavelet-Based Compression of Hyperspectral Images *

Xiaoli Tang and William A. Pearlman

Center for Image Processing Research
Rensselaer Polytechnic Institute
Troy, NY 12180-3590

1 Introduction

Hyperspectral imaging is a powerful technique and has been widely used in a large number of applications, such as detection and identification of the surface and atmospheric constituents present, analysis of soil type, monitoring agriculture and forest status, environmental studies, and military surveillance. Hyperspectral images are generated by collecting hundreds of narrow and contiguous spectral bands of data such that a complete reflectance spectrum can be obtained for each point in the region being viewed by the instrument. However, at the time we gain high resolution spectrum information, we generate massively large image data sets. Access and transport of these data sets will stress existing processing, storage and transmission capabilities. As an example, the Airborne Visible InfraRed Imaging Spectrometer (AVIRIS) instrument, a typical hyperspectral imaging system, can yield about 16 Gigabytes of data per day. Therefore, efficient compression should be applied to these data sets before storage and transmission [19].

However, utilization of the data in compressed form can often be inconvenient and intractable, if it requires full decompression. One would like the bit stream to have properties of scalability and random access. There are two types of scalability of interest here - rate or quality scalability and resolution scalability. Rate scalability means that a portion of the bit stream can be decoded to provide a reconstruction at lower rate or quality. That would allow faster or lower bandwidth transmission or

---

* This work was performed at Rensselaer Polytechnic Institute and was supported in part by National Science Foundation Grant No. EEC-981276. The government has certain rights in this material.

a quick look at the entire data set at lower quality. Resolution scalabilty would permit decoding at reduced resolution from a portion of the compressed bit stream. These scalability properties enable transmission and retrieval that are progressive by quality or resolution.

Compression techniques can be broadly classified as either lossless or lossy. As the name suggests, lossless compression (lossless coding) reduces the redundancy of data sets without losing any information. The original images can be reconstructed exactly. This is a reversible process, and usually lossless compression can provide a compression ratio of about 2~3:1. On the other hand, if we are willing to lose some information, we can gain significantly higher compression ratio than that of lossless compression. This is so-called lossy compression (lossy coding). Many analytical applications for hyperspectral images, like classification and/or feature extraction, can perform reliably [10, 21] on images compressed to very low bit rates. Visualization applications, such as image browsing, are able to function successfully with lossy representations as well. However, hyperspectral image data are very different from other remote sensing images, such as gray-level PAN images, multi-spectral images, SAR images, etc. Hyperspectral data carry rich information in the spectral domain. A ground sample point in a hyperspectral data set has a distinct spectral profile, which is the fingerprint information of the point. Some hyperspectral data users will rely on the spectrum of each point to create application products using their remote sensing algorithms. When we compress hyperspectral images, we would like to preserve the important spectral profiles. Furthermore, given the extraordinary expense of acquiring hyperspectral imagery, it makes more sense to require lossless coding for archival applications. Therefore, in this study, we present both lossless and lossy compression for hyperspectral images.

Some Vector Quantization (VQ) based algorithms were proposed for lossy or lossless hyperspectral image compression. Ryan and Arnold [23] proposed mean-normalized vector quantization (M-NVQ) for lossless AVIRIS compression. The sample mean is scalar quantized before subtraction from the input vector so that any error in quantization of the mean is incorporated into the error vector. Each block of the image is converted into a vector with zero mean and unit standard variation. The mean and variance are scalar quantized and the input vector is vector quantized for transmission. M-NVQ results compare favorably with other compression techniques. Motta *et al.* [18] proposed a VQ based algorithm that involved locally optimal design of a partitioned vector quantizer for the encoding of source vectors drawn from hyperspectral images. Pickering and Ryan [22] jointly optimized spatial M-NVQ and spectral Discrete Cosine Transform (DCT) to produce compression ratios significantly better than those obtained by the optimized spatial M-NVQ technique alone. Pickering and Ryan's new technique can be applied on both lossless and lossy hyperspectral compression. An end-use remote sensing application, maximum likelihood classification (MLC), was used to test the efficiency of the algorithm. Results shown that distortions in the data caused by the compression process result in only minor losses in classification accuracy. Other than VQ based methods, Harsanyi and Chang [8] applied Principle Component Analysis (PCA) on hyperspectral images to simultaneously reduce the data dimensionality, suppress undesired or interfering spectral signature, and classify the spectral signature of interest. This approach is applicable to both spectrally pure as well as mixed pixels. A training sequence based entropy constrained predictive trellis coded quantization scheme was also proposed recently by Abousleman *et al.* [1] for hyperspectral image compression. All these algorithms have promising performance on hyperspectral image compression. However, none of them generates embedded bit stream, and therefore cannot provide progressive transmission.

To incorporate the embedded requirement and maintain other compression performances, many promising image compression algorithms based on wavelet transform [17] were proposed recently. They are simple, efficient and have been widely used in many applications. One of them is Shapiro's Embedded Zerotree Wavelet (EZW) [28]. Said and Pearlman [26] refined and extended EZW subsequently to SPIHT. Islam and Pearlman [11, 12] proposed another low complexity image encoder with similar features – Set Partitioned Embedded bloCK (SPECK). Related in various degrees to these earlier works on scalable image compression, the EBCOT algorithm [30] (adopted as the basis for the JPEG2000 image compression standard) also uses a wavelet transform to generate the subband samples which are to be quantized and coded. EBCOT stands for Embedded Block Coding with Optimized Truncation, which identifies some of the major contributions of the algorithm. It is resolution and

SNR scalable and has the random access property. EBCOT partitions each subband into relatively small blocks (typically, 32×32 or 64×64 pixels[1] are used), and generates a separate highly scalable (or embedded) bit stream for each block. The bit streams can be independently truncated to a set of rates calculated by a bit allocation algorithm and interleaved to achieve embedding.

The state-of-the-art encoder, SPIHT, has many attractive properties. It is an efficient embedded technique. The original SPIHT was proposed for two-dimensional image compression, and it has been extended to 3D applications by Kim and Pearlman [14]. 3D-SPIHT is the modern-day benchmark for three dimensional image compression. It has been applied on multispectral image compression by Dragotti et al. [6]. They use vector quantization (VQ) and Karhunen-Loéve transform (KLT) on the spectral dimension to explore the correlation between multispectral bands. In the spatial domain, they use discrete wavelet transform, and the 3D-SPIHT sorting algorithm is applied on the transformed coefficients. Dragotti et al.'s algorithms are comparable to 3D-SPIHT in multispectral image compression in rate distortion performance. Applying KLT on the spectral domain of multispectral images is acceptable because multispectral images only have a small number of bands. However, for hyperspectral imagery such as AVIRIS, computing KLT for 224 bands is usually not practical. Fry [7] adopts 3D-SPIHT directly on hyperspectral image compression. His work demonstrates the speed and computational complexity advantages of 3D-SPIHT. Results show that 3D-DWT is a fast and efficient means to exploit the correlations between hyperspectral bands. We show in this study that the lossy version of 3D-SPIHT also guarantees to preserve the spectral information for remote sensing applications.

The EBCOT algorithm has also been extended to 3D applications. Annex N of Part II of JPEG2000 standard [2] is for multi-component imagery compression. 3D-DWT is applied to decorrelate the separate components for multi-component images. Extended JPEG2000 partitioning and sorting algorithm to 3D sources is used to generate the embedded bit streams. JPEG2000 multi-component is a good candidate for hyper-

---

[1] The terms "pixel" and "coefficient" within the wavelet transform will be used interchangeably. The distinction between pixel as location and coefficient as value is often blurred.

spectral image compression. We will compare our algorithm to multi-component JPEG2000 in this study. Three Dimensional Cube Splitting EBCOT (3D CS-EBCOT) [27] initially partitions the wavelet coefficient prism into equally sized small code cubes of $64 \times 64 \times 64$ elements. The cube splitting technique is applied on each code cube to generate separate scalable bit streams. Like EBCOT, the bit streams may be independently truncated to any of a collection of different lengths to optimize the rate distortion criteria. Xu *et al.* [35] used a different method to extend EBCOT to video coding – Three-Dimensional Embedded Subband Coding with Optimized Truncation (3-D ESCOT). They treat each subband as a code cube and generate embedded bit streams for each code cube independently by using fractional bit-plane coding. Candidate truncation points are formed at the end of each fractional bit-plane.

A recently proposed 2D embedded wavelet based coder, tarp coder [29] has also been extended to 3D for hyperspectral image compression [31]. The tarp filtering operation is employed to estimate the probability of coefficient significance for arithmetic coder. The 3D tarp coder is comparable to 3D-SPIHT and JPEG2000 multi-component.

In this study, we extend SPECK to 3D sources and apply it to hyperspectral images. For an image sequence, 3D-DWT is applied to obtain a wavelet coefficient prism. Since our applications are hyperspectral images, there is not motion, but tight statistical dependency along the wavelength axis of this prism. Therefore, 3D-DWT can exploit the consequent correlation along the wavelength axis, as well as along the spatial axes. To start the algorithm, the subbands of the wavelet coefficient prism are tested for significance in order of increasing spatial frequency and, when significant, recursively partititioned into smaller (three-dimensional) code blocks[2] The resulting code blocks of different sizes (including 1x1 single points) are sorted using an extended and modified version of the SPECK algorithm, which we call 3D-SPECK.

In this chapter, we shall present some compression techniques based on three-dimensional wavelet transforms that produce compressed bit streams with many useful properties. These properties are progressive quality encoding and decoding, progressive lossy-to-lossless encoding, and progressive resolution decoding. Although the compression algo-

---

[2] It is customary to call the unit to be coded a block. This terminology is adopted here for the three-dimensional blocks in the shape of rectangular prisms.

rithms treated here are capable of producing bitstreams with the random access property, we shall not treat that subject here. We shall feature the embedded, block-based, low-complexity 3D-SPECK image coding algorithm. We describe the use of this coding algorithm in two implementations: first in a purely quality or rate scalable mode; and secondly in a resolution scalable mode. We utilize both integer and floating point wavelet transforms, whereby the former one enables lossy and lossless decompression from the same bit stream, and the latter one achieves better performance in lossy compression. The structure of hyperspectral images reveals spectral responses that would seem ideal candidates for compression by 3D-SPECK. We demonstrate that 3D-SPECK, a wavelet domain algorithm, like other time domain algorithms, can preserve spectral profiles well. Compared with the lossless version of the benchmark JPEG2000 (multi-component), the 3D-SPECK lossless algorithm produces average of 3.0% decrease in compressed file size for AVIRIS images, the typical hyperspectral imagery. We also conduct comparisons of the lossy implementation with other state-of-the-art algorithms such as Three-Dimensional Set Partitioning In Hierarchical Trees (3D-SPIHT) and JPEG2000. We conclude that this algorithm, in addition to being very flexible, retains all the desirable features of these algorithms and is highly competitive to 3D-SPIHT and better than JPEG2000 in compression efficiency.

2   MATERIAL AND METHODS

2.1   Discrete Wavelet Analysis

Wavelet transform coding provides many attractive advantages over other transform methods. This motivates intense research on this area. Many widely known coding schemes such as EZW, SPIHT, SPECK and EBCOT are all wavelet based schemes. The 9/7 tap biorthogonal filters [5], which produce floating point wavelet coefficients, are widely used in image compression techniques [26, 11, 12, 14] to generate a wavelet transform. This transform has proved to provide excellent performance for image compression. Hence, in this study, 9/7 tap biorthogonal filters will provide the transform for our lossy implementation of the new algorithm. For lossless implementations, the S+P [25] filter will be utilized.

The most frequently used wavelet decomposition structure is dyadic decomposition [17]. All coding algorithms mentioned above support dyadic decomposition. Occasionally, we need the wavelet packet decomposition which provides a richer range of possibilities for signal analysis. As hyper-spectral data carries rich information in the spectral domain, one may want to apply a wavelet packet instead of a dyadic wavelet transform on the spectral domain of the data. We tested both transforms on the spectral domain for our algorithm. For floating point filter implemen-tation, the experiments show that compared to the dyadic transform, the wavelet packet transform on spectral domain yields average of 2% increase in compressed file size for AVIRIS data for lossless compression and average of 0.36 dB lower SNR for lossy compression at rate 0.1 bits per pixel per band (bpppb). Therefore, the typical dyadic decomposition structure will be used for the floating point filter implementation. For integer filters, however, the dyadic structure provides a transform that is not unitary, so we need to apply a wavelet packet structure and scaling (by bit shifts) of the wavelet coefficients to make the transform unitary. More specifically, for spatial axes, we still maintain the 2D dyadic wavelet transform for each slice with scaling of the integer wavelet coefficients; for spectral axis, we use a 1D packet structure, and again with scaling of the integer wavelet coefficients. This packet structure and scaling make the transform approximately unitary.

2.2   The SPIHT Algorithm

Both the SPIHT and SPECK algorithms are highly efficient encoders. They are low in complexity, fast in encoding and decoding, and are fully embedded.

The SPIHT algorithm is the modern-day benchmark. It is essen-tially a wavelet transform-based embedded bit-plane encoding technique. SPIHT partitions transformed coefficients into spatial orientation tree sets (Fig. 1) based on the structure of the multi-resolution wavelet de-composition [26].

The SPIHT algorithm searches for "significant" coefficients of the wavelet transform along trees rooted at coefficients in the lowest fre-quency subband and branching into higher frequency subbands along the axes. Figure 1 depicts spatial orientation trees descending from a

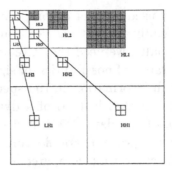

Figure 1: 2D Spatial orientation tree

2x2 group of coefficients in the root subband to the higher frequency subbands. "Significant" coefficents are those that exceed in magnitude the current threshold, initially the magnitude corresponding to the most significant bit of the largest coefficient in the image transform. After initial testing of the coefficients of the root subband for significance, each tree descending from a root is searched for a significant coefficent. If there is none, the coordinates of the root are placed on a list of insignificant sets (LIS) for later testing at the next lower threshold, which is half the current one. If there is any significant coefficient in the tree, the tree is divided into the children of the roots and the sub-trees descending from them. The children and sub-trees are then tested for significance in the same way. When a single coefficient is not significant, its coordinate is put on a list of insignificant points (LIP) to be tested later at the next lower threshold. When significant, its sign is output and its coordinate is put on a list of significant points (LSP). Whenever any test outcome is significant, a "1" is transmitted (placed into output bit-stream); whenever insignificant, a "0" is transmitted. The threshold is successively lowered by a factor of 2 and two of these lists are visited for similar testing in the order of LIP first, then LIS. Coefficients in the LSP found significant at prior higher thresholds are then refined by sending to the codestream their magnitude bits in the bit plane corresponding to the current threshold. Therefore, as the threshold decreases, the encoded bits belong to successively smaller bit planes and represent decreasingly smaller value changes to their associated coefficients. Such a code stream is said to be embedded.

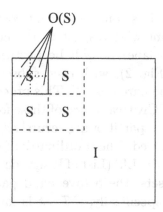

Figure 2: Set Partitioning rules for SPECK algorithm

One of the salient features of SPIHT is that the encoder and decoder have the same sorting algorithm. Therefore, the encoder does not need to transmit the order of the sorting. The decoder can recover the ordering information from the execution path, which is put into the bit-stream through the binary outputs of the significance tests.

2.3   The SPECK Algorithm

The SPECK algorithm has its roots primarily in the ideas developed in SPIHT and therefore has many features and properties similar to SPIHT. These two algorithms are both wavelet based techniques, and the transformed images all have hierarchical pyramidal structures. Their difference lies in the way of partitioning the wavelet coefficients. As stated above, SPIHT partitions wavelet coefficients into spatial orientation tree sets and sorts coefficients along the trees according to the results of significance tests. On the other hand, SPECK partitions wavelet coefficients into blocks and sorts coefficients by using the quadtree partitioning algorithm to be described.

As shown by solid lines in Figure 2, SPECK starts by partitioning the image of transformed coefficients into two sets: the set S which is the root (the topmost band) of the pyramid, and set $\mathcal{I}$ which is everything that is left of the image after taking out the root. Then, SPECK sorts the coefficients by testing the significance of set S first. The set is declared significant if there is at least one significant coefficient in this set. If S is found to be significant with respect to the current bit plane n (the highest "1" is in this plane), it will be partitioned into four subsets $\mathcal{O}(S)$ (dotted lines in Fig. 2), with each subset having approximately one-fourth the size of the parent set S. This procedure is called quadtree partitioning. Then, SPECK treats each of these four subsets as type S set and applies the quadtree partitioning recursively to each of them until significant pixels are located. The coordinates of insignificant coefficients and sets are recorded in the LIS (List of Insignificant Sets). After finishing testing of the type S sets, the octave band partitioning is applied to test type $\mathcal{I}$ sets. More specifically, if $\mathcal{I}$ set is found to be significant, it will be partitioned into three type S sets and one type $\mathcal{I}$ set as shown in Fig. 2 with dashed lines. The quadtree partitioning and octave band partitioning will be applied to these new sets respectively until significant pixels are isolated. Further details of SPECK may be read in Pearlman et al.[12].

By the end of the first pass, many type S sets of varying sizes are generated. In the next pass, SPECK will check their significance against the next bit plane according to their sizes. This process will be repeated to test the insignificant sets in the LIS in the same way at the next lower threshold until either the desired rate is reached or all coefficients have been transmitted.

3   The 3D-SPECK Algorithm

In this section, we present the 3D-SPECK coding algorithm. We describe the set-up and terminology first, followed by the main body of the algorithm, some detailed discussions, and the general 3D integer wavelet packet transform structure implementation that allows bit shifting of wavelet coefficients to approximate a 3D unitary transformation.

3.1   Set-up and Terminology

Consider a hyperspectral image sequence which has been adequately transformed using the discrete wavelet transform (can be either an integer or floating point wavelet transform). The transformed image sequence is said to exhibit a hierarchical pyramidal structure defined by the levels

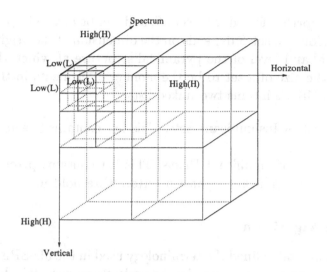

Figure 3: Subband Structure for 3D-SPECK.

of decomposition, with the topmost level being the root. Figure 3 illustrates such a structure with three-level decomposition. The finest pixels lie at the bottom level of the pyramid while the coarsest pixels lie at the top (root) level. The image sequence is represented by an indexed set of transformed coefficients $c_{i,j,k}$, located at pixel position (i, j, k) in the transformed image sequence.

Pixels are grouped together in sets which comprise regions in the transformed images. Unlike 2D-SPECK, 3D-SPECK has only one type of set: $\mathcal{S}$ set. We say a set $\mathcal{S}$ is significant with respect to n, if

$$\max_{(i,j,k)\in\mathcal{S}} |c_{i,j,k}| \geq 2^n \tag{1}$$

Where $c_{i,j,k}$ denotes the transformed coefficients at coordinate (i, j, k). Otherwise it is insignificant. For convenience, we can define the significance function of a set $\mathcal{S}$ as:

$$\Gamma_n(\mathcal{S}) = \begin{cases} 1 & : \quad \text{if } 2^n \leq \max_{(i,j,k)\in\mathcal{S}} |c_{i,j,k}| < 2^{n+1} \\ 0 & : \quad \text{else} \end{cases} \tag{2}$$

3D-SPECK makes use of rectangular prisms in the wavelet transform. Each subband in the pyramidal structure is treated as a code block or prism, henceforth referred to as sets $\mathcal{S}$, and can be of varying dimensions. The dimension of a set $\mathcal{S}$ depends on the dimension of the original images and the subband level of the pyramidal structure at which the set lies. We define the size of a set to be the number of elements in the set.

3D-SPECK maintains two linked lists:

- **LIS** – List of Insignificant Sets. This list contains $\mathcal{S}$ sets of varying sizes.
- **LSP** – List of Significant Pixels. This list contains pixels that have been found significant against a certain threshold n.

3.2 The Algorithm

Having set up and defined the terminology used in the 3D-SPECK coding method, we are now in a position to understand the main body of the actual algorithm.

The main body of 3D-SPECK consists of four steps: the initialization step; the sorting pass; the refinement pass; and the quantization step. These steps call two functions, ProcessS() and CodeS(), which are described in detail in the following.

The algorithm starts by adding all sets $\mathcal{S}$ to the LIS.

1. **Initialization**
   - Output $n = \lfloor \log_2(\max | c_{i,j,k} |) \rfloor$
   - Set LSP $= \emptyset$
   - Set LIS $= \{$all subbands of transformed images of wavelet coefficients $\}$
2. **Sorting Pass**
   In increasing order of size of sets, for each set $\mathcal{S} \in$ LIS, ProcessS($\mathcal{S}$)

   ProcessS($\mathcal{S}$)
   {
   - Output $\Gamma_n(\mathcal{S})$ (Whether the set is significant respect to current n or not)
   - if $\Gamma_n(\mathcal{S}) = 1$
     • if $\mathcal{S}$ is a pixel, output sign of $\mathcal{S}$ and add $\mathcal{S}$ to LSP
     • else CodeS($\mathcal{S}$)
     • if $\mathcal{S} \in$ LIS, remove $\mathcal{S}$ from LIS

```
}
```
CodeS($\mathcal{S}$)
```
{
```
- Partition $\mathcal{S}$ into eight approximately equal subsets $\mathcal{O}(\mathcal{S})$. For the situation that the original set size is odd × odd × odd, we can partition this kind of sets into different but approximately equal sizes of subsets (see Fig 4). For the situation that the size of the third dimension of the set is 1, we can partition the set into 4 approximately equal sizes of subsets.
- For each $\mathcal{O}(\mathcal{S})$
  - Output $\Gamma_n(\mathcal{O}(\mathcal{S}))$
  - if $\Gamma_n(\mathcal{O}(\mathcal{S})) = 1$
    * if $\mathcal{O}(\mathcal{S})$ is a pixel, output sign of $\mathcal{O}(\mathcal{S})$ and add $\mathcal{O}(\mathcal{S})$ to LSP
    * else CodeS($\mathcal{O}(\mathcal{S})$)
  - else
    * add $\mathcal{O}(\mathcal{S})$ to LIS
```
}
```

3. **Refinement Pass**
   For each entry $(i, j, k) \in$ LSP, except those included in the last sorting pass, output the nth MSB of $| c_{i,j,k} |$.
4. **Quantization Step**
   Decrement n by 1 and go to step 2.

The initial sets $\mathcal{S}$ in the LIS are the subbands of the 3D wavelet decomposition. In the first pass at the highest n, 3D-SPECK tests the significance of sets $\mathcal{S}$ in the LIS following the order of lowpass bands to highpass bands. As an example, for one-level decomposition, the scanning order is LLL, LHL, HLL, LLH, HHL, HLH, LHH, HHH. For higher level decomposition, the scanning path starts from the top of the pyramid down to its bottom by following the same order from lowpass bands to highpass bands.

ProcessS and CodeS are extensions of the two-dimensional procedures ProcessS and CodeS of SPECK. 3D-SPECK processes a type $\mathcal{S}$ set by calling ProcessS to test its significance with respect to a threshold n. If not significant, it stays in the LIS. Otherwise, ProcessS will call CodeS to partition set $\mathcal{S}$ into eight approximately equal subsets $\mathcal{O}(\mathcal{S})$

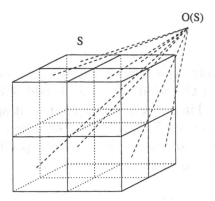

Figure 4: Partitioning of set S

(Fig 4). 3D-SPECK then treats each of these subsets as new type S set, and in turn, tests their significance. This process will be executed recursively until reaching pixel level where the significant pixel in the original set S is located. The algorithm then sends the significant pixel to the LSP, outputs a bit 1 to indicate the significance of the pixel, and outputs another bit to represent the sign of the pixel.

After finished the processing of all sets in the LIS, 3D-SPECK executes the refinement pass. The algorithm outputs the nth most significant bit of the absolute value of each entry (i, j, k) in the LSP, except those included in the just-completed sorting pass. The procedure refines significant pixels that were found during previous passes progressively.

The last step of the algorithm is to decrease n by 1 and return to the sorting pass of the current LIS, making the whole process run recursively.

The decoder is designed to have the same mechanism as the encoder. Based on the outcome of the significance tests in the received bit stream, the decoder can follow exactly the same execution path as the encoder and therefore reconstruct the image sequence progressively.

3.3   Processing Order of Sets

During the sorting pass, we claim that sets should be tested in increasing order of size. This follows the argument in [11, 12]. After the first pass, many sets of type S of varying sizes are generated and added to the LIS. For instance, the algorithm searches a set S and finds some significant pixels against the current threshold n belonging to set S. Neighboring pixels in set S not found to be significant in the current pass and sent to the LIS are very likely to be found as significant against the next lower threshold. Furthermore, our experiments show that a large number of sets with size of one are generated after the first iteration. Therefore, testing sets in increasing order of size can test pixel level first and locate new significant pixels immediately.

We do not use any sorting mechanism to process sets of type S in increasing order of their sizes. Even the fastest sorting algorithm will slow down the coding procedure significantly. This is not desirable in fast implementation of coders. However, there are simple ways of completely avoiding this sorting procedure. SPECK uses an array of lists to avoid sorting, whereas we use a different and simpler approach to achieve this goal. 3D-SPECK only maintains one list instead of an array of lists.

Note that the way sets S are constructed, they lie completely within a sub-band. Thus, every set S is located at a particular level of the pyramidal structure. Each time the algorithm partitions a set S, it generates eight smaller sets in approximate equal sizes, and the sizes of these sets S corresponds to a higher level of the pyramid. Based on this fact, to process sets of type S in increasing order of their sizes, we only need to search the same LIS several times at each iteration. Each time we only test sets with sizes corresponding to a particular level of the pyramid. This implementation completely eliminates the need for any sorting mechanism for processing the sets S. Thus, we can test sets in increasing order of size while keeping our algorithm running fast.

3.4   Entropy Coding

As with other coding methods such as SPIHT and SPECK, the efficiency of our algorithm can be improved by entropy-coding its output [16, 20, 24, 30]. We use the adaptive arithmetic coding algorithm of Witten *et al.* [32] to code the significance map. Referring to the function CodeS in our algorithm, instead of coding the significance test results of the eight subsets separately, we code them together first before further processing the subsets. Simple context is applied for conditional coding of the significance test result of this subset group. More specifically, we encode the significance test result of the first subset without any context, but encode the significance test result of the second subset by using the context (whether the first subset is significant or not) of the first coded subset and so on. Other outputs from the encoder are entropy coded by applying simple arithmetic coding without any context.

Also, we make the same argument as SPECK that if a set S is significant and its first seven subsets are insignificant, then this means that the last subset must be significant. Therefore, we do not need to test the significance of the last subset. This reduces the bit rate somewhat and provides corresponding gains.

We have chosen here not to entropy-code the sign and magnitude refinement bits, as small coding gains are achieved only with substantial increase in complexity. The SPECK variant, EZBC [9], has chosen this route, along with a more complicated context for the significance map quadtree coding. The application will dictate whether the increase in coding performance is worth the added complexity.

3.5   Computational Complexity and Memory

3D-SPECK has low computational complexity. The algorithm is very simple, consisting mainly of comparisons, and does not require any complex computation. Since the analysis in detail has already been done in [11] and [12], we do not repeat it here. Readers are referred to these two papers for more information.

3D-SPECK also has low dynamic memory requirements. At any given time during the coding process, only one connected prism is processed.

3.6   Scaling Wavelet Coefficients by Bit Shifts

The integer filter transform with dyadic decomposition structure is not unitary. This does not affect the performance of lossless compression. However, to achieve good lossy coding performance, it is important to have an unitary transform. If the transform is not unitary, the quantization error in the wavelet domain is, thus, not equal to the mean squared error (MSE) in the time domain. Therefore, the lossy coding performance will be compromised. Appropriate transform structure and scaling the integer wavelet coefficients can make the transform approximately unitary before quantization. It is therefore possible to keep track of the final quantizer coding error with the integer transform.

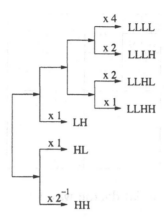

Figure 5: 1D wavelet packet structure along the spectral axis that makes the transform approximately unitary by shifting of the integer wavelet coefficients.

We adopt the transform structure mentioned in [34]. As shown in Figure 5, a 4-level 1D wavelet packet tree structure is applied on the spectral axis. The scaling factors for each subband is indicated in the figure. As each scaling factor is some power of two, we can implement the scaling factor by bit shifting.

For the spatial axes, we keep the same 2D dyadic wavelet transform to each slice. As shown in Figure 6, 4-level dyadic decomposition structure with scaling factor for each subband is plotted. Each of the scaling factors is some power of two and therefore can be implemented by bit shifting.

To summarize, the 3D integer wavelet packet transform we use here is first to apply 1D packet decomposition and bit shifting along the spectral axis, followed by the basic 2D dyadic decomposition and bit shifting on the spatial axes. An example is shown in Figure 7, where scaling factors associated with some subbands are indicated. The factors are the multiplications of the corresponding scaling factors in Fig. 5 and Fig. 6. The actual implementation of scaling factors is to shift all coefficients to some positive numbers of power two. In other words, for our case, all factors used in the implementation are four times of the factors shown in Fig. 7. This 3D integer wavelet packet structure makes

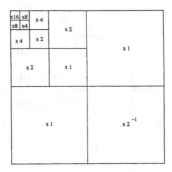

Figure 6: Same 2D spatial dyadic wavelet transform for each slice.

the transform approximately unitary, and thus leads to much better lossy coding performance.

3.7 Resolution Progressive 3D-SPECK

Although the subband transform structure is inherently scalable of resolution, most embedded coders in the literature are unable to efficiently provide resolution scalable code streams. This is a consequence of entanglement in coding, modeling, and data structure across different resolutions. As an example, EZW and SPIHT, the classical zerotree coders with individual zerotrees spanning several subband scales are not efficient for resolution scalable coding.

However, we can modify our implementation of 3D-SPECK quite easily to enable resolution scalability. The idea is just to run the 3D-SPECK algorithm on each subband separately. Instead of maintaining the same significance threshold across subbands until we exhaust them, we maintain separate LIS and LSP lists for each subband and proceed through the lower thresholds in every subband before moving to the next one. Therefore, we generate an array of lists, $\{LSP_k\}$ and $\{LIS_k\}$, where k is the subband index. We move through the subbands in the same order as before, from lowest to highest scale. Therefore, we can truncate the bit stream corresponding to a reduced scale and decode to that scale.

The generation of the bit stream successively by subbands in order of increasing scale is illustrated in Figure 8 for a two level dyadic decomposition into $K = 15$ subbands. The code stream for each subband

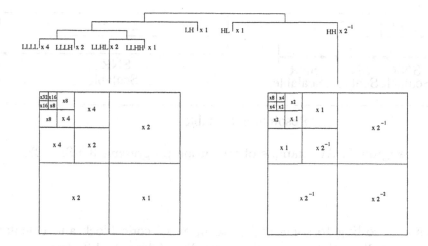

Figure 7: 3D integer wavelet packet transform.

is SNR scalable, and the full bit stream is resolution scalable, because it can be terminated at any subband corresponding to lower than full scale and be decoded to that scale.

In order to effect multi-resolution decoding, bit stream boundaries are maintained between subbands. Adaptive arithmetic coding models are accumulated from samples within the same resolution scale. Finally, the modeling contexts do not include any neighbor from the finer scales. These conditions guarantee the decodability of the truncated code stream.

Although the full bit stream is resolution progressive, it is now not SNR progressive. The bit streams in the subbands are individually SNR progressive, so the bits belonging to the same bit planes in different subbands could be interleaved at the decoder after truncation to the desired scale to produce an SNR scalable bit stream.

For the SNR progressive coding mode, the bits are allocated optimally across subbands, according to the significance threshold of the coefficients. But, for the resolution progressive mode, for a given target bit rate, we need now to apply an explicit bit allocation algorithm to assign different bit rates to different subbands to minimize mean squared error. The solution is the same rate-distortion slope for every subband receiving non-zero rate. That slope depends on the target rate. JPEG2000

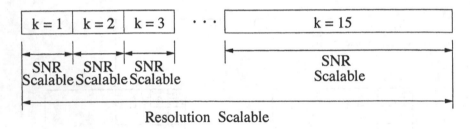

Figure 8: An example of resolution progressive 3D-SPECK

uses over-coding to some high rate in every code block and calculates these rate-distortion slopes while encoding. Then the bit stream in each code block is truncated to the correct point in an iterative procedure.

For the sake of expediency, we adopt a different procedure [37, 36] to solve the rate allocation. Let us assume that the subbands are numbered acording to decreasing variance to size ratio σ_k^2/n_k, $k = 1, 2, \ldots, K$. At low rates, the subbands numbered from some subband, say m, to K, will receive zero rate. Thus, if the first m subbands obtain a nonzero rate, the optimum rate allocation is

$$r_k = \begin{cases} \frac{N}{N_{s,m}}R + \frac{1}{2}\log_2 \frac{\sigma_k^2/n_k}{\gamma_{wgm,m}^2}, & 1 \le k \le m \\ 0, & m < k \le K \end{cases} \tag{3}$$

where γ_m^2 is a size weighted geometric mean of the variances of the first m subbands and is defined as

$$\gamma_m^2 = [\prod_{k=1}^{m} (\sigma_k^2/n_k)^{n_k}]^{1/N_{s,m}}$$

where n_k is the number coefficients in subband k and $N_{s,m} = \sum_{k=1}^{m} n_k$ is the number of coefficients in the first m subbands.

In order to find m, we use the following iterative procedure.

1. Set $m = K$.
2. Allocate rate using Equation 3.
3. If all m bands are allocated non-negative rates, the rate allocation is complete. Otherwise, decrement m by 1 and go to step 2.

To decode the image sequence to a particular level at a given rate, we need to encode each subband at a higher rate so that the algorithm can truncate the sub-bitstream to the assigned rate. However, unlike the JPEG2000 method, with this method we can achieve the target rate at the encoding stage without over-coding.

4 Numerical Results

We performed coding experiments on three signed 16-bit reflectance AVIRIS image volumes. AVIRIS has 224 bands and 614 × 512 pixel resolution that corresponds to an area of approximately 11 km × 10 km on the ground. We have 1997 runs of Moffett Field scene 1 and 3 and Jasper Ridge scene 1. For our experiments, we cropped each scene to 512 × 512 × 224 pixels.

4.1 Comparison of Lossless Compression Performance

Table 1 presents the lossless performances of 3D-SPECK, 3D-SPIHT[3], JPEG2000 multi-component (JP2K-Multi) [13], 2D-SPIHT and JPEG-2000 [13]. JP2K-Multi implemented by first applying S+P filter on spectral dimension to decorrelate spectral correlation and followed by JPEG-2000 on spatial dimensions. S+P integer filters are used for 3D-SPECK, 3D-SPIHT and 2D-SPIHT, while for JPEG2000, the integer filter (5,3) [4] is used. For all 3D algorithms, including 3D-SPECK, 3D-SPIHT and JP2K-Multi, the results of AVIRIS data are obtained by coding all 224 bands as a single unit, and for the two 2D algorithms, the results are obtained by first coding the AVIRIS data band by band and then averaging over the entire volume.

Overall, 3D algorithms perform better than 2D algorithms. Compared with 2D-SPIHT and JPEG2000, 3D-SPECK yields, on average, 13.1% and 18.6% decreases in compressed file sizes for AVIRIS test image volumes. 3D-SPECK and 3D-SPIHT are fairly comparable as their results are quite close. They both outperform the benchmark JPEG2000 multi-component, averaged over the three image volumes, by 3.0% and 3.2% decreases in file size, respectively. Surprisingly, considering its considerably higher complexity, JPEG2000 is not as efficient as 2D-SPIHT.

---

[3] We use symmetric tree 3D-SPIHT here.

File Name	Coding Methods				
	3D-SPECK	3D-SPIHT	JP2K-Multi	2D-SPIHT	JPEG 2000
moffett scene 1	6.9102	6.9411	7.1748	7.9714	8.7905
moffett scene 3	6.8209	6.7402	7.0021	7.5847	7.7258
jasper scene 1	6.7014	6.7157	6.8965	7.9770	8.5860

Table 1: Comparison of methods for Lossless coding of test 16 bit image volumes. The data are given in bits per pixel per band (bpppb), averaged over the entire image volume.

As shown in the table, 2D-SPIHT always yields smaller bits per pixel per band (bpppb) than that of JPEG2000.

4.2 Comparison of Lossy Compression Performance

As we stated above, many hyperspectral image applications can perform reliably on images compressed to very low bit rates. Therefore, we present lossy versions of our algorithm as well by comparing the performances with other lossy algorithms.

To quantify fidelity, the coding reconstruction quality is reported using Signal-to-Noise ratio (SNR) for the whole sequence :

$$\text{SNR} = 10 \log_{10} \frac{P_x}{\text{MSE}} \text{ dB} \tag{4}$$

where P_x is the average squared value (power) of the original AVIRIS sequence, and MSE is the mean squared error over the entire sequence.

We present the lossy compression performance of 3D-SPECK by using both integer filter implementation, which enables lossy-to-lossless compression, and floating point filter implementation, which provides better lossy performance. For both implementations, the coding results are compared with 3D-SPIHT and JP2K-Multi.

The rate-distortion results for 3D-SPECK, 3D-SPIHT, and JP2K-Multi integer implementations are listed in Table 2 for our three test image volumes. For each algorithm with a desired bit rate, we truncate

Method	SNR (dB) vs. Rate (bpppb)					
	0.1	0.2	0.5	1.0	2.0	4.0
moffett scene 1						
3D-SPECK	15.717	20.778	29.199	37.284	44.731	54.605
3D-SPIHT	15.509	20.605	29.105	37.198	44.671	54.544
JP2K-Multi	14.770	19.655	27.999	36.312	44.460	53.686
moffett scene 3						
3D-SPECK	10.622	16.557	25.998	34.845	42.002	49.721
3D-SPIHT	10.828	16.740	26.102	34.946	42.094	49.892
JP2K-Multi	10.264	15.952	25.208	33.835	41.535	49.240
jasper scene 1						
3D-SPECK	19.022	22.675	30.400	36.697	43.622	51.857
3D-SPIHT	18.905	22.553	30.279	36.647	43.566	51.742
JP2K-Multi	17.825	21.869	29.035	36.039	42.516	51.124

Table 2: Comparative evaluation the rate distortions of integer filter versions of 3D-SPECK, 3D-SPIHT and JPEG2000 multi-component.

the same embedded information sequence obtained in Ssection 4.1 at appropriate points and reconstruct the data to the corresponding accuracy. If no information loss is allowed, the whole embedded sequence will be used to fully recover the original image volume.

Overall, both 3D-SPECK and 3D-SPIHT perform better than JP2K-multi, providing higher SNR all the time. For all three test image volumes, the results show that 3D-SPECK is comparable to 3D-SPIHT, being slightly worse for moffett scene 3, but slightly better for moffett scene 1 and jasper scene 1.

Table 3 shows the rate-distortion results of the lossy implementations for 3D-SPECK, 3D-SPIHT and JPEG2000 multi-component. All results are obtained by using all 224 bands as a single coding unit and 5-level pyramid decompositions with the 9/7 tap biorthogonal filters and using a reflection extension at the image edges. Since every codec is embedded, the results for various bit rates can be obtained from a single encoded file.

Method	SNR (dB) vs. Rate (bpppb)					
	0.1	0.2	0.5	1.0	2.0	4.0
moffett scene 1						
3D-SPECK	16.671	21.520	29.913	38.595	47.178	55.574
3D-SPIHT	16.570	21.461	29.880	38.539	47.136	55.527
JP2K-Multi	15.286	19.920	28.194	36.558	45.430	55.177
moffett scene 3						
3D-SPECK	12.604	17.983	26.988	35.370	44.095	50.786
3D-SPIHT	12.924	18.249	27.277	35.620	44.371	51.037
JP2K-Multi	10.791	16.810	25.822	33.439	38.778	40.826
jasper scene 1						
3D-SPECK	19.702	23.658	31.750	38.552	45.997	52.361
3D-SPIHT	19.589	23.586	31.480	38.363	45.853	52.261
JP2K-Multi	18.246	22.172	29.813	36.625	43.369	51.963

Table 3: Comparative evaluation the rate distortions of floating point filter versions of 3D-SPECK, 3D-SPIHT and JPEG2000 multi-component.

Comparing with integer filter results at different reconstruction rates, 3D-SPECK and 3D-SPIHT floating point implementations have better performances, both yielding an approximate range of 1.5 to 3.5 dB higher SNR. For JPEG2000 multi-component, the gains over the integer filter implementation are smaller. 3D-SPECK and 3D-SPIHT are competitive as they demonstrate quite close rate-distortions results for all AVIRIS sequences. 3D-SPECK performs slightly worse for moffett scene 3 but slightly better for moffett scene 1 and jasper scene 1. JPEG2000 is again worse than the 3D-SPIHT and 3D-SPECK in all trials.

These coding gains will produce better performance for hyperspectral applications. Therefore, for hyperspectral applications such as classification and feature extraction that can function reliably with lossy representations, the floating pointer filter version is a better choice.

Figure 9: A visual example of resolution progressive 3D-SPECK using floating point wavelet transform. From left to right: 1/8 resolution, 1/4 resolution, 1/2 resolution, at 0.5 bpppb and full resolution (original).

4.3 Resolution Progressive 3D-SPECK Results - Floating Point Filters

As before, the coding performances of resolution progressive 3D-SPECK are reported in signal-to-noise ratio (SNR), using mean square error (MSE) calculated over the whole sequence.

Figure 9 shows the reconstructed band 20 of jasper scene 1 decoded from a single scalable code stream at a variety of resolutions at 0.5 bpppb. The SNR values for 0.5 bpppb for the whole sequence are listed in Table 4 along with results of other bit rates. The corresponding bit budget for the individual resolutions are provided in Table 5. We can see that the computational cost of decoding reduces from one resolution level to the next lower one.

The SNR values listed in Table 4 for low resolution image sequences are calculated with respect to the reference image generated by the same analysis filter bank and synthesized to the same scale. The total bit cost decreases rapidly with a reduction in resolution. However, the image quality is increasingly degraded from one resolution to the next lower

Bit Rate (bpppb)	SNR (dB) vs. scale			
	1/8	1/4	1/2	Full
0.1	8.46	12.94	16.75	19.29
0.5	18.29	23.04	27.24	31.53
1.0	21.97	26.41	31.97	38.37
2.0	29.02	34.15	39.61	45.82

Table 4: SNR in dB for coding jasper scene 1 at a variety of resolution and coding bit rates using resolution progressive 3D-SPECK with floating point filters.

Bit Rate (bpppb)	Bit budget (Kbits) vs. scale			
	1/8	1/4	1/2	Full
0.1	11	91	734	5872
0.5	57	459	3670	29360
1.0	115	918	7340	58720
2.0	229	1835	14680	117441

Table 5: Corresponding bit budgets for Table 4

one. If we look at the sample images in Fig. 9, when the reconstructed sequences are presented at same display resolution, the perceived distortion for viewing a sample image at half resolution is equivalent to that at full resolution but from twice a distance. The low resolution sequences can thus allowed to be coded relatively coarsely. The multi-resolution coding with such a perceptual concept has been reported in [9].

4.4   Resolution Progressive 3D-SPECK Results - Integer Filters

The basic function of integer filter implementation of resolution progressive is the same as the floating point implementation. The difference is that the former one supports lossy-to-lossless encoding/decoding, and

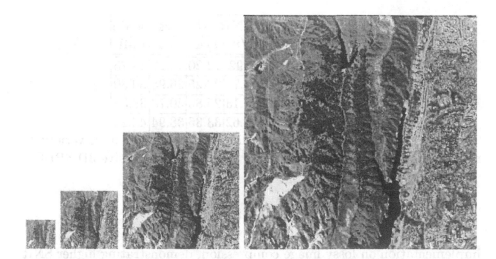

Figure 10: A visual example of resolution progressive 3D-SPECK with integer wavelet transform. From left to right: 1/8 resolution, 1/4 resolution, 1/2 resolution, and full resolution (original).

thus lossy and lossless reconstructions can be generated from the same embedded bit stream.

Again we use the AVIRIS jasper scene 1 as an example. Coding the entire sequence as one unit of 224 frames. To assess the visual quality of the reconstructed sequence, we show one band of the sequence. Figure 10 shows the reconstructed band 20 of jasper scene 1 losslessly decoded at a variety of resolutions.

For the lossy reconstruction from the same bit stream, Table 6 lists the SNR results of the whole jasper scene 1 sequence reconstructed to different resolution levels at different bit rates. The SNR values decrease from one resolution to the next lower one. If we look at the sample images, when the reconstructed sequences are presented at same display resolution, the perceived distortion for viewing a sample image at half resolution is equivalent to that at full resolution but from twice a distance. These results are similar to the floating point 3D-SPECK results. However, comparing to the values listed in Table 9, we could see that the floating point implementation performs better than the integer filter

Bit Rate (bpppb)	SNR (dB) vs. scale			
	1/8	1/4	1/2	Full
0.1	7.92	12.20	16.27	18.75
0.5	17.72	22.25	26.95	30.30
1.0	21.13	25.86	30.78	36.52
2.0	28.62	33.36	38.94	43.22

Table 6: SNR values in dB for coding jasper scene 1 at a variety of resolution and coding bit rates using resolution progressive 3D-SPECK with integer filters.

implementation on lossy image compression, demonstrating higher SNR values at the same bit rates.

Table 7 lists the related CPU times for Table 6 at the percentages of decoding time of lossless decoding at full resolution. We can see that the computational cost of decoding reduces from one resolution level to the next lower one.

4.5   The Coding Gain

We wish to establish the effectiveness of extending SPECK from 2D to 3D coding. We use jasper scene 1 as an example to show the lossy compression performance of 2D-SPECK and 3D-SPECK.

Table 8 shows the rate distortions results by comparing the results of 3D-SPECK and 2D-SPECK. The gap between 3D-SPECK and 2D-SPECK has the approximate range of 12 to 26 dB SNR, all depending on different bit rates. This demonstrates the big benefit of using 3D algorithm. 3D algorithm exploits the correlations along the spectral axis and therefore achieves much better coding performance.

4.6   Spectral Profile Integrity and Classification Performance

As the most important information for hyperspectral users is the spectral profile, we illustrate the performance for the integer filter version of 3D-SPECK by plotting the original spectral profiles of individual pixels,

Bit Rate (bpppb)	Decoding time (%) vs. scale			
	1/8	1/4	1/2	Full
0.1	0.23	1.59	3.17	3.44
0.5	0.25	1.64	13.22	13.52
1.0	0.28	1.69	13.23	34.77
2.0	0.33	1.84	13.28	70.44
lossless	0.43	2.19	13.52	100

Table 7: Decoding times in percentage (%) of lossless decoding at full resolution for coding jasper scene 1 at a variety of resolution using resolution progressive 3D-SPECK.

Method	SNR (dB) vs. Rate (bpppb)					
	0.1	0.2	0.5	1.0	2.0	4.0
3D-SPECK	19.702	23.658	31.750	38.552	45.997	52.361
2D-SPECK	7.503	9.237	11.075	13.824	18.427	28.525

Table 8: Comparative evaluation the rate distortions of floating point filter versions of 3D-SPECK and 2D-SPECK.

along with associated reconstructed and error profiles. Figures 11 and 12 show the profiles for one asphalt pixel and one vegetation pixel of Jasper scene 1, respectively. The spectral profiles are preserved excellently even at 1.0 bppp, with only several larger values of errors occur at the spectral valleys around bands 160 and 224. The largest error corresponds to 2.4% of the maximum value. Increasing the bit rate, the error (difference) values drop quickly. The absolute values of errors are already within 25 at 2.0 bppp, corresponding to 0.7% and 0.6% of the maximum values for asphalt pixel and vegetation pixel, respectively. For bit rate of 4.0 bppp, as shown in Figure 11 and Figure 12, the differences between the original profiles and the reconstructed ones are barely distinguishable, and the errors are very small.

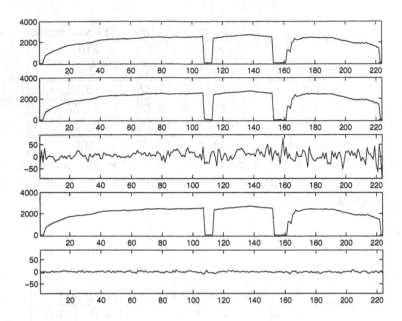

Figure 11: The original, reconstructed and the difference values between the original and reconstructed pixels for an asphalt pixel for Jasper scene 1. The first graph is the original, the second one is the reconstructed pixel at 1.0 bppp, the third one is the difference values at 1.0 bppp, the fourth one is the reconstructed pixel at 4.0 bppp, and the last one is the difference values at 4.0 bppp.

To address how our compression algorithm impacts remote sensing applications, it is important to provide an experiment for an end-use application. We use a well-known remote sensing classification method, Spectral Angle Mapper (SAM) [3], to test the proposed algorithm 3D-SPECK as well as 3D-SPIHT and JPEG2000 multi-component (JP2K-Multi). SAM determines the similarity of the original and reconstructed spectrum by computing the normalized inner product between the two spectra. We assume first that the classification on the original image is correct, and then report the classification performance as percentage of "correctly" classified pixels. In other words, we report the percentage of pixels whose classification is the same by using both the original and reconstructed spectrum.

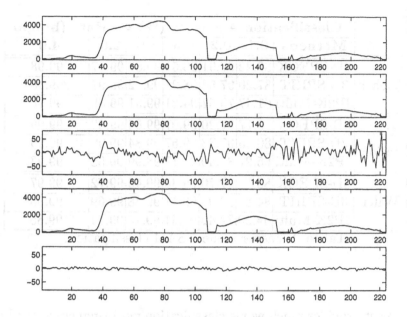

Figure 12: The original, reconstructed and the difference values between the original and reconstructed pixels for a vegetation pixel for Jasper scene 1. The first graph is the original, the second one is the reconstructed pixel at 1.0 bppp, the third one is the difference values at 1.0 bppp, the fourth one is the reconstructed pixel at 4.0 bppp, and the last one is the difference values at 4.0 bppp.

Table 9 lists the classification results for three classes (asphalt, vegetation and water) of Jasper scene 1. All algorithms tested here are integer filter implementations. We can see that the classification tasks investigated are robust with respect to lossy compression of the source image. The percentage of correctly classified pixels converges to 100% at the rates higher than 1 bppp for all three algorithms, with JPEG2000 multicomponent being slightly worse than that of 3D-SPECK and 3D-SPIHT. For 3D-SPECK and 3D-SPIHT, the distortions in the reconstructed data caused by the compression process result in only minor losses in classification accuracy even at low bit rate such as 1 bppp, with the classification accuracy higher than 99% almost all the time. For 3D-SPECK and 3D-SPIHT at very low bit rate such as 0.2 bppp, the percentages of classification accuracy are already higher than 97%. JPEG2000 multi-

	Classification Accuracy (%) vs. Rate (bpppb)					
	Methods	0.1	0.2	0.5	1.0	2.0	4.0
Asphalt	3D-SPECK	89.22	97.91	98.51	99.87	99.97	99.98
	3D-SPIHT	87.20	97.56	98.27	99.42	99.97	99.98
	JP2K-Multi	61.47	75.57	94.21	99.31	99.88	99.96
Vegetation	3D-SPECK	75.77	97.20	99.07	99.64	99.82	99.99
	3D-SPIHT	80.35	97.83	99.57	99.84	99.90	99.99
	JP2K-Multi	65.27	84.40	95.17	98.99	99.58	99.93
Water	3D-SPECK	85.77	97.70	99.36	99.45	99.72	99.97
	3D-SPIHT	84.88	96.94	99.11	99.38	99.69	99.95
	JP2K-Multi	64.20	72.42	98.31	99.23	99.74	99.85

Table 9: Jasper scene 1 SAM classification.

component provides much worse classification performances at 0.2 bppp. Overall, JPEG2000 multi-component performs not as well as the other two algorithms, rendering much poorer classification accuracy at very low bit rates and slightly lower percentage of classification accuracy at higher bit rate. Therefore, massively large image data sets can be reduced to manageable sizes with only minor reductions in classifier performance.

5 Conclusion

This chapter proposed a three dimensional set partitioned embedded block coder for hyperspectral image compression. The three dimensional wavelet transform automatically exploits inter-band dependence. Two versions of the algorithm were implemented. The integer filter implementation enables lossy-to-lossless compression, and the floating point filter implementation provides better performance for lossy representation. Wavelet packet structure and bit shifting were applied on the integer filter implementation to make the transform approximately unitary.

Rate distortion results of both lossless and lossy compression of hyperspectral imagery have been presented, and all results were compared with other state-of-the-art three dimensional compression algorithms such as 3D-SPIHT and JPEG2000 multi-component. 3D-SPECK is competitive to 3D-SPIHT and better than JPEG2000 in compression efficiency. The plots of original, reconstructed and error spectral profiles shown that the proposed algorithm preserved spectral profiles well.

The proposed 3D-SPECK is completely embedded and can be used for progressive transmission. These features make the proposed coder a good candidate to compress (encode) hyperspectral images before transmission and to decompress (decode) them at another end for image storage.

References

[1] G.P. Abousleman, MW. Marcellin, and B.R. Hunt, *Hyperspectral image compression using entropy-constrained predictive trellis coded quantization*, IEEE Trans. Image Processing, Vol. 6, No. 4, April 1997.

[2] ISO/IEC 15444-2, Information Technology – JPEG 2000 Image Coding System – Part 2: Extensions, December 2000, Final Committee Draft.

[3] J.W. Boardman, F.A. Kruse and R.O. Green, *Mapping target signatures via partial unmixing of AVIRIS data*, Fifth JPL Airborne Earth Science Workshop, JPL Publication, pp.23-26, 1995.

[4] R. Calderbank, I. Daubechies, W. Sweldens, and B.-L. Yeo, *Wavelet transforms that map integers to integers*, J. Appl. Computa. Harmonics Anal. 5, pp.332-369, 1998.

[5] M. Antonini, M. Barlaud, P. Mathieu, and I. Daubechies, *Image coding using wavelet transform*, IEEE Trans. Image Processing, vol. 1, pp.205-220, 1992.

[6] P.L. Dragotti, G. Poggi, and A.R.P. Ragozini, *Compression of multispectral images by three-dimensional SPIHT algorithm*, IEEE Trans. on Geoscience and remote sensing, vol. 38, No. 1, Jan 2000.

[7] Thomas W. Fry, *Hyperspectral image compression on reconfigurable platforms*, Master Thesis, Electrical Engineering, University of Washington, 2001.

[8] J.C. Harsanyi, and C.I. Chang, *Hyperspectral image classification and dimensionality reduction: an orthogonal subspace projection approach*, IEEE Trans. Geoscience and Remote Sensing. Vol. 32, No. 4, July 1994.

[9] S-T. Hsiang and J.W. Woods, *Embedded image coding using zer-oblocks of subband/wavelet coefficients and context modeling*, IEEE Int. Conf. on Circuits and Systems (ISCAS2000), vol. 3, pp.662-665, May 2000.

[10] P.F. Hsieh, *Classification of high dimensional data*, Ph.D. Thesis, Purdue University, 1998.

[11] A. Islam and W.A. Pearlman, *An embedded and efficient low-complexity hierarchical image coder*, in Proc. SPIE Visual Comm. and Image Processing, vol. 3653, pp. 294-305, 1999.

[12] W. A. Pearlman, A. Islam, N. Nagaraj, and A. Said, *Efficient, Low-Complexity Image Coding with a Set-Partitioning Embedded Block Coder*, IEEE Trans. on Circuits and Systems for Video Technology, vol. 14, pp. 1219-1235, Nov. 2004.

[13] Kakadu JPEG2000 v3.4, http://www.kakadusoftware.com/.

[14] B. Kim and W.A. Pearlman, *An embedded wavelet video coder using three-dimensional set partitioning in hierarchical tree*, IEEE Data Compression Conference, pp.251-260, March 1997.

[15] Y. Kim and W.A. Pearlman, *Lossless volumetric medical image compression*, Ph.D Dissertation, Department of Electrical, Computer, and Systems Engineering, Rensselaer Polytechnic Institute, Troy, 2001.

[16] J. Li and S. Lei, *Rate-distortion optimized embedding*, in Proc. Picture Coding Symp., Berlin, Germany, pp.201-206, Sept. 10-12, 1997.

[17] S. Mallat, *Multifrequency channel decompositions of images and wavelet models*, IEEE Trans. Acoust., Speech, Signal Processing, vol. 37, pp.2091-2110, Dec. 1989.

[18] G. Motta, F. Rizzo, and J.A. Storer, *Compression of hyperspectral imagery*, Data Compression Conference. Proceedings. DCC 2003, pp. 25-27, March 2003.

[19] A.N. Netravali and B.G. Haskell, *Digital pictures, representation and compression*, in Image Processing, Proc. of Data Compression Conference, pp.252-260, 1997.

[20] E. Ordentlich, M. Weinberger, and G. Seroussi, *A low-complexity modeling approach for embedded coding of wavelet coefficients*, in Proc. IEEE Data Compression Conf., Snowbird, UT, pp.408-417, Mar. 1998.

[21] M.D. Pal, C.M. Brislawn, and S.P. Brumby, *Feature extraction from hyperspectral images compressed using the JPEG-2000 standard*, IEEE Southwest Symposium on Image Analysis and Interpretation, 5, pp.168-172, April. 2002.

[22] M.R. Pickering and M.J. Ryan, *Efficient spatial-spectral compression of hyperspectral data*, IEEE Trans. Geoscience and Remote Sensing, Vol. 39, No. 7, July 2001.

[23] M.J. Ryan and J.F. Arnold, *The lossless compression of AVIRIS images by vector quantization*, IEEE Trans. Geoscience and Remote Sensing, Vol. 35, No. 3, May 1997.

[24] *Proposal of the arithmetic coder for JPEG2000*, ISO/IEC/JTC1/SC29/WG1 N762, Mar. 1998.

[25] A. Said and W.A. Pearlman, *An image multiresolution representation for lossless and lossy compression*, IEEE Trans. Image Process. 5, pp.1303-1310, 1996.

[26] A. Said and W.A. Pearlman, *A new, fast and efficient image codec based on set partitioning in hierarchical trees*, IEEE Trans. on Circuits and Systems for Video Technology 6, pp.243-250, June 1996.

[27] P. Schelkens, *Multi-dimensional wavelet coding algorithms and implementations*, Ph.D dissertation, Department of Electronics and Information Processing, Vrije Universiteit Brussel, Brussels, 2001.

[28] J.M. Shapiro, *Embedded image coding using zerotrees of wavelet coefficients*, IEEE Trans. Signal Processing, vol. 41, pp.3445-3462, Dec. 1993.

[29] P. Simard, D. Steinkraus, and H. Malvar, *On-line adaptation in image coding with a 2-D tarp filter*, in Proceedings of the IEEE Data Compression conference, J.A. Storer and M.Cohn, Eds., Snowbird, UT, pp. 23-32, April 2002.

[30] D. Taubman, *High performance scalable image compression with EBCOT*, IEEE Trans. on Image Processing, vol. 9, pp.1158-1170, July, 2000.

[31] Yonghui Wang, Justin T. Rucker, and James E. Fowler, *3D tarp coding for the compression of hyperspectral images*, Submitted to IEEE Trans. on Geoscience and Remote Sensing, July 2003.

[32] I.H. Witten, R.M. Neal, and J.G. Cleary, *Arithmetic coding for data compression*, Commun. ACM, vol. 30, pp.520-540, June 1987.

[33] Z. Xiong, X. Wu, D.Y. Tun, and W.A. Pearlman, *Progressive coding of medical volumetric data using three-dimensional integer wavelet*

packet transform, Medical Technology Symposium, 1998. Proceedings. Pacific, PP.384 -387, 1998.

[34] Z Xiong, X. Wu, S. Cheng, and J. Hua, *Lossy-to-lossless compression of medical volumetric data using three-dimensional integer wavelet transforms*, IEEE Trans. on Medical Imaging, Vol. 22, No. 3, March 2003.

[35] J. Xu, Z. Xiong, S. Li, and Y. Zhang, *Three-dimensional embedded subband coding with optimized truncation (3-D ESCOT)*, J. Applied and Computational Harmonic Analysis: Special Issue on Wavelet Applications in Engineering. vol. 10, pp.290-315, May 2001.

[36] W.A. Pearlman, *Performance Bounds for Subband Coding*, Chapter 1 in *Subband Image Coding*, J. W. Woods and Ed., Kluwer Academic Publishers, 1991.

[37] M. Balakrishnan and W.A. Pearlman, *Hexagonal subband image coding with perceptual weighting*, Optical Engineering, Vol. 32, No. 7, pp.1430-1437, July, 1993.

Spectral/Spatial Hyperspectral Image Compression

Bharath Ramakrishna[1] Antonio J. Plaza[1,2] Chein-I Chang[1] Hsuan Ren[3]
Qian Du[4] Chein-Chi Chang[5]

[1]Remote Sensing Signal and Image Processing Laboratory
Department of Computer Science and Electrical Engineering
University of Maryland, Baltimore County, Baltimore, MD 21250
[2]Computer Science Department, University of Extremadura
Avda. de la Universidad s/n,10.071 Caceres, SPAIN
[3]Center for Space and Remote Sensing Research
Graduate Institute of Space Science
Department of Computer Science and Information Engineering
National Central University, Chungli, Taiwan, ROC
[4]Department of Electrical and Computer Engineering
Mississippi State University, Mississippi State, MS 39762
[5]Department of Civil and Environmental Engineering
University of Maryland, Baltimore County, Baltimore, MD 21250

1.   INTRODUCTION

Hyperspectral image compression has received considerable interest in recent years due to enormous data volumes collected by imaging spectrometers which consists of hundreds of contiguous spectral bands with very high between-band spectral correlation. Due to such significantly improved spatial and spectral resolution provided by a hyperspectral imaging sensor, hyperspectral imagery expands the capability of multispectral imagery in many ways, such as subpixel target detection, object discrimination, mixed pixel classification, material quantification, etc. It also presents new challenges to image analysts, particularly, how to effectively deal with its enormous data volume so as to achieve their desired goals. One common practice is to compress data prior to image analysis. Two types of data compression can be performed, lossless and lossy in accordance with redundancy removal. More specifically, lossless data compression is generally considered as data compaction which eliminates *unnecessary* redundancy without loss of information. By contrast, lossy data compression removes *unwanted* information or *insignificant* information which results in entropy reduction. Which compression should be used depends heavily upon various applications. For example, in medical imaging, lossless compression is preferred to lossy compression in order to avoid potential lawsuits against doctors. However, in this case, only small compression ratios can be achieved, generally less than 3:1. On the other hand, video processing such as HDTV (High Definition TV) can benefit from lossy compression. For remotely sensed imagery, both types of compression can be beneficial and have been studied and investigated extensively in the past [1-8]. Since we are interested in exploitation-based applications, data analysis is generally determined by features of objects in the image data rather than the image itself. As a result, lossless compression may not offer significant advantages over lossy compression in the sense of feature extraction. So, in this chapter the main interest will be focused on lossy hyperspectral image compression.

The success of a lossy compression technique is generally measured by whether or not its effectiveness meets a preset desired goal which in turn determines which criterion should be used for compression. As an example, Principal Components Analysis (PCA) is a compression technique that represents data in a few principal components determined by data variances [9-10]. Its underlying assumption is based on the fact that the data are well-represented and structured in terms of variance, where most of data points are clustered and can be packed in a low dimensional space. Unfortunately, it was recently shown in [11-13] that Signal-to-Noise Ratio (SNR) was a better measure than data variance to measure image quality in multispectral imagery. Similarly, the Mean Squared Error (MSE) has been also widely used as a criterion for optimality in communications and signal processing such as quantization. However, it is also known that it may not be appropriate to be used as a measure of image interpretation. This is particularly true for hyperspectral imagery which can uncover many unknown signal sources, some of which may be very important in data analysis such as anomalies, small targets which generally contribute very little to SNR or MSE. In the PCA these targets may only be retained in minor components instead of principal components. So, preserving only the first few principal components may lose these targets. In SNR or MSE, such targets may very likely be suppressed by lossy compression if no extra care is taken since missing these targets may only cause inappreciable loss of signal energy or small error.

By realizing the importance of hyperspectral data compression, many efforts have been devoted to design and development of compression algorithms for hyperspectral imagery. Two major approaches have been studied. One is a direct extension of 2D image compression to 3D image compression where many 2D image compression algorithms that have proven to be efficient and effective in 2D images are extended to 3D algorithms. Another is spectral/spatial compression which deals with spectral and spatial compression separately. While the former considers a hyperspectral image as an image cube as a whole, the latter performs spectral/spatial compression on a hyperspectral image with 1D compression on spectral information and 2D compression on spatial information. Despite a hyperspectral image can be considered as an image cube, a direct application of 3-D image compression to such a 1-D spectral/2-D spatial image cube may not be applicable in some cases as shown by examples. This is largely due to the fact that the spectral correlation of a hyperspectral image cube provides more crucial information than the spatial information in many exploitation-based applications. Therefore, an effective hyperspectral image compression technique must be able to explore and retain critical spectral information while the images are compressed spatially. This paper investigates these two approaches and provides evidence that 3D compression does not necessarily perform better than spectral/spatial compression in hyperspectral image compression from an exploitation point of view. In particular, using MSE or SNR as a compression criterion may result in significant loss of spectral information in data analysis. Additionally, in many cases, separating spectral and spatial compression may achieve better results in terms of preserving spectral information that is crucial in hyperspectral data exploitation. In order to demonstrate that it is indeed the case, this chapter studies various scenarios via a synthetic image simulated by a real HYperspectral Digital Image Collection Experiment (HYDICE) image to show that a simple spectral/spatial compression technique may perform as well as or even better than 3D lossy compression. Finally, we further develop several PCA-based spectral/spatial hyperspectral image compression techniques for hyperspectral image compression which are easy to implement, but yet achieve at least same results than a 3D lossy compression technique that is extended from its 2D compression counterpart. Experiments show that the proposed spectral/spatial hyperspectral image compression generally performs better than standard 3D hyperspectral image compression.

The remainder of this chapter is organized as follows. Section 2 reviews two well-known 2D image compression techniques, wavelet-based JPEG 2000 and set partitioning in hierarchical tree (SPIHT), and their extensions to 3D compression. Section 3 develops two principal components analysis (PCA)-based spectral/spatial compression techniques for hyperspectral image compression, referred to as Inverse PCA (IPCA)/spatial compression and PCA/spatial compression. Section 4 demonstrates that 3D lossy compression does not necessarily perform better than the PCA-based spectral/spatial compression techniques in terms of mixed pixel classification via experiments. Section 5 conducts real image experiments for comparative analysis. Finally, Section 6 concludes with some remarks.

2.   3D COMPRESSION TECHNIQUES

3D compression techniques are generally extended from their 2-D counterparts. Two techniques of particular interest that will be used in our investigation are the JPEG2000 Multicomponent which is an extension of the wavelet-based 2D-JPEG2000 and the 3D-SPIHT [14] which is extended by 2D-SPIHT developed by Said and Pearlman [15].

The JPEG2000 is a new still image compression standard that has replaced the commonly used DCT-based JPEG. It is a wavelet-based compression technique that adds/improves features such as coding of regions of interest, progressive coding, scalability etc. The entire coding can be divided into three stages: discrete wavelets transform (DWT), quantization and block coding. The 5/3 integer wavelet transform is used for reversible transformation and 9/7 floating point transform is used for irreversible transformation. After the 2D DWT, all wavelet coefficients are subjected to uniform scalar quantization employing a fixed dead-zone about the origin. One quantization step size is allowed for each subband. The quantized sub-bands are split further into partitions. A partition is formed by collections of blocks from different sub-bands. Each subband contributes one block to the partition. Partitions are split further into code-blocks. Block coding is then performed independently on each of the code-blocks. The used block coding is based on the principles of Embedded Block Coding with Optimized Truncation (EBCOT) [16-17]. For the case of hyperspectral imagery the Part II of JPEG2000 [18-19] is implemented to allow multi-component image compression which involves grouping of arbitrary subsets of components into component collections and applying point transforms along the spectral direction like wavelet transform.

Recently, an approach developed by Said and Pearlman [15], Set Partitioning in Hierarchical Trees (SPIHT) has become very popular. Two main features are introduced in the SPIHT algorithm. First, it utilizes a partial ordering of coefficients by magnitude and transmits the most significant bits first. Second, the ordering data are not explicitly transmitted. The decoder running the same algorithm can trace the ordering information from the transmitted information. Xiong et al [14] later extended the 2D-SPIHT to 3D-SPIHT for video compression in a relatively straightforward manner. There is no constraint imposed on the SPIHT algorithm regarding the dimensionality of the data. If all pixels are lined up in decreasing order of magnitude, 3D-SPIHT performs exactly the same as does 2D-SPIHT. In the case of 3D subband structure, one can use a wavelet packet transform to allow a different number of decompositions between the spatial and spectral dimensions.

In summary, a flowchart to describe an application of 3D compression to a hyperspectral image can be depicted in block diagram 1.

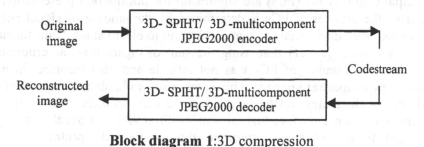

Block diagram 1:3D compression

3. SPECTRAL/SPATIAL HYPERSPECTRAL IMAGE COMPRESSION

Despite the fact that a hyperspectral image can be viewed as a 3D image cube, there are some major unique features that distinguish a hyperspectral image from commonly used 3D images such as videos. Unlike pure voxels considered in traditional 3D images, a hyperspectral image pixel vector is characterized by spectral properties such as subpixels and mixed pixels which are generally not encountered in pure voxels. Additionally, many material substances of interest that are present in hyperspectral imagery can be only explored by their spectral properties, not spatial properties such as combat vehicles embedded in single pixels and decoys in surveillance applications. Most importantly, many objects that are considered to be relatively small but yet provide significant information generally cannot be identified by prior knowledge, but can only be uncovered and revealed by their spectral properties such as chemical plumes or biological agents.

Therefore, whether or not a hyperspectral image compression technique is effective may not be necessarily determined by its spatial compression, but rather its spectral compression. Accordingly, performing spectral and spatial compression separately may be more desirable than compressing spectral and spatial information simultaneously. In this section, we develop several methods which implement the PCA to perform spectral compression in conjunction with 3D or 2D compression techniques to perform spatial compression.

3.1.   Determination of Number of PCs to be Preserved

One of primary obstacles to implement PCA is to determine how many Principal Components (PCs) are significant for information preservation. In the past, the number of PCs is determined by the amount of signal energy calculated from data variances that correspond to eigenvalues. Unfortunately, it was shown in [20-21] that using the sum of eigenvalues as criterion to determine the number of PCs was not reliable and also incorrect in most cases in hyperspectral imagery. This is because subtle objects that contribute little eigenvalues may not be retained in the PCs. In order to mitigate this dilemma, the concept of Virtual Dimensionality (VD) was developed in [20-21] and further used to determine the number of spectrally distinct signatures. If we assume that each spectrally distinct signature is accommodated by a single PC, then the total number of PCs required to accommodate all the spectrally distinct signatures will be determined by the VD. One such method is the one developed by Harsanyi, Farrand and Chang in [22] (HFC) method.

The HFC method first calculates the sample correlation matrix, $\mathbf{R}$, and sample covariance matrix, $\mathbf{K}$, then finds the difference between their corresponding eigenvalues where L is the number of spectral channels. Let $\hat{\lambda}_1 \geq \hat{\lambda}_2 \geq \cdots \geq \hat{\lambda}_L$ and $\lambda_1 \geq \lambda_2 \geq \cdots \geq \lambda_L$ be two sets of eigenvalues generated by $\mathbf{R}$ and $\mathbf{K}$, called correlation eigenvalues and covariance eigenvalues, respectively. By assuming that signal sources are nonrandom unknown positive constants and noise is white with zero mean, we can expect that

$$\hat{\lambda}_l > \lambda_l \text{ for } l = 1, \cdots, \text{VD}, \tag{1}$$

and

$$\hat{\lambda}_l = \lambda_l \text{ for } l = \text{VD} + 1, \cdots, L. \tag{2}$$

Using Eqs. (1-2), the eigenvalues in the l-th spectral channel can be related by

$$\hat{\lambda}_l > \lambda_l > \sigma_{n_l}^2 \text{ for } l = 1, \cdots, \text{VD}, \tag{3}$$

and

$$\hat{\lambda}_l = \lambda_l = \sigma_{n_l}^2 \text{ for } l = \text{VD} + 1, \cdots, L. \tag{4}$$

where $\sigma_{n_l}^2$ is the noise variance in the l-th spectral channel.

In order to determine the VD, Harsanyi et al. [22] formulated the VD determination problem as a binary hypothesis problem as follows.

$$H_0 : z_l = \hat{\lambda}_l - \lambda_l = 0$$

$versus$ for $l = 1, \cdots, L$ (5)

$$H_1 : z_l = \hat{\lambda}_l - \lambda_l > 0$$

where the null hypothesis H_0 and the alternative hypothesis H_1 represent the case that the correlation-eigenvalue is equal to its corresponding covariance eigenvalue and the case that the correlation-eigenvalue is greater than its corresponding covariance eigenvalue, respectively. In other words, when H_1 is true (i.e., H_0 fails), it implies that there is an endmember contributing to the correlation-eigenvalue in addition to noise, since the noise energy represented by the eigenvalue of **R** in that particular component is the same as the one represented by the eigenvalue of **K** in its corresponding component.

Despite the fact that the $\hat{\lambda}_l$ and λ_l in Eqs. (1)-(4) are unknown constants, according to [23], we can model each pair of eigenvalues, $\hat{\lambda}_l$ and λ_l, under hypotheses H_0 and H_1 as random variables by the asymptotic conditional probability densities given by

$$p_0(z_l) = p(z_l \mid H_0) \cong N(0; \sigma_{z_l}^2) \text{ for } l = 1, \cdots, L \tag{6}$$

and

$$p_1(z_l) = p(z_l \mid H_1) \cong N(\mu_l; \sigma_{z_l}^2) \text{ for } l = 1, \cdots, L \tag{7}$$

respectively, where μ_l is an unknown constant and the variance $\sigma_{z_l}^2$ is given by

$$\sigma_{z_l}^2 = var\left[\hat{\lambda}_l - \lambda_l\right] = var\left[\hat{\lambda}_l\right] + var\left[\lambda_l\right] - 2\,cov\left(\hat{\lambda}_l, \lambda_l\right) \text{ for } l = 1,\cdots,L. \quad (8)$$

It is shown in [23] that when the total number of samples, N is sufficiently large, $var[\hat{\lambda}_l] \cong \dfrac{2\hat{\lambda}_l^2}{N}$ and $var[\lambda_l] \cong \dfrac{2\lambda_l^2}{N}$. Therefore, the noise variance $\sigma_{z_l}^2$ in Eq. (7) can be estimated and approximated using Eq. (8).

Now, we use Schwarz's inequality to bound $cov\left(\hat{\lambda}_l, \lambda_l\right)$ in Eq. (8) as follows

$$cov\left(\hat{\lambda}_l, \lambda_l\right) \le \sqrt{var\,[\hat{\lambda}_l] + var\,[\lambda_l]} \cong \frac{2}{N}\left(\hat{\lambda}_l \lambda_l\right) \qquad (9)$$

If we further assume that the estimators $\hat{\lambda}_l$ and λ_l are consistent in mean square, the variances of $\hat{\lambda}_l$ and λ_l are asymptotically zero. In other words, $var[\hat{\lambda}_l] \cong \dfrac{2\hat{\lambda}_l^2}{N}$ and $var[\lambda_l] \cong \dfrac{2\lambda_l^2}{N}$ converge to zero as $N \to \infty$. This further implies that $cov\left(\hat{\lambda}_l, \lambda_l\right) \to 0$ as well as

$$\sigma_{z_l}^2 = var[\hat{\lambda}] + var[\lambda] \approx \frac{2\hat{\lambda}_l^2}{N} + \frac{2\lambda_l^2}{N} \to 0 \text{ for } l = 1,\cdots,L \text{ as } N \to \infty. \quad (10)$$

From Eqs. (6), (7) and (10), we define the false alarm probability and detection power (i.e., detection probability) as follows:

$$P_F = \int_{\tau_l}^{\infty} p_0(z)dz \qquad (11)$$

$$P_D = \int_{\tau_l}^{\infty} p_1(z)dz. \qquad (12)$$

A Neyman-Pearson detector for $\hat{\lambda}_l - \lambda_l$, denoted by $\delta_{NP}\left(\hat{\lambda}_l - \lambda_l\right)$ for the binary composite hypothesis testing problem specified by Eq. (5) can be obtained by maximizing the detection power P_D in Eq. (12), while the false alarm probability P_F in Eq. (11) is fixed at a specific given value, which determines the threshold value τ_l in Eqs. (11)-(12). So a case of $\hat{\lambda}_l - \lambda_l > \tau_l$ indicating that $\delta_{NP}\left(\hat{\lambda}_l - \lambda_l\right)$ fails the test, in which case there is signal energy assumed to contribute to the eigenvalue, $\hat{\lambda}_l$, in the l-th data dimension. It should be noted that the test for Eq. (5) must be performed for each of L spectral dimensions. Therefore, for each pair of $\hat{\lambda}_l - \lambda_l$, the threshold τ is different and should be l-dependent, that is τ_l.

3.2.   PCA-Spectral/Spatial Compression

Using the PCA to de-correlate spectral information between bands has been a common practice in data compression [24]. However, it has been a long standing problem with how to determine the number of principal components (PCs) for information preservation. This section proposes a new idea to resolve this issue. It uses the concept of the VD to determine the number of PCs required for compression. Since the PCs resulting from the PCA are spectrally de-correlated, we can compress these VD-determined PCs in three different ways described in the following subsections.

3.2.1.   Inverse PCA (IPCA)/3D Compression

One straightforward approach is to use PCA in conjunction with a 3D compression technique. More specifically, the PCA is first used to de-correlate a hyperspectral image for spectral compression. Then the VD determines how many PCs must be retained for compression. Then a 3D lossy compression technique is applied to an image cube formed by VD-determined PC images for further spatial compression. Finally, an inverse PCA is implemented to reconstruct a 3D image with the same number of spectral bands as the original image. This approach is referred to as Inverse PCA (IPCA)/3D compression. A flow chart of the IPCA/3D compression is depicted in Block diagram 2.

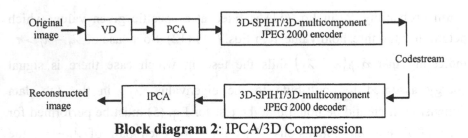

Block diagram 2: IPCA/3D Compression

The details of its implementation can be summarized as follows.

IPCA/3D Compression Algorithm

1. Determine the VD of an L-band hyperspectral image, p.
2. Form the first p PCA-generated PC images as a 3D image cube, referred to as 3D p-PC image cube.
3. Use a 3D compression technique to the 3D p-PC image cube.
4. Apply IPCA to the 3D image obtained in step 3 to reconstruct a 3D L-band image cube.
5. Exploit the resulting compressed 3D L-band image cube for various applications.

Depending upon which 3D compression is used, two IPCA/3D compression algorithms can be implemented, IPCA/3D-SPIHT and IPCA/3D-multicomponent JPEG2000. However, since 3D SPIHT requires dimensions to be multiples of 2^{n+1} with n being the number of levels in wavelet decomposition, the IPCA/3D SPIHT may not be applicable when the number of spectral bands does not meet this constraint.

3.2.2.   Inverse PCA (IPCA)/2D Compression

In addition to PCA/3D compression as described above, a second approach is to implement the PCA for spectral de-correlation in conjunction with 2D spatial compression [25-26]. More precisely, instead of applying 3D compression directly to a PCs-formed image cube as is done in IPCA/3D compression, the proposed PCA/2D compression applies a 2D compression technique to each of the VD-determined PCs for spatial compression. Then an inverse PCA is applied to an image cube formed by the VD-determined 2D compressed images to reconstruct a 3D image with the same number of spectral bands as the original image. Such an approach is referred to as Inverse PCA (IPCA)/2D compression. A flowchart of the IPCA/2D compression is delineated in block diagram 3.

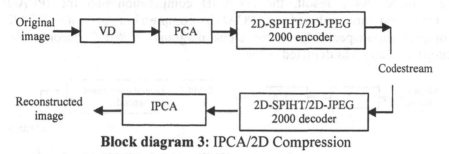

Block diagram 3: IPCA/2D Compression

The detailed implementation of the IPCA/2D compression is described as follows.

IPCA/2D Compression Algorithm

1. Determine the VD of an L-band multispectral/hyperspectral image.

2. Use a 2D image compression technique to each of the first p PC images obtained in step 1.

3. Form a 3D image cube by the p compressed PC image.

4. Apply IPCA to the 3D image obtained in step 3 to reconstruct a 3D L-band image cube.

5. Exploit the resulting compressed 3D L-band image cube for various applications.

In analogy with the IPCA/3D compression, two IPCA/2D compression algorithms can be also implemented, referred to as IPCA/2D-SPIHT and IPCA/2D-JPEG2000.

3.2.3. PCA/2D Compression

The IPCA/3D compression and IPCA/2D compression described previously require an inverse PCA to reconstruct a 3D image from the compressed PC images so that the resulting 3D image has the same number of spectral bands as the original image does. In fact, it may not be necessary to do so in many

applications. As an alternative, we can simply de-compress the compressed
PC images for image analysis. In this case, the last step of processing IPCA,
i.e., step 4 in the IPCA/3D compression and the IPCA/2D compression can
be skipped. As a result, the IPCA/3D compression and the IPCA/2D
compression are reduced to PCA/3D compression and the PCA/2D
compression respectively where block diagrams 2 and 3 become block
diagrams 4 and 5 as depicted below.

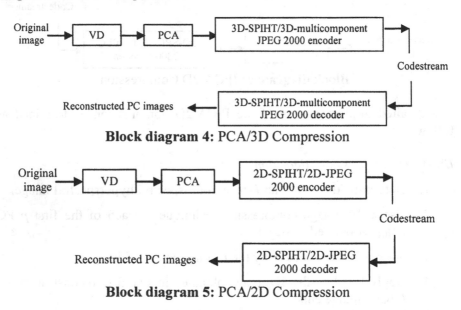

Block diagram 4: PCA/3D Compression

Block diagram 5: PCA/2D Compression

In analogy with IPCA/3D compression and IPCA/2D compression, two
PCA/3D compression and two PCA/2D compression algorithms can be also
implemented, referred to as PCA/3D-SPIHT, PCA/3D-multicomponent
JPEG2000, PCA/2D-SPHIT and PCA/2D-JPEG2000 respectively.

4.   COMPARATIVE ANALYSIS VIA SYNTHETIC IMAGES

In this section, computer simulations via a synthetic image are presented to
demonstrate that a direct application of 3-D data compression to a
hyperspectral image without extra care may result in significant loss of
information. Furthermore, it may not perform as well as compression of
spectral and spatial separately. Additionally, the same example will also

show that the commonly used variance-based measure, i.e., sum of eigenvalues to determine the number of PCs required to be preserved for spectral compression is generally not an adequate criterion. Instead, the proposed VD is more appropriate and effective.

The experiments were based on a synthetic image that was simulated from a HYperspectral Digital Image Collection Experiment (HYDICE) image scene in [21]. It is an image scene shown in Fig. 1(a), which has a size of 64×64 pixel vectors with 15 panels in the scene and the ground truth map in Fig. 1(b).

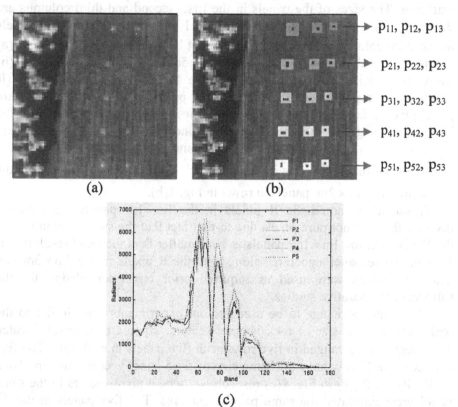

(a)   (b)

(c)

Figure 1: (a) A HYDICE panel scene which contains 15 panels; (b) Ground truth map of spatial locations of the 15 panels; (c) five panel signatures $\{P_i\}_{i=1}^{5}$

It was acquired by 210 spectral bands with a spectral coverage from 0.4μm to 2.5 μm. Low signal/high noise bands: bands 1-3 and bands 202-

210; and water vapor absorption bands: bands 101-112 and bands 137-153 were removed. So, a total of 169 bands were used. The spatial resolution is 1.56m and the spectral resolution is 10nm. Within the scene in Fig. 1(a) there is a large grass field background, and a forest on the left edge. Each element in this matrix is a square panel and denoted by p_{ij} with rows indexed by i and columns indexed by j. For each row $i = 1,2,\cdots,5$, there are three panels p_{i1}, p_{i2}, p_{i3}, painted by the same material but with three different sizes. For each column $j = 1,2,3$, the 5 panels p_{1j}, p_{2j}, p_{3j}, p_{4j}, p_{5j} have the same size but with five different materials. Nevertheless, they were still considered as different materials. The sizes of the panels in the first, second and third columns are $3m \times 3m$, $2m \times 2m$ and $1m \times 1m$ respectively. Since the size of the panels in the third column is $1m \times 1m$, they cannot be seen visually from Fig. 1(a) due to the fact that its size is less than the 1.56m spatial resolution. Fig. 1(b) shows the precise spatial locations of these 15 panels where red pixels (R pixels) are the panel center pixels and the pixels in yellow (Y pixels) are panel pixels mixed with the background. The 1.56m-spatial resolution of the image scene suggests that most of the 15 panels are one pixel in size except that p_{21}, p_{31}, p_{41}, p_{51} which are two-pixel panels. Fig. 1(c) plots the 5 panel spectral signatures $\{P_i\}_{i=1}^5$ with P_i obtained by averaging R pixels in the $3m \times 3m$ and $2m \times 2m$ panels in row i in Fig. 1(b).

It should be noted the R pixels in the $1m \times 1m$ panels are included because they are not pure pixels due to that fact that the spatial resolution of the R pixels in the $1m \times 1m$ panels is 1 m smaller than the pixel resolution is 1.56 m. These panel signatures along with the R pixels in the $3m \times 3m$ and $2m \times 2m$ panels were used as required prior target knowledge for the following comparative studies.

The synthetic image to be used for our experiments was similar to the real scene and has size of 64×64 pixel vectors. There are 10 panels located at its center and arranged in five rows with five panels in each row. The five panels in the 1st row have the same size of 5×5 pixel vectors and simulated by P_1, P_2, P_3, P_4, P_5 in Fig. 1(c) respectively where pixel vectors in the same panel were simulated the same panel signatures. The five panels in the 2nd row are all single-pixel panels, denoted by p_{21}, p_{22}, p_{23}, p_{24}, and p_{25} with abundance fractions 100%, 80%, 60%, 40% and 20% by P_1, P_2, P_3, P_4, P_5 respectively. In other words, the panels in the j-th column were all simulated by the j-th panel signature P_j. The background in the synthetic image was simulated by a grass field signature **b** in the image scene in Fig. 1 with an added Gaussian noise to achieve signal-to-noise ratio (SNR) 30:1 as defined in [29]. Fig. 2(a-b) shows the 10 simulated panels and the background image. Fig. 2(c) is a synthetic image obtained by implanting the 10 simulated panels in Fig. 2(a) in the background image in Fig. 2(b) where their corresponding background pixels were removed to accommodate the implanted panel pixels. It should be noted that the noise background in Fig. 2(c) has been visually suppressed because of high intensity gray level values of panel pixels.

(a)   (b)   (c)

Figure 2: A 10-panel synthetic image

Here two major compression techniques 3D-SPIHT and 3D-multicomponent JPEG2000 will be implemented and compared to our proposed PCA based techniques. For the 1D wavelet transform used in 3D-multicomponent JPEG2000 the QccPack [27] was implemented. It should be noted that the 3D-SPIHT algorithm requires all dimensions to be multiples of 2^{n+1}, where n is the number of decomposition levels. Since the HYDICE image has169 bands (after removal of water absorption and noisy bands), it does not meet this requirement. Therefore, the last 9 bands of the HYDICE image were removed to accommodate its implementation. For 3D-SPIHT, 4-level spectral and 5-level spatial wavelet packet decomposition was performed. In particular, the wavelet packet decomposition instead of the dyadic decomposition was used because it could be better tailored to the data and the wavelet packet decomposition is considered to be more suitable for hyperspectral images.

The JPEG2000 is an embedded wavelet-based coder that supports the coding of hyperspectral images in Part II of the standard. This standard specifies arbitrary decorrelating transforms in the spectral direction, thus permitting implementation of wavelet transforms. The currently available implementations of the JPEG2000 standard do not yet implement the Part II of the standard. The JPEG2000 implementation used for our experiments was the Kakadu version 4.2.1 [28]. Since the Kakadu software implements only

Part I of the JPEG2000 standard, a 1-D spectral transform was performed separately on the data before feeding the data to the Kakadu coder. Additionally, the popular Cohen-Daubechies-Feauveau 9-7 wavelet with symmetric extension was used. In our experiments a 4-level wavelet decomposition in the spectral domain was first performed and followed by the Kakadu coder.

The compression obtained from the PCA-based methods was through two stages, PCA/VD spectral compression and the 2D-JPEG2000 or 3D-multicomponent JPEG2000 spatial compression. Since the compression obtained by the PCA is fixed for a given hyperspectral image, a variable bit-rate lossy compression technique was applied in the 2D-JPEG2000/3D-multicomponent JPEG2000 stage.

Four scenarios were conducted to evaluate performance of 3D compression and our proposed PCA/spatial compression algorithms.

Scenario 1: Classification based on 3D de-compressed image cubes

In this scenario, two 3D compression techniques, 3D-SPIHT and 3D multicomponent JPEG2000 described in block diagram 1 were directly applied to the 10-panel image in Fig. 2(c) with compression ratio (CR) equal to 20, 40, 80 and 160. Then such compressed images were de-compressed to reconstruct the original image and used for unsupervised mixed pixel classification where the unsupervised fully constrained least squares (UFCLS) mixed pixel classification method in [21,29,30] was used to classify the 10 panels where among the first six signatures generated by the UFCLS, five of them were found to correspond to the five panel signatures. It should be noted that the UFCLS must be unsupervised since there is no prior knowledge available during compression. It was performed on de-compressed images. Figs. 3 and 4 show their respective classification results with compression ratio (CR) equal to 20, 40, 80 and 160.

As shown in Figs. 3-4, both 3D-SPIHT and 3D-multicomponent JPEG2000 performed very similarly for all cases where there was no visible difference among CR = 20, 40 and 80. Nevertheless, the two 3D algorithms performed very poorly for the case of CR = 160.

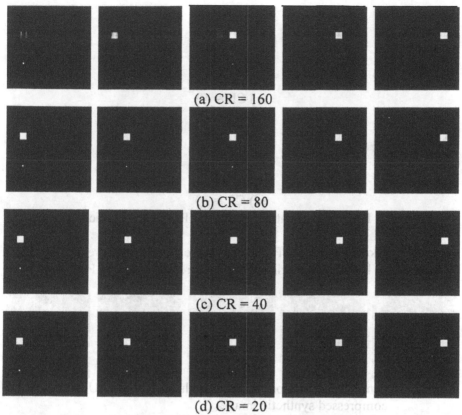

Figure 3: Panel classification results of 3D-SPIHT

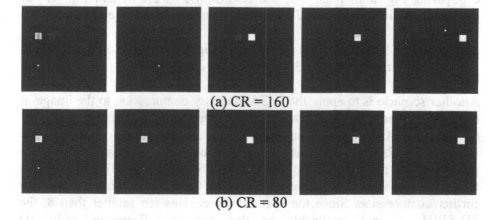

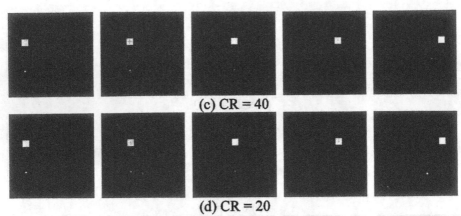

(c) CR = 40

(d) CR = 20

Figure 4: Panel classification results of JPEG2000 Multicomponent

In order to make comparison, Fig. 5 shows the classification results produced by the UFCLS based on the original un-compressed image in Fig. 2(c).

Figure 5: Panel classification results produced by the UFCLS on un-compressed synthetic image

Comparing Fig. 5 to Figs. 3-4, the results in Fig. 3(b-d) and Fig. 4(b-d) produced by CR = 80, 40 and 20 was very comparable to those in Fig. 5.

Scenario 2: Classification based on 3D images reconstructed by applying inverse PCA to 3D compressed image cubes

Another scenario is to apply the IPCA/3D lossy compression to the image in Fig. 2(c) where the VD was used to determine how many principal components (PCs) needed to be preserved for compression. For the synthetic image in Fig. 2(c), the VD was estimated to be 6. So, the first six PCs were preserved and formed as a 3D image cube so that a lossy 3D compression technique was applied to compress the 6-PC formed image cube to achieve further compression. Since the spectral dimensions are smaller than 8, the 3D-SPIHT is not applicable to this scenario. Therefore, only 3D multicomponent JPEG2000 was applied to this scenario. Finally, an inverse PCA (IPCA) was then applied to reconstruct an image with 160 bands that is a compressed image of the original image in Fig. 2(c). This approach is called IPCA/3D-multicomponent JPEG2000 in Block diagram 2. The resulting IPCA/3D-multicomponent JPEG2000 compressed image was then used for the UFCLS classification. Since only five out of the first six PCs contained panels, only the five classification images are provided to show the classification of panels. Fig. 6 shows the classification results produced by IPCA/3D-multicomponent JPEG2000 were very close to those in Fig. 5 produced by the UFCLS operating on the original un-compressed image. Additionally, the IPCA/3D-multicomponent JPEG2000 also significantly improved those results obtained for CR = 160 in Figs. 3-4.

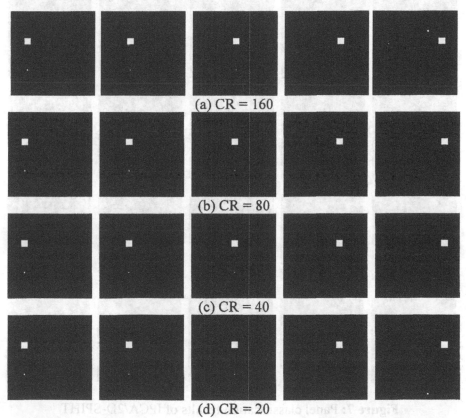

(a) CR = 160

(b) CR = 80

(c) CR = 40

(d) CR = 20

Figure 6: Panel classification results of IPCA/3D multicomponent-JPEG2000

Scenario 3: Classification based 3D images reconstructed by applying IPCA to 3D image cubes formed by a set of 2D compressed PC images

A third scenario was to apply the IPCA/2D-SPIHT and IPCA/2D-JPEG2000 lossy compression techniques to compress individually and separately the six PCs. Then an inverse PCA was applied to an image cube that was formed by the six resulting 2D compressed PCs to reconstruct a de-compressed image with 160 bands for unsupervised mixed pixel classification where the UFCLS method used for Figs. 3-6 was also applied here. The classification results of the IPCA/2D-SPIHT and the IPCA/2D-JPEG2000 for panels are shown in Figs. 7 and 8 respectively.

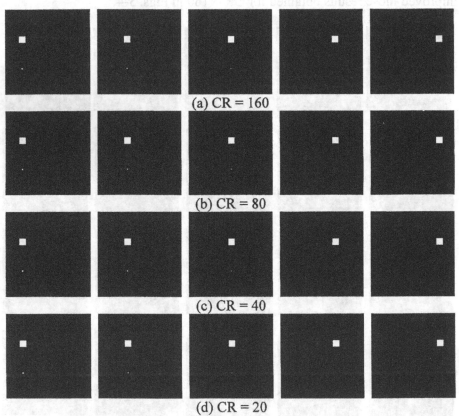

(a) CR = 160

(b) CR = 80

(c) CR = 40

(d) CR = 20

Figure 7: Panel classification results of IPCA/2D-SPIHT

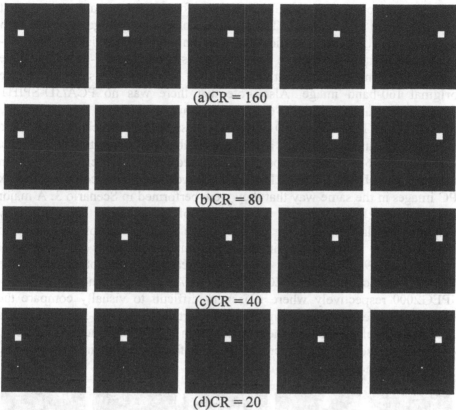

(a)CR = 160

(b)CR = 80

(c)CR = 40

(d)CR = 20

Figure 8: Panel classification results of IPCA/2D-JPEG2000

Similar to Fig. 6, both the IPCA/2D-SPIHT and the IPCA/2D-JPEG2000
performed well on the case of CR = 160 and their results were very
comparable to the IPCA/3D multicomponent-JPEG2000 in Fig. 6.
Comparing Figs. 7-8 to Figs. 3-4, the most visible and significant
improvement was the case of CR = 160 where the PCA/2D-JPEG2000 and
PCA/3D lossy compression performed as well as the cases of CR = 20, 40
and 80.

<u>Scenario 4</u>: Classification based image cubes formed by a set of 2D
compressed PC images

This scenario is different from all three scenarios described above. It
applied the PCA/3D-multicomponent JPEG2000 in Block diagram 4 where

the 3D-multicomponent JPEG2000 was performed in the same way that it was performed in Scenario 1. The resulting compressed image cube was then used for the UFCLS classification. The only difference is that the 3D-multicomponent JPEG2000 in Scenario 4 was applied to a 6-PC image cube while the 3D multicomponent JPEG2000 in Scenario 1 was applied to the original 160-band image. Also note that there was no PCA/3D-SPIHT because the number of PCs, 6 is smaller than 8. Another was to use the PCA/2D-SPIHT and PCA/2D-JPEG2000 described in Block diagram 5 to compress PC images to form a 3D image cube with 6 spectral dimensions. The resulting 6-PC image cube was then used for UFCLS classification. In this case, the 2D-SPHIT and 2D-JPEG2000 were applied to compress the six PC images in the same way that they were performed in Scenario 3. A major advantage of this approach is reduction of computation complexity by skipping the last process in all the above three scenarios, which is to reconstruct an image cube with the same number of bands as the original image. Figs. 9-11 show the panel classification results obtained by the PCA/3D-multicomponent JPEG2000, the PCA/2D-SPHIT and the PCA/2D-JPEG2000 respectively where it is very difficult to visually compare the classification results among Figs. 9-11. In particular, the five subpixel panels are single-pixel panels and their detection in abundance fractions could be easily suppressed by the detected abundance fractions of their corresponding 5×5 large panels.

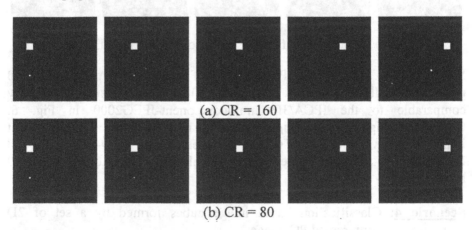

(a) CR = 160

(b) CR = 80

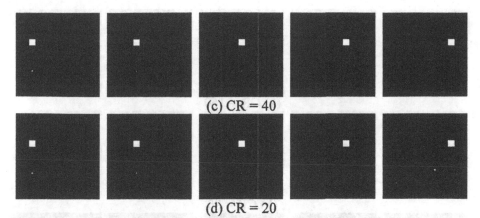

(c) CR = 40

(d) CR = 20

Figure 9: Panel classification results of PCA/ 3D multicomponent-JPEG2000

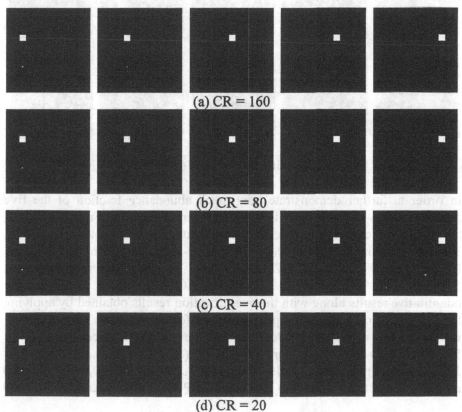

(a) CR = 160

(b) CR = 80

(c) CR = 40

(d) CR = 20

Figure 10: Panel classification results of PCA/2D-SPIHT

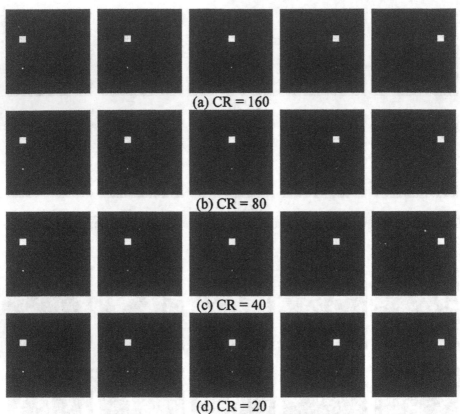

(a) CR = 160

(b) CR = 80

(c) CR = 40

(d) CR = 20

Figure 11: Panel classification results of PCA/2D-JPEG2000

In order to further demonstrate how much abundance fraction of the five subpixel panels in the 2nd row in the scene were detected in Figs. 3-11 by all the eight lossy compression techniques evaluated in this chapter, 3D-SPIHT, 3D-multicomponent JPEG2000, IPCA/3D-multicomponent JPEG2000, IPCA/2D-SPHIT, IPCA/2D-JPEG2000, PCA/3D-multicomponent JPEG2000, PCA/2D-SPIHT and PCA/2D-JPEG2000, Table 1 tabulates their quantitative results along with the quantification results obtained by applying the UFCLS to original uncompressed image for comparison. For simplicity, we have used numerals 1-8 to represent the results produced by (1) 3D-SPIHT, (2) 3D-multicomponent JPEG2000, (3) IPCA/3D multicomponent-JPEG2000, (4) IPCA/2D-SPHIT, (5) IPCA/2D-JPEG2000, (6) PCA/3D multicomponent JPEG2000, (7) PCA/2D-SPIHT, (8) PCA/2D-JPEG2000 and numeral 9 to represent the results produced by the UFCLS on the original uncompressed image respectively.

CR	Subpixel panels	1	2	3	4	5	6	7	8	9
160	p_{21}	100	100	98	98	97	98	98	97	100
	p_{22}	0	38	71	74	75	71	74	75	75
	p_{23}	49	0	59	58	59	59	59	59	59
	p_{24}	22	29	39	39	40	39	39	40	39
	p_{25}	17	0	10	15	13	11	15	12	14
80	p_{21}	92	100	100	100	100	100	100	100	100
	p_{22}	73	62	75	75	74	74	75	74	75
	p_{23}	56	52	59	59	59	59	59	59	59
	p_{24}	34	30	39	39	39	34	34	34	39
	p_{25}	19	18	15	15	15	15	15	15	14
40	p_{21}	94	100	100	100	100	100	100	100	100
	p_{22}	73	69	74	74	74	74	74	74	75
	p_{23}	57	56	59	59	59	59	59	59	59
	p_{24}	37	38	39	39	39	34	34	34	39
	p_{25}	18	19	15	15	15	15	15	15	14
20	p_{21}	98	100	100	100	100	100	100	100	100
	p_{22}	74	70	74	74	74	74	74	74	75
	p_{23}	59	58	59	59	59	59	59	59	59
	p_{24}	38	36	39	39	39	34	34	34	39
	p_{25}	19	19	15	15	15	15	15	15	14

Table 1: Abundance fractions of the 5 subpixel panels in the 2nd row

Finally, we tabulate SNR and MSE for each CR in Table 2 for Figs. 3-4 and Figs. 6-11.

CR	160		80		40		20	
	SNR	MSE	SNR	MSE	SNR	MSE	SNR	MSE
1	42.50	37017	43.16	31809	43.76	27734	44.91	21255
2	41.66	44967	42.96	33288	43.53	29235	44.61	22787
3	43.38	30240	43.46	29675	43.47	29659	43.47	29659
4	43.38	30215	43.46	29675	43.47	29654	43.47	29656
5	43.33	30619	43.46	29706	43.46	29690	43.46	29690
6	33.67	587	47.36	25	54.14	5	54.14	5
7	33.85	563	47.61	24	56.67	3	56.94	3
8	31.49	969	43.91	56	45.22	41	45.22	41

Table 2: SNR and MSE for Figs. 3-4 and Figs. 6-11

In Table 2, the same numerals used in Table 1 were used for consistency where (1) 3D-SPIHT, (2) 3D multicomponent-JPEG2000, (3) IPCA/3D multicomponent-JPEG2000, (4) IPCA/2D-SPHIT, (5) IPCA/2D-JPEG2000, (6) PCA/3D multicomponent JPEG2000, (7) PCA/2D-SPIHT and (8) PCA/2D-JPEG2000. Apparently, (6) the PCA/3D-multicomponent JPEG2000, (7) PCA/2D-SPIHT and (8) PCA/2D-JPEG2000 produced much smaller MSEs. Additionally, since (6) the PCA/3D-multicomponent JPEG2000, (7) PCA/2D-SPIHT and (8) PCA/2D-JPEG2000 operated on only PC images not on de-compressed images with the original number of bands, their produced SNRs were generally lower than expected.

In the previous experiments, the number of PCs was determined by the VD which was 6. In order to demonstrate the advantage of using the VD, a general and widely used approach to determination of the number of PCs was considered, which calculates the sum of the largest eigenvalues to measure how much percentage of energy is required to be preserved during compression. Table 3 tabulates the energy contributed by the first 33 PCs where the energy was calculated by summing all eigenvalues of the PCs up to the PC being considered and normalizing the sum to 100%.

PC	Eigenvalue	energy	PC	eigenvalue	percent	PC	eigenvalue	energy
1	1267555.526	90.70%	12	260.5764	97.99%	23	243.1267	98.21%
2	91517.509	97.25%	13	259.0156	98.01%	24	241.7741	98.22%
3	5201.5112	97.63%	14	257.0252	98.03%	25	240.2581	98.24%
4	2044.3714	97.77%	15	256.3777	98.05%	26	239.7718	98.26%
5	1147.3887	97.86%	16	255.104	98.06%	27	238.8506	98.28%
6	273.5699	97.88%	17	253.4133	98.08%	28	237.9477	98.29%
7	271.5065	97.89%	18	252.4769	98.10%	29	237.5739	98.31%
8	269.7012	97.91%	19	251.3845	98.12%	30	236.3263	98.33%
9	268.3106	97.93%	20	249.2878	98.14%	31	234.688	98.34%
10	265.0195	97.95%	21	247.9757	98.15%	32	233.8727	98.36%
11	262.3911	97.97%	22	245.5467	98.17%	33	232.3503	98.38%

Table 3: Energy contributed by eigenvalues in the first 33 PCs

According to Table 3, Fig. 12(a-b) also plots the eigenvalue distribution of the first 33 PCs and their energy distribution respectively.

As shown in Table 3 and Fig. 12, there was a sudden and drastic drop between 2 and 3. Therefore, an obvious choice for the number of PCs was 2. Of course, it was not correct because there were at least five distinct panel signatures in the synthetic image scene. This fact implied that using sum of eigenvalues to calculate signature energies as a criterion to determine the number of PCs was not a good measure. Similar observations were also witnessed in [20-21].

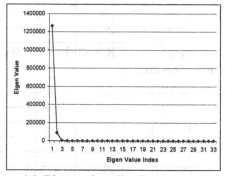
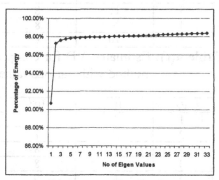

(a) Eigenvalue distribution   (b) energy distribution

Figure 12: Eigenvalue distribution and energy distribution of the first 33 PCs

In order to see whether there was a change in the VD estimate for lossy compressed images, Table 4(a-d) also tabulates the results of the VD estimated with for various false alarm probabilities by the HFC method based on the de-compressed images with CR = 160, 80, 40, and 20 produced by (1)3D-SPIHT, (2)3D-multicomponent-JPEG2000, (3)IPCA/3D multicomponent-JPEG2000, (4)IPCA/2D-SPHIT, (5)IPCA/2D-JPEG2000.

P_F	10^{-1}	10^{-2}	10^{-3}	10^{-4}	10^{-5}
1	26	17	12	12	11
2	25	16	14	13	11
3	10	8	8	8	7
4	10	8	8	7	7
5	10	9	7	7	7

Table 4(a): Estimated VD for compressed image with CR = 160 by the HFC method with various false alarm probabilities

P_F	10^{-1}	10^{-2}	10^{-3}	10^{-4}	10^{-5}
1	13	8	8	7	7
2	21	16	11	8	8
3	9	8	7	7	7
4	10	8	7	7	7
5	10	7	7	7	7

Table 4(b): Estimated VD for compressed image with CR = 80 by the HFC method with various false alarm probabilities

P_F	10^{-1}	10^{-2}	10^{-3}	10^{-4}	10^{-5}
1	8	7	7	7	7
2	11	9	9	9	8
3	11	8	8	7	7
4	9	8	7	7	7
5	10	9	7	7	7

Table 4(c): Estimated VD for compressed image with CR = 40 by the HFC method with various false alarm probabilities

P_F	10^{-1}	10^{-2}	10^{-3}	10^{-4}	10^{-5}
1	7	7	7	7	7
2	7	7	7	7	7
3	11	8	8	7	7
4	11	8	7	7	7
5	11	9	7	7	7

Table 4(d): Estimated VD for compressed image with CR = 20 by the HFC method with various false alarm probabilities

It is clearly shown in Table 4(a-d) that the VD estimates were more consistent when the CR was low. It should be also noted that the PCA/3D compression and PCA/2D compression were not applicable since they did not apply IPCA to recover the PCA-compressed image in the original image space with 160 spectral bands.

5.   REAL HYPERSPECTRAL IMAGE EXPERIMENTS

In this section, the 15-panel HYDICE image scene in Fig. 1 was used for experiments. The VD was estimated by the HFC method is tabulated in Table 5 where the VD was empirically selected to be 9.

P_F	10^{-1}	10^{-2}	10^{-3}	10^{-4}	10^{-5}
HYDICE	14	11	9	9	7

Table 5: VD estimates for the HYDICE image by the HFC method

Fig. 13 shows the panel classification results of the UFCLS based on the original un-compressed image where the UFCLS generated 9 signatures for unsupervised mixed pixel classification. For simplicity of demonstration, only those abundance fraction maps that detected panels are shown in figures.

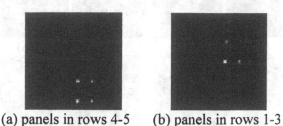

(a) panels in rows 4-5   (b) panels in rows 1-3

Figure 13: Panel classification results produced by the UFCLS using the original un-compressed image

As shown in Fig. 13, the UFCLS could neither separate those panels in rows 1-3 nor the panels in rows 4-5 due to the fact that the panel signatures P_1-P_3 were very similar and so are P_4 and P_5 [21]. In order to see the performance of the UFCLS on images compressed and de-compressed by a compression algorithm, the same experiments done for Fig. 13 were also conducted for the images compressed and de-compressed by the eight algorithms, (1) 3D-SPIHT, (2) 3D-multicomponent-JPEG2000, (3) IPCA/3D-multicomponent JPEG2000, (4) IPCA/2D-SPHIT, (5) IPCA/2D-JPEG2000, (6) PCA/3D-multicomponent JPEG2000, (7) PCA/2D-SPIHT and (8) PCA/2D-JPEG2000. For simplicity of demonstration, Figs. 14-17 only show those abundance fraction maps that detected panels with CR = 160, 80, 40 and 20 respectively. The numerals under figures indicate which algorithm was used to compress and decompress the images.

It is interesting to see that in Fig. 14 with CR = 160 the second algorithm, 3D-multicomponent JPEG2000 could only produced one panel classification map that classified panels in rows 4-5 and missed all panels in rows 1-3. Other than the 3D-multicomponent JPEG2000, all the other 7 algorithms produced very similar results which were close to the two panel classification maps in Fig. 13 that were produced by the UFCLS operating on the un-compressed HYDICE image.

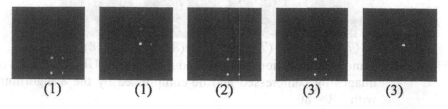

(1)   (1)   (2)   (3)   (3)

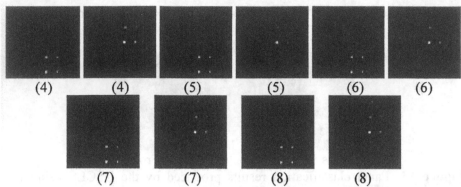

Figure 14: Panel classification results produced by the UFCLS based on
images by compressed and de-compressed by the 8 algorithms
with CR = 160

For images compressed by the eight algorithms with CR = 80 and 40, the
panel classification results in Figs. 15-16 produced by the UFCLS were
nearly the same as the two classification maps in Fig. 13. This implied that
there was no much difference for the UFCLS operating on the un-
compressed image or compressed images as long as CR was lower than 80:1.

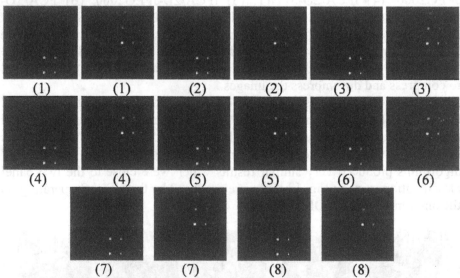

Figure 15: Panel classification results produced by the UFCLS based on
images by compressed and de-compressed by the 8 algorithms
with CR = 80

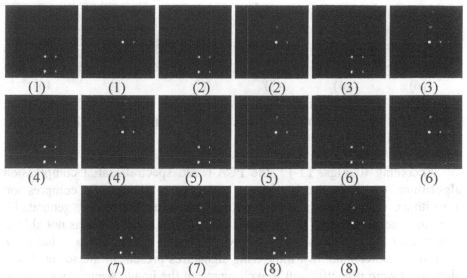

Figure 16: Panel classification results produced by the UFCLS based on
images by compressed and de-compressed by the 8 algorithms
with CR = 40

When the CR = 20, Fig. 17 shows an interesting result produced by the
UFCLS based on the compressed image by the first algorithm, the 3D-SPIHT
where three panel classification maps were generated by the UFCLS
compared to only two maps generated by the UFCLS based on the un-
compressed image. These three classification maps were able to classify the
panels in row 1 from the panels in rows 2-3, a task that could not be
accomplished in Fig. 13. This implied that the UFCLS actually performed
better on the 3D-SPIHT-compressed image than on the un-compressed image.

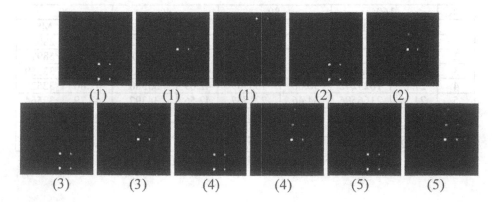

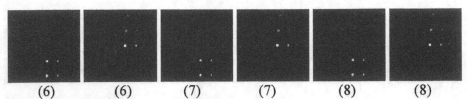

| (6) | (6) | (7) | (7) | (8) | (8) |

Figure 17: Panel classification results produced by the UFCLS based on images by compressed and de-compressed by the 8 algorithms with CR = 20

According to Figs. 13-17, the PCA-based spectral/spatial compression algorithms generally performed at least as well as 3D compression algorithms. One comment is noteworthy. Since the UFCLS only generated 9 signatures according to VD = 9, its mixed pixel classification was not able to separate all the panels in the five rows. This was due to the fact that there were many other unknown interfering signatures present in the scene. The 9 signatures were not sufficient to well represent the image scene. As shown in [21], if we allowed the UFCLS to extract 34 signatures for mixed pixel classification, then the classification images in Figs. 13-17 could have been able to separate all the 15 panels in the five rows in separate images. This was because the additional generated signatures would have been used in the UFCLS for interference annihilation to significantly improve classification results. A detailed study can be found in [31].

To conclude our experiments, we further calculated the SNR and MSE for performance of the eight algorithms with CR = 160, 80, 40 and 20. Table 6 tabulates their respective results which showed that PCA-based spectral/spatial compression always produced smaller MSE than 3D compression.

CR	160		80		40		20	
	SNR	MSE	SNR	MSE	SNR	MSE	SNR	MSE
1	28.85	807374	33.28	290854	38.19	94022	43.45	28023
2	27.08	1214986	30.47	555363	34.92	199507	40.21	58973
3	35.44	177005	41.62	42683	42.79	32613	42.79	32559
4	27.82	1023242	36.66	133739	42.69	33380	42.80	32525
5	24.56	2166596	34.46	221737	42.56	34397	42.79	32564
6	24.91	144479	36.44	10162	56.84	93	61.23	34
7	16.55	990819	26.46	101220	47.16	860	69.94	5
8	13.22	2134410	23.74	189222	43.78	1873	60.38	41

Table 6: SNR and MSE for the HYDICE image

As also shown in Table 6, for most of cases except CR =160, PCA-based spectral/spatial compression performed better than 3D compression in the sense that the former produced higher SNR than did the latter.

Like Table 2, since (6) the PCA/3D-multicomponent JPEG2000, (7) PCA/2D-SPIHT and (8) PCA/2D-JPEG2000 operated on only PC images not on de-compressed images with the original number of bands, their produced SNRs in Table 6 were generally lower than expected.

In order to see whether or not there was a change in the estimation of the VD for de-compressed images, Table 7 tabulates the VD estimated by the HFC method with various false alarm probabilities based on the decompressed images by (1) 3D-SPIHT, (2) 3D-multicomponent JPEG2000, (3) IPCA/3D multicomponent-JPEG2000, (4) IPCA/2D-SPHIT, (5) IPCA/2D-JPEG2000. Similar to Table 4(a-d), Table 7(a-d) also demonstrates that the VD estimates were more consistent when the CR was low.

P_F	10^{-1}	10^{-2}	10^{-3}	10^{-4}	10^{-5}
1	53	42	36	34	30
2	54	41	32	25	22
3	12	12	12	12	12
4	17	15	14	13	13
5	20	18	18	18	18

Table 7(a): Estimated VD for compressed image with CR = 160 by the HFC method with various false alarm probabilities

P_F	10^{-1}	10^{-2}	10^{-3}	10^{-4}	10^{-5}
1	47	31	27	23	22
2	47	34	28	24	20
3	10	10	10	9	9
4	10	9	9	9	8
5	11	9	9	9	8

Table 7(b): Estimated VD for compressed image with CR = 80 by the HFC method with various false alarm probabilities

P_F	10^{-1}	10^{-2}	10^{-3}	10^{-4}	10^{-5}
1	29	26	19	16	14
2	32	20	15	13	13
3	9	9	9	9	8
4	10	9	9	9	8
5	10	9	9	9	8

Table 7(c): Estimated VD for compressed image with CR = 40 by the HFC method with various false alarm probabilities

P_F	10^{-1}	10^{-2}	10^{-3}	10^{-4}	10^{-5}
1	10	10	8	8	7
2	10	9	9	9	8
3	11	9	9	9	8
4	10	9	9	9	8
5	10	9	9	9	8

Table 7(d): Estimated VD for compressed image with CR = 20 by the HFC method with various false alarm probabilities

It is also noted that the PCA/3D compression and PCA/2D compression were not applicable since they did not apply IPCA to recover the PCA-compressed image in the original image space with 160 spectral bands.

Finally, we also calculated the eigenvalue distribution and energy distribution of the first 33 PCs for the HYDICE image in Fig. 1 and the results are tabulated in Table 8 and plotted in Fig. 18.

PC	Eigenvalue	Percent	PC	Eigenvalue	Percent	PC	Eigenvalue	Percent
1	57995933.33	81.98%	12	2828.34	99.95%	23	617.0386	99.98%
2	12121150.07	99.14%	13	1986.268	99.95%	24	552.206	99.98%
3	173987.8	99.53%	14	1580.478	99.96%	25	508.911	99.98%
4	72008.77	99.69%	15	1377.929	99.96%	26	478.4526	99.98%
5	46640.85	99.80%	16	1139.912	99.96%	27	467.6903	99.98%
6	24729.75	99.85%	17	1054.234	99.97%	28	413.1114	99.98%
7	15673.41	99.89%	18	963.4904	99.97%	29	397.1537	99.98%
8	12623.25	99.92%	19	890.6664	99.97%	30	388.2148	99.98%
9	5230.008	99.93%	20	803.1869	99.97%	31	363.9604	99.98%
10	4051.45	99.94%	21	695.9851	99.97%	32	329.4372	99.98%
11	2975.395	99.94%	22	660.3904	99.97%	33	323.8451	99.99%

Table 8: Eigenvalues and energy percentages of the first 33 PCs

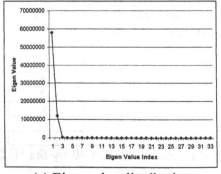

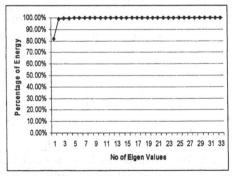

(a) Eigenvalue distribution   (b) energy distribution
Figure 18: Eigenvalue distribution and energy distribution of the first 33 PCs

From Table 8 and Fig. 18, there was a sudden drop between 2 and 3. So, an obvious choice for the number of PCs was 2, which is certainly not accurate. A detailed analysis and study on this issue was conducted by Ramakrishna in [31].

6. CONCLUSIONS

This chapter investigates the applicability of direct application of 3D compression techniques to hyperspectral imagery and develops PCA-based spectral/spatial compression techniques in conjunction with the virtual dimensionality (VD) for hyperspectral image compression where the VD is used to estimate number of principal components required to be preserved. In particular, we conduct computer simulations based on a synthetic image and real image experiments to demonstrate that simple PCA-based spectral/spatial lossy compression techniques can perform at least as well as 3D lossy compression techniques in applications such as mixed pixel classification and quantification. This interesting finding provides evidence that PCA-based spectral/spatial compression can be as competitive as the 3D compression for hyperspectral image compression. Additionally, this chapter also further demonstrates that the number of PCs required to be preserved by lossy compression is crucial and the proposed VD provides a much better estimate than the commonly used criterion determined by the sum of largest eigenvalues. For more details we refer to [31].

ACKNOWLEDGEMENT

The authors would like to acknowledge the use of the QccPack developed by Dr. J.E. Fowler with Mississippi State University for the experiments conducted in this work. A. Plaza would like to thank for support received from the Spanish Ministry of Education and Science (PR2003-0360 Fellowship).

REFERENCES
[1] V.D. Vaughn and T.S. Wilkinson, "System considerations for multspectral image compression designs," *IEEE Signal Processing Magazine*, pp. 19-31, January 1995.

[2] J.A. Saghri, A.G. Tescher and J.T. Reagan, "Practical transform coding of multispectral imagery," *IEEE Signal Processing Magazine*, pp. 32-43, January 1995.

[3] J.A. Saghri and A.G. Tescher, "Near-lossless handwidth compression for raiometric data," *Optical Engineering*, vol. 30, no. 7, pp. 934-939, July 1991.

[4] J.A. Saghri, A.G. Tescher and A. Boujarwah, "Spectral-signature-preserving compression of multispectral data," *Optical Engineering*, vol. 38, no. 12, pp. 2081-2088, December 1999.

[5] G.P. Abousleman, E. Gifford and B.R. Hunt, "Enhancement and compression techniques for hyperspectral data," *Optical Engineering*, vol. 33, no. 8, pp. 2562-2571, August 1994.

[6] G.P. Abousleman, M.W. Marcellin and B.R. Hunt, "Hyperspectral image compression using entropy-constrained predictive trellis coded quantization," *IEEE Trans. on Image Processing*, vol.6, no. 4, pp. 566-573, April 1994.

[7] G.P. Abousleman, M.W. Marcellin and B.R. Hunt, "Compression of hyperspectral imagery using the 3-D DCT and hybrid DPCM/DCT," *IEEE Trans. on Geoscience and Remote Sensing*, vol.33, no. 1, pp. 26-34, April 1994.

[8] S.-E. Qian, A.B. Hollinger, D. Williams and D. Manak, "Fast three-dimensional data compression of hyperspectral imagery using vector quantization with spectral-feature-based binary coding," *Optical Engineering*, vol. 35, no. 7, pp. 3242-3249, November 1996.

[9] R.O. Duda and R.E. Hart, *Pattern Classification and Scene Analysis*, John Wiley & Sons, New York, 1973.

[10] J.A. Richards, *Remote Sensing Digital Image Analysis*, 2nd ed. Springer-Verlag. 1993.

[11] A.A. Green, M. Berman, P. Switzer and M.D. Craig, "A transformation for ordering multispectral data in terms of image quality with implications for noise removal," *IEEE Trans. on Geoscience and Remote Sensing*, vol. 26, no. 1, pp. 65-74, January 1988.

[12] J.B. Lee, A.S. Woodyatt and M. Berman, "Enhancement of high spectral resolution remote sensing data by a noise-adjusted principal components transform," *IEEE Trans. on Geoscience and Remote Sensing*, vol. 28, no. 3, pp. 295-304, May 1990.

[13] C.-I Chang, Q. Du, T.S. Sun and M.L.G. Althouse, "A joint band prioritization and band decorrelation approach to band selection for

hyperspectral image classification," *IEEE Trans. on Geoscience and Remote Sensing*, vol. 37, no. 6, pp. 2631-2641, November 1999.

[14] B.-J. Kim, Z. Xiong, and W.A.Pearlman, "Low bit-rate scalable video coding with 3-D set partitioning in hierarchical trees (3-D SPIHT)," *IEEE Transactions on Circuits and Systems for Video Technology*, vol. 10, no. 8, pp.1374-1387, December 2000.

[15] A. Said and W.A. Pearlman, "A new, fast, and efficient image codec based on set partitioning in hierarchical trees," *IEEE Trans. on Circuits and systems for Video Technology*, vol. 6, no. 3, pp. 243-350, June 1996.

[16] D. Taubman, "High performance scalable image compression with EBCOT", IEEE Trans. Image Proc., 9, 1158-1170

[17] D. S. Taubman and M. W. Marcellin, JPEG2000: Image Compression Fundamentals, Standard and Practice. Boston, MA: Kluwer, 2002.

[18] ISO, Information Technology—JPEG 2000 Image Coding System - Part 1: Core Coding System, ISO, Geneva, Switzerland, 2000.

[19] ISO, Information Technology—JPEG 2000 Image Coding System - Part 2: Extensions; Final Committee Draft, ISO, Geneva, Switzerland, Dec. 2000.

[20] C.-I Chang and Q. Du, "Estimation of number of spectrally distinct signal sources in hyperspectral imagery," *IEEE Trans. on Geoscience and Remote Sensing*, vol. 42, no. 3, pp. 608-619, March 2004.

[21] C.-I Chang, *Hyperspectral Imaging: Techniques for Spectral Detection and Classification*, Kluwer Academic/Plenum Publishers, New York, N.Y., 2003

[22] J.C. Harsanyi, W. Farrand and C.-I Chang, "Detection of subpixel spectral signatures in hyperspectral image sequences," *Annual Meeting, Proceedings of American Society of Photogrammetry & Remote Sensing*, Reno, pp. 236-247, 1994.

[23] T.W. Anderson, *Multivariate Analysis*, Academic Press, 2nd ed., 1984.

[24] C.-I Chang, Q. Du, T.S. Sun and M.L.G. Althouse, "A joint band prioritization and band decorrelation approach to band selection for hyperspectral image classification," *IEEE Trans. on Geoscience and Remote Sensing*, vol. 37, no. 6, pp. 2631-2641, November 1999.

[25] S. S. Shen and B. S. Beard, "Effects of hyperspectral compression on non-literal exploitation," *Proceedings of SPIE,* vol. 3438, pp. 191-199, 1998.

[26] Arto Kaarna, Pekka J. Toivanen, Pekka Keranen, "Compression of multispectral AVIRIS images," *Proceedings of SPIE*, vol. 4725, pp.588-599, 2002

[27] J.E. Fowler, "QccPack: An open-source software library for quantization, compression, and coding," in *Applications of Digital Image Processing XXIII*, vol. 4115, pp.249-301, San Diego, CA, 2000.

[28] Kakadu software: A Comprehensive Framework for JPEG2000, www.Kakadusoftware.com, Implementation of JPEG2000.

[29] J.C. Harsanyi and C.-I Chang, "Hyperspectral image classification and dimensionality reduction: an orthogonal subspace projection," *IEEE Trans on Geoscience and Remote Sensing*, vol. 32, no. 4, pp. 779-785, July 1994.

[30] D. Heinz and C.-I Chang, "Fully constrained least squares linear mixture analysis for material quantification in hyperspectral imagery," *IEEE Trans. on Geoscience and Remote Sensing*, vol. 39, no. 3, pp. 529-545, March 2001.

[31] Bharath Ramakrishna, *Principal Components Analysis (PCA)-Based Spectral/Spatial Hyperspectral Image Compression*, MS. Thesis, Department of Computer Science and Electrical Engineering, University of Maryland, Baltimore County, Baltimore, MD, 2004.

Compression of Earth Science Data with JPEG2000

Prajit Kulkarni[1], Ali Bilgin[1], Michael W. Marcellin[1], Joseph C. Dagher[1],
James H. Kasner[2], Thomas J. Flohr[3], Janet C. Rountree[3]

[1]Dept. of Electrical and Computer Engineering, The University of Arizona, Tucson,
AZ 85721

[2]Eastman Kodak Co., 1300 N. 17th Suite 1040, Arlington, VA 22209

[3]Science Applications International Corporation, 101 N. Wilmot Suite 400, Tucson,
AZ 85711

1. Introduction

With the increased use of remote sensing, the need for efficient transmission of such data has gathered greater importance in recent times. Remote sensing images are typically large and are often multispectral or hyperspectral in nature. Hyperspectral imaging sensors generate data at hundreds of wavelengths simultaneously, resulting in very large data sets. Transmission of such earth science data over bandwidth-limited channels requires the employment of compression technology.

JPEG2000 is the latest international standard for image compression [1,2]. It offers many advantages over earlier image compression standards. Perhaps the most important advantage offered by JPEG2000 is that it is designed to act as an image processing system rather than as just an input-output image compression filter. That is, unlike earlier image compression standards, decisions regarding image quality, compression ratio and image resolution need not be made at compression time. With JPEG2000, such decisions can be made after compression. This provides tremendous flexibility and facilitates the adaptation of the standard to specific imaging applications.

The JPEG2000 standard is published in several parts. Part I describes the minimal compliant decoder and the codestream syntax. Part II consists of "value-added" technologies that improve the performance for some applications. Other parts of the standard define extensions such as those defined in Part III (referred to as *Motion JPEG2000*) for enabling the use of the standard with video sequences and the JPEG2000 Interactive Protocol (JPIP) defined in Part IX. Our goal here is to provide a brief overview of the standard and its capabilities as it relates to compression of earth science data. Thus, we will only discuss the relevant sections of the standard. For a comprehensive discussion of the standard, the interested reader is referred to [2,3].

The rest of this chapter is organized as follows: Section 2 provides an overview of the JPEG2000 standard. Although the standard specifies only the decoder and codestream syntax, this section focuses on the description of a representative encoder, since this makes the description more comprehensible. In Section 2, we discuss both Part I and Part II of the standard as they relate to encoding of earth science data. Part II of the standard specifies additional functionalities that are particularly important for compression of earth science data. In Section 3, we present methods that enable scan-based processing of JPEG2000. Since remote sensing data are often captured incrementally by sensors in a push-broom fashion, scan-based processing enables efficient implementation of the standard.

2.   Overview of JPEG2000

Figure 1 shows the block diagram of a JPEG2000 encoder. As seen in the figure, JPEG2000 compression consists of several steps. Each step is described below.

2.1. Tiling

The input image can (optionally) be divided into non-overlapping rectangular regions called tiles. A tile can have arbitrary dimensions without exceeding $2^{32}-1$ pixels in either dimension. A tile may even include the whole image. If tiles are used, each tile is processed separately. This facilitates low-memory processing and also enables spatial random access in the compressed codestream[1].

The main disadvantage of using tiles, however, is that tiles can lead to the appearance of border artifacts. Since each tile is compressed

---

[1] JPEG2000 offers other alternatives for low-memory processing and spatial random access as discussed later.

Prajit Kulkarni, Ali Bilgin, Michael W. Marcellin, Joseph C. Dagher,
James H. Kasner, Thomas J. Flohr, and Janet C. Rountree

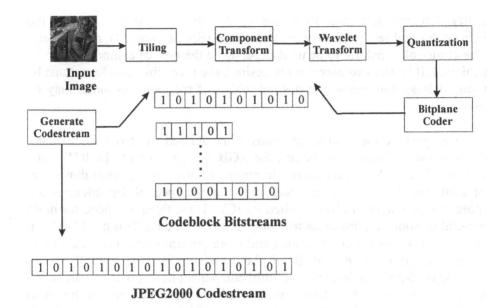

Figure 1: A Simple JPEG2000 Encoder.

independently, visible discontinuities can appear at tile boundaries. These effects are particularly visible at low bit rates.

When the image being compressed has multiple components (RGB, hyperspectral etc.), all samples from a component that lie in the region covered by a tile form a *tile-component*.

2.2 Component Transform

For multi-component images, an optional component transform can be applied to each tile to decorrelate the components of the image. This decorrelation removes spectral redundancy and increases coding efficiency. Part I of the standard allows one of two optional component transforms to be applied to the first three components of the image. These component transforms are named irreversible color transform (ICT) and reversible color transform (RCT). Both transforms are invertible in the mathematical sense, but the RCT maps integer pixel values to integer transform coefficients, and is perfectly invertible using only finite (low) precision arithmetic. In

JPEG2000, the ICT and RCT are used only in conjunction with the irreversible and reversible wavelet transforms (See Section 2.3), respectively. The choice of transform to be used depends on the type of compression to be achieved. If lossless compression is desired, the reversible transform must be used. If lossy compression is desired, either of the two transforms may be used.

The goal of the component transforms defined in Part I is to allow decorrelation of color components for RGB images. In fact, the ICT is the familiar RGB to YC_bC_r transform. In many instances, the spectral dimension of earth science data is larger than three and the spectral dependencies are more complex than can be exploited by ICT. Thus, there is a need for more general component transforms for compressing such data. This need has been recognized by the JPEG committee and more general component transforms have been allowed in Part II of the standard. In fact, Part II allows remarkable flexibility in choice of multi component transforms. In Part II, the multiple component transforms are carried out in stages, as illustrated in Figure 2. Each transform stage outputs a set of intermediate components. It should be noted that the number of output components of each stage is allowed to be different than the number of input components.

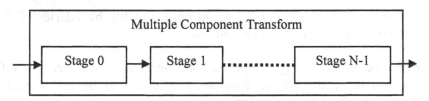

Figure 2: Multiple Component Transform Stages in Part II.

Within each stage, it is possible to gather different input components to form *component collections*. A different transform can then be applied to each component collection. This is illustrated in Figure 3. This flexible structure allows grouping of interrelated components for efficient decorrelation.

There are two types of transforms that can be used for a given component collection: wavelet-based transforms and array-based transforms. The wavelet-based transforms enable the application of a one-dimensional wavelet transform in the component direction. Coupling of the one-dimensional wavelet transform with the two-dimensional wavelet transform described in the next section results in a three-dimensional transform. The wavelet transform used across the component direction is defined as a special case of the spatial wavelet transform. Thus, we delay the discussion of the wavelet transform until the next section.

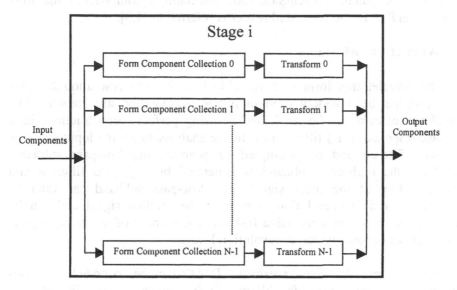

Figure 3: Use of Component Collections within Each Stage.

Array-based transforms in Part II of the JPEG2000 standard are defined as linear combinations of the input components. There are two types of array-based transforms documented in the standard – a decorrelation transform and a dependency transform.

The array-based decorrelation transform is a matrix multiplication operation on the input components. The outputs of the decorrelation transform are linear combinations of the inputs, with a possible DC offset. The most common decorrelation transform recognized by JPEG2000 is the Karhunen-Loeve Transform (KLT). The KLT is applied along the components to achieve spectral decorrelation. This decorrelated data is then passed on to the two-dimensional wavelet transform stage. The array-based dependency transform can be thought of as a sequential prediction of the next input component from those already available. The idea is very similar to that of differential pulse code modulation (DPCM). The prediction error is passed on to the two-dimensional wavelet transform stage for further processing. For both of these transforms, the transform information required for inverse processing is sent to the decoder as side information.

For a more detailed discussion about the multiple component transforms available in Part II, the interested reader is referred to [4,5].

2.3. Wavelet Transform

The wavelet transform is a valuable tool for multiresolution analysis [6,7] that has been widely used in image compression applications. The wavelet transform can be implemented using perfect reconstruction finite impulse response (FIR) filter banks. In the analysis stage, the input signal is low-pass filtered and downsampled to generate the low-pass subband. Similarly, the high-pass subband is generated by high-pass filtering and downsampling of the input signal. The low-pass subband can then be considered as a low-resolution version of the original signal and can be further decomposed in a recursive fashion. The number of recursive steps is referred to as decomposition or resolution levels.

The Discrete Wavelet Transform (DWT) can be extended to multi-dimensions using separable filters. Each dimension is filtered and downsampled separately. Figure 4 shows the basic operation of the two-dimensional DWT. Applying one level of DWT decomposes the image into four *subbands* (indicated as LL_1, HL_1, LH_1 and HH_1 in the figure). In Figure 4, the subband identified as LL_1 (or the *low-low* subband) stands for the set of samples obtained by applying a second low-pass filter (in the horizontal direction) to the output of the low-pass filter from the first 1-D DWT operation (in the vertical direction). The subband identified as HL_1 stands for the set of samples obtained after low-pass filtering in the vertical direction and successive high-pass filtering in the horizontal direction. The other two subbands are labeled accordingly. Because of the manner in which they are produced, the HL subbands contain information about vertical edges, the LH subbands contain information about horizontal edges and the HH subbands describe diagonal edges.

It is possible to further decompose each subband. In Part I of the JPEG2000 standard, the DWT is applied recursively to the LL subband

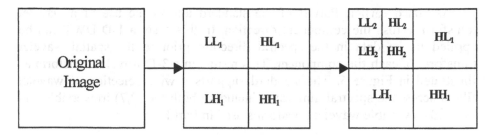

Figure 4: Subbands Produced after 2 Levels of DWT Decomposition.

samples. This is illustrated in Figure 4 where the second level of DWT decomposes the LL_1 subband into the LL_2, HL_2, LH_2 and HH_2 subbands. Part II of the standard allows more general decompositions which allow further decompositions of the HL, LH, and HH subbands as well.

The LL_1 subband in Figure 4 can be considered as a reduced resolution version of the original image. Similarly, the LL_2 subband can be considered as a reduced resolution version of the LL_1 subband. This is the basis of the *resolution scalability* principle employed in JPEG2000. If only the LL_2 subband is received at the decoder, a low-resolution version of the original image is obtained. If in addition to the LL_2 subband, the HL_2, LH_2 and HH_2 subbands are received, the decoder can use these four subbands to reconstruct the LL_1 subband which is a higher resolution version of the image. When the HL_1, LH_1, and HH_1 subbands are also received at the decoder, the image can be reconstructed at full resolution.

In JPEG2000, the wavelet transform is applied separately to each tile component. There are two choices of wavelet filters available in Part I of the standard. The (9,7) wavelet transform, also known as the irreversible wavelet transform, has real valued impulse responses of lengths 9 and 7 for the high-pass and low-pass filters respectively. The irreversible wavelet transform is beneficial when high performance lossy compression is desired. The (5,3) wavelet transform, also known as the reversible wavelet transform, is implemented using integer arithmetic and is reversible, enabling lossless (as well as lossy) compression. In general, the lossy compression performance of the irreversible transform is superior to that of the reversible transform. However, the lossy performance of the reversible transform is still quite good. Part II of the standard enables more general selection of wavelet filters.

As stated earlier, Part II of the standard allows the use of a wavelet transform across the component direction. In this case, a 1-D DWT can be applied to the data in the spectral direction prior to the spatial wavelet transform of each tile-component. This results in a 3-D wavelet transform as illustrated in Figure 5. The standard supports a wide selection of wavelet filters across the spectral dimension including both the (9,7) irreversible and the (5,3) reversible wavelet transforms used in Part I.

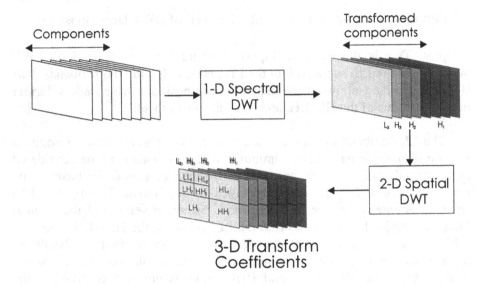

Figure 5: 3-D Wavelet Transform Available in Part II.

2.3.1 Data Partitioning in the Wavelet Domain

Data in the wavelet domain are partitioned into geometric structures to enable many of the desirable features of JPEG2000. The smallest geometric structure used in JPEG2000 is called a *codeblock*. Codeblocks are obtained by dividing each wavelet transform subband into rectangular regions. The dimensions of a codeblock do not change across resolutions and are constant for all subbands. However, it is required that each dimension of a codeblock is a power of two. As we will discuss later, the data in each codeblock are entropy coded independently of others. Thus, each codeblock can be decoded independently of others. Many of the desirable features of JPEG2000 are due to this independent encoding of codeblocks.

Another geometric structure used in JPEG2000 is called a *precinct*. Precincts are formed by partitioning each resolution of a tile-component into rectangular regions. Precincts are similar to tiles in the sense that they contain data corresponding to a particular spatial region in the image. Unlike tiles however, precincts are formed in the wavelet domain, and, thus, there is no "break" in the transform at precinct boundaries (as there is at tile boundaries). As a result, precincts do not cause block (tile) artifacts. The precinct size can be chosen independently by resolution, but each dimension

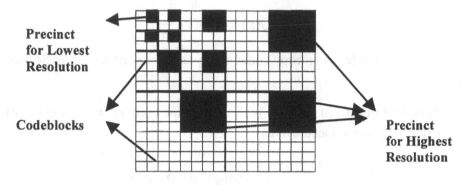

Figure 6: Relationship between Precincts and Codeblocks.

of the precinct size must be a power of two. Due to the fact that both the precincts and codeblock dimensions are required to be powers of two, the codeblock and precinct partitions "line up." This is illustrated in Figure 6. If the codeblock size in a subband exceeds the precinct size in that subband, codeblocks are "truncated" to fit into precincts.

Compressed data from each precinct are grouped together to form *packets*. Packets are the fundamental building blocks of a JPEG2000 codestream. Only the compressed data from a precinct need to be buffered before a packet can be formed. This facilitates low-memory compression. Precincts also form another mechanism for spatial random access.

2.4. Quantization

Quantization is the process of reducing the precision of wavelet coefficients before entropy coding is performed. Thus, quantization is the source of the loss in lossy compression in JPEG2000. Once the wavelet coefficients become available, they are quantized using either a deadzone uniform scalar quantizer that is available in Part I or the Trellis Coded Quantization (TCQ) methods described in Part II.

The deadzone uniform scalar quantizer in Part I helps produce embedded bitstreams enabling the quality progression feature of JPEG2000. For a given wavelet coefficient z and quantizer step size Δ, the quantized value of z is termed the quantized index, and is a signed integer q, given by

$$q = Q(z) = \text{sign}(z)\left\lfloor \frac{|z|}{\Delta} \right\rfloor.$$

This quantized index is entropy coded using techniques described in Section 2.5.

When the quantized index q is received at the decoder, an estimate $\hat{z}$ of the value of z is produced using

$$\hat{z} = Q^{-1}(q) = \begin{cases} 0 & q = 0 \\ \text{sign}(q)(|q| + \delta)\Delta & q \neq 0 \end{cases},$$

where δ is a user selectable parameter. This particular type of quantization, known as *deadzone uniform scalar quantization*, enables the quality progression feature of JPEG2000. For such quantizers, the quantization index of every quantization with step size Δ has embedded within it, the index of every quantization with step size $2^p \Delta$, $p = 0,1,2,\ldots$.

Assume that z has been quantized with step size Δ to get q. If the decoder is missing the p Least Significant Bits (LSBs) of q (i.e., they are not decoded yet), it is still possible to produce an estimate $\hat{z}$ of the value of z. This is done using the dequantizer with step size $2^p \Delta$ to get

$$\hat{z} = Q^{-1}(q^{(p)}) = \begin{cases} 0 & q^{(p)} = 0 \\ \text{sign}(q^{(p)})(|q^{(p)}| + \delta)2^p \Delta & q^{(p)} \neq 0 \end{cases}$$

where $q^{(p)} = \lfloor q/2^p \rfloor$ denotes the quantization index q with p LSBs missing. The estimate $\hat{z}$ achieved in this fashion is identical to what it would have resulted if the step size had been $2^p \Delta$ in the first place.

When irreversible wavelets are utilized, JPEG2000 allows a different step size to be chosen for each subband. However, when reversible wavelets are utilized, a step size of $\Delta = 1$ is used. Since the wavelet coefficients are integers in this case, this choice of the step size results in no quantization at all unless one or more LSBs of the wavelet coefficients are omitted. This enables lossless compression. A detailed review of deadzone scalar quantization employed in JPEG2000 can be found in [8].

As mentioned earlier, Part II of the standard allows the use of TCQ. TCQ has been shown to be an efficient method for encoding memoryless sources [9]. It is based on the ideas of an expanded signal set and set partitioning from coded modulation, and has excellent mean squared error (MSE) performance with modest complexity.

For encoding a memoryless source using TCQ a scalar codebook is partitioned into four disjoint subsets D_0, D_1, D_2, D_3. This is illustrated in Figure 7. These subsets are used to label the branches of a trellis. Figure 8 shows an eight-state trellis with branch labeling.

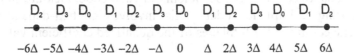

Figure 7: Subset Partitioning of TCQ.

For a given sequence of data, the Viterbi algorithm is used to choose the trellis path (sequence of codewords) that minimizes the mean-squared error between the input data and the output codewords. In any given trellis state, the output codeword is selected from one of two *supersets* $S_0 = D_0 \cup D_2$ or $S_1 = D_1 \cup D_3$. For example, if the current state is 0 in Figure 8, only the codewords that are in S_0 can be chosen. Specifying a codeword in a superset is enough to determine from which subset the codeword was selected, which, in turn determines the next trellis state. Thus, the output from TCQ consists of the superset indices taking the form of a sequence of signed integers. For a detailed overview of TCQ, the interested reader is referred to [9,10,11,12].

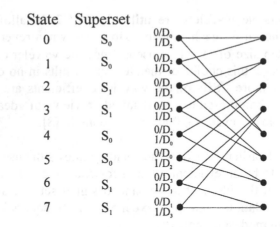

Figure 8: Eight State Trellis and Branch Labeling.

2.5. Bit-plane Coding

The quantized wavelet coefficients in each codeblock are independently coded using a bitplane coder. This involves context-dependent, binary, arithmetic coding of the bitplanes of the quantized coefficient values.

The independent compression of wavelet domain codeblocks is one of the most important features of JPEG2000. Each codeblock is encoded independently and by the same token, it can be decoded independently as well. As mentioned earlier, entropy coding of each codeblock is carried out as the context-dependent binary arithmetic coding of bitplanes obtained after the quantization of subband samples. The arithmetic coder employed is the MQ-coder as specified in the JBIG-2 standard.

Figure 9 illustrates the concept of bitplanes as applied to JPEG2000 compression. For a given codeblock, the quantization indices can be regarded as an array of signed integers. Let $q[\mathbf{n}]$ denote the quantization index at location $\mathbf{n} = [n_1, n_2]$ of a given codeblock. We can represent $q[\mathbf{n}]$ using a sign and a magnitude array. Let $\chi[\mathbf{n}] \overset{\Delta}{=} \text{sign}(q[\mathbf{n}])$ denote the sign array and $v[\mathbf{n}] \overset{\Delta}{=} |q[\mathbf{n}]|$ denote the magnitude array. The sign array $\chi[\mathbf{n}]$ can be considered as a binary array where the value of the array at each point indicates whether the quantization index is positive or negative. Similar to the sign array, the magnitude array can also be divided into a sequence of binary arrays with one bit from each quantization index. Each such array is referred to as a *bitplane*. For a given subband, let K_{max} denote the number of magnitude bitplanes. Then, the K_{max} magnitude bitplanes can be ordered from the one corresponding to the Most Significant Bit (MSB) to the one corresponding to the LSB as in Figure 9.

Each bitplane is encoded using three passes, referred to as *coding passes*, starting from the most significant bitplane that has at least a single 1 bit. For each bitplane, samples are visited according to the scan pattern shown in

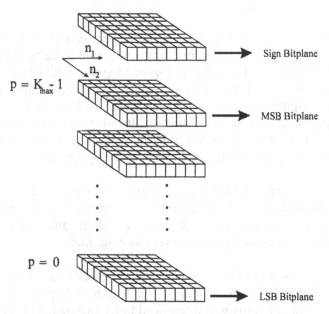

Figure 9: Bitplane Representation of a Codeblock.

Figure 10. The encoder visits each sample along this pattern during all three coding passes and determines which of the three passes the current bit will be coded in. This decision is made based on the significance of the current and neighboring samples.

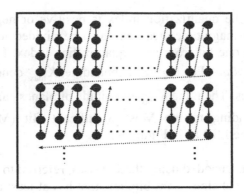

Figure 10: Scan Pattern of a Codeblock for Bitplane Coding.

The first pass in a new bitplane is called a *significance propagation pass*. A sample at a particular location in a bitplane is said to be "significant" with respect to that bitplane if the first non-zero magnitude bit of the sample has been encoded in one of the previous (more significant) bitplanes. For the significance propagation pass, a bit is encoded at a location if its location is not yet significant and at least one of its eight-connected neighbors is significant. If the bit that is coded is 1, the sign bit of the current sample is coded and the sample is deemed to have become significant.

In the second pass, called the *magnitude refinement pass*, all bits from locations that have become significant in a previous bitplane are coded. As the name implies, the magnitude of each significant sample is refined since one more bit is now available to represent its magnitude.

The third pass is the *clean-up pass*, which encodes all bits not coded in the first two passes. In certain cases, run length coding is employed here since a long string of zeros will often need to be encoded. This pass is also a significance pass since all samples that were not predicted to become significant during the significance propagation pass, but have actually become significant, are coded in this pass. The run-coding mode is used when all four locations in a column of the scan are insignificant and have insignificant neighbors. In run coding mode, a single bit is coded to indicate whether the entire column is identically zero or not. If the entire column is not identically zero, the length of the zero run (0 to 3) is coded. The run mode is then terminated immediately following the 1 bit that ended the zero run.

Different context models are employed depending on the type of coding pass and the subband type. Nine different contexts are used for significance coding (i.e., significance propagation and clean-up passes). As mentioned earlier, the sign bit of a sample is coded immediately after its first non-zero bit is coded (sample becomes significant). JPEG2000 also uses five contexts for sign coding and three contexts to code a magnitude refinement pass. The interested reader is referred to [2] for details about these contexts and how they are computed.

In JPEG2000, rate-distortion optimization is performed after the coding passes are formed. Thus, this optimization is referred to as *Post Compression Rate Distortion (PCRD)* optimization. Every coding pass, if included in the final codestream, reduces the distortion of the reconstructed image by a certain amount. At the same time, it consumes a certain number of bytes in the codestream. Thus, each coding pass has a *distortion-length slope* (or *distortion-rate slope*) associated with it. The distortion-length slope of a coding pass is defined as

$$S = \frac{\Delta D}{\Delta L},$$

where ΔD is the reduction in distortion obtained by including the coding pass, and ΔL is the number of bytes used to code the coding pass. The encoder computes the distortion-length slope of every coding pass. It is easy to see that the higher the slope value of a coding pass, the more "important" it is, since its inclusion leads to a greater reduction in distortion per bit than that obtained by including a coding pass with a smaller slope value. Thus, conceptually the PCRD optimization algorithm is performed by sorting the coding passes in descending order of distortion-rate slope, and including coding passes starting from the top of the list, until the byte budget is exhausted.

Once the encoder decides on which coding passes will be included in the codestream, the final task is to form the codestream. The fundamental unit used in the construction of the codestream is a packet. A packet contains compressed data from a varying number of coding passes from each codeblock in one precinct of one tile-component. Any number of passes (including zero) can be included in a packet from each codeblock. The packets are then organized into *layers*. A layer is defined as the collection of all the packets, one from every precinct, of every resolution of every tile-component of a tile. Therefore, a packet provides one quality increment for one spatial region (precinct), at one resolution of one tile-component. Since a layer consists of one packet from every precinct of each resolution of each tile-component, it provides one quality increment for an entire tile. The introduction of layers into a codestream facilitates progression by quality (SNR scalability) decoding. The layered codestream can be used to enable many applications. For example, a layered codestream can be used for transmission of data over a time-varying communication channel. Depending on the available bandwidth, varying numbers of layers can be transmitted and decoded. Similarly, a layered codestream can be used in a multicast environment where different channels have different bandwidths. In this case, a single multi-layered codestream would meet the bandwidth requirements of all the channels, with each layer meeting the target rate of a different channel.

Besides compressed coding passes, the JPEG2000 codestream includes information necessary for decompression of the codestream. The codestream starts with the main header. The main header contains global information that is necessary for decompression. This includes the sizes of the geometric structures (image, tile, precinct, codeblock), as well as coding parameters. The main header is followed by a sequence of tile-streams. Each tile-stream starts with a tile header that contains information related to that particular tile. Tile headers can be used to overwrite some of the coding parameters specified in the main header. The body of a tile-stream contains the packets belonging to the tile. A two-byte marker called the EOC (End of codestream) terminates the codestream.

3. Scan-Based Processing in JPEG2000

Remote sensing data are often captured incrementally by sensors in a push-broom fashion. One way to handle such acquisition is to buffer the entire image and then perform the compression operation on the data. This, however, is highly undesirable. Since remote sensing data are often quite large, buffering of the entire image requires large amount of on-board storage. Secondly, buffering introduces a delay into the processing system. Thus, it is very advantageous to design a compression system that can handle the incremental acquisition of the data.

In this section, we present methods that enable the use of JPEG2000 with incrementally acquired data. As soon as data from the push-broom sensors become available, they are incrementally transformed to the wavelet domain, quantized, and entropy-coded. One of the main challenges in such a system is the design of the rate allocation methods to ensure that the image quality is fairly constant from "top" to "bottom" in an image. Thus, the goal of this section is to introduce modified PCRD optimization methods that work in a "sliding-window" fashion.

3.1. Scan Elements

The first step in designing an encoder that works on incremental data is to determine the "unit" of incremental image data. As mentioned earlier, tiles can be used as incremental inputs to the encoder since each tile is processed independently. But employing tiles can cause border artifacts, especially at low rates. To avoid this, precincts can be used in place of tiles. Precincts also enable low-memory operation but do not cause artifacts because they are defined in the wavelet domain.

Raw image data are acquired until a (user-defined) precinct can be formed in the highest resolution wavelet subband. An incremental wavelet transform [13] is performed on the available data, and subsets of wavelet coefficients are collected into *scan elements*. Each scan element consists of data from a certain number of rows from each resolution subband nominally corresponding to a "stripe" of the image in the spatial domain. The contribution to the scan element from a resolution level comes from one precinct at that resolution level.

The spatial region of the image nominally covered by each scan element depends on the number of rows of wavelet coefficients taken from each subband. Figure 11 shows a number of scan elements for one component with two levels of wavelet transform. Here, regions in different subbands shaded with the same color correspond to the same region of the image in the spatial domain. The formation of scan elements using small amounts of data from different subbands is possible because of the use of an incremental wavelet transform. This concept of scan elements can be extended to any number of resolution levels, with contributions from subbands getting smaller (by powers of two) as we go down to lower resolutions.

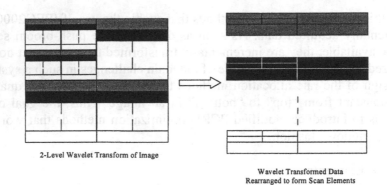

2-Level Wavelet Transform of Image

Wavelet Transformed Data
Rearranged to form Scan Elements

Figure 11: Relationship between Scan Elements and Resolution Subbands
for a Single Component.

3.2. Fixed Rate Encoding

The simplest rate control method is to encode each scan element at a
fixed rate. As soon as a scan element becomes available, it is wavelet
transformed, quantized, and passed through the bitplane coder. The PCRD
optimization is performed on the resulting coding passes, and the coding
passes that will be included in the codestream are selected.

Unfortunately, this simple method has some disadvantages. In many
instances, the image content varies considerably between different areas in
the image. Thus, when each scan element is encoded at a fixed rate, the
reconstructed image varies in quality from top to bottom. Since maintaining a
fairly constant quality across the image is quite important, the available bit
budget needs to be distributed among the scan elements to allow such
constant quality. This can be achieved by employing a "leaky bucket" rate
control method.

3.3. Leaky-Bucket Rate Control Methods

Figure 12 shows the block diagram of the proposed scheme for low-
memory incremental processing of large multi-component images. The
buffer control mechanism performs rate control on the incremental
compressed data at the output of the bitplane coder and fills up the rate
control buffer. Thus, the buffer operates in the compressed domain. Each

Prajit Kulkarni, Ali Bilgin, Michael W. Marcellin, Joseph C. Dagher,
James H. Kasner, Thomas J. Flohr, and Janet C. Rountree

365

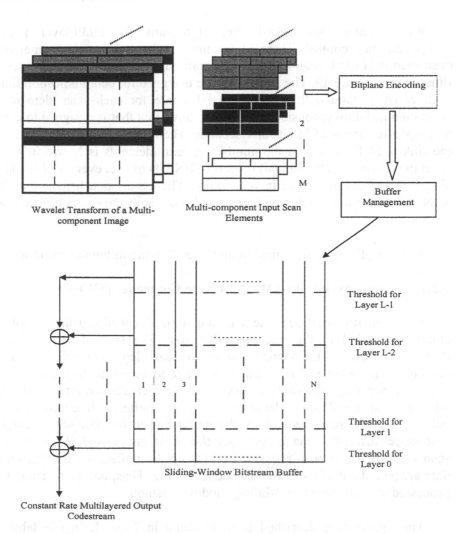

Figure 12: Block Diagram of Leaky-Bucket Rate Control Algorithm for Incremental Processing of Large Multi-Component Images with Multiple Quality Layers.

scan element is encoded at a different rate (with the total rate fixed) depending on how "difficult" it is to compress. Data are taken out of the buffer at a constant rate. To facilitate the desirable features of JPEG2000 enabled by layers, the proposed method also introduces layers into the output JPEG2000 codestream.

We consider two leaky-bucket algorithms for multi-layer multi-component rate control. These algorithms are extensions of the methods described in [14,15]. A simple block diagram of these rate control schemes is illustrated in Figure 12. The algorithms are designed for communication links with constant bandwidth. The nominal bit rate for each scan element is computed as follows; consider a fixed-rate downlink that is designed to carry a compressed image of M bits in T seconds. The fixed rate of transmission on the link is M/T bits/sec. If the number of scan elements is N, we (remove from the rate control buffer and) transmit M/N bits of data every T/N seconds since we process the image incrementally. The assumption here is that the M/N bits transmitted each time correspond (nominally) to one complete scan element.

The algorithms are described in more detail in the following sections.

3.3.1.   Multi-Layer Sliding Window Rate Controller (SWRC)

In this method, each scan element is quantized, encoded using a bitplane coder and added to the rate control buffer. The size of the buffer is determined based on the nominal number of scan elements needed to fill up the buffer. Each time a new scan element is to be added to the buffer, a distortion-rate slope threshold is calculated for each desired layer such that all the compressed scan elements fit in the buffer. All coding passes belonging to the scan elements in the buffer and to the new scan element, with slopes lower than the *lowest layer threshold*, are deleted. When enough scan elements have been processed to fill up the buffer, the multi-layered data are pulled out of the buffer at a constant rate. Thus, one scan element is processed at every time in a "sliding window" fashion.

The algorithm is described in more detail in Table 1. In this table, a quantity called *excess bytes* is used. The data being removed from the buffer corresponds (nominally) to one compressed scan element. However, since each scan element is encoded at a different rate, the data may correspond to only a portion of a scan element. In that case, only a part of the scan element is removed from the buffer to meet rate requirements. The remaining portion of the scan element is "frozen" in the buffer and no more rate-distortion optimization decisions are made on this data when the next scan element is added to the buffer. This portion of data is flushed along with the next scan element to be flushed out. The portion of the buffer occupied by this frozen chunk of data is not available when the next PCRD-optimization is performed on the buffer. The excess bytes value for each layer stores the size of the contribution from that layer to this frozen portion of the buffer and is used when layer thresholds are calculated. Similarly, the data rate may be such that the scan element to be released may not be large enough to utilize the entire available bandwidth. In this case, portions of an additional scan element (or elements, depending on their sizes) have to be released in order to maintain a constant rate output. Again, if a portion of a scan element is left behind after the previous flush operation, the part of the buffer occupied by this data is frozen and the excess bytes value for each of the layers is updated to reflect this change. This process is repeated until all scan elements are processed.

Let the total number of scan elements for an image be N, each corresponding to P pixels. Let the number of layers to be generated be L, with corresponding rates (in bpp) R_0, R_1,..., $R_{(L-1)}$. Let the nominal number of scan elements in the buffer be S. Let the target sizes corresponding to the buffered portion of the L layers be B_0, B_1,..., $B_{(L-1)}$ bytes. We have $B_l = PS R_l/8$, $l=0$, 1, 2,..., $L-1$.

The nominal number of bytes contributed by each layer of a single scan element to the final composite codestream (flush bytes) is given by $F_l = PR_l/8$, $l=0$, 1, 2,..., $L-1$.

The fixed transmission rate is such that $PR_{(L-1)}/8$ bytes are removed from the buffer before each new scan element is added.

Then, the Sliding Window Rate Control algorithm is described as follows:

1. Start with buffer empty and reset the value of the excess bytes for each layer, i.e., $E_l = 0$, $l=0$, 1, 2,..., $L-1$.

2. When the first scan element has been processed and is ready to be buffered, compute the distortion-rate slope threshold for each layer, $T_{DR}(l)$, such that the total size of the coding passes from the scan element that contribute to each layer, and have slopes $\geq T_{DR}(l)$ does not exceed the target size for that layer, B_l. Delete all coding passes of the scan element, with slope values $< T_{DR}(L-1)$, the lowest threshold among all the layer thresholds. If $S = 1$, go to Step (6).

3. When the next scan element has been processed and is ready to be buffered, for each layer l, $l=0$, 1, 2,..., $L-1$, perform the following operations:
a. Calculate the new layer target size as $b_l = B_l - E_l$.
b. Compute the distortion-rate threshold, $T_{DR}(l)$, such that the total size of all qualifying coding passes, from the new scan element and from all the unfrozen scan elements already in the buffer, that contribute to this layer, does not exceed the target size for this layer, b_l.

4. Delete all coding passes of the new scan element and those of the unfrozen scan elements in the buffer, with slope values $< T_{DR}(L-1)$.

5. If buffer has not been initialized, repeat Steps 3 and 4 until S scan elements have been processed and buffered. Now, the buffer is initialized and data transmission can begin.

6. For each layer l, $l \in \{0,1,\ldots,L-1\}$, perform the following operations:
a. Flush out E_l bytes of data (if any) which form the remaining portion of a previous (partially flushed) scan element. Update the value of number of bytes to be flushed, given by, $f_l = F_l - E_l$.
b. Compute the contribution, O_l, of the qualifying coding passes from the next scan element to be flushed, to this layer.

7. If $O_{(L-1)} = f_{(L-1)}$, the size of scan element being released fits the output byte requirement exactly. For each layer l, $l \in \{0,1,\ldots,L-1\}$, update value $E_l = 0$. Go to step (10). Else, go to step (8).

8. If $O_{(L-1)} > f_{(L-1)}$, the total number of bytes being released is greater than the allotted number and some data from the current scan element being flushed will remain in the buffer. For each layer l, $l \in \{0,1,\ldots,L-1\}$, update value $E_l = O_l - f_l$. Go to step (10). Else, go to step (9).

9. If $O_{(L-1)} < f_{(L-1)}$, releasing one scan element does not meet the output byte requirement. We need to release an additional scan element from the buffer. For each layer l, $l \in \{0,1,\ldots,L-1\}$, compute the total contribution, O_l, from this layer. Go to step (7).

10. Release scan element (or elements, as required) from the buffer. Repeat steps (3) through (9) until all scan elements have been processed and buffered. No further calculation is then required. Flush out $F_{(L-1)}$ bytes at a time, until all data have been flushed.

Table 1: SWRC Algorithm for Multiple Layers

3.3.2. Multi-Layer Extended Sliding Window Rate Controller (EWRC)

With the Multi-Layer SWRC, all coding passes with slopes lower than the lowest threshold are deleted at each step. However, under certain conditions, we may prefer to keep a few of the coding passes that were deleted in previous optimization steps. This situation may arise when most of the coding passes of the new scan element being added to the buffer have slopes lower than the current lowest threshold, i.e., the new scan element is "easy" to compress. Since we have already deleted the required coding passes, we are left to include "extra" coding passes from the "easy" scan element. To avoid this, we use the EWRC algorithm where an extended buffer is maintained. This algorithm can be understood as maintaining an extra layer in an enlarged buffer with all the processing being identical to that in SWRC using $L+1$ layers. But data from only L layers are transmitted. This extra layer in the buffer is used to hold some of the coding passes, from the scan elements in the buffer, which normally would have been discarded if the SWRC were used. When an easily compressible scan element is added to the buffer, these coding passes can be allocated to the first L layers. The use of the extended buffer improves the performance of the rate control algorithm. Compared to SWRC, tighter quality control is achieved and the variation in quality between scan elements decreases.

The algorithm is described in more detail in Table 2. In this table, a quantity called the *Effective Buffer Ratio (EBR)* has been used. It is defined as follows:

$$EBR = \frac{B_2}{B_1} \text{, where, } B_2 = \text{size of buffer used in EWRC}$$

$$B_1 = \text{size of buffer used in SWRC.}$$

EBR has a value greater than or equal to 1. When *EBR* = *1*, the EWRC algorithm is identical to the SWRC algorithm.

Let the total number of scan elements for an image be N, each corresponding to P pixels. Let the number of layers to be generated be L, with corresponding rates (in *bpp*) $R_0, R_1,..., R_{(L-1)}$. Let the nominal number of scan elements in the buffer be S. Let the target sizes corresponding to the buffered portion of the L layers be $B_0, B_1,..., B_{(L-1)}$ bytes. We have $B_l = PS R_l/8$, $l=0, 1, 2,..., L-1$. Let the *effective buffer ratio* be EBR.
The nominal number of bytes contributed by each layer of a single scan element to the final composite codestream (flush bytes) is given by $F_l = PR_l/8$, $l=0, 1, 2,..., L-1$.

The fixed transmission rate is such that $PR_{(L-1)}/8$ bytes are removed from the buffer before each new scan element is added.

Then, the Extended Sliding Window Rate Control algorithm is described as follows:

1. Start with buffer empty and reset the value of the excess bytes for each layer, i.e., $E_l = 0$, $l=0, 1, 2,..., L-1$.

2. When the first scan element has been processed and is ready to be buffered, compute the distortion-rate slope threshold for each layer, $T_{DR}(l)$, such that the total size of the coding passes from the scan element that contribute to each layer, and have slopes $\geq T_{DR}(l)$ does not exceed the target size for that layer, B_l. Also compute the threshold $T_{EBR}(L-1)$ for the extended buffer of size $EBR * B_{L-1}$. Since $EBR > 1$, $T_{EBR}(L-1) < T_{DR}(L-1)$. Delete all coding passes belonging to the scan element, which have slope values smaller than $T_{EBR}(L-1)$. If $S = 1$, go to Step (6).

3. When the next scan element has been processed and is ready to be buffered, for each layer l, $l \in \{0,1,\ldots,L-1\}$, perform the following operations:

a. Calculate the new buffer size as $b_l = B_l - E_l$.

b. Compute the distortion-rate threshold, $T_{DR}(l)$, such that the total size of all qualifying coding passes, from the new scan element and from all the unfrozen scan elements already in the buffer, that contribute to this layer, does not exceed the target size for this layer, b_l.

4. Compute the threshold $T_{EBR}(L-1)$ and delete all coding passes belonging to the new scan element and to the unfrozen scan elements in the primary and secondary buffers, with slope values $< T_{EBR}(L-1)$.

5. If buffer has not been initialized, repeat Steps 3 and 4 until S scan elements have been processed and buffered. Now, the buffer is initialized and data transmission can begin.

6. For each layer l, $l \in \{0,1,\ldots,L-1\}$, perform the following operations:

a. Flush out E_l bytes of data (if any), which form the remaining portion of a previous (partially flushed) scan element. Update the value of the number of bytes to be flushed, given by $f_l = F_l - E_l$.

b. Compute the contribution, O_l, of the next scan element to be flushed, to this layer.

7. From the rate control buffer, delete all the coding passes belonging to the scan element that is being flushed, but with slope values that lie between the threshold for layer $L-1$ ($T_{DR}(L-1)$) and the threshold for the extended buffer ($T_{EBR}(L-1)$).

8. If $O_{(L-1)} = f_{(L-1)}$, the size of scan element being released fits the output byte requirement exactly. For each layer l, $l \in \{0,1,\ldots,L-1\}$, update value $E_l = 0$. Go to step (11).

9. If $O_{(L-1)} \geq f_{(L-1)}$, the total number of bytes being released is greater than the allotted number and some data from the current scan element being flushed will remain in the buffer. For each layer l, $l \in \{0,1,\ldots,L-1\}$, update value $E_l = O_l - f_l$. Go to step (11). Else go to step (10).

10. If $O_{(L-1)} < f_{(L-1)}$, releasing one scan element does not meet the output byte requirement. We need to release an additional scan element from the buffer. For each layer l, $l \in \{0,1,\ldots,L-1\}$, compute the total contribution, O_l, from this layer. Go to step (7).

11. Release scan element (or scan elements, as required) from the buffer. Repeat steps (3) through (10) until all scan elements have been processed and buffered. No further calculation is then required. Flush out $F_{(L-1)}$ bytes at a time, until all data have been flushed.

Table 2: EWRC Algorithm for Multiple Layers

The main advantage of EWRC over SWRC is that it *reduces the variation in PSNR* across scan elements. By maintaining a few more coding passes than is necessary, the EWRC algorithm is able to take bits away from easily compressible scan elements and give them to scan elements that are harder to compress. Therefore, there is a better allocation of the bit budget between scan elements.

3.4. Comparison of Different Rate Control Algorithms

The two leaky-bucket algorithms described above have several advantages over methods that require the buffering of the entire image. These advantages do not come at the cost of significant complexity increase. The leaky-bucket methods do not require additional computations to determine the content complexity of each frame. The encoder already produces the rate-distortion information corresponding to every coding pass, and this information is simply passed to the rate controller. The rate controller is able to use the coding pass information to assess the importance of each elementary bitstream.

One important advantage of the proposed methods is that in both cases, rate control is strictly a post-compression operation. Since the rate controller operates on the compressed bitstream, a single encoder running at a rate slightly higher than the target rate is sufficient to achieve constant quality. Unlike existing schemes, the encoder does not need continuous feedback from the rate controller and it need not encode the input data repeatedly at varying quantization sizes. This reduces computational complexity and enables real-time processing.

Another advantage is that the algorithms can accommodate the fine scalability features of JPEG2000. The algorithms can be used to generate codestream with many layers.

In order to quantitatively compare the performance of the rate control methods presented in this chapter, we used them to compress a hyperspectral AVIRIS [16] data set ("Low Altitude"). This data set has 224 components and the dimensions of the image are 3584 pixels (high) by 614 pixels (wide). A scan element corresponding to 32 rows of image data is employed. Therefore, 112 scan elements are required to completely cover the image. Two levels of wavelet transform are applied with a codeblock size of 16x256. Four quality (SNR scalable) layers are used, corresponding to 0.5 bpp/component (112 bpp), 1.0 bpp/component (224 bpp), 1.5 bpp/component (336 bpp) and 2.0 bpp/component (448 bpp), respectively. In all figures, results are reported for a rate of 448 bpp (2 bpp/component). This is the highest quality layer among the four layers in the codestream. In all cases, Peak Signal-to-Noise Ratio (PSNR) is used to measure quantitative compression performance.

Figure 13 compares the overall PSNR of components reconstructed from two different codestreams – one obtained by incremental processing using fixed rate encoding for each scan element, and the other obtained by

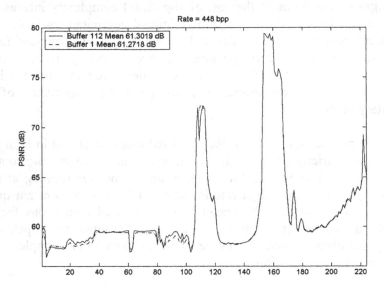

Figure 13: Comparison of Overall Component PSNR values for Fixed-Rate Encoding of Scan Elements.

buffering all the data before creation of the final codestream (which is similar to the "normal" mode of JPEG2000). It is seen that the mean PSNR over all components is only about 0.03 dB away from what is obtained when all the data are buffered. There is almost no difference in the individual component PSNR values either.

While the average PSNR over all components does not change considerably between the two methods, there is substantial difference in PSNR variation across scan elements. This is illustrated in Figure 14 for component 84. In the figure, it can be seen that while the scan element PSNRs remain fairly constant when all compressed data is buffered (buffer size = 112), there is significant variation for fixed-rate encoding (buffer size

= 1). In other words, the quality of the image varies substantially from top to bottom when a fixed-rate is assigned to each scan element.

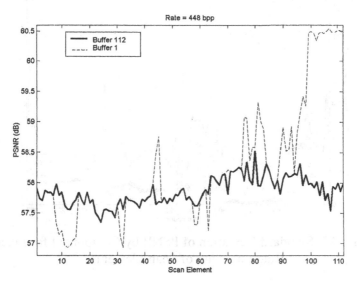

Figure 14: Scan Element PSNRs for Component 84 with Fixed-Rate Encoding.

The PSNR variation across scan elements for each component is plotted in Figure 15. It can be seen from the figure that, similar to component 84 in Figure 14, the fixed-rate encoding results in large PSNR variations in almost all components. Next, we present experimental results that demonstrate the performance of the two leaky-bucket rate allocation methods (SWRC and EWRC) presented earlier on the same AVIRIS data set.

Figure 16 is a plot of the overall PSNR values of all components obtained using the SWRC for various buffer sizes. For buffer sizes of 5 and 20, the mean overall PSNR (averaged over all components) is only about 0.03 dB and 0.01 dB away from that obtained when the entire image is buffered (indicated by buffer size 112). Additionally, the individual components PSNRs are very close even with a small buffer. Thus, for component PSNRs and mean PSNR, there is little to be gained by buffering more than 1 scan element.

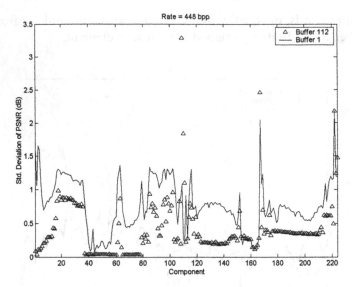

Figure 15: Standard Deviation of PSNR by Component for Fixed-Rate Encoding of Scan Elements.

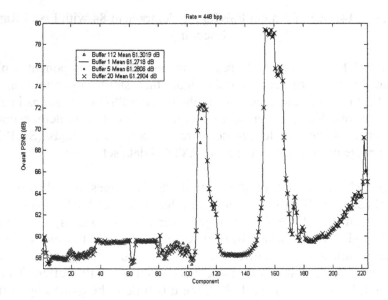

Figure 16: Comparison of Overall Component PSNR for SWRC.

Fig. 17 shows the variation in PSNR across scan elements for each component obtained with the SWRC for various buffer sizes. It is seen that

Prajit Kulkarni, Ali Bilgin, Michael W. Marcellin, Joseph C. Dagher,   375
James H. Kasner, Thomas J. Flohr, and Janet C. Rountree

the variation in PSNR decreases as the buffer size is increased. This is because a bigger buffer results in a better allocation of the bit budget between scan elements.

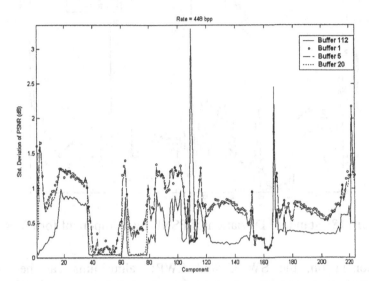

Figure 17: Standard Deviation of PSNR by Component for SWRC.

As with the SWRC, there is very little to be gained in terms of mean PSNR performance by buffering more than 1 scan element when EWRC is used. The main advantage of EWRC over SWRC, however, is that it reduces the variation in PSNR across scan elements. Figure 18 shows the PSNR variation across scan elements for the 224 components for EWRC. As expected, the standard deviation is the least when all the data are buffered. Comparing Figure 18 to Figure 17, we see that there is smaller variation in image quality across the image when EWRC is used.

For the intermediate layers (corresponding to 112 bpp, 224 bpp and 336 bpp respectively), the PSNR values for SWRC and EWRC are identical. This is because these layers, by virtue of having layers above them, always operate in "EWRC mode." Therefore, there is nothing to be gained by using a larger buffer under the EWRC scheme for these layers. The benefits of EWRC are observed for the final layer only.

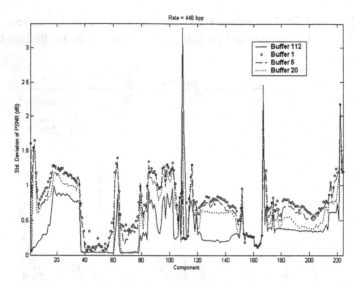

Figure 18: Standard Deviation of PSNR by Component for EWRC.

In conclusion, the SWRC and EWRC algorithms can be used to incrementally compress earth science data using only a small fraction of the memory that would be required if the entire raw image were to be buffered before compression. Experimental results show that there is very little loss in PSNR performance due to the incremental processing. With the schemes being amenable to real-time applications, these algorithms make a strong case for their inclusion in practical remote-sensing acquisition systems.

References

[1]   ISO/IEC 15444-1. JPEG2000 Image Coding System, 2000.

[2]   D. S. Taubman and M. W. Marcellin, JPEG2000: Image Compression Fundamentals, Standards and Practice, Kluwer Academic Publishers, Massachusetts, 2002.

[3]   http://www.jpeg.org/jpeg2000/index.html

[4]   T. S. Wilkinson, J. H. Kasner, B. V. Brower, S. S. Shen, "Multi-component Compression in JPEG2000 Part II," Applications of Digital Image Processing XXIV, Proceedings of SPIE, Vol. 4472, pp. 224–235, 2001.

[5]   S. S. Shen, J. H. Kasner, "Effects of 3D Wavelets and KLT Based JPEG-2000 Hyperspectral Compression on Exploitation," Imaging Spectrometry VI, Proceedings of SPIE, Vol. 4132, pp. 167–176, 2000.

[6]   M. Vetterli and J. Kovacevic, *Wavelets and Subband Coding*, Prentice-Hall, New Jersey, 1995.

[7]   G. Strang and T. Nguyen, *Wavelets and Filter Banks*, Wellesley-Cambridge Press, Wellesley, Massachusetts, 1996.

[8]   M. W. Marcellin, M. A. Lepley, A. Bilgin, T. J. Flohr, T. T. Chinen, J. H. Kasner, "An Overview of Quantization in JPEG-2000," Signal Processing: Image Communications, Special Issue on JPEG-2000, Vol. 17, Issue 1, pp. 73–84, January 2002.

[9]   M. W. Marcellin and T. R. Fischer, "Trellis coded quantization of memoryless and Gauss-Markov sources," IEEE Trans. Commun., Vol. 38, pp. 82–93, Jan. 1990.

[10] R. L. Joshi, V. J. Crump, and T. R. Fischer, "Image subband coding using arithmetic coded trellis coded quantization," IEEE Trans. Circuits Syst. Video Technol., Vol. 5, pp. 515–523, Dec. 1995.

[11] J. H. Kasner, M. W. Marcellin, and B. R. Hunt, "Universal trellis coded quantization," IEEE Trans. Image Processing, Vol. 8, No. 12, pp. 1677–1687, December 1999.

[12] A. Bilgin, P. J. Sementilli, M. W. Marcellin, "Progressive Image Coding Using Trellis Coded Quantization," IEEE Transactions on Image Processing, Vol. 8, No. 11, pp. 1638–1643, November 1999.

[13] C. Chrysafis and A. Ortega, "Line-based reduced memory wavelet image compression," in Proceedings of IEEE Data Compression Conference, Snowbird, UT, pp. 308–407, 1998.

[14] T. J. Flohr, M. W. Marcellin, J. C. Rountree, "Scan-based processing with JPEG2000," Applications of Digital Image Processing XXIII, Proceedings of SPIE, Vol. 4115, pp. 347–355, July 2000.

[15] J. C. Dagher, A. Bilgin, M. W. Marcellin, "Resource Constrained Rate Control for Motion JPEG2000," IEEE Transactions on Image Processing, Vol. 12, No. 12, pp. 1522–1529, December 2003.

[16] http://aviris.jpl.nasa.gov

Spectral Ringing Artifacts in Hyperspectral Image Data Compression

Matthew Klimesh, Aaron Kiely, Hua Xie, and Nazeeh Aranki

Jet Propulsion Laboratory, California Institute of Technology,
Pasadena, CA, USA

1 Introduction

Straightforward extension of wavelet-based two-dimensional (2-D) image compression to hyperspectral image compression based on a three-dimensional (3-D) wavelet decomposition can result in inefficient coding of some subbands and can lead to reconstructed spectral bands with systematic biases. In this chapter we describe this problem in detail, and discuss some methods to resolve it.

The effects we describe are consequences of the fact that the wavelet transform doesn't account for systematic differences in signal level in different spectral bands. We remark that using a wavelet transform for spectral decorrelation of hyperspectral data has other shortcomings as well. For example, the spectral dependencies that exist are not limited to the small spectral neighborhood exploited by the wavelet transform. However, the 3-D wavelet transform has practical advantages compared to other transforms: it offers reasonably effective compression with modest computational and implementation complexity.

Our analysis and results are presented with respect to the ICER-3D compressor, which was created as an extension of the ICER image compressor to hyperspectral images. ICER is a wavelet-based, progressive (embedded), 2-D image compressor; see [1] for a description. ICER is being used onboard the Mars Exploration Rovers for compression of a large majority of the images returned [2]. ICER-3D inherits much of its design from ICER, but uses a 3-D wavelet decomposition to provide decorrelation in the spectral dimension as well as both spatial dimensions. Further development of ICER-3D is ongoing.

Other investigations of 3-D wavelet-based compression of hyperspectral imagery include [3–5].

The examples presented in this chapter use Airborne Visible/Infrared

Imaging Spectrometer (AVIRIS) data [6]. AVIRIS hyperspectral images have a width of 614 pixels and include 224 spectral bands covering wavelengths from 370 nm to 2500 nm. For most of our examples we use the first 512 line scene of the calibrated 1997 Moffett Field radiance data set.[1] In this chapter we number bands, columns, rows, and planes starting from 1 (rather than 0).

For all examples in this chapter, wavelet transforms are performed using the integer 2/6 discrete wavelet transform (DWT) filter pair described in [7] (and referred to as "filter A" in [1, 8]).

2   ICER Overview

We start with a brief overview of some relevant concepts from the basic (2-D) ICER.

In ICER, multiple stages of a 2-D wavelet transform are applied to the image. The first stage is applied to the whole image, while subsequent stages are applied only to the (horizontally and vertically) low-pass subband from the previous stage. This results in the pyramidal decomposition first suggested by Mallat [9] and currently in common use. The resulting subbands include one small low-pass subband and several subbands that are high-pass in at least one dimension. A three-level 2-D wavelet decomposition of an image is shown in Figure 1.

To limit the effect of data losses that can occur in transmission of data to Earth, ICER partitions image data into a user-defined number of error-containment segments, which are compressed independently. These segments are defined in the transform domain, and each segment approximately corresponds to a rectangular region of the original image. Figure 2 illustrates this correspondence. Note that the partitioning into segments is performed automatically based on the image dimensions and number of segments requested; this operation has no relation to the concept of segmentation for distinguishing objects or regions in an image. Segments are analogous to "precincts" in JPEG2000 [10].

Subbands that are high-pass in at least one dimension typically contain transform coefficients with a distribution that is roughly symmetric,

---

[1]The Moffett Field data set is available from the AVIRIS web site, http://aviris.jpl.nasa.gov/html/aviris.freedata.html.

(a)   (b)

Figure 1: Example of a three-level, 2-D wavelet decomposition; (a) is the original image, spectral band 41 (740 nm) from the Moffett Field scene, and (b) is result of the wavelet decomposition. In (b), in all subbands except the low-pass subband, absolute values are shown, contrast-enhanced by a factor of 3 relative to the low-pass subband.

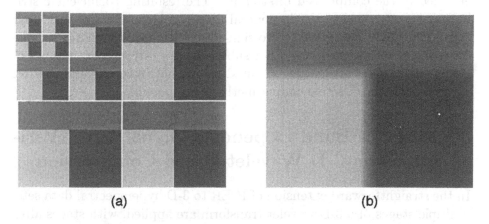

(a)   (b)

Figure 2: Example of regions formed by dividing an image into 3 error-containment segments: (a) shows the regions with hard boundaries in the wavelet transform domain, while (b) shows the resulting regions with soft boundaries in the image domain.

has zero mean, and has a single sharp peak at zero. An approximately Laplacian distribution is prototypical.

In ICER, DWT coefficients are converted to sign-magnitude form and encoded one bit plane at a time starting with the most significant magnitude bit plane. (A bit plane is formed by taking the ith most significant magnitude bit of each coefficient of a subband, for some i.) When the first '1' bit of a coefficient is encoded, the sign bit is encoded immediately afterward. If encoding is stopped after completing some number of bit planes, the resulting effective quantization is uniform except for a central deadzone. Bit-plane encoding is known to be an effective method for progressive compression of values for which the distribution has a sharp peak at zero; see e.g. [11]. A common non-progressive method is to quantize the coefficients and encode them in one pass. Either of these methods can be very effective, especially when combined with predictive coding and context modeling.

The low-pass subband resembles a low-resolution version of the original image and thus its DWT coefficient distribution can vary significantly from image to image. In ICER, for each error-containment segment of the low-pass subband a mean value is computed and subtracted (and encoded in the compressed bitstream). The resulting coefficient distribution has zero mean, but in general does not have a sharp peak near zero. The values are converted to sign-magnitude form and encoded one bit plane at a time as in the other subbands. The strong correlation between adjacent coefficients is exploited via predictive coding and context modeling. Other effective coding methods are possible.

3   Effect of Band-Dependent Signal Level Variations on 3-D Wavelet-Based Compression

In the straightforward extension of ICER to 3-D hyperspectral data sets, multiple stages of a 3-D wavelet transform are applied, with stages after the first applied only to the (spatially and spectrally) low-pass subband from the previous stage. The resulting decomposition is a 3-D Mallat decomposition (see Figure 3); it is analogous to the 2-D Mallat decomposition of Figure 1. Error-containment segments are defined spatially (in the wavelet transform domain) so segments extend through all spectral bands. In our baseline implementation, in each segment of the low-pass subband the mean value is computed and subtracted.

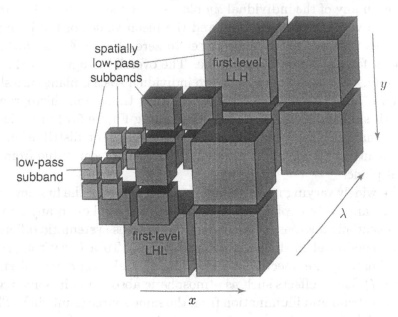

Figure 3: The 3-D Mallat wavelet decomposition, illustrated here with three levels of decomposition. The x, y, and λ labels identify the horizontal, vertical, and spectral axes respectively.

In this section, for our examples we make use of the first level LLH (spatially low-pass, spectrally high-pass) subband and the first level LHL (horizontally low-pass, vertically high-pass, spectrally low-pass) subband.

3.1 Distributions of DWT Coefficients in Planes of Subbands

In any subband that is high-pass in at least one dimension, the mean value of the DWT coefficients will tend to be close to zero (see the Appendix). However, in a subband that is high-pass in only one dimension, individual planes that are orthogonal to the high-pass filter direction, such as xy planes (spatial planes) of the first level LLH subband and $x\lambda$ planes (horizontal-spectral planes) of the first level LHL subband, do not necessarily have mean values that are close to zero. In both of these subbands, the overall mean value is approximately zero, but in the LLH subband many of the individual xy planes have mean values that are far from zero while in the LHL subband the mean values of the individual $x\lambda$ planes turn out to be much closer to zero. Figure 4 illustrates this situation for the Moffett Field scene. The overall histogram of the LLH subband as well as histograms of two individual spatial planes are shown in Figure 5(a). Note from Figure 5(b) that the overall histogram for the LHL subband is well-behaved. Comparing Figure 5(a) and Figure 6 we see that the LLH subband has a much narrower distribution (and consequently a higher peak) after subtracting the mean value from each spatial plane.

The widely varying mean values of spatial planes of the first level LLH subband are easily explained. The explanation applies to any subband that is spatially low-pass. The underlying cause is systematic differences in the signal level in different spectral bands. To a (very rough) first approximation, the spectra at individual spatial points are all similar (Figure 7) due to effects such as atmospheric absorption in some regions of the spectrum and illumination from the same source (sunlight). Therefore, applying a wavelet decomposition in the spectral dimension results in similar transformed spectra (Figure 8). In some spatial planes of the subband, the systematic content of the transformed spectra swamps the spatial variation that arises from the scene content; in other words, the magnitude of the mean value of some planes is relatively large compared to the variation of DWT coefficient values in the plane. High-pass filtering in either spatial direction effectively removes this systematic variation, so it is only an issue in spatially low-pass subbands.

The planes corresponding to spatial rows and columns of a hyperspectral image generally should not exhibit significant systematic differences in the signal level; thus, no analogous issues should arise with wavelet transforms in the spatial dimensions.

For a similar reason, an analogous effect generally does not arise in wavelet-based compression of 2-D images. However, it is instructive to consider the case of a 2-D image that has systematic variations in pixel intensities that depend on the row index or column index. Such variations do not occur in most types of images, but they are exhibited in a spatial-spectral plane of a hyperspectral image. An example of

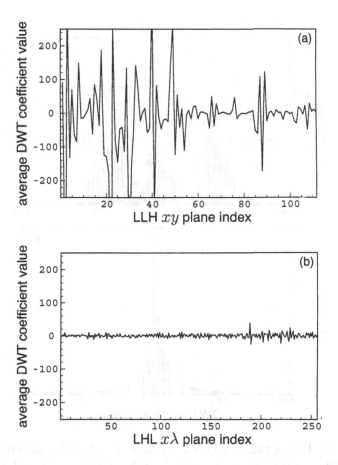

Figure 4: Means of (a) the individual xy planes in the first level LLH subband and (b) the individual $x\lambda$ planes in the first level LHL subband. For both cases the dataset is the Moffett Field scene.

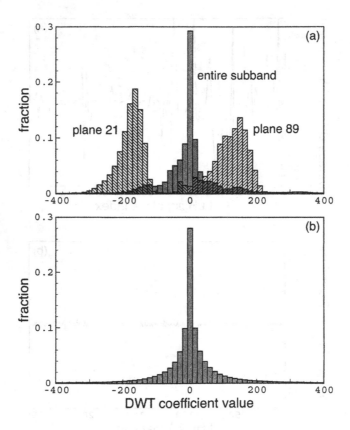

Figure 5: Histograms of DWT coefficient values in subbands from the Moffett Field scene: (a) the first level LLH subband and two individual spatial planes of this subband, and (b) the first level LHL subband.

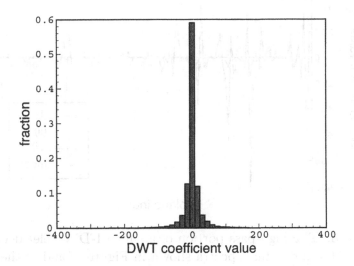

Figure 6: Histogram of DWT coefficient values in the first level LLH subband from the Moffett Field scene after subtracting the mean value from each spatial plane.

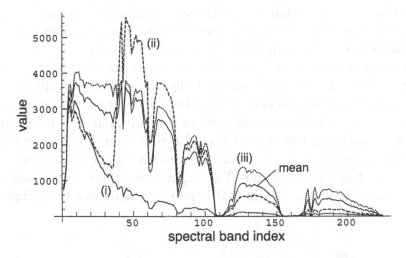

Figure 7: Examples of individual spectra, labeled (i)–(iii), and the overall mean spectrum, from the Moffett Field scene.

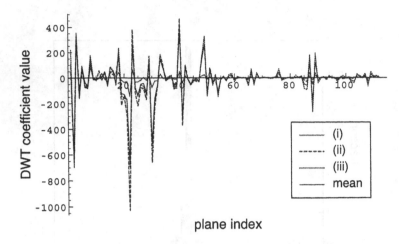

Figure 8: The high-pass portion of a single 1-D wavelet decomposition of the individual spectra shown in Figure 7, and of the mean spectrum for the whole scene.

such a spatial-spectral plane is given in Figure 9. Figure 10 shows the result of a 2-D wavelet decomposition of this spatial-spectral plane. Note that the systematic signal level differences in the spectral bands produce bright lines in the spatial (vertical) dimension in the spatially low-pass, spectrally high-pass subbands; these lines correspond to columns of these subbands that have mean values that are not close to zero.

We remark that although in this case there are also significant lines in the spectral dimension of the spatially high-pass, spectrally low-pass subbands, the analogous phenomenon in the 3-D case is much weaker: in the 2-D case, these lines can be produced by a prominent spatial feature at a single location, but in the 3-D case it would take a prominent feature in a whole row of spatial locations to create a similar effect in an entire $x\lambda$ plane of an LHL subband. Thus, in a sense, there is more asymmetry among the dimensions in 3-D hyperspectral images than Figure 10 suggests.

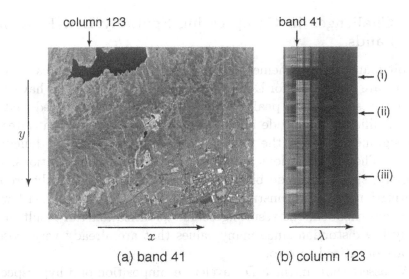

(a) band 41   (b) column 123

Figure 9: Planes of the Moffett Field scene: (a) spectral band 41 and (b) column 123. Column 123 is the spatial-spectral plane consisting of column 123 from each spectral band. The arrows above the images indicate where they intersect. The labels (i)–(iii) identify the individual spectra used in Figures 7 and 8.

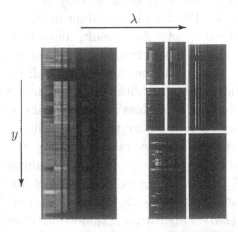

Figure 10: The spatial-spectral plane of Figure 9 and its two level 2-D wavelet decomposition. In all subbands except the low-pass subband, absolute values are shown, contrast-enhanced by a factor of 8 relative to the low-pass subband.

3.2   Challenges in Compressing Spatially Low-Pass Subbands

The bit-plane coding schemes used by ICER and other progressive compressors are best suited for DWT coefficient distributions that have mean zero and a single sharp peak at zero. It is implicitly assumed that the more significant magnitude bits are likely to be zero, and that after the most significant '1' bit, the values of less significant bits are difficult to predict. These assumptions are appropriate for such distributions. Furthermore, sign-magnitude bit-plane coding schemes effectively produce quantization with a reconstruction point at zero, so even when few bit planes are encoded, the resulting coarse quantization can result in relatively low distortion since many values that are already very close to zero are quantized to zero.

We assert that, in the 3-D wavelet decomposition of a hyperspectral image, many spatial planes of spatially low-pass subbands have DWT coefficient distributions that are not well matched to ICER's bit-plane coding scheme. As a result, the compression effectiveness suffers. In particular, for planes with distributions that have a peak away from zero, the most significant '1' bits occur earlier, and subsequent (refinement) bits are somewhat predictable because they often describe coefficient values near the peak. The bit-plane coding model does not adequately capture either of these effects. As a result, many bits are spent early for encoding spatially low-pass, spectrally high-pass subbands; this encoding is not as effective as it could be, hurting rate-distortion performance, especially at low bit rates. In addition, coarse quantization can result in relatively large distortion and a bias in the plane if there does not happen to be a reconstruction point near the peak value. Any bias in these planes can become a bias in several consecutive spectral bands in the reconstructed hyperspectral image. We give examples illustrating such biases in Section 5. These effects would occur not only with ICER's bit-plane coding scheme, but also with the schemes used by the Embedded Zerotree Wavelet (EZW) algorithm [12], Set Partitioning in Hierarchical Trees (SPIHT) [13], Embedded Block Coding with Optimized Truncation (EBCOT) [14], and JPEG2000 [10].

The biases described above can be considered to be a manifestation of a phenomenon we call *spectral ringing*. This term comes from the term "ringing" which describes the more familiar 2-D image compression phenomenon in which an edge in an image produces spurious oscillations adjacent and parallel to the edges in the reconstructed image due to quantization effects. In hyperspectral data, the individual spectral bands play the role of edges and the resulting ringing occurs in the spectral dimension. We note that any spectral transform that does not take into account the systematic variations in the relative signal levels of the spectral bands would produce transform coefficient planes with systematic large-magnitude means, creating the possibility for analogous spectral compression artifacts.

Finally, we point out that the individual spatial planes of spatially low-pass subbands retain much of the qualitative appearance that is present in the original spectral bands. This contrasts with spatial planes of other subbands. Representative examples of spatial planes from the first level LHL and LLH subbands are shown in Figure 11. The structure present in the spatial planes of spatially low-pass subbands suggests that exploiting the remaining correlation is important for effective compression.

(a)   (b)

Figure 11: Spatial planes of (a) the first level LLH and (b) the first level LHL subbands from the Moffett Field scene. Absolute values of DWT coefficients are shown. In both cases plane 89 (of 112) is shown.

4   Handling Band-Dependent Signal Level Variations

In the preceding section, we saw that systematic variations in signal levels of different spectral bands can cause widely-varying mean values in spatial planes of spatially low-pass subbands. We saw that this can have detrimental effects on image compression. We now describe two methods of mitigating these effects. Compression results illustrating the benefits of these methods are presented in Section 5.

The two methods are as follows:

A. **Mean Subtraction.** The basic idea of this method is simply to subtract the mean values from spatial planes of spatially low-pass subbands prior to encoding, thus compensating for the fact that such spatial planes often have mean values that are far from zero. The resulting data (e.g., see Figure 6) are better suited for compression by methods that are effective for subbands of 2-D images.

B. **Modified Decomposition.** Under this method, the subband decomposition is changed from the 3-D Mallat decomposition so that in stages of decomposition after the first, not only is the low-pass subband further decomposed, but spatially low-pass, spectrally high-pass subbands are also further decomposed spatially. An illustration of this subband decomposition is provided in Figure 12; it should be compared to the Mallat decomposition shown in Figure 3. The decomposition can be alternately described as follows: first, a 2-D Mallat decomposition with the desired number of levels is performed (spatially) on every spectral band. Then, a single level of spectral decomposition is applied across the first level spatial subbands; a two-level 1-D Mallat decomposition is applied spectrally across the second level spatial subbands; and so on.

These two methods can be combined: we can perform the modified decomposition and then subtract the mean values from spatial planes of the spatially low-pass subbands.

In the context of ICER-3D, the mean subtraction method is implemented as follows. After the 3-D wavelet decomposition is performed,

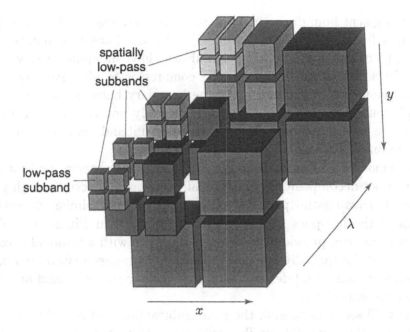

Figure 12: The 3-D wavelet decomposition scheme used by the modified decomposition method, illustrated here with three levels of decomposition.

mean values are computed for and subtracted from each spatial plane of each error-containment segment of each spatially low-pass subband. The resulting data is converted to sign-magnitude form and compressed as in the baseline ICER-3D. The mean values are encoded in the compressed bitstream and added back to the data at the appropriate decompression step. The overhead incurred by encoding the mean values is only a few bits per spectral band per segment, which is negligible because of the huge size of hyperspectral data sets.

Note that it is important to subtract the means *after* all stages of subband decomposition; otherwise, if two adjacent error-containment segments have significantly different means, a sharp edge would appear after subtracting the means, artificially increasing high-frequency signal content in further stages of spatial decomposition.

The mean subtraction method is easy to implement. However, when used with the Mallat decomposition it has some tendency to produce visible segment boundaries in some reconstructed spectral bands at low bit rates (see Figure 16 in Section 5). When adjacent segments in a spatial plane of a spatially low-pass subband have different mean values, the subtraction of means causes the compressor to effectively use different quantizers, which can make the boundary between the segments conspicuous. Segment boundaries are generally not visible when mean values are subtracted only for the low-pass subband, as is the case for the baseline ICER-3D.

The modified decomposition is motivated by the observation that in a 3-D wavelet decomposition, the spatially low-pass, spectrally high-pass subbands have spatial planes that look qualitatively similar to spatial planes in the low-pass subband, as demonstrated in Figure 11. This suggests that compression effectiveness improves with additional decompositions of the spatially low-pass, spectrally high-pass spatial planes, as it does with additional decompositions of the low-pass subband in a 2-D Mallat decomposition.

As we'll see in Section 5, the mean subtraction and modified decomposition methods provide similar improvements in rate-distortion performance, but the latter appears to have a slight advantage in the subjective appearance of individual reconstructed bands. This is explained as follows. Because the spatially low-pass subbands are relatively small under the modified decomposition, they can be encoded to high fidelity with relatively few bits (and reasonable coding schemes will give these subbands high priority). As a result, low-pass data in the individual spectral bands will tend to be reproduced with high fidelity. Thus the mean values of small regions of the reconstructed spectral bands will tend to be close to the corresponding values in the original image (where the size of the "small regions" increases with the number of levels of wavelet decomposition). The net result is that even at fairly low bit rates, no noticeable bias will be present in small regions of the individual reconstructed spectral bands.

We note that, when the two methods are combined under ICER-3D, the fact that spatially low-pass subbands are represented with high fidelity means that segment boundaries will not be readily visible. Furthermore, whatever segment boundaries might be visible in the low-pass versions of the individual spectral bands will tend to be washed out by the blurring effect of several levels of the inverse wavelet transform.

Other researchers have also devised hyperspectral image compression schemes that use 3-D wavelet decompositions that are modifications to the Mallat decomposition. For example, in [3, 4] the wavelet decomposition used is equivalent to a 2-D Mallat decomposition in the spatial domain followed by a 1-D Mallat decomposition in the spectral dimension. The resulting overall decomposition has further decomposed subbands compared to our modified decomposition with the same number of stages. Because all of the transform steps of our modified decomposition are included in the decomposition of [3, 4], the latter enables a similar advantage in compression effectiveness. Alternatives to the Mallat 3-D wavelet decompositions have also been used for compression of 3-D medical data sets (e.g. [15]), and video coding (e.g. [16, 17]). In video coding the number of samples in the temporal dimension has generally been very small.

Finally, we outline an approach to encoding spatially low-pass subbands that is an alternative to the mean subtraction method. As we have observed above, spatial planes of spatially low-pass subbands look rather image-like, and the distributions of DWT coefficients in such spatial planes often do not have zero means and single sharp peaks. Rather than adjusting the effective quantizers by subtracting mean values, one could alter the way these subbands are encoded so as to be based on (possibly progressive) uniform quantization that does not depend on subband content. One method of doing this is bit-plane coding of the subbands without mean subtraction or conversion to sign-magnitude form. For effective compression under this method, one would want to use predictive coding and context modeling modules that can effectively exploit the image-like appearance of the spatial planes of these subbands. This modification could be applied to either the standard Mallat decomposition or the modified decomposition.

Since all error-containment segments in a subband would be using the same quantizer under this alternative encoding approach (so long as they are all compressed to the same fidelity), it eliminates any possible boundary artifacts between segments. However, this coding approach might not encode the affected (i.e., spatially low-pass) subbands as effectively. In particular, under the mean subtraction method a sharp peak in the DWT coefficient distribution would tend to be exploited by quantization that includes a reconstruction point at the peak value, but under uniform quantization, having a reconstruction point near the peak values would be less likely, and as a result there could be higher distortion and a systematic bias in some spectral bands of the reconstructed image.

5   Results

The methods described in Section 4 provide a noticeable improvement in rate-distortion performance compared to the baseline approach, especially at moderate to low bit rates (roughly 1 bit/pixel/band and below). In Figure 13 we compare the rate-distortion performance of these methods to the baseline approach for the Moffett Field scene and for a 512 line radiance data scene of Arizaro, Argentina taken on February 7, 2001.[2] The points shown on the curves were produced by encoding all subband bit planes that have significance exceeding a given value. It is seen that mean subtraction, modified decomposition, and the combination of the two provide very similar rate-distortion performance, and, for example, give roughly a 10% improvement in rate compared to the baseline method at 1 bit/pixel/band. When the number of wavelet decompositions is small, the rate-distortion performance of the modified decomposition alone is slightly worse than that of mean subtraction alone or the combination of the two methods.

Overall, the use of either method from Section 4 with ICER-3D provides a moderate subjective image quality improvement consistent with the improvement in mean squared error (MSE) distortion. In some cases, however, the improvement is more dramatic, especially with regard to reduction of bias in reconstructed spectral bands when compressed at low bit rates. This is illustrated in Figures 14, 15, and 16. These images are of spectral band 81, which was chosen because its reconstruction exhibits a noticeable bias when using the baseline ICER-3D. In this case, the bias appears as a brighter overall reconstructed image. To a lesser degree, regional biases can be seen under the mean subtraction method.

As the discussion in Section 4 suggests, error-containment segment boundaries are sometimes visible when mean subtraction is used alone. This is illustrated in the reconstruction of Figure 16, where some seg-

---

[2]AVIRIS flight number f010207t01p02_r06.

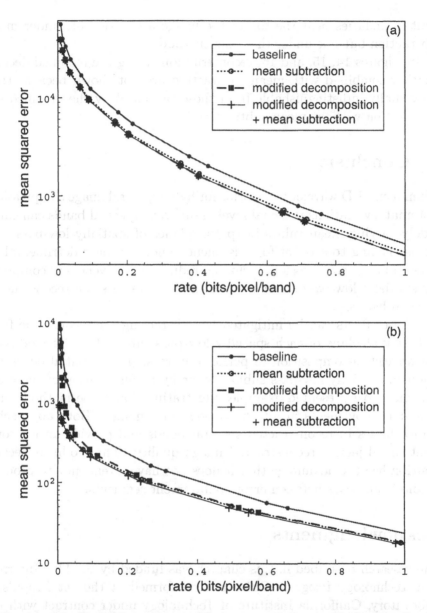

Figure 13: Rate-distortion performance of the methods described in Section 4 and baseline ICER-3D: (a) for the Moffett Field scene using 5 stages of wavelet decomposition and a single error-containment segment, (b) for the Arizaro scene using 3 stages of wavelet decomposition and 4 error-containment segments.

ment boundaries near the top of the image are noticeable under mean subtraction but not under the other methods.

In Figures 14, 15, and 16, reconstructions using the modified decomposition combined with mean subtraction are not shown because they are visually indistinguishable from those produced by the modified decomposition without mean subtraction.

6 Conclusion

When using 3-D wavelet transforms for hyperspectral image compression, systematic variations in signal level of different spectral bands can cause widely-varying mean values in spatial planes of spatially low-pass subbands. Failing to account for this phenomenon can have detrimental effects on image compression, including reduced effectiveness in compressing spatially low-pass subband data, and biases in some reconstructed spectral bands.

These effects can be mitigated by subtracting the mean value from each spatial plane of each spatially low-pass subband, or by modifying the wavelet decomposition to perform extra stages of spatial decomposition in spatially low-pass subbands, or by a combination of these approaches. We presented examples illustrating that these methods offer similar improvements in rate-distortion performance. Both approaches reduce biases in reconstructed spectral bands and provide an improvement in subjective reconstructed image quality. The modified decomposition has the advantage that it does not have a tendency to produce visible boundaries between error-containment segments.

Acknowledgments

The research described in this chapter was funded by the IND Information Technology Program Office and performed at the Jet Propulsion Laboratory, California Institute of Technology under contract with the National Aeronautics and Space Administration.

The authors would like to thank Robert Green for providing the Arizaro image used in Section 5.

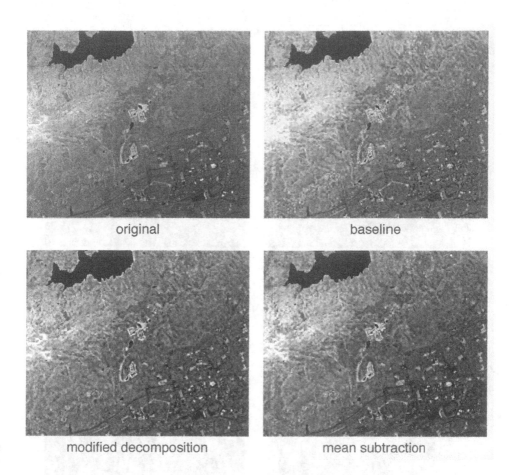

Figure 14: Reconstructed images of band 81 from the Moffett Field scene using the baseline ICER-3D, and ICER-3D with mean subtraction and modified decomposition. In all three cases the entire hyperspectral scene was compressed to 0.1 bits/pixel/band using 5 stages of wavelet decomposition and a single error-containment segment.

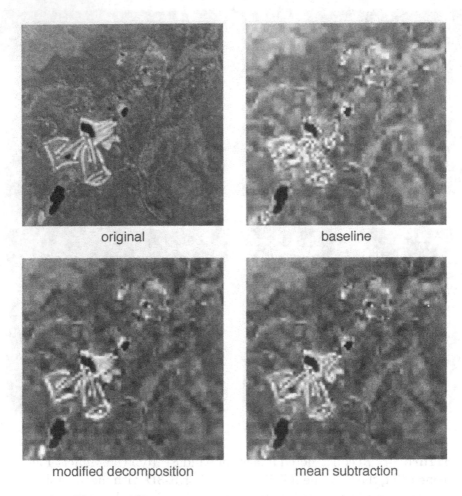

original   baseline

modified decomposition   mean subtraction

Figure 15: Detail region from the reconstructed images of Figure 14.

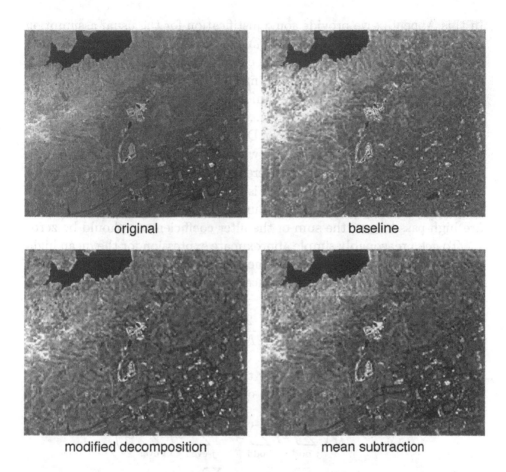

Figure 16: Reconstructed images of band 81 from the Moffett Field scene using the baseline ICER-3D, and ICER-3D with mean subtraction and modified decomposition. In all three cases the entire hyperspectral scene was compressed to 0.0625 bits/pixel/band using 5 stages of wavelet decomposition and 16 error-containment segments.

Appendix: Mean Value of High-Pass DWT Coefficients

In this Appendix we provide some justification for the usual assumption that a subband that is high-pass in at least one direction will have a mean DWT coefficient value that is close to zero. We do this by deriving an approximate expression for the mean high-pass coefficient value of a single decomposition in the one-dimensional case.

Consider a length N signal $x_1, \ldots, x_N$. For convenience we assume N is even. For a fairly general linear DWT, a high-pass coefficient h_n can be computed as $h_n = \sum_i c_i x_{2n+i}$, where the sum is over the indices of the wavelet filter coefficients c_i. Here we have assumed that the number of filter coefficients is small, and n is in the range $1, \ldots, N/2$ but not so near the edge of that range that boundary effects matter. Because these are high-pass values, the sum of the filter coefficients c_i should be zero.

To get a reasonably simple approximate expression for the mean high-pass coefficient value $\bar{h}$, we make the approximation that each x_j makes the same contribution to $\bar{h}$. Specifically,

$$\bar{h} = \frac{2}{N} \sum_{n=1}^{N/2} h_n \approx \frac{2}{N} \sum_n \sum_i c_i x_{2n+i},$$

where the last pair of sums is over those n and i for which $2n + i$ is in the range $1, \ldots, N$. Separating the odd and even indices of x gives

$$
\begin{aligned}
\bar{h} &\approx \frac{2}{N} \left(\sum_{j \text{ odd}} x_j \sum_{i \text{ odd}} c_i + \sum_{j \text{ even}} x_j \sum_{i \text{ even}} c_i \right) \\
&= \bar{x}_{\text{odd}} \sum_{i \text{ odd}} c_i + \bar{x}_{\text{even}} \sum_{i \text{ even}} c_i \\
&= \bar{x}_{\text{odd}} \sum_i c_i + (\bar{x}_{\text{even}} - \bar{x}_{\text{odd}}) \sum_{i \text{ even}} c_i \\
&= (\bar{x}_{\text{even}} - \bar{x}_{\text{odd}}) \sum_{i \text{ even}} c_i,
\end{aligned}
$$

where $\bar{x}_{\text{even}}$ and $\bar{x}_{\text{odd}}$ denote the mean even- and odd-indexed signal values respectively, and we have used the fact that the c_i sum to zero.

In most situations we would expect $\bar{x}_{even}$ and $\bar{x}_{odd}$ to be about equal due to the effect of averaging many samples, which implies that $\bar{h}$ is close to zero. This in turn implies that a subband that is high-pass in at least one direction will have a mean DWT coefficient value that is close to zero.

References

[1] A. Kiely and M. Klimesh, "The ICER progressive wavelet image compressor," *The Interplanetary Network Progress Report 42-155*, vol. July–September 2003, pp. 1–46, November 15, 2003, Jet Propulsion Laboratory, Pasadena, California.
http://ipnpr.jpl.nasa.gov/tmo/progress_report/42-155/155J.pdf.

[2] ———, "Preliminary image compression results from the Mars Exploration Rovers," *The Interplanetary Network Progress Report*, vol. 42-156, pp. 1–8, February 15, 2004, Jet Propulsion Laboratory, Pasadena, California.
http://ipnpr.jpl.nasa.gov/tmo/progress_report/42-156/156I.pdf.

[3] X. Tang, S. Cho, and W. A. Pearlman, "3D set partitioning coding methods in hyperspectral image compression," in *Proc. 2003 International Conference on Image Processing*, vol. II, 14–17 Sept. 2003, pp. II–239–II–242.

[4] Y. Wang, J. T. Rucker, and J. E. Fowler, "Three-dimensional tarp coding for the compression of hyperspectral images," *IEEE Geoscience and Remote Sensing Letters*, vol. 1, no. 2, pp. 136–140, April 2004.

[5] S. Lim, K. Sohn, and C. Lee, "Compression for hyperspectral images using three dimensional wavelet transform," in *Proc. IEEE 2001 International Geoscience and Remote Sensing Symposium (IGARSS '01)*, vol. 1, 2001, pp. 109–111.

[6] G. Vane, R. Green, T. Chrien, H. Enmark, E. Hansen, and W. Porter, "The Airborne Visible/Infrared Imaging Spectrometer (AVIRIS)," *Remote Sensing of Environment*, vol. 44, pp. 127–143, 1993.

[7] M. D. Adams and F. Kossentini, "Reversible integer-to-integer wavelet transforms for image compression: Performance evaluation and analysis," *IEEE Transactions on Image Processing*, vol. 9, no. 7, pp. 1010–1024, June 2000.

[8] A. Said and W. Pearlman, "An image multiresolution representation for lossless and lossy compression," *IEEE Transactions on Image Processing*, vol. 9, no. 5, pp. 1303–1310, September 1996.

[9] S. G. Mallat, "A theory for multiresolution signal decomposition: The wavelet representation," *IEEE Transactions on Pattern Analysis and Machine Intelligence*, vol. 11, no. 7, pp. 674–693, July 1989.

[10] D. S. Taubman and M. W. Marcellin, *JPEG2000: Image Compression Fundamentals, Standards and Practice.* Boston, MA: Kluwer Academic Publishers, 2002.

[11] A. Kiely, "Progressive transmission and compression of images," *TDA Progress Report 42-124*, vol. October–December 1995, pp. 88–103, February 15 1995, jet Propulsion Laboratory, Pasadena, California.
http://tmo.jpl.nasa.gov/tmo/progress_report/42-124/124E.pdf.

[12] J. M. Shapiro, "Embedded image coding using zerotrees of wavelet coefficients," *IEEE Transactions on Signal Processing*, vol. 41, no. 12, pp. 3445–3462, December 1993.

[13] A. Said and W. Pearlman, "A new, fast, and efficient image codec based on set partitioning in hierarchical trees," *IEEE Transactions on Circuits and Systems for Video Technology*, vol. 6, no. 3, pp. 243–250, June 1993.

[14] D. Taubman, "High performance scalable image compression with EBCOT," *IEEE Transactions on Image Processing*, vol. 9, no. 7, pp. 1158–1170, July 2000.

[15] Z. Xiong, X. Wu, S. Cheng, and J. Hua, "Lossy-to-lossless compression of medical volumetric data using three-dimensional integer wavelet transforms," *IEEE Transactions on Medical Imaging*, vol. 22, no. 3, pp. 459–470, March 2003.

[16] B.-J. Kim, Z. Xiong, and W. A. Pearlman, "Low bit-rate scalable video coding with 3-D set partitioning in hierarchical trees (3-D SPIHT)," *IEEE Transactions on Circuits and Systems for Video Technology*, vol. 10, no. 8, pp. 1374–1387, December 2000.

[17] J. Y. Tham, S. Ranganath, and A. A. Kassim, "Highly scalable wavelet-based video codec for very low bit-rate environment," *IEEE Journal on Selected Areas in Communications*, vol. 16, no. 1, pp. 12–27, January 1998.

INDEX